D1520194

Bloody Lowndes

Bloody Lowndes

*Civil Rights and Black Power
in Alabama's Black Belt*

Hasan Kwame Jeffries

NEW YORK UNIVERSITY PRESS

New York and London

NEW YORK UNIVERSITY PRESS
New York and London
www.nyupress.org

Library of Congress Cataloging-in-Publication Data

Jeffries, Hasan Kwame, 1973–
Bloody Lowndes : civil rights and Black power in Alabama's Black
Belt / Hasan Kwame Jeffries.
p. cm.
Includes bibliographical references and index.
ISBN-13: 978-0-8147-4305-8 (cl : alk. paper)
ISBN-10: 0-8147-4305-6 (cl : alk. paper)
1. African Americans—Civil rights—Alabama—Lowndes County—
History—20th century. 2. Civil rights movements—Alabama—Lowndes
County—History—20th century. 3. Lowndes County (Ala.)—
Race relations—History—20th century. 4. Black Belt (Ala. and Miss.)—
Race relations—History—20th century. 5. African Americans—
Alabama—Lowndes County—Politics and government—20th century.
6. Lowndes County (Ala.)—Politics and government—20th century.
7. Black Belt (Ala. and Miss.)—Politics and government—20th century.
I. Title.
E185.93.A3J44   2009
323.11970761'465—dc22   2009000735

New York University Press books are printed on acid-free paper, and
their binding materials are chosen for strength and durability. We
strive to use environmentally responsible suppliers and materials to
the greatest extent possible in publishing our books.

Manufactured in the United States of America
10 9 8 7 6 5 4 3

To Uncle Lenny,
For Everything

Oh, Freedom

Oh, freedom, Oh, freedom,
Oh freedom over me.
And before I'd be a slave
I'll be buried in my grave
And go home to my Lord and be free.

—Anonymous

Contents

Maps and Illustrations

Maps

Figures

Abbreviations

ACES	Agricultural and Cooperative Extension Service
ACMHR	Alabama Christian Movement for Human Rights
ACRE	Alabama Center for Rural Enterprise
ADAH	Alabama Department of Archives and History
ADCI	Alabama Democratic Conference Inc.
ADDSCO	Alabama Dry Dock and Shipbuilding Company
ASCS	Agricultural Stabilization and Conservation Service
BPP	Black Panther Party for Self-Defense
CAP	Community Action Program
CIO	Congress of Industrial Organizations
COAPO	Coalition of Alabama Political Organizations
ESCRU	Episcopal Society for Cultural and Racial Unity
ESEA	Elementary and Secondary Education Act
HEW	U.S. Department of Health, Education, and Welfare
IUMSWA	International Union of Marine and Shipbuilding Workers of America
LCCMHR	Lowndes County Christian Movement for Human Rights
LCFO	Lowndes County Freedom Organization
LCFP	Lowndes County Freedom Party
LCTS	Lowndes County Training School
MCDC	Macon County Democratic Club
MFDP	Mississippi Freedom Democratic Party
NAACP	National Association for the Advancement of Colored People

NCNE	National Center for Neighborhood Enterprise
NDPA	National Democratic Party of Alabama
NOI	Nation of Islam
OEO	Office of Economic Opportunity
SCLC	Southern Christian Leadership Conference
SCU	Sharecroppers' Union
SNCC	Student Nonviolent Coordinating Committee
TCA .	Tuskegee Civic Association
UAW	United Auto Workers
VRA	Voting Rights Act of 1965
WATS	Wide Area Telephone Service
WCC	White Citizens' Council

Acknowledgments

This book simply would not exist were it not for the support and encouragement of many people, beginning with my family. I am forever grateful to my parents, Marland and Laneda, for investing a lifetime of love in me; my brother, Hakeem, for being my role model; my sister-in-law, Kenni, for her encouraging words; my nephews, Jeremiah and Joshua, for making me laugh and smile; Uncle Lenny and Aunt Rosalind for teaching me to embrace my history and my people; Aunt Shirley, Aunt Shelly, and Lani for believing in me; Hal for watching over me while I lived in Atlanta; Uncle Frank, Adrienne, Terri, and Barry for making Florida feel like home; and Grandma Connie for her loving words. I am equally thankful for, and cherish the memory of, Nano, Grandma Lee, Grandpa Jeffries, Grandma Penny, Grandpa Gomes, Aunt Leigh, Nathan, Aunt Kay Kay, and Uncle Tom. The family of my wife, Rashida, has been wonderfully supportive from the moment we met. For their kindness and love, I thank my in-laws, Martha Rachedi, and David and Lougenia Barton; brothers-in-law, Dan, David, and Chris; sister-in-law, Nina; nephews, Victor and Caleb; Grandma Versie; uncles, Stan, John, and Ronnie; and Kelvin, Jacquie, Duane, and Evan. I also treasure the time that I was able to spend with Granddad Alexander and Abuela Julia. Like so many other families, mine transcends ties of blood. For always being there, I thank my brother, David Blaine. For their prayers and well wishes, I thank aunts Juanita, Gloria, Jane, Ama, and Cathy, as well as Rev. Harry S. Wright and the Cornerstone Baptist Church family.

Some people are fortunate to have one or two lifelong friends; I am blessed to have several. For their camaraderie, I thank Bryant Marks, Howard Craft, Kamau Bobb, Lewis Bingham, Ludge Olivier, Mike Johnson, Richard Williams, and Wesley Smith. For making my experience as a history major at Morehouse College unforgettable, I thank Malcolm Larvadain, Eric Grant, Scott Smith, and Fred Knight. For making graduate school at Duke University enjoyable, I thank Quaku Pletcher, Derek

Chang, Rochelle Hayes, Nikki Taylor, Paul Ortiz, Chuck McKinney, Patrick Hannah, Blair Murphy, Britt Britton, Martez Hill, and Aunt Shirley and Uncle Pete.

The intellectual journey that produced this book began while I was an undergraduate at Morehouse. For setting me on this course, I thank Alton P. Hornsby, Jr., Marcellus Barksdale, Giles Conwill, Daniel Klenbort, Augustine Konneh, and Cindy Lutenbacher. As a graduate student at Duke, I continued to learn from the very best. For helping me develop and hone my skills as a historian, I thank Lawrence Goodwyn, Raymond Gavins, Charles Payne, Sidney Nathans, Steven Lawson, Lee Baker, William Chafe, Robert Korstad, Jacqueline Dowd Hall, Nancy Hewitt, David Barry Gaspar, and Peter Wood.

Writing a book is never easy, but my colleagues helped ease the pain of the process. For their generosity and kindness during my time at the University of Alabama, I thank Lisa Lindquist-Dorr, Greg Dorr, Joshua and Rebecca Rothman, George Williamson, Scott O'Bryan, Paul and Diane Hagenloh, Kari Frederickson, Larry Clayton, and George Rable. I also thank my friends Anne and Ralph, and former students Tim Robinson and LaRue Haigler. For making Ohio State University a wonderful place to work, I thank, from the history department, Leslie Alexander, Alcira Duenas, Lilia Fernandez, Derek Heng, Ousman Kobo, Mytheli Sreenivas, Ahmad Sikainga, and Judy Wu. I also thank Ken Andrien, Mansel Blackford, Kevin Boyle, Mark Grimsley, Donna Guy, Margaret Newell, Claire Robertson, Stephanie Shaw, Stephanie Smith, David Steigerwald, and Warren Van Tine. From the Kirwan Institute, I thank john powell, Andrew Grant-Thomas, Ming Trammel, Tom Rudd, Jason Reece, Tara McCoy, Hiram Osorio, Lauren Hill, Stephen Menendian, Rajeev Ravisankar, Rebecca Reno, Denis Rhoden, Christy Rogers, and Angela Stanley, as well as fellow joint appointees Wendy Smooth and Michelle Alexander. From the African American and African Studies Department, I thank Walter Rucker, Rebecca Wanzo, Ken Goings, Nick Nelson, and Ted McDaniel. Also from the Ohio State community, I thank Koritha Mitchell, John Roberts, Maurice Stevens, Jacqueline Royster, Mac Stewart, and Larry Williamson. For making Ohio State a fantastic place at which to teach, I thank my graduate students Jason Perkins, Rebecca Barrett, Tiffany Preston, Tony Gass, and William Sturkey, as well as Robert Bennett, Christianna Thomas, Angela Ryan, Jennifer Huff, Gisell Jeter, and Kelly Eager. And for making Columbus a great place to live, I thank Laura Espy and family, Doug and Erica Geyer, and Steve Fink.

As I wrote this book, I was in conversation with a terrific group of historians whose work on the African American experience helped me tremendously. For their scholarship and expertise, I thank Elsa Barkley Brown, Emilye Crosby, John Dittmer, Kim Ellis, V. P. Franklin, Damon Freeman, Charles Jones, Wesley Hogan, Clarence Lang, Waldo Martin, Tiyi Morris, Todd Moye, Frederick Douglass Opie, Charles Payne, Barbara Ransby, Patricia Sullivan, Chris Strain, Jeanne Theoharis, James Turner, Tim Tyson, and Rob Widell. I have also benefited greatly from ongoing discussions and debates with a dynamic group of scholars studying various aspects of Black Power. For their keen insights, I thank Scot Brown, Matthew Countryman, Jelani Favors, Devin Fergus, Peniel Joseph, Minkah Makalani, Keith Mayes, Donna Murch, Derek Musgrove, Jeffrey O. G. Ogbar, Robyn Spencer, Stephen Ward, Fanon Wilkins, Rhonda Williams, Derrick White, and Komozi Woodard. Several people read multiple drafts of this book, and the final product is exponentially better as a result. For their time and suggestions, I thank Leslie Alexander, Kevin Boyle, John Dittmer, Glenda Gilmore, Derek Musgrove, David Steigerwald, and Stephanie Shaw. I especially want to thank Emilye Crosby and the students of her fall 2007 class on the black freedom struggle for their many brilliant insights.

The institutional support that I received for this project has been invaluable. For funding the research for this book, I thank the Graduate School at Duke University, the history department at the University of Alabama, and the College of Humanities at Ohio State University. I also thank the Ford Foundation, which provided fellowships that helped me start and finish this project. For enabling me to receive feedback on the theoretical underpinnings of this work, I thank the National Endowment for Humanities for fellowships to participate in stimulating and memorable summer conversations at the Africana Studies and Research Center at Cornell University and at the W. E. B. Du Bois Institute at Harvard University. For preserving and helping me locate much of the material in this book, I thank the archivists at the Martin Luther King, Jr., Center for Nonviolent Social Change, the Auburn University Archives, the Schomburg Center for Research in Black Culture, and the Moorland-Spingarn Research Center at Howard University. In addition, I am especially grateful for the assistance provided by the staff at the Alabama Department of Archives and History, including John Hardin, Frazine Taylor, Debbie Pendleton, Rickie Brunner, Sherrie Hamil, Norwood Kerr, and Ed Bridges. For providing me with many of the photographs included herein, I thank

Estizer Smith, who has her father's keen eye for the historical, and John Phillips, whose portfolio of Selma and Lowndes County prints is simply stunning.

As I traveled the country conducting research, someone always made a place for me to rest and work. For their hospitality, I thank Rolfe Barber, Danny Calhoun, and Bryant Marks. I thank especially Jocelyn Cash, who took me in for an entire year and treated me just like one of her sons. This project would not be the same, and may never have gotten off the ground, had it not been for her kindness and generosity.

As a study of a local movement, this book could not have been written without the assistance of the people who made the movement happen, including past and present grassroots organizers. For helping me recover the story of the Lowndes movement, I thank John Hulett, John Jackson, Timothy Mays, Harriet and Elbert Means, Bob Mants, and Willie Mukassa Ricks. I am also indebted to those who matched my enthusiasm for documenting the freedom struggle in Lowndes County and who shared my vision for this book. For their commitment and encouragement, I thank Catherine Coleman Flowers, Taylor Branch, Jeremiah Day, and Barbara Evans.

Several people who believed deeply and passionately in this project made sure, when it mattered most, that this book was published. For all that they did, I am forever grateful to Kevin Boyle, Emilye Crosby, John Dittmer, Steven Lawson, Komozi Woodard, and my editor, Debbie Gershenowitz.

I have lived with this project for nearly a decade, and so has my wife. For her patience, endurance, support, encouragement, and most of all for her abiding love, I thank the love of my life and my best friend, Rashida.

Alabama's Black Belt counties

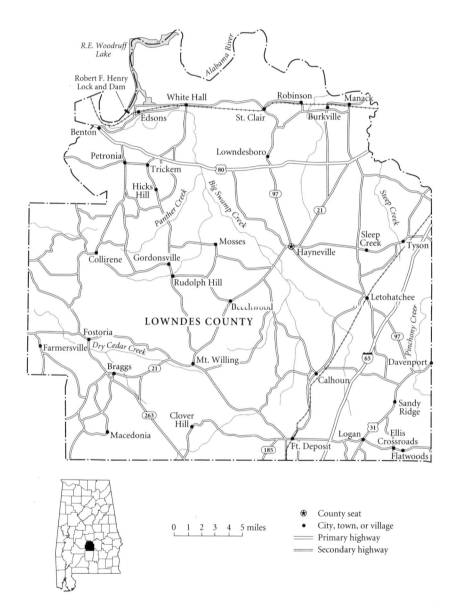

R.E. Woodruff
Lake

Robert F. Henry
Lock and Dam

White Hall   Robinson   Manack
Edsons   St. Clair   Burkville
Benton

Petronia   Lowndesboro
Trickem   80

Hicks
Hill   Panther Creek   Big Swamp Creek   97
                                        21   Sleep Creek

Mosses   Sleep Creek   Tyson
Collirene Gordonsville   Hayneville

Rudolph Hill

Beechwood   Letohatchee

LOWNDES COUNTY   Pinchony Creek

Fostoria   97
Farmersville Dry Cedar Creek
                    Mt. Willing   65
Braggs 21   Davenport
                              Calhoun

                                        Sandy
                                        Ridge
          263   Clover
                Hill
Macedonia   Logan 31   Ellis
                                        Crossroads
                        185   Ft. Deposit
                                        Flatwoods

County seat
0 1 2 3 4 5 miles   ● City, town, or village
                          ═══ Primary highway
                          ═══ Secondary highway

Lowndes County, Alabama

Introduction

Jim Crow was a grim reality in Lowndes County, Alabama, at the beginning of 1965. African Americans attended separate and unequal schools, lived in dilapidated and deteriorating housing, and toiled as underpaid and overworked domestics and farm laborers. They were also completely shut out of the political process. There were five thousand African Americans of voting age in the overwhelmingly black rural county, but not a single one was registered.[1] Most were too scared even to try. Francis Moss, born nearly seventy years earlier, was among those immobilized by an overwhelming fear of white violence. "I used to run in the house whenever I saw a white man coming down the road," she said. "I was afraid I'd be killed. And I wasn't a baby then, but a grown woman."[2]

By the end of 1966, however, Jim Crow was crumbling. The most obvious sign of its demise could be found on the voter rolls, which listed the names of nearly three thousand African Americans. In a remarkable display of collective courage, African Americans managed to set aside their fear and act on the powerful impulse to end segregation immediately. "Negroes ain't planning on scaring no more," said a black farmer. Their fierce determination to take action also led them to embark on a radical experiment in democracy. With the help of the Student Nonviolent Coordinating Committee (SNCC), they created the Lowndes County Freedom Organization (LCFO), an all-black, independent political party whose ballot symbol was a snarling black panther. "We ain't backing up," said Sidney Logan, Jr., the LCFO candidate for sheriff. "We're looking for power."[3] Their bold bid to take over the local government transformed Lowndes County from an unheard of bastion of white supremacy to the center of southern black militancy.

This startling change seemed to appear out of nowhere, but it was actually more than a century in the making. When the Civil War ended, emancipated African Americans laid the groundwork for the movement in Lowndes County by initiating a broadly configured struggle to exercise

1

the privileges of American citizenship and enjoy the full benefits of their human rights.[4] But after Reconstruction, white violence rose steadily, forcing African Americans to make strategic decisions about which rights to pursue publicly. The surge in white violence did not abate quickly. Instead, it endured in extreme form far into the twentieth century, earning the county the epithet "Bloody Lowndes" and causing African Americans to refrain from challenging white supremacy openly.[5]

African Americans resumed protesting publicly in 1965, several years after collective action surfaced elsewhere in the South. Although "Bloody Lowndes" remained extraordinarily violent, black protest quickly reached an intensity that surpassed that of any other period. Very soon, a genuine social movement emerged.[6] SNCC field secretaries, led by twenty-three-year-old Stokely Carmichael, helped organize the grassroots insurgency. They also helped radicalize the uprising by introducing the idea of forming an independent political party.[7]

The creation of the LCFO was the defining event of the Lowndes movement. It transformed local black political behavior by providing African Americans with a framework for a new kind of political engagement. It inspired black activists and emboldened black radicals nationwide, including Oakland-based organizers Bobby Seale and Huey P. Newton, who named the Black Panther Party for Self-Defense after the LCFO ballot symbol. It also provided SNCC organizers with a new, more radical, organizing program that they famously called Black Power.[8]

African Americans continued to fight for basic civil and human rights long after the movement's heyday.[9] In the early 1970s, however, the leaders of the movement made electoral politics, rather than freedom rights, their singular focus. This fateful decision profoundly affected the freedom struggle, and its consequences are still being felt today.[10]

Lowndes (pronounced "Loundz") is tucked away in south central Alabama, nestled quietly between Montgomery to the east and Selma to the west. The twists and turns of the Alabama River form much of its northern border, while a simple straight line separates it from Butler County to the south. The tiny town of Fort Deposit sits just above the southern boundary, right where the Louisville & Nashville Railroad built a switching station long ago. In 1960, Fort Deposit had only 1,446 inhabitants, yet it was the most populated town in the county. Although small by every measure—the town is only five square miles—it was the county's commercial hub. In addition, Fort Deposit's black population, which hovered around 60 percent, fell noticeably below the local standard; at the time, the black population in the entire county was 80 percent. The relatively low concentration of African Americans made Fort Deposit an oasis of sorts for whites and a particularly dangerous place for blacks.[11]

Hayneville, the county seat, is about a dozen miles north of Fort Deposit. It has never been much more than a town square ringed by storefronts and anchored at one end by the turn-of-the-century, two-story county courthouse. For the longest time, the best way to get to Hayneville from Fort Deposit was through the unincorporated village of Calhoun, the county's oldest black landowning community. White Hall, the other leading settlement of black landowners, is located some thirty miles away in the northwest corner of the county. Both Calhoun and White Hall were epicenters of black protest, due in no small part to the greater economic independence that owning land conferred on black farmers.

U.S. Route 80, the county's main east-west thoroughfare, passes about six miles north of Hayneville. Also known as the Jefferson Davis Highway, it provides local people with direct access to Selma and Montgomery. In 1965, this two-lane stretch of blacktop entered the nation's consciousness when civil rights activists from around the country traversed it by foot during the Selma to Montgomery March. Route 80 also runs just south of Lowndesboro, an old antebellum town that served as the seat of the white aristocracy for more than a century. Well-preserved plantation mansions and long-forgotten sharecroppers' shacks dot its landscape. More than any place else, Lowndesboro embodies the tremendous wealth and acute poverty that has always existed in the area.

Lowndes County is also situated in the heart of the Alabama Black Belt, a string of seventeen counties with fertile black clay soil that stretches 170 miles from the border with Georgia to the Mississippi state line. Like Lowndes County, Black Belt counties are decidedly rural; Montgomery and Dallas counties are the only ones with sizeable urban centers. These rural counties have extremely large black populations (many of which exceed 60 percent), they are remarkably poor (consistently ranking dead last in per capita income in the state and near the bottom in per capita income in the nation), and, until recently, their economies revolved almost exclusively around low-wage cotton production.[12]

Lowndes County is representative of the Black Belt in another important way: the freedom struggle in the county was emblematic of local struggles throughout the region.[13] The arc of black protest followed the same general trajectory—there was an explosion of organizing after emancipation, an eerie absence of visible protest during the World War II era, and the emergence of a genuine social movement in the mid-1960s. African Americans also pursued a similar set of broadly configured goals, faced the usual entrenched white opposition, tapped into the same kinds of indigenous social networks to recruit people and mobilize resources, and attempted to use the War on Poverty to improve local conditions.

At the same time, the freedom struggle in the county was distinct. Traditional black leaders—preachers, teachers, and businesspersons—were peripheral to the movement, whereas outside organizers played a vital role. African Americans also rejected nonviolence and embraced armed self-defense. Although they never created a formal defense group, such as the Louisiana-based Deacons for Defense and Justice, they were fully prepared to meet violence with violence. And of course, they formed their own political party.[14]

In the pages ahead, I tell the story of the Lowndes County freedom struggle. My purpose is fourfold. First, I aim to provide a more comprehensive framework for understanding the civil rights movement. This new paradigm revolves around the concept of freedom rights—the assortment of civil and human rights that emancipated African Americans identified as the crux of freedom. Framing the civil rights movement as a fight for freedom rights acknowledges the centrality of slavery and emancipation to conceptualizations of freedom; incorporates the long history of black protest dating back to the daybreak of freedom and extending beyond the Black Power era; recognizes African Americans' civil and human rights objectives; and captures the universality of these goals. Moreover, it allows for regional and temporal differentiation, moments of ideological radicalization, and periods of social movement formation.[15]

Second, I strive to offer new insights into the mechanics of the civil rights movement. The struggle in Lowndes County elucidates the movement's key organizing elements, including recruitment efforts that tapped into the Diaspora of black southerners who migrated north. It underscores the breadth of black protest, which extended far beyond voting rights. It draws attention to the special character of grassroots insurgency in the rural South.[16] It highlights the outside forces that affected movement activism, especially white resistance and federal involvement. It helps explain the demise of movement organizing. And it complicates the movement's standard chronology, partly by underscoring the importance of exploring black protest in the post–Voting Rights Act era.[17]

Third, I seek to provide a better understanding of SNCC and the emergence of Black Power. The Lowndes County freedom struggle shines much needed light on SNCC organizing outside Mississippi and after 1964. It renders plain the actual origin and meaning of SNCC's call for Black Power. It shows how civil rights and Black Power activism were interrelated yet distinct forms of protest. It reveals the unique nature of Black Power in the rural South. It debunks the popular notion that SNCC's decline was the result of a sharp move away from grassroots organizing caused by frustration, disillusionment, and a sudden infatuation with sloganeering. And it makes clear that the radicalization of local people stemmed from specific movement experiences rather than from general interaction with supposed movement messiahs.[18]

Lastly, I aim to retrieve a remarkable experiment in democracy from the margins of history. The creation of the LCFO gave rise to what I call freedom politics. This new kind of political engagement combined SNCC's egalitarian organizing methods with the people's civil and human rights goals. Freedom politics was a substitute for the undemocratic traditions that defined American politics, which ranged from disenfranchising poor people to choosing candidates exclusively from the propertied and the privileged. By embracing the LCFO, African Americans transformed local black political behavior. More importantly, they created a model for exporting freedom politics beyond the black community to democratize American politics.

African Americans were at the center of the Lowndes County freedom struggle. Local people, from the former slaves who tried to acquire a parcel of land to the domestic workers who helped organize the first voter registration campaign, were its lifeblood. Their experiences, therefore, are the focus of this narrative and the pivot around which it turns. During the Lowndes movement, though, local people worked closely and effectively with SNCC field secretaries. As a result, the organizing experiences of SNCC workers are a key component of this narrative. Lowndes County whites were central actors in this drama as well. Their approach to negotiating the color line helped shape the contours of the freedom struggle. For this reason, they too are an integral part of this narrative.

The Lowndes County freedom struggle unfolds chronologically in the pages that follow. The narrative begins with the evolution of black protest before the civil rights era, from emancipation in 1865 to the advent of the Lowndes movement a century later. It continues with the development of the local movement, from the initial voter registration campaign in March 1965 to the attempt by the LCFO to win control of the county courthouse in November 1966. The chapters in this section form the heart of the book and are arranged both chronologically and thematically to capture the full impact that organizing experiences had on the maturation and radicalization of the movement. The narrative concludes with the transition from black protest to black electoral politics during the 1970s, which dramatically affected the tenor, tempo, and effectiveness of the movement.

The Lowndes County freedom struggle is a remarkable story of persistence and possibility. It is also a cautionary tale of the perils of power. In fundamental ways, the experiences of African Americans in this out-of-the-way county in Alabama represent a common black experience and a basic American experience.

1

Conditions Unfavorable to the Rise of the Negro

The Pursuit of Freedom Rights before the Civil Rights Era

A stranger wearing a blue coat reminiscent of Union Army attire passed through southeastern Lowndes County in April 1882 heralding news that African Americans wanted to hear since the day of jubilee. According to the visitor, the federal government planned to implement a bold plan for redistributing plantation land. In two weeks, someone from Washington would arrive by rail and divide among them the land they had worked as slaves and sharecroppers. Word of the announcement spread rapidly throughout that corner of the county. Some people, though, doubted the veracity of the rumor because they lacked faith in the mysterious messenger. Others questioned what they heard because they distrusted a government that had turned a blind eye and a deaf ear toward their plight. Nonetheless, nearly two hundred black men and women laid down their hoes and camped out at the Letohatchee railroad station on the day that the federal agent was due to arrive. When the regularly scheduled locomotive pulled into the station without the emissary, disappointment crept over the crowd, but despair gave way to hope when word spread that the envoy would arrive the following week. Apparently, there had been some confusion regarding his itinerary. Encouraged, the crowd dispersed, but when they reassembled one week later, the official once again failed to show.[1]

Local whites mocked the behavior of their black workers. "They flocked to the station, and there they stood on the tiptoe of expectancy all the live long day," began an editorial entitled "Negro Credulity" that appeared in the Hayneville *Examiner*, the county weekly. Whites also scoffed at the idea that those whom they blamed for causing the Civil War should receive some recompense for their suffering during slavery. According to the editorialist, "The great trains came thundering by, bearing the bread and the meat produced by the thrift of the Northern white man, and brought to feed the stupid and credulous beings who stood listlessly there awaiting the further bounty of those who had shed a river of blood and wasted billons of money in a struggle which had its origins in the black man." The author added that African Americans were so naive that the stranger who had started the rumors "could return among these simple people, tell them some other foolish tale [and it] would pass as current as the story he has already told." He also suggested a reason for their gullibility: "Nothing is more readily believed by the blacks than some tale which promises them a lift on top of buckra, and they will be the victims of idle rascals as long as they are taught by the foes of the South that a natural hatred should exist in their hearts against the whites." Although scorn and disdain filled the editorial, the opinion piece hinted at a truth that whites completely misunderstood. The return of the interloper would have indeed prompted African Americans to flock once again to the Letohatchee station, but not because of a natural proclivity for foolishness. On the contrary, they would have returned because of their hunger to fulfill their dream of owning land and becoming economically independent.[2]

The eagerness that African Americans displayed for land redistribution derived from their experiences as slaves. At the moment of emancipation, they reflected on their enslavement and identified their freedom rights, or those civil and human rights that slaveholders denied them. These rights included those enumerated in the U.S. Constitution and in various state constitutions, such as freedom of speech, religion, and assembly, and the right to due process, keep and bear arms, and vote. They also included rights that everyone is born entitled to, such as the right to own property, choose employment, enjoy economic security, marry and start a family, move without restriction, and receive an education. African Americans recognized the importance of freedom rights during slavery. Their bondage made clear that freedom rights were not only essential to living meaningful lives, but also the key to power within society. The violence of slavery, however, circumscribed their efforts to secure these rights. Only after emancipation were they able to claim them publicly. Unencumbered by the shackles of the Peculiar Institution, they insisted on a decent standard of living, pushed for social autonomy, pursued basic literacy, fought for political power, and sought protection from white violence. Even after the euphoria surrounding the jubilee subsided, their primary focus remained the guarantee of freedom rights.

The racial animus expressed by the editorialist reflected the persistence of a slaveholder mentality among Lowndes County whites. Although whites realized that slavery was dead, they felt no compulsion to abandon their sense of entitlement to black labor or obligation to relinquish their belief in using violence to control black workers. Their refusal to adjust their antebellum mind-set stemmed from their deeply rooted belief in white supremacy. Their antebellum way of thinking also helped shape the environment in which African Americans lived, labored, and strived for equality by dictating the terms of white interaction across the color line.[3]

No one understood the context in which the local fight for freedom rights occurred better than Atlanta University professor W. E. B. Du Bois, who lived in Lowndes County in 1906 while collecting data on local life for a book project commissioned by the U.S. Department of Labor.[4] Drawing on this field research, the thirty-eight-year-old scholar offered a startling appraisal of the fortunes of local people at the dawn of the new century. "I know something of the South from ten years' residence and study," he said, "and outside of some sections of the Mississippi and Red River valley, I do not think it would be easy to find a place where conditions were on the whole more unfavorable to the rise of the Negro."[5]

Du Bois's bleak assessment reflected the trying conditions in Lowndes County. Nearly fifty years after emancipation, African Americans had made very few gains beyond those achieved during the first few years of freedom. At the time of Du Bois's visit, hardly any African Americans attended school for more than a few weeks a year, most lived in abject poverty, and practically none participated in electoral politics. In addition, every man, woman, and child was a potential target of racial violence. "The white element was lawless," explained Du Bois, "and up until recent times the body of a dead Negro did not even call for an arrest."[6]

The dreadful conditions that Du Bois encountered stretched backward to emancipation and forward beyond the New Deal. Thus, the obstacles that African Americans sought to overcome during the civil rights era were neither new nor short-lived. These harsh restrictions, however, failed to extinguish the desire of African Americans to live autonomous lives. Although the limitations that whites imposed on African Americans influenced the timing, tactics, and goals of the Lowndes movement, they were not solely responsible for shaping its contours. Equally important was the unique understanding of freedom that African Americans developed during slavery, which served as the basis of their post-emancipation political agenda.

• • •

After the Civil War, Lowndes County whites moved quickly to reestablish the exploitative labor arrangements that undergirded slavery. Very often, they set aside the annual labor contracts that the federal government, in the interest of fair play, insisted they sign. Planter William Bonnell Hall, for example, refused to pay former slaves Frank, Pfeaster, Abner, Ann, and Cicily at the end of 1865, as agreed to in contracts he signed earlier that year.[7] Whites also withheld significant portions of freedmen's monthly wages until the end of the year, a practice that forced their workers to stay put until after the harvest. In addition, they regularly charged workers for goods they never purchased and for time lost that had been spent at work. So many and so much were these deductions that quite a few planters paid their workers no year-end wages at all, but instead handed them a bill of debt that tied them to their land for another year. Large landowners also colluded with one another to reduce the bargaining power of their workers. One group of Lowndes County planters agreed not to hire African Americans within ten miles of their homes, hoping to secure a monopoly over the labor of their former slaves. Others organized vigilance committees that, together with the county militia and the sheriff's posse, terrorized African Americans traveling the roadways. These groups raided freedmen's cabins under the auspices of searching for signs of plotting; after beating the occupants, they seized firearms and stole what little cash and coin they found. "The Negro does not know whether to leave the plantation and be harassed or remain on the plantation and be brutalized," reported W. A. Poillon, a Freedman's Bureau agent stationed nearby in Mobile.[8]

African Americans responded to white efforts to deny them their freedom rights by mobilizing their resources, but upon emancipation most African Americans possessed little more than their social ties. Instead of money, they had marriage; rather than land, they had laughter and love; and in lieu of military protection, they had family and community. The value of the capital they invested in one another, however, was priceless. Bonds among real and fictive kin enabled black families and communities to survive the horrors of slavery, including forced separation. In the aftermath of emancipation, social networks based on these personal relationships provided African Americans with an organizing infrastructure through which they mobilized their scarce resources.

Emancipated African Americans understood the value of personal relationships, especially the importance of marriages. Unions between men and women were the building blocks of families and communities, but during slavery, African American marriages existed on the precipice of perpetual dissolution because law and custom did not recognize their legitimacy. Therefore, freedmen and -women acted quickly to stabilize and strengthen the bonds between them by obtaining legal recognition of their marriages. Samuel Jackson and Louisa Emerson, for example, marched into the Lowndes County courthouse on August 12, 1865, and made their mark in the *Book of Marriage Licenses for Colored Persons*. Others scoured the countryside searching determinedly for forcibly separated spouses, siblings, children, and extended kin. At least a few left Lowndes County altogether in order to search for lost family. One mother walked as far as Charleston, South Carolina, in a quest to find her five sons.[9] Unfortunately, separation in slavery too often proved permanent in freedom, leading the overwhelming majority of African Americans to take up residence on the plantations of their enslavement, where they had some kinfolk. By documenting their marriages for white people to see, reuniting with separated loved ones, and remaining on plantations, African Americans guaranteed that the social networks they forged in slavery would survive the turbulent transition to freedom. Their efforts were not enough, however, to preserve these networks indefinitely. For antebellum social networks to endure they had to be institutionalized, and soon after the Civil War they found a permanent home in black churches.

Before the war, Emma Howard had no choice but to attend Hope Hull Baptist Church with her master and mistress, William and Georgiana Shepherd. Sitting in the segregated section of Hope Hull's sanctuary, she suffered through countless sermons counseling hard work and blind obedience to her master's will. Her desire to worship as she pleased, however, led her to exploit opportunities to do so, and she was not alone.[10] During the war, African Americans across the county began testing the limits of slaveholder authority in white churches. A local history of Bethany Baptist Church in Collirene records that "with the outbreak of hostilities the church began having trouble . . . especially with the colored members." Yet, for several years after the end of the conflict, African Americans from various plantations continued to attend Bethany. As the majority of the church membership, they viewed Sunday service as an important socializing opportunity. The hypocrisy of the white clergy and white parishioners, however, eventually led them to break away. In 1871, they elected their own pastor and deacon board and conducted a grand baptismal service. Their assertiveness led Bethany's white members to capitulate to complete racial separation, and in 1872 white parishioner Josiah Todd gave five acres to the black congregants, which they used to build Bethel Baptist

Church. The founders of Bethel were among the last African Americans to gain religious autonomy. The minutes of a meeting that took place at the all-white Lowndesboro Presbyterian Church one year earlier testify to the completeness of the break with white churches. "Our relations with the colored people remain unchanged," noted the official proceedings. "They have churches and preachers of their own, and seem determined to maintain a separate organization."[11]

Black churches were rarely more than simple, clapboard, one-room structures covered in thin coats of white paint with a dozen or so roughly hewn wooden benches masquerading as pews. But these unpretentious buildings quickly emerged as centerpieces of African American social life. Sunday services brought family and friends together for all-day fellowship. At Fort Deposit's African Methodist Episcopal Zion (AMEZ) church, children's Bible school met at 9:30 a.m., the morning worship convened at 11:00 a.m., the choir practiced at 1:00 p.m., the adult Bible school started at 4:00 p.m., and the evening worship began at 8:30 p.m. Annual revivals brought the members of different congregations together. On revival Sunday, African Americans gathered in the early afternoon and remained late into the night. As the preaching, singing, and shouting bellowed from the packed sanctuary, nonchurchgoers fellowshipped outside over cards and dice. Their numbers swelled throughout the day as churchgoing men slipped away from their families to join them. The sinners shared these Sundays with the saints. "They did as much preparing for the holiday as the deacons, the sisters or the preachers of the church," recalled a local resident. "It was a chance for everybody to socialize."[12]

Sabbath activities provided African Americans with the time and space to strengthen the personal relationships that resided at the heart of social networks. Church-based groups, however, were principally responsible for institutionalizing these networks. Mixed-sex benevolent associations, which provided vital community services, ranging from helping the sick and the shut-in to paying for funeral expenses, met at black churches. The Rising Star Benevolent Society, for instance, was a fixture at Fort Deposit's AMEZ church. By obligating people to help one another, these groups made the custom of communalism a formal practice. Masonic orders also met at black churches. Scattered across the county were chapters of the Knights of Wise Men, the Knights of Pythias, and the Odd Fellows, and branches of their female counterparts, the Messiah Household of Ruth and the Knights of Tabor. These highly ritualized secret societies provided services similar to those offered by benevolent groups, but because they relied heavily on ceremony, they played an even greater role in institutionalizing social networks. Once established, these formal networks became a permanent presence in the black community.[13]

With an organizing infrastructure in place, African Americans marshaled the human and material resources essential to fighting effectively for freedom rights, but they did not pursue their goals with equal vigor. Instead, they carefully assessed the risks and rewards associated with each and focused on obtaining social autonomy, as evidenced by their wholesale withdrawal from white churches; controlling their own labor, as demonstrated by their refusal to work in gangs and the departure of women from the cotton fields; and acquiring the basics of reading and writing, as made clear by their high rates of attendance at the handful of grossly overcrowded and understaffed public schools.[14] In the first few years of freedom, though, they did not expend much energy agitating for political power because ex-Confederates retained absolute control over the state and local government.

Local whites tightened their grip on the county government in order to restore and safeguard the labor controls that had been lost with abolition. Ironically, their early efforts did not involve excluding African Americans from electoral politics. In 1865, Lowndes County legislators supported a proposal to enfranchise black men, believing that they could control their votes. Their view changed in March 1867, however, when Congress extended the franchise to black men through the Reconstruction Acts and it became clear that they intended to vote as they pleased. At this critical juncture, local whites began organizing against black political participation. Drawing on paramilitary traditions that had given rise before the Civil War to the Muster Men, a countywide military company, and during the war to the Hayneville Guards, they formed branches of terror organizations such as the Knights of the White Camellia and the Ku Klux Klan in order to intimidate black voters. They also responded swiftly and brutally to symbolic manifestations of the political threat posed by the black electorate. In 1868, whites shot and killed an African American simply because he appeared uninvited at a meeting of county Democrats. Despite the use of terror tactics, Lowndes County whites failed to keep African Americans away from the ballot box. In fact, African Americans began pursuing political power more aggressively than any other freedom right.[15]

African Americans mobilized with remarkable efficiency in the wake of the revolutionary congressional measures. They held several mass meetings in the county seat during which they discussed the implications of the new laws. They also registered en masse. By the summer of 1867, some four thousand black men had added their names to the voting roll. Moreover, they responded to the paramilitary politics of whites with their own shotgun diplomacy. In 1868, a group of armed black men assembled in front of the county courthouse and demanded that Democrats vacate local offices in accordance with the provisions of the Reconstruction Acts. White officeholders refused to surrender their seats that day, but many did vacate eventually and African Americans voted out those who refused to step down voluntarily.[16]

The enthusiastic response of African Americans to enfranchisement reflected the depth of their interest in obtaining political power. So too did the publication of two countywide, politically oriented black newspapers, the *Republican Sentinel* and the Hayneville *Times*, and the high rate of black subscriptions to the local white weekly. Their reaction also spoke volumes about the extent of their political readiness. African Americans had been preparing for the franchise, not just hoping for it. Rev. Mansfield Tyler, for one, had been readying his Lowndesboro congregation and community for the vote for some time, in part by hosting political meetings at his humble cottage home. The election of the former slave to the Alabama legislature for a single term beginning in 1870 testifies to his organizing efforts.[17]

With the vote in hand, African Americans threw their support behind the Republican Party. They expected great things from the party that had delivered emancipation, but the postwar agenda advocated by white Republicans conflicted with their own. African Americans wanted plantation land confiscated and redistributed, but the party's white leaders favored policies that kept freed people landless and working for their former masters. In addition, the white men in command of the party's county apparatus were more interested in political self-preservation than in serving their black constituents. The Republican Party, though, was the best available option for black voters.

John McDuffie, the Lowndes County probate judge from 1868 to 1880 and the boss of the local Republican Party, was no friend of African Americans, especially African American politicians. "Whenever McDuffie had a chance to defeat a black man for a position he did so, and those he could not control were beheaded first," explained Ben DeLemos, a fellow carpetbagger and a political disciple of the former Union Army officer. DeLemos added that the Iowa native never supported a Republican for office unless it advanced his own interests, and that he managed to drive the "best Republicans" out of the party because "they would not knuckle under to him." McDuffie's personal opposition to James Rapier's bid for Congress in 1872 prompted him to leave the black politician's name off the Republican Party's nomination ballot and to list instead the name of the Democratic nominee, a former Confederate general. Two years later, McDuffie led a raucous and drawn-out nomination convention during which he tried twice to nominate a straight Democratic ticket. He even took to the floor at the end of the meeting, after most of the black partici-pants had returned home, and declared that the convention had selected two of the county's largest former slaveholders for the state legislature. Those remaining in the audience shouted him down. According to De-Lemos, "The colored voters of the county were not disposed to excuse what they considered . . . an uncalled for attack on the party of Judge McDuffie, who tried to transfer 4500 Republican voters into the ranks [of] the Democratic party." Without a doubt, McDuffie was more interested in preserving his political career than in advancing the interests of Afri-can Americans. His skullduggery coupled with the policies of the national party, which buttressed the political program of planters rather than that of plantation workers, hamstrung African Americans and prevented them from converting their voting strength into real political power.[18]

Lowndes County was one of the last counties in Alabama to be re-deemed. Democrats had seized control of the state's majority white coun-ties by 1870, but they had been unable to make headway in the Black Belt until taking back the statehouse in 1874. Once in command of the legis-lature, they diluted the voting strength of the black electorate by gerry-mandering the county's congressional district and by expelling its black legislators, including William Gaskin, who lost his seat on a fabricated charge of taking a bribe, and Hugh A. Carson, who fell victim to the false claim that he was a felon. Ex-Confederates filled the vacancies created by the expulsions. Prominent Lowndes County planter J. F. Haigler replaced Rep. Carson. Democrats also eliminated the county's board of commis-sioners and substituted it with a panel appointed by the governor, thereby stripping Republicans of the power to govern locally. The legislature did not reestablish the county commission until after native whites regained control of the local government.[19]

By 1880, the machinations of Democrats at the state level had cleared the way for local whites to make a run at the county courthouse. Seiz-ing the moment, Willis Brewer, the head of the county Democrats, along with his friend A. E. Caffey, hatched a plan to steal that year's general election. Earlier, Brewer hosted a secret meeting of the county's wealthiest and most influential white men during which he collected $1,500 for a slush fund from which to pay white Republicans to resign from office. The group succeeded in enticing the Republican sheriff to step down and replacing him with Democrat M. A. Graves. This move gave the conspirators control of the election because it was the duty of the sheriff to select poll sites, appoint poll inspectors, and collect ballot boxes. Judge McDuffie contributed to the conspiracy by leaving the names of the Republican nominees off the printed ballots. Even more was needed, however, since black voters outnumbered white voters by several hundred. Thus, on Election Day, whites brazenly stuffed the voting boxes, intimidated black voters, and altered and discarded black ballots. Democrat Walter L. Bragg encouraged the fraud. From the steps of the courthouse he shouted, "Yes, boys, stuff the ballot boxes, stuff them until they burst, stuff them like you would a fattening goose. Lowndes County must be cleaned." Bragg had his way. Democrats won each race by about 1,600 votes. In previous years, they had lost these races by 3,000 votes. Reveling in the triumph, coconspirator Caffey wrote, "We threw [off] the yoke of Yankee masters and native renegades. The struggle was worth a thousand times over what it cost us."[20]

Democrats guarded their victory aggressively in order to prevent a return to what the Hayneville *Examiner* termed "political barbarism." Relying once again on massive voting fraud, they swept every electoral precinct by decisive majorities in 1882. Significantly, after that year's election, the state Republican Party, which was already a shadow of its former self, collapsed completely. These developments, however, did not keep African Americans from seeking political power. They continued to vote in impressive numbers for independent and third-party candidates, and they also continued to map strategy at public gatherings. Politics was the watchword among the 2,500 African Americans from all parts of Lowndes County and three neighboring counties who attended the October 1884 Colored Baptist Association meeting in Calhoun.[21]

Black political participation remained high through the Populist era even though African Americans knew that Democrats routinely stole their votes. In 1901, however, this involvement ended abruptly. Local whites joined the statewide effort to exclude African Americans from electoral politics by inserting into the state constitution provisions adopted from Mississippi's disenfranchisement constitution of 1890 requiring prospective voters to pay a $1.50 cumulative poll tax, pass a literacy test, and provide proof of good moral character. Although the impetus for constitutional disenfranchisement came from upstate whites who had grown weary of Black Belt oligarchs using stolen black ballots to decide the outcome of statewide elections, local whites needed very little cajoling to support the effort. They understood that as long as African Americans retained the vote, their own power to control the courthouse was at risk. In addition, they concluded that it was far more important to maintain power over local African Americans than to hold sway over upstate whites. The impact of constitutional disenfranchisement was immediate and shocking. In 1900, Lowndes County had more than five thousand registered black voters. A half dozen years later, the county had only fifty-seven.[22]

African Americans were well aware of the injustice inherent in disenfranchisement, but they refrained from criticizing the new constitution publicly. Their decision to keep quiet reflected the harsh reality of life in Lowndes County. The regular use of violence by whites to control black labor and regulate black behavior eliminated the space that African Americans needed to safely express their opposition to the new constitution. Above all else, lynching made it abundantly clear that public protest was foolishly dangerous. Indeed, during the years surrounding the turn of the century, whites routinely resorted to lynching in response to breaches of the racial code. On March 29, 1888, the Lowndes County sheriff handed his jailhouse keys to a mob of two hundred armed white men that had gathered in Hayneville to lynch Theo Calloway, an African American from Sandy Ridge who had shot and killed Mitchell Gresham, a white man of local standing, in a clear case of self-defense. With free run of the jail, the mob dragged Calloway from his cell, carried him to the front of the courthouse, hanged him from a blossoming chinaberry tree, and riddled his body with bullets. The mangled corpse dangled undisturbed until the next day when whites allowed local African Americans to cut it down and give it to the young man's parents when they arrived that afternoon for their son's trial.[23] Another of the county's more sensational lynchings occurred on December 18, 1914, when a mob of "infuriated citizens" hanged Will Jones, a black laborer recent to the county from Rome, Georgia, after Olie Mae Sullivan, a white girl of high school age and a member of a politically connected family, claimed that someone had broken into her bedroom and frightened her. Lawmen fingered Jones for the attempted assault after finding a set of shoeprints in the mud outside of the girl's window that supposedly led directly to his cabin. Any doubt of the laborer's guilt disappeared when a search of his belongings turned up a pair of muddy socks.[24] Similarly, on July 23, 1917, a gang of one hundred men seized Will and Jesse Powell from two deputies outside of Hayneville and lynched them for drawing their pistols on A. H. Jenkins, the son of a local justice of the peace, who pulled a handgun on the pair and struck one of them following a minor wagon collision. Unlike the mob that lynched Jones, this group of murderers did not even bother to concoct a rape story.[25]

Lynching reinforced the notion that whites would deal with the slightest transgression of the racial code, whether real or perceived, swiftly and severely. It also demonstrated the high probability of summary execution for challenging the status quo publicly. Lynching, however, was only the most sensational element of the culture of racial violence that permeated the county and forestalled public protest. More commonly, white landowners beat black workers to compel compliance just as they did before emancipation. According to U.S. district attorney Warren S. Reese, Jr., who led a federal investigation of peonage in the Alabama Black Belt in 1903, Lowndes County was "honeycombed with slavery." In a report to his superiors, Reese explained that the "miserable business and custom" of using violence to keep black agricultural workers from leaving was "not confined to one or two periodical and independent instances," but was an institutionalized system over which the county's most "reputable men" had full command.[26] The case of black laborer Dillard Freeman illustrates his point.

In 1903, Freeman contracted with sheriff J. W. Dickson to work off the cost of a fine and court fees that the officer paid for him following his arrest and conviction on a trumped-up charge.[27] While laboring for the sheriff, the young man sought permission on multiple occasions to visit his sick brother who was convalescing at his mother's home only a few miles away, but Dickson denied every request. Frustrated and desperate, Freeman sneaked away from the farm, but the sheriff tracked him to his mother's house and beat him mercilessly in her presence. After the beating, he tied the young man's hands behind his back, fastened a rope around his neck, and handed the loose end to a henchman sitting astride a mule. Dickson then forced him to run more than six miles back to his plantation and whipped him whenever his pace slowed. Upon their return, Dickson beat Freeman again, this time with a piece of gin belt attached to a wooden handle. When the sheriff tired, he handed the whip to another of his men who finished administering the punishment. The most compelling evidence of the severity of the flogging was Freeman's back, which an eyewitness described as "one mass of scars from his thighs to his neck." Two days after the beating, the sheriff forced Freeman back into the fields, but because he never received medical attention, field hands had to grease his back so that he could bend to work. At night, Dickson chained Freeman to the foot of the boss's bed to prevent a second escape.[28]

Racial violence together with constitutional disenfranchisement prompted African Americans to table their pursuit of political power. At the turn of the century, it made more sense to give up a valueless vote than to sacrifice a valuable life. As demoralizing as these developments were, they did not cause African Americans to stop agitating for other freedom rights. Once pursuing political power became too dangerous, they redirected much of their energy toward securing quality education.

Lowndes County's segregated public schools were outrageously inadequate and had been so from their inception. During Reconstruction, Congress cared too little about black education to challenge the orthodox view that public education was a matter reserved to the states and neither subject to national regulation nor an object of federal support. Consequently, Congress did not commit the financial and personnel resources needed to establish an infrastructure capable of meeting the demands of African Americans. Alabama's black legislators did what they could, but by the early 1870s this amounted to only twenty schools for the county's eight thousand black youngsters. The first generation of the county's public schools also failed to provide African Americans with the curricula they wanted. Instead of lessons on contracts, court proceedings, county government, and electoral politics, the schools taught Bible study and etiquette.[29]

Segregated public schools grew worse with time partly because large landowners vehemently opposed educating African Americans for anything other than menial labor. Rev. R. D. Harper, the federal government's superintendent of education for Alabama, explained that as early as 1868 a violent atmosphere of "determined hostility" plagued those who supported black education, resulting in burned schoolhouses and more than a few murders.[30] Politics also played a major role in perpetuating poor-quality public schools because disenfranchisement robbed African Americans of the political power they needed in order to challenge the discriminatory state appropriation process, which allowed county officials to funnel state money away from black schools to white schools. In 1907, for instance, the

Students at a single-teacher segregated public school in Lowndes County in 1910. Courtesy of the Alabama Department of Archives and History.

county's superintendent of education earmarked twenty-eight thousand dollars in state funds for white schools and only eight thousand dollars for black schools. This amounted to twenty dollars for each white student and sixty-seven cents for each black student.[31]

To enhance the quality of black education, African Americans mobilized their community resources. In Sandy Ridge, they formed their own school board and taxed themselves to start a school and pay a black teacher twenty-five dollars a month, twice what the county paid black educators. Within six years, the school offered seven consecutive months of instruction, a significant improvement over the three-month public school term. The schoolhouse, however, was not much better than the typical log cabins used by the county. Wanting more for their children, community members raised two hundred dollars in 1908 to establish an Anna T. Jeanes school, and the following year they built a well-lighted, properly heated, and fully furnished building.[32] Black communities from Gordonsville to Mt. Zion engaged in similar efforts and succeeded in drastically improving the quality of black education.[33] Their hard work, however, fell well short of bridging the gap between what segregated public schools offered and what black children needed. The Calhoun community was the lone exception because of a private industrial training school that opened there in 1892.

In the aftermath of the Theo Calloway lynching in 1888, the members of Ramah Baptist Church in Calhoun held a two-week prayer vigil during which they asked the Almighty for protection, mercy, and relief in the form of a school.[34] Around the same time, Ramah's pastor wrote to Booker T. Washington, the president of Tuskegee Institute, to inform him of the series of murders that followed the lynching and to share with him the congregation's prayers. If God would not listen, surely Mr. Washington would.[35] Moved by the preacher's appeal, the Wizard of Tuskegee traveled to Lowndes County and called on N. J. Bell, the principal white man in the area. During his visit, Washington persuaded Bell to donate ten acres to the Calhoun community for a school.[36] Soon thereafter, he convinced Charlotte Thorn and Mabel Dillingham, two white teachers from his alma mater, Hampton Institute, to serve as coprincipals. Under their able stewardship, the Calhoun School enrolled three hundred students its inaugural year, twice as many as expected but well shy of the hundreds who wanted desperately to attend.[37]

The new school provided black children with an education that exceeded public school standards in every way, from facilities and classroom resources to pupil-teacher ratio and length of school term. Philanthropic organizations, including the Slater Foundation and the General Education Board, gave sustaining contributions, while African Americans, despite their considerable poverty, contributed tuition payments averaging four dollars per child and totaling more than one thousand dollars annually. The curriculum was decidedly Washingtonian, with the theories and practices of agriculture and domestic work the baseline of instruction. The principals explained that Calhoun sought to educate students "not for the Northern city, but for the Southern farm,—not away from the world about them, but definitely and with enthusiasm for the land and people of Lowndes County." Calhoun also sought to inculcate students with New England morals and ethics. To instill "Christian and American ideas and ideals of manhood, womanhood, of home, farm, school, and church" is how one report phrased it.[38]

Calhoun produced a cadre of well-trained teachers and preachers committed to working locally. "Do not forget, do not be ashamed of, do not run away from those below you in want and darkness," exhorted Principal Thorn. "By your education fit yourselves in order to give yourself freely and in any simplest and humblest way to the lifting up of your own flesh and blood in your own climate and on your own soil."[39] The school's graduates embraced Thorn's Bookerite charge. Fully half the alumni accepted jobs teaching in the county's public schools and ministering at local churches, but only after matriculating at industrial training institutes, usually Tuskegee and Hampton; liberal arts colleges, particularly Morehouse and Spelman; and divinity schools, including Bible Institute in Chicago. In this way, they transformed many of the county's classrooms and pulpits. Calhoun graduates also made a lasting impact on the school itself. During the 1920s, they convinced school officials to de-emphasize cooking and cobbling and to stress social studies, African American history, economics, and sociology instead. They also persuaded them to hire more black instructors.[40] These efforts helped weed white supremacy out of the curriculum.

The Calhoun School made it possible for hundreds of black families to realize their goal of providing their children with a quality education. It also enabled some of these same families to achieve their lifelong dream of economic independence through a unique land-buying program. Sharecropping, which replaced contracting as the dominant labor arrangement during Reconstruction, sharply curtailed African American autonomy by snaring black workers in a vicious cycle of recurring debt.[41] "The keynote of the Black Belt is debt," explained Du Bois, "not commercial credit but debt in the sense of continued inability on the part of the mass of the population to make income over expense."[42] Typically, at the start of each agricultural season, white landowners advanced black farmers $250 against the coming year's crop. After the harvest, they sold the sharecroppers' cotton to buyers in Montgomery and Mobile and then deducted from the proceeds whatever they decided the farmers owed. Invariably, through deceit and fraud, sharecroppers owed more than they earned, a financial quandary that forced most to remain in the employ of the landowner from whom they received the advance. In this way, debt perpetuated the exploitation of black labor. At the same time, it generated tremendous wealth for local whites. It is no coincidence that William Brewer, one of the wealthiest people in the county, held nearly $30,000 in outstanding loans made almost exclusively to black farmers.[43]

Three years after the Calhoun School opened, its founders established the Calhoun Land Trust and raised $750 locally for a down payment on a one-thousand-acre plantation. The supervisors of the cooperative divided the plantation into several family farms and sold the parcels to black

A typical home of a black tenant farmer in Lowndes County in 1917. Courtesy of the General Research and Reference Division, Schomburg Center for Research in Black Culture, New York Public Library, Astor, Lenox, and Tilden foundations.

A typical home of a Calhoun Land Trust landowner in 1917, complete with glass windows and brick chimney. Courtesy of the General Research and Reference Division, Schomburg Center for Research in Black Culture, New York Public Library, Astor, Lenox, and Tilden foundations.

tenant farmers. To ensure that the farmers did not fall victim to preda-
tory financiers, they provided the mortgages and extended the annual advances. By 1906, exactly eighty-five black farmers had secured deeds to
the Calhoun farms and had begun to replace their threadbare shacks with
attractive houses complete with glass windows and brick chimneys. The
cooperative fell on hard times after World War I, however, when plum-
meting prices for agricultural products made it extremely difficult for
participants to meet mortgage payments and nearly impossible for tenant farmers to purchase farms; during the Great Depression, it collapsed
completely. Nevertheless, the land trust lasted longer than many expected
and along the way helped nearly two hundred black families climb out
of debt, purchase farms, and construct decent housing. It is little wonder
that field hands toiling on nearby plantations referred to the farms as the
"free land."[44]

The success of the land trust inspired New Deal policy makers to
launch a similar land-buying program on the opposite end of the county.
In 1935, the Resettlement Administration, which sought to transform tenant farmers into self-sufficient landowners, purchased a large plantation in
White Hall, divided it into small farms, and extended loans to almost 250
black families so that they could purchase the homesteads. Unfortunately,
participation in the program did not translate immediately into economic
independence. Although African Americans had demonstrated their financial acumen for several generations by surviving off their meager
earnings, federal officials doubted their commitment to thrift and their
ability to save. Consequently, they made them follow a strict and closely
supervised plan of farm and home management. They also denied cash
advances to nearly half the participants, forcing them to earn what they
needed for the year by laboring for fifty cents a day on a government-
owned plantation. Despite the paternalistic meddling of federal officials,
roughly 75 percent of the tenant farmers who enrolled in the program became self-supporting within two years.[45]

The land-buying programs initiated by the Resettlement Administration and the Calhoun School gave rise to the only sizeable black landowning communities in the county. Those who were able to participate in the
programs made the most of the opportunity. Unfortunately, landownership neither conferred the right to vote nor trumped Jim Crow customs.
It also failed to shield black farmers from white violence. In fact, landownership often increased the likelihood of becoming a target of racial
terrorism because economic independence undermined white authority.

"The more a Negro owned, the more humble he had to act in order to keep in the good graces of white people," said African American educator Benjamin Elijah Mays, who had kinfolk in Lowndes County.[46] The immediate impact of joining the ranks of landowners, therefore, was much less than revolutionary, yet it was vitally important to future organizing. Black landowners in White Hall and Calhoun were not as beholden to whites, which gave them slightly more space to agitate. For this reason, it is hardly surprising that these two communities emerged as epicenters of black protest in the 1960s.

White Hall and Calhoun were exceptions to the norm. Everywhere else, African Americans remained landless and handcuffed by debt to white financiers. Sharecropper Wesley Smith, who lived near the Calhoun farms in the early 1930s, earned just forty cents a day working from "sun to sun."[47] The Great Depression worsened the prevailing condition of poverty. In fact, the collapse of the southern agricultural economy pushed

African American women picking cotton on a plantation in Alabama, circa 1930s. © Associated Press.

many black families to the brink of destitution. The federal government exacerbated matters by instituting economic policies that legitimized and reinforced the exploitative labor practices of large landowners. The Agricultural Adjustment Act of 1933, for instance, mandated county-level management of New Deal relief and subsidy programs. This stipulation allowed white landowners to discriminate against African Americans by giving them the power to declare black farmers ineligible for cash payments and bestowing on them the authority to reject their applications for subsidized loans. In addition, it permitted whites to force black tenant farmers to reduce the amount of acreage they planted while withholding payments for the reductions.[48]

Lynching added to black folks' misery. Mobs targeted everyone in the black community, including women and children. On August 5, 1931, a group of unmasked white men tied sixteen–year-old Neal Guin to the trunk of a tree in his father's field and shot him more than one hundred times for allegedly attempting to rape the eleven–year-old daughter of a white neighbor.[49] Whippings and beatings compounded local difficulties. Sharecroppers living in the small plantation town of Benton experienced such brutality regularly. During the first few months of 1933, the town's white landowners flogged more than a dozen black men and women. And on August 9, several well respected white men, including Edwin Mealings, Archie Bryant, Arthur Hall, and Asa May, seized sharecropper Joe "Buck" Seles, hauled him to Asa May's barn, which doubled as the "whipping place" for African Americans in that part of the county, and beat him to death. A letter to Alabama governor B. M. Miller written collectively by Benton sharecroppers in response to the murder summed up the prevailing conditions. According to these farmers, African Americans were "yet in slavery."[50]

The prospect of African Americans enjoying their freedom rights seemed as distant in the 1930s as a dimly lit star. Nevertheless, they continued to agitate and organize. During the height of the Great Depression, when nearly everyone faced the prospect of falling into the abyss of absolute poverty, they redoubled their efforts to improve their economic lot. Usually this involved subterfuge. An elderly African American who worked as a clerk at N. J. Bell's plantation store always gave black customers a little extra of whatever they purchased, and he feigned forgetfulness when interrogated about missing inventory.[51] During the summer of 1935, sharecroppers in Calhoun raised the stakes by joining the Sharecroppers' Union (SCU) and striking for better wages and working conditions. "We couldn't go on living at the price we were getting," explained sharecropper Wesley Smith.[52] When the laborers initiated a work stoppage on August 19, 1935, sheriff Robert Woodruff, along with thirty-five white landowners, rode through the area searching for the strike's leaders and whipping anyone unfortunate enough to cross their path. The sortie was the beginning of a weeklong rampage during which white men ambushed Jim Press Meriwether, a leader of the Calhoun branch of the scu, beat him unconscious, and filled his body with lead. Landowners and lawmen also detained Meriwether's wife, Annie May, a captain in the scu women's auxiliary, stripped her naked, whipped her with a knotted rope, and hanged her until she lost consciousness. In addition, a group led by Sheriff Woodruff shot and killed local resident and scu organizer Ed Bracey. Before their bloodlust had been quenched, the county's leading white men had murdered at least six people, beaten scores more, forced dozens to flee the county forever, and made everyone else return to the fields under pre-strike terms.[53] The bloody suppression of the strike snuffed out collective agitation. After the mayhem, African Americans turned completely away from public protest. It was clear that Lowndes County remained entirely too dangerous to challenge white power openly.[54]

As the United States entered World War II, African Americans were only marginally closer than they had been decades earlier to realizing the dreams they inherited from their enslaved forebears. The demand that the war generated for industrial workers in southern cities and northern metropolises, however, enabled nearly seven thousand African Americans to escape the grinding poverty and fierce brutality of Lowndes County. Like the ten thousand people who left Lowndes County around World War I, these mid-century migrants had grown weary of rural poverty, Jim Crow, and racial terrorism. At the same time, they hoped to take advantage of opportunities specific to urban life, especially factory work. They sought in the city that which had been denied them in the country. Unfortunately, urban America turned out to be much less than the fabled promised land. Try as they might, they could not outrun white supremacy.[55]

Mobile was a favorite destination of local migrants who wanted to stay in Alabama. Once there, they joined the one hundred thousand black and white workers who crowded into the city during the war years in search of work in the shipyards. Charles Smith, an even-tempered farmer's son from Calhoun, was a part of the tidal wave of humanity that crested Mobile's shores. Born in 1914, Smith grew up on land that his father purchased from the Calhoun Land Trust. Belonging to a landowning family had its privileges, but it did not shelter him from racial violence. He witnessed the shooting of an scu organizer in 1935 and observed the beating of a uniformed black serviceman in the courthouse by the county sheriff for using a whites-only restroom.[56]

Smith attended school intermittently until he dropped out in the ninth grade to marry, though he still had more schooling than most. After his wedding, he worked on his father's farm before testing his luck on the Gulf Coast. In Mobile, he secured work as a hull erector at the Alabama Dry Dock and Shipbuilding Company (addsco), one of the largest employers in the city. In 1942, at its peak capacity, the addsco employed thirty thousand people, but only seven thousand African Americans, all of whom worked as unskilled laborers. Racial discrimination on the docks prompted Smith to join the Industrial Union of Marine and Shipbuilding Workers of America (iumswa), an affiliate of the Congress of Industrial Organizations (cio). The iumswa was not a vanguard union on racial issues; like most industrial unions in the South, the leaders of the iumswa were generally hostile to black demands for greater equality. The attitude of the iumswa's white members and the dock's unaffiliated workers was even worse. In 1943, a riot broke out at the addsco dockyard after the company bent to federal pressure and promoted twelve deserving African Americans to skilled positions as welders. Despite racial animosity emanating from within the union hall, Smith and his black coworkers recognized the value of union membership. Indeed, fully 90 percent of the addsco's black employees joined the iumswa, whereas fewer than half of the addsco's white workers did.[57]

The end of the war forced Smith off the docks, but not before he had saved enough money to purchase a farm back in Calhoun. He had also saved enough to buy a truck, which he used to launch a marginally profitable logging business. The modicum of wealth that he accumulated in Mobile allowed him to enjoy a significant degree of economic independence upon his return home, which created space for him to become a leader in the Lowndes movement once it materialized. Thus, working outside of the county was critical to his movement activism—union membership, though, was not. Smith's racial politics took shape long before he joined the iumswa. His belief that African Americans needed to work together to achieve even the smallest gains prompted him to join the union. Besides, the iumswa did more to reinforce white privilege than it did to promote racial equality. Conversely, Smith's membership in the

Mobile branch of the National Association for the Advancement of Colored People (NAACP), which he joined as soon as he arrived in the city, contributed significantly to his political education.[58]

John Hulett also joined the NAACP the first chance he got. In 1948, just two years after graduating from high school, the hardworking twenty-one–year-old left his family's farm in Gordonsville and moved to Birmingham. His experiences with the Birmingham branch of the NAACP and with the Birmingham-based Alabama Christian Movement for Human Rights (ACMHR) provide important insight into the ways that civil rights groups operating outside Lowndes County helped politicize migrants.[59]

In the Magic City, Hulett found employment in the furnace rooms at the Birmingham Stove and Range Company. Foundry work was physically taxing and exhausted even the strongest men, but he endured it for six years because the pay was considerably better than anything available back home. Still, wages remained significantly lower for African Americans than for whites, and opportunities for promotion to skilled jobs were nonexistent. Workplace discrimination prompted Hulett to join Local 1489 of the foundry workers' union, and racism outside his place of employment led him to become a member of the NAACP. Working under the supervision of state NAACP leader W. C. Patton, Hulett canvassed Pratt City, the segregated neighborhood where he lived, and encouraged African Americans to register to vote. He also went door-to-door generating support for campaigns to build a playground for black children and to pave neighborhood roads. After Alabama banned the NAACP in 1956, he joined the ACMHR, which filled the organizational void created by the absence of the nation's leading civil rights group. As the Birmingham movement intensified in the late 1950s, so did Hulett's activism. Although he never participated in public demonstrations, he guarded mass meetings, watched the homes of movement leaders, including that of firebrand Rev. Fred Shuttlesworth, and protected visiting dignitaries, most notably Dr. Martin Luther King, Jr.—all of which he did with a .12–gauge shotgun by his side. When he returned to Lowndes County in 1959 to care for his ailing father and to manage his family's farm, he brought with him all that he had learned about the power of collective action, the mechanics of Jim Crow, and the importance of voter registration. He also brought his shotgun.[60]

Lowndes County migrants who left the South usually relocated to Detroit. In fact, the Motor City had been the preferred destination of local black migrants since the automobile industry began hiring African

Americans in the late 1910s and early 1920s. The experiences of transplants in Detroit were similar to those of migrants who moved to Mobile and Birmingham. For instance, they were able to secure better-paying jobs. In fact, it was possible for a Detroit factory worker to earn ten times as much as a Lowndes County farmhand.[61] At the same time, they were always the last hired and the first fired, and housing was just as cramped and crowded as it was in southern cities, although it too was better than the sharecroppers' shacks. Migrants to Detroit were also politicized, but unlike those who settled in Mobile and Birmingham, unions figured prominently in this process.

Simon Owens joined the exodus to Detroit in 1924. The seventeen-year-old left the N. J. Bell plantation that he grew up on not only to escape farm labor, but also to earn enough money to help his parents feed and clothe his siblings. In the bustling metropolis, Owens earned five dollars a day working in the foundries, much more than he ever earned in the county. Although city life was not easy, he did not entertain thoughts of returning south until the Depression, which forced him to rejoin his father in the fields. In 1943, after the desegregation of the defense industry, he gladly returned to Detroit.[62]

Owens knew very little about unions when he began working in a factory gluing cloth to the moveable flaps on the wings of airplanes, but he knew a lot about racial discrimination and was irritated by the factory's policy of placing newly hired white women in the sewing room while keeping black women with more seniority in the toxic dope room. To remedy the situation, he organized a wildcat strike of black workers. To avoid a walkout, the company transferred the dope room's black women to another plant and promised to promote them to a sewing room. Owens's coworkers never received their promotions, but the Wayne County CIO noticed his organizing skills. Even though Owens was unclear about exactly what unions did, union officials made him a delegate to the organization's national convention.[63]

Owens became more involved in union activities after the war. He fought racial discrimination at the automobile plants where he worked, and he helped eliminate Jim Crow customs at restaurants that catered to factory workers. Not surprisingly, these endeavors typically involved black workers organizing black workers, a fact that did not escape him. Owens was keenly aware that white workers and white union officials contributed much less than they could have to the fight against white supremacy. In fact, he viewed the CIO, especially the national leadership of the United

Auto Workers (UAW), as unresponsive to calls for action to stop racial discrimination and as hostile to African Americans organizing among themselves. The willingness of African Americans to work together, therefore, added to Owens's understanding of the power of collective action, further radicalized his politics, and helped mold him into the civil rights leader that he would become. Unlike Hulett and Smith, the shop floor was the principal site of his political education.[64]

Ironically, Owens found problematic the politics of Detroit's civil rights groups, particularly the NAACP. In his opinion, the local branch of the nation's largest civil rights organization was "completely guided by the UAW bureaucrats," which caused the association's leaders to avoid independent, radical action. It was clear to him that the NAACP would sooner support UAW officials than the union's regular black members. His views were not out of step with the opinions of his fellow migrants. Even people who joined the NAACP made Detroit's factories the focal point of their activism.[65]

By the 1950s, Lowndes County natives had established a vibrant community in Detroit, which they sustained through social networks. As in the South, black churches played a prominent role in formalizing these networks. Former residents gravitated to a select few churches where they became active members, participating in Alabama clubs and creating Lowndes County clubs. These groups sponsored an array of activities, including regular trips home, which drew migrants closer to one another and kept them connected to family. Outside the church, the Detroit chapter of the Calhoun School Alumni Association was an important vehicle for integrating new arrivals into the community. Various incarnations of a Lowndes County social club served a similar function. The vitality of the Detroit community made it the center of the Lowndes Diaspora, and after the Lowndes movement emerged, Detroit became its most important source of material and financial support.[66]

Back in the county, nearly every aspect of black life remained unchanged. Most noticeably, political exclusion remained absolute. Not even the Supreme Court's 1944 ruling in *Smith v. Allwright*, holding that primary elections must be open to voters of all races, affected the status quo. There were no registered black voters before the decision and no registered black voters two decades later.[67] White residents reconfirmed their desire to keep African Americans out of politics in 1946 by rallying behind the proposed Boswell Amendment to the Alabama Constitution. The new policy expanded the requirement for voter registration by insisting that applicants not only copy a portion of the state charter, but also demonstrate an understanding of the document and an ability to explain it.[68] It was no secret that the supporters of the amendment hoped that it would undermine *Allwright*. "We do not profess to know whether the Boswell Amendment, if passed, will be enough to stop a very determined drive to break down all Southern customs in regard to racial segregation," wrote Kenneth Perry, the editor of the Lowndes *Signal*. "We do believe that this amendment is very necessary to prevent the wholesale registration of negroes [*sic*], and their assuming control of some of the Blackbelt counties."[69] Local whites agreed and voted six to one in favor of the amendment, which the state electorate adopted by a narrow majority.[70] A federal court eventually declared the amendment unconstitutional, but the ruling did not matter much because the state's preexisting voter registration requirements contained enough hurdles to ensure the exclusion of African Americans from the ballot box for another generation.[71]

The exploitation of black labor also continued apace. Although federal subsidies, agricultural mechanization, and the conversion to livestock farming steadily reduced the dependency of large landowners on black workers, the former still relied heavily on the latter, albeit on fewer of them.[72] It is hardly surprising, then, that whites continued to use violence, including lynching, to regulate African American behavior. On February 8, 1942, a posse that included dozens of Fort Deposit businessmen scoured the countryside searching for Roosevelt Thompson, a former employee of white landowner Charley Hartsell. When they found the day laborer, they shot him dead. Hartsell had accused Thompson of attempting to rape his wife, but an investigator sent by the Association of Southern Women for the Prevention of Lynching (ASWPL) discovered that the true motive for the murder was Thompson's demand that Hartsell pay him eighty dollars in outstanding wages.[73] Similarly, on December 4, 1947, Elmore Bolling, a thirty-year-old black businessperson who owned a general merchandise store and made a small fortune hauling goods to and from Montgomery for black and white customers, was murdered in cold blood near his Lowndesboro home. An NAACP report documenting the lynching described Bolling's body as "riddled by shotgun and pistol shots." Clarke Luckie, one of Bolling's white neighbors, admitted publicly to having orchestrated the murder and justified his actions by claiming that Bolling had insulted his wife over the telephone. NAACP investigators discovered that Bolling's wealth was the real motive behind the slaying. He was "too prosperous as a Negro farmer," they concluded.[74]

Entrepreneur Elmore Bolling in Hayneville circa 1937, a decade before he was murdered by whites for being too successful. Courtesy of Josephine Bolling McCall.

Lynching, however, was becoming outdated. The federal government began to frown on mob violence in the wake of Cold War Soviet propaganda, and Alabama politicians started to do the same because of concerns expressed by northern investors.[75] Under increasing pressure, local whites eventually stopped spectacle murders, but they did not cease using violence to preserve the racial hierarchy. "A new type of lynching is developing," explained a Montgomery activist in the wake of the murder of Elmore Bolling. "The mob get one or two men to do the work."[76]

Rather than rely on groups of citizens, whites also turned to the local police. The involvement of peace officers in acts of racial terrorism was acceptable to both state and federal officials because their participation gave the impression of order and legality. They were also up to the task. Automobiles and paved roads allowed them for the first time to establish a physical presence in every corner of the county, and telephones, which enabled instantaneous countywide communication, made rapid response possible. Thus, as the second half of the twentieth century commenced, police violence emerged as the dominant form of racial terrorism.

In a typical act of postwar police violence, two Lowndes County deputy sheriffs attacked Montgomery resident Willie Brown for failing to comply quickly enough with an order to leave Fort Deposit. In a sworn affidavit, Brown explained that on September 20, 1947, a Fort Deposit deputy questioned him about his business in the county and then told him to leave immediately. Having not broken any laws, Brown appealed to a second officer, but that constable, who was considered by some in the black community to be a reasonable white man, provided no relief. Shortly thereafter, as Brown bid farewell to his friends, both officers approached him, ordered him into their vehicle, and drove him to a nearby cemetery where they beat him bloody. After the attack, Brown sought refuge at the home of Les Reynolds, a friend who lived on the outskirts of town. News of the assault did not surprise Reynolds. A few weeks earlier one of the same deputies had shot him; his crime was eyeing a young black woman who had piqued the officer's sexual interest. Thankful to be alive but still fearing for his life, Brown fled Lowndes County the next morning by paying a black farmer to drive him to a bus stop five miles outside Fort Deposit. As he was leaving, his friend Reynolds "begged" him "to send help."[77]

Among the white men who wore badges, the county sheriff was by far the most abusive. At mid-century, the principal practitioner of police violence was sheriff Otto Moorer, a six-foot, 250-pound hellion who had a well-deserved reputation for beating African Americans, especially men, for reasons that make sense only when viewed through the prism of white supremacy.[78] "If you were walking at night and you saw some car lights, you better hit the ditch. It could be the sheriff," explained John Hulett. "More than one time, I've laid down to hide. I ain't gon' lie. Those were some pretty sad times, you know."[79] An anonymous letter sent to the national headquarters of the NAACP in July 1944 testifies to the abuses of Sheriff Moorer: "I am writing this association to see if any thing can be don [sic] about the High Sheriff of Lowndes County in Alabama. He is beating people unmerciful just because they are [unprotected] by the law." The author, who withheld his name out of fear of retaliation, cited one example of Moorer jumping out of his patrol car and giving a "licking" to a black man who was on his way to the doctor simply because the man was not at work.[80]

Police violence kept memories of lynching, peonage, and the violent suppression of the sharecropper strike fresh on the minds of African Americans. It also reminded them that the room they needed to confront white power openly still did not exist. Consequently, there was a total absence of organized public protest. During the 1940s, 1950s, and early 1960s, defiant veterans never marched on the county courthouse demanding the right to vote. Teachers and businesspersons never formed a voters' league to coordinate registration drives. Small landowners never established a chapter of the NAACP.[81] Parents never submitted petitions to the board of education demanding school desegregation in the wake of the U.S. Supreme Court ruling in *Brown v. Board of Education of Topeka, Kansas*. And students never conducted sit-ins, stand-ins, wade-ins, or pray-ins.

The eerie silence, however, did not mean that African Americans were uninterested in organized public protest. They paid close attention to the civil rights struggles emerging in neighboring cities and nearby towns. A determined handful even participated surreptitiously in some of these protests. In 1956, during the Montgomery bus boycott, dozens of people traveled east along Route 80 to the capital city to attend mass meetings, and even more gave rides to boycotters when they drove to Montgomery for work or to shop. A decade later, during the Selma voting rights campaign, some of the same people traveled west along the same stretch of roadway to attend mass meetings in Dallas County. In the late 1950s, two people even attempted to register to vote, but courthouse officials turned them away and no one dared follow their lead. Consequently, for twenty years after World War II, there was no obvious sign that African Americans would ever start a movement.[82]

Ironically, the closest thing to a social movement emanated from the white community. Responding to the threat that *Brown* posed to the racial caste system, whites organized a countywide chapter of the White Citizens' Council (wcc). More than two hundred white men attended the founding meeting held at the county courthouse on February 3, 1956, and nearly all of them paid the three dollars required to join. Twice as many people showed up for the next meeting two weeks later. White women were mostly responsible for the surge in attendance, having convinced their husbands, fathers, and brothers to allow them to join. The chapter pulled its membership from every socio-economic class but drew its leadership from the ranks of the wealthy and well connected. The officers of the first executive committee represented the county's economically powerful and politically influential families. Included in this group were O. P. Woodruff, the son of former sheriff Robert Woodruff, and E. R. Meadows, the son of Howard H. Meadows, a leading dairy farmer. Initially, the wcc confined its activities to sponsoring lectures by white supremacist demagogues, including Robert Patterson, the founder and executive secretary of Mississippi's Citizens' Council, and speeches by George Wallace and Eugene "Bull" Connor, Alabama's poster boys for segregation. It was not until after the start of the local voter registration campaign in the mid 1960s that the chapter began to retaliate systematically against African Americans who challenged the established order. The formation of the wcc chapter in 1956, therefore, was a preemptive strike designed to forestall black insurgency, which further compressed the space that African Americans needed to organize.[83]

Change seemed remote at the start of the civil rights era. Local whites continued to feel entitled to the fruits of black labor and remained committed to using violence to regulate black behavior. Although the passage of time reduced their dependency on black workers and transferred the primary task of enforcing the status quo to the sheriff and his deputies, it did not diminish their slaveholder mentality. As a result, they worked hard to preserve the exploitative labor arrangements that their parents and grandparents recreated in response to emancipation. Violence, of course, was the key to maintaining the racial hierarchy. It was simply too dangerous to organize publicly. Disenfranchisement was equally important. Excluding African Americans from the ballot box ensured white political hegemony, which was necessary to reestablish and protect the social restrictions and labor controls that emancipation erased.

Despite the intractable nature of white supremacy and the dearth of black protest, change was actually close at hand because the crucial ingredients for making a social movement were in place. African Americans possessed a clear set of unifying objectives. Like those who lived and labored in Lowndes County before them, they wanted their freedom rights. They aspired to enjoy the fundamental civil rights and the basic human rights that whites continued to deny them, including the franchise, quality education, and the chance to earn a decent living. They had access to an organizing infrastructure. Well-established social networks institutionalized in the church and extending beyond the county line were available for marshalling the human and material resources essential to fighting effectively for freedom rights. A critical mass of African Americans also possessed grassroots organizing skills. John Hulett was among those who learned the craft of organizing when he left the county during the Great Migration. Upon their return, these nascent organizers began searching for opportunities to mobilize family, friends, and neighbors. Inevitably, black protest fit the times. African Americans made shrewd tactical decisions based on careful assessments of risks and rewards. At the turn of the century, this prompted them to eschew protesting disenfranchisement and to focus instead on improving African American education. And at the start of 1965, this led them to renew the struggle for the ballot

2

I Didn't Come Here to Knock
The Making of a Grassroots Social Movement

They met in the rear parking lot of the county courthouse. Some speculated that one hundred would gather, but only thirty-nine showed up. They all drove, picking up a neighbor here and a friend there. No one knew everyone but everyone knew someone. At eight o'clock, with the sun still inching heavenward, four of them circled the old building and entered through its twin front doors. The rest waited in their cars, some talking quietly, others lost in thought, but all anxious. These ordinary rural folk had come to register to vote—or at least to try, since no African American had registered successfully in Lowndes County in recent memory. It was risky business and they knew it. They had all heard the rumor that the first African American who tried to register would be dead by nightfall. As lifelong residents of "Bloody Lowndes," they knew to take such talk seriously.[1]

Once inside the courthouse, the four men proceeded directly to the registrars' office. They knew exactly where to go, having visited the courthouse before to handle personal affairs, but they walked through the halls cautiously, knowing that their presence would cause a stir. When they reached their destination John Hulett, who had returned to the county a half dozen years earlier, entered unannounced, declaring his presence with nothing more than a steely, penetrating stare. Carl Golson, one of the county's three registrars, was the only one in that morning. The car dealership owner and former state senator was a hulk of a man, even at fifty-nine years of age, and had a reputation for being angered easily by breaches of racial etiquette. Visibly disturbed by the incomprehensible intrusion, he said, "Don't you know how to knock when you come into an office?" Unintimidated, Hulett replied, "I came here to get registered. I didn't come here to knock."[2]

To no one's surprise, Golson turned the would-be registrants away. Nevertheless, the March 1, 1965, voter registration attempt was a pivotal moment in the local freedom struggle, for it marked the beginning of a new era of protest. African Americans elsewhere in the South had engaged in civil rights organizing for several decades, but in Lowndes County they did not begin agitating publicly for civil rights until two decades after World War II and a decade after the Montgomery bus boycott. To be sure, they had been fighting for freedom rights for a century, but the voter registration attempt was the opening salvo of the most public effort to secure freedom rights ever to surface locally. As such, it signaled the start of the Lowndes movement, which not only involved voting rights agitation, but also organizing for quality education, economic opportunity, and control of county government. The Lowndes movement, though, did not emerge fully formed immediately after the action at the courthouse. It materialized deliberately between 1965 and 1966, beginning with informal conversations about black exclusion from the political process, which led to the first voter registration attempt. It then expanded beyond voting rights to incorporate the full spectrum of freedom rights.

Although only a handful of African Americans tested the waters of public resistance prior to March 1965, many people discussed social change. By the early 1960s, black political chatter had increased significantly, fueled by neighboring and national events, from the Montgomery bus boycott and the Freedom Rides, to Mississippi's Freedom Summer and the Selma voting rights campaign. Conversations about civil rights activities occurred everywhere black folk were and white folk were not. African Americans talked about the movement at church, at black-owned shops, in fields, on front porches, across dinner tables, and after school. Some of the most serious political discussions, however, took place at mutual aid society meetings, which typically convened at black homes, the most private spaces in the black community.

Mutual aid groups usually consisted of a half dozen married couples, people who had known each other for years and shared strong bonds of trust, which allowed them to discuss racially sensitive topics without having to worry about white employers or landlords learning what they said. That members participated as couples is also important because it mitigated the usual sexual banter that dominated conversations in same-sex settings, such as Masonic halls and beauty salons, and in spaces where singles mixed, including juke joints. It is equally significant that the societies met for purposes other than social and psychological escape. Although African Americans regularly discussed civil rights issues at clubs on Saturday night and at church the next morning, talking politics was not the primary purpose of these social spaces—these places existed as sanctuaries from life's pain. The raison d'etre of mutual aid societies, however, was to address the problems afflicting the black community—their very mission was to confront life's pain. In these settings, people accepted, if not expected, politically charged conversations.[3]

Hulett and his wife, Eddie Mae, were charter members of the Daylight Savings Club, a mutual aid society that met regularly at the home of Frank Miles, Jr., a thirty-five-year-old furniture dealer. As club members, the Huletts contributed a portion of their income to help the elderly, the infirm, and the poor of Gordonsville meet their material needs. In 1964, as Christmas neared and the club finalized its plans for the holiday season, Hulett raised the subject of voter registration. Ever since returning to the county, he wanted to mobilize a group to attempt to register. Initially, he discussed the idea with a handful of teachers and shopkeepers, but they spurned his overtures. "I had talked with other people, more or less professional people, and they were afraid to even take [a] chance [at registering to vote]," he recalled. Indifference by black professionals prompted him to approach the members of the Savings Club. To his relief, they agreed to meet after Christmas to evaluate the risks and rewards of such an endeavor.[4]

On a chilly Sunday evening in the middle of February 1965, fourteen members of the Savings Club gathered to discuss registering. They talked generally about the ballot and political power, and specifically about Alabama's voter registration exam. Hulett was the only registered voter among them, having registered while living in Birmingham, so he led them in a careful review of the state test. By evening's end, a consensus had emerged in favor of trying to register, and the decision had been made to meet in the parking lot of the courthouse on Monday, March 1, when the registrars' office reopened for the first of its two monthly sessions.[5]

A chance encounter the day after the meeting extended the registration attempt beyond the close-knit circle of Savings Club members and Gordonsville residents. Traveling home from work, Hulett happened upon a family acquaintance from White Hall, the largest community of landowning black farmers in the county. Excited about the group's decision to attempt to register, he shared the details of the plan. His enthusiasm soared when the family friend named others whom she believed would be interested in joining them. Before parting company, she agreed to gather these people together for a meeting later that week and he promised to join them to discuss the coming action. The meeting took place as planned, and eight White Hall residents pledged to rendezvous with Hulett and the group from Gordonsville at the courthouse. They also asked Hulett to return to White Hall to meet with another group. Unfortunately, when the time for that meeting arrived, Hulett was unable to attend, but his absence did not stop the second group from convening. William Cosby, a well-established and well-liked shopkeeper and farmer from the small residential town of Trickem, which borders White Hall, facilitated in his stead. Drawing on what he had learned at the earlier gathering, he outlined the registration plan, and the small group agreed to join the attempt.[6]

As March 1 neared, the number of people willing to defy local custom and try to register continued to grow. Personal contacts were responsible for the slow but steady rise in volunteers. Savings Club members and those who attended the two meetings in White Hall encouraged people they trusted to participate in the impending action. In doing so, they established a pattern of recruitment that became the basis for building the movement. At the same time, they increased the likelihood that whites would hear about their plans.[7]

The voting rights campaign in neighboring Selma had sensitized whites to upswings in civil rights talk within the black community. As February ended, local whites suspected that some type of action was in the offing, but they possessed no specific intelligence. Convinced that the impetus for black protest would come from beyond the county line, they searched for outsiders. Unable to locate any, they redirected their attention toward finding a local person with links to the Selma movement. They found their man in the person of Rev. Lorenzo Harrison, the pastor of Mt. Carmel Baptist Church in Gordonsville. To them, Rev. Harrison was as likely a civil rights leader as anyone. Not only had they spotted him at demonstrations and mass meetings in Selma, but he was also a preacher, which placed him in the company of Dr. Martin Luther King, Jr., the most despised social activist in the South. Consequently, on February 28, the day before the registration attempt, several truckloads of white men armed with shotguns interrupted Sunday service at Mt. Carmel and demanded an audience with the church deacons. The mob delivered a simple message: "Get this nigger out of town," one of the gunmen told the church caretakers, "or he will get killed." The deacons knew that this was not a threat but a promise. After hurrying back inside, some with tears in their eyes, they held an emergency caucus and decided not only to get the young minister out of the county, but also to sever all ties with him. "We don't want anything to happen," explained a deacon to the congregation. After a few quick goodbyes, they hustled Rev. Harrison off to Selma.[8]

Speaking later that evening at a mass meeting, the exiled minister referred to the episode as the darkest day in his life. He vowed to keep fighting, however. So too did Hulett, who was a deacon at Mt. Carmel. In fact, Hulett was at the church that day and helped whisk Rev. Harrison out of town, but he wisely kept silent about his organizing activities and the forthcoming registration attempt. He was certain that no good would come from telling the mob that he was the person they really wanted. Besides, he knew they would find out about him soon enough.[9]

It is very likely that the visit to Mt. Carmel kept some would-be registrants away from the courthouse the next day, but it did not scare off everyone. On Monday, thirty-nine intrepid souls caravanned to Hayneville. After the brief encounter with Registrar Golson, Hulett and his fellow emissaries informed them that no one would be registering that morning. The news did not surprise many, though it did dampen spirits. Although success was unlikely, they clung tenaciously to the hope that it was possible. The delegation also reported that those wishing to register when the office reopened in two weeks had to submit their names and addresses in writing before they departed. This was no small request. If the would-be registrants consented, every white person in the county would know who they were and where they lived, probably before lunch. There was security in anonymity and now they were being forced to give that up. Yet, in a remarkable display of courage and determination, almost everyone surrendered their information. The significance of this seemingly simple act cannot be overstated. By providing their names and addresses they made an irrevocable, public commitment to fight white supremacy.

The next two weeks tested their resolve. As expected, a list bearing their names and addresses circulated among merchants, employers, and landlords. Visits followed. The message that whites delivered was always the same: stop trying to register or face severe consequences. Specifics about reprisals were rarely revealed, but details were unnecessary. Black shopkeepers, employees, and renters understood that if they tried to register again, whites would boycott their businesses, fire them from their jobs, or evict them from their homes.[10] Then came Bloody Sunday. On March 7, 1965, a phalanx of Alabama state troopers brutally beat scores of demonstrators in Dallas County as they crossed Selma's steeply arched Edmond Pettus Bridge en route to Montgomery. The marchers were protesting the murder of Jimmie Lee Jackson, a twenty-six-year-old native of nearby Perry County who had died less than two weeks earlier from gunshot wounds inflicted by state police. The episode was a sobering reminder of how vicious the state regime could be in its support of local oligarchs.[11] Two days later, white youths attacked Rev. James Reeb, a white Unitarian minister from Boston, in downtown Selma shortly after the aborted second march to Montgomery. Reeb later died from injuries sustained during the assault. His murder underscored the willingness of ordinary whites to kill in order to maintain the established order.[12] The coup de grace came the next registration day when local officials announced that they had moved the registrars' office to the county's crumbling jailhouse located on the outskirts of Hayneville. The old brick jail, with its blood-stained cells, was the one place in Lowndes County that evoked more fear in African Americans than the courthouse.[13]

Given local intimidation tactics and nearby acts of violence, it would not have been a surprise if those who tried to register on March 1 simply stayed at home when the registrars' office reopened two weeks later, but even more people than before lined up outside the jail. The specific forces that compelled them to do so varied widely. For some it was determination, for others it was fear, and for still others it was faith. The range of emotions that people felt as they waited to be examined also covered a vast spectrum. Everyone was frustrated, however, because the registrars refused to process their applications expeditiously. That day they examined only seventeen people. They also failed to announce whether any of these applications had been approved. In fact, several weeks passed before county officials revealed that they had rejected every application except Hulett's (because he had registered previously in Birmingham) and John C. Lawson's, a sixty-five-year-old blind preacher and Daylight Savings Club member (because he answered correctly the literacy test questions read to him). When the people returned home late that afternoon, their only comfort was knowing that they had acted and lived to tell about it.[14]

The drama and excitement surrounding the first two attempts to register fully occupied the attention of those seeking the franchise, but after the second registration try, several people began discussing ways to sustain their efforts and increase their numbers. It did not take them long to conclude that they needed to form an organization to coordinate future registration attempts. Toward this end, they called a meeting for Friday,

March 19, 1965. Alerting those who had already tried to register about the meeting was not too difficult, but finding a place to host the gathering was nearly impossible. Those who organized the event hoped to hold it at a church, but every minister and deacon board they approached turned them away. The stewards of the county's black churches feared that whites would bomb and burn their places of worship just as they had done in Birmingham and Montgomery. The unwillingness of black churches to open their doors was profoundly disappointing and marked the beginning of a pattern of institutional ostracism that lasted nearly as long as the movement did. Eventually, the meeting planners secured access to an old, abandoned store on the edge of White Hall. Retiree Frank Haralson, who owned the forgotten shop, had paid off the mortgage on the building many years prior and, as a result, was not afraid of losing it should whites discover that it had been the site of a civil rights gathering.[15]

The meeting started promptly at 7:30 p.m. The attendees included twenty-eight local African Americans, almost all of whom took part in one or both of the registration attempts. Hulett was among them, but he was one of only a handful not from the White Hall area. Representatives from the Southern Christian Leadership Conference (SCLC) were also present. It is unclear who invited them but it is not surprising that they were there. A month earlier, Dr. King, SCLC's president, informed his circle of advisers that he wanted to revive the Selma voting rights movement, which had reached an impasse, by mobilizing the rural counties surrounding the city. In late February 1965, he sent a team of scouts, led by Rev. Andrew Young, into Lowndes County to gauge interest, and on March 1, 1965, he visited the courthouse hoping to meet the people trying to register but missed them by a few hours. SCLC's representatives did not come alone. They were joined by eight members of the Episcopal Society for Cultural and Racial Unity (ESCRU) who had answered Dr. King's call to come to Alabama for the march.[16]

The meeting opened with the movement anthem "We Shall Overcome," a prayer by Rev. James David Armstrong of New York, and a scripture reading by Rev. Ronald Hafer of Massachusetts. After taking a moment for introductions, the group began the process of forming a social movement organization by selecting officers. In a move indicative of the democratic tendencies that came to characterize the local struggle, they decided that the people they chose that evening would only hold office temporarily; they would wait until they held a mass meeting to elect permanent officers. To lead them as interim chairperson, they turned to Hulett. Although most people met him only recently, his commitment to fight white supremacy was plain to see. Indeed, everyone knew he was the catalyst behind the registration attempts. Besides, he was willing to serve and most people were not. The group tapped White Hall shopkeeper William Cosby for the vice chair, a decision that reflected how highly Cosby's friends, neighbors, and customers regarded him. His selection also evidenced the disproportionate number of White Hall residents in attendance. For chaplain, they turned to John Hinson, a lay preacher of sorts, and for assistant secretary they elected Jesse Favors, a railroad laborer and member of the Daylight Savings Club. They found their treasurer in the person of Elzie Lee McGill, a fifty-nine-year-old farmer who owned two hundred acres in White Hall, which he purchased in 1943 from a Resettlement program participant. Finally, for secretary, the group elected McGill's daughter Lillian, who volunteered at the start of the meeting to serve as note taker because, she said, that's what women did. Though no one realized it at the time, her appointment to the executive committee was one of the most important decisions made that evening.

Lillian McGill was born in White Hall in 1933. She attended grade school at White Hall Elementary and church across the street at Unity Baptist. The economic independence that landownership bestowed on her parents, combined with the supplemental income that her father's work as a laborer provided, enabled her to attend junior high school and high school in Selma and college in Montgomery at Alabama State University. After marrying, she settled in the capital city, cleaning and cooking for white families to help support her own. Like most of Montgomery's domestic workers, she participated in the bus boycott by walking to work for the better part of a year and by attending mass meetings whenever possible. She returned to White Hall in 1964 shortly after her mother's death to help her father with his farm. At the time, she was working part-time as a clerical worker for the Department of Agriculture. She was also a single mother of three small children, having separated from her husband not long before returning home. Her desire to have her children receive a quality education without having to leave the county served as a major catalyst for her movement participation.[17]

Choosing a name for the new organization was the next agenda item. The group bandied about several possibilities before settling on the Lowndes County Christian Movement for Human Rights (LCCMHR). Fred Shuttlesworth's Birmingham-based civil rights group, the Alabama Christian Movement for Human Rights, which was at the forefront of the freedom struggle in the state, inspired the choice. The name's appeal, however, reached beyond simply paying homage to the fiery preacher and his association. Including "Lowndes County" in the appellation touched a responsive chord with those who wanted to emphasize the indigenous nature of the new organization, while "Christian" not only resonated with the representatives of SCLC and ESCRU, but also spoke to the Christian ethic that undergirded the involvement of the more religious residents in attendance. Finally, "Human Rights" satisfied those who wanted the new organization to fight for more than voting rights. It reflected their understanding of the struggle as a fight for freedom rights.[18]

The creation of the LCCMHR was a watershed event in the evolution of the freedom struggle. It transformed local protest by providing African Americans with a formal social movement organization through which they could mobilize a sizeable segment of the black population in a sustained, organized, public effort to secure freedom rights. In this way, it signaled the transition in the local struggle from a loosely organized campaign of voter registration attempts to a bona fide social movement. African Americans had a long history of protest, but never before had black protest coalesced into a social campaign. This development set the coming years apart from other periods. In fact, it made this era the highpoint of the local freedom struggle.

Ed Moore King understood the importance of this moment. The army veteran grew up in Sardis, a small town in Dallas County, but had lived in Gordonsville and taught elementary school in Hayneville and Fort Deposit since the late 1950s. The youngest of ten siblings and the son of landowning farmers, the thirty-three-year-old parlayed the GI Bill into a master's degree from Alabama State. Working in the county's resource-poor, segregated schools was not easy, especially because he rarely received teaching assignments near his home. The eagerness of his students, however, made his job worth the hassles. At the same time, it placed a heavy burden on his shoulders. When asked why he took part in the voter registration activities of March 1965, he replied, "I didn't think I could do an effective job teaching our children without being a registered voter." He added, "I hated to see my children grow up in a place where they couldn't be registered voters. I wasn't only thinking about myself, but I was thinking about trying to make things better for all the young people."[19]

King recognized that the embryonic movement was the key to improving local conditions and knew instinctively that the LCCMHR needed a church home to sustain the energy generated that month. Consequently, when he met with the leadership of White Hall's Mt. Gilliard Missionary Baptist Church the morning after the LCCMHR founding meeting, he insisted that his pastor and fellow deacons invite the new organization to hold its meetings at the church. "The people have nowhere to go and need to keep up momentum," he recalled telling them. Surprisingly, he did not have a hard sell, thanks mainly to pastor Theodore Roosevelt "R. V." Harrison.[20]

Dr. Harrison was a hands-on preacher who enjoyed a good rapport with Mt. Gilliard's deacon board and congregation. The sixty-year-old cleric had pastored the church seemingly since its cornerstone had been laid in 1901. His sermons were not radical, but he believed in racial equality in Heaven as well as on Earth. When exactly he decided to commit the church to the freedom struggle is unclear, but any uncertainty about doing so disappeared forever on February 28, 1965, when local whites chased his son, Rev. Lorenzo Harrison, out of the pulpit of Mt. Carmel. After that day, he was ready to move and awaited only the opportunity that Ed Moore King presented. When that time came, he urged the deacons to embrace the teacher's proposition, which they did. Their consent, however, did not blind them to the danger that Mt. Gilliard now faced. The same day that they agreed to open the church to the LCCMHR, they instructed King to purchase insurance on the building.[21]

This simple, unassuming, brick church built jointly by the residents of White Hall and Trickem provided the LCCMHR with a much-needed public gathering place. Gaining access to Mt. Gilliard, however, meant much more than merely securing a better venue for meetings. The church anchored two fiercely independent black communities, including the largest community of black landowners in the county. By opening its doors to the LCCMHR, the church legitimized the new organization, because African Americans put greater trust into that which was associated with a bedrock church like Mt. Gilliard than into that which was not.

As the Lowndes movement began to take shape, the nation turned its attention to the Alabama Black Belt due to the Selma to Montgomery March, which finally got underway on March 21, 1965. That Sunday, some 3,000 demonstrators resumed the trek to the Alabama capitol that state police had beat back two weeks earlier. At sunset, most of the demonstrators returned to Selma, but about 450 camped out on an eighty-acre farm owned by David and Rosa Belle Hall, located seven miles east of the Edmond Pettus Bridge. They broke camp early the next morning and by noon reached the Dallas County line. As they crossed into Lowndes

County, they sang, "We are not afraid." Their hymnal choice was purposeful. They were well aware of the county's violent reputation and turned to these lyrics to stiffen their resolve.[22]

The appearance of the marchers angered Lowndes County whites. "I feel like any other good citizen," said sheriff Frank Ryals. "This march is uncalled for. It's a lot of expense for nothing. It's disrupting people in their homes and on the highway." Fueling their bitterness was the belief that if these "beatniks and screwballs," as Ryals called them, were allowed to continue their professional agitation they would destroy the harmonious race relations that existed locally. "We have been getting along fine here," said the police chief. "And we will continue to unless they come in here with a lot of this unlawful stuff and this provocation."[23]

Some African Americans undoubtedly believed that the march was a bad idea because it upset whites, but most welcomed the demonstration as a harbinger of changing times. As an expression of support, a handful made their way to Route 80. Mattie Lee Moorer, a fifty-year-old beautician, was among those who waited for hours on the sloping shoulder of the two-lane highway to cheer the marchers. When they finally came into view, she rejoiced, and when she saw Dr. King leading them, she wept. "It's him! It's him!" she shouted as she ran to hug the famous preacher. Dr. King kindly received her embrace, which surely meant the world to her.[24]

Many people shared Mrs. Moorer's excitement but few actually lined the side of the roadway. Fear kept most people away. With good reason, they were afraid of being spotted by employers and creditors because of the consequences of being associated with "that mess." Others simply could not afford to skip work. In the evenings, however, scores visited the marchers' campsite. On their first night in Lowndes County, the weary demonstrators bedded down in Trickem on farmland owned by Rosie Steele, an active member of White Hall's First Baptist Church and the proprietor of a grocery store that whites tried to burn out of business immediately after the march. Ed Moore King and his family, along with several members of Mt. Gilliard, joined those who fellowshipped with the protesters on Monday. On Tuesday, the McGills drove across the county to keep company with them as they camped in a pasture owned by A. G. Gaston, the black millionaire headquartered in Birmingham. That evening, the marchers were exhausted, cold, and soaked to the bone. A pitiful sight to see, they seemed more like a motley crew than a fearsome force of freedom fighters. Yet, local visitors found mingling among them

Participants in the Selma to Montgomery March make their way in the rain along U.S. Route 80 in Lowndes County on March 23, 1965. © Associated Press.

breathtaking. Their appearance might have been unimpressive, but their purpose was inspiring and left an indelible imprint on the hearts and minds of those who dared meet them.[25] The marchers departed the county on Wednesday and found sanctuary that night at St. Jude Catholic School in western Montgomery. The next morning they wound their way through downtown Montgomery, up Dexter Avenue, and assembled on the stark white steps of the state capitol. Joining the three hundred people who walked the entire fifty-four miles were thousands of supporters from the city, the surrounding counties, and across the country. Together they sang freedom songs and listened to a bevy of speeches, including an unforgettable sermon by Dr. King, who gave voice to the spirit that drew so many from so far. SCLC's chairperson began by calling attention to the marchers' weary bodies but rested souls. He named those who had fallen in the freedom struggle, including Jimmie Lee Jackson and Rev. James Reeb. He offered a history of disenfranchisement and explained that the right to vote was the key issue going forward. How long will freedom and justice take, he asked, and then he answered with the memorable refrain, "Not long," because truth and righteousness were on their side. That afternoon, change appeared on the horizon, but by evening, a white civil rights volunteer was dead in Lowndes County and the idea that change would visit Alabama seemed fanciful.[26]

Viola Liuzzo was the only white woman murdered in the 1960s for supporting the African American freedom struggle. The thirty-nine-year-old mother of five, who drove by herself from Detroit to Alabama to attend the march, was just discovering her activist self. The previous year she had been arrested for homeschooling her children in protest over a Michigan law that lowered the minimum age a student could be in order to drop out of school without parental consent (Liuzzo had left school when she was only fourteen and regretted the decision). News of racial violence and injustice in the South troubled the recent college enrollee, who had a touch of the spirit of a radical humanist. Confident that drawing attention to discrimination against black southerners would help eliminate the problem, she accepted Dr. King's open invitation to join the Alabama protest. By answering the preacher's call, she challenged both standard gender conventions and the norms governing interracial interaction—middle-aged, middle-class white women from the North simply did not leave their children to march in solidarity with African Americans in the South. She did so, however, because she believed that it was her prerogative to do what she wanted and what was right. But following her conscience cost Liuzzo her life.[27]

Liuzzo and nineteen-year-old Leroy Moton, an SCLC staffer, had just dropped off a carload of marchers in Selma and were returning to Montgomery to pick up others when a red-and-white Impala driven by four Klansmen from Birmingham's notorious Eastview Klavern 13 fell in behind them. Liuzzo immediately hammered the accelerator of her 1963 green Oldsmobile, sending the car flying along Route 80, but she was unable to elude her pursuers. Halfway through Lowndes County, the Impala pulled alongside the Olds, and Collie Wilkins, an unemployed mechanic from Birmingham who had just turned twenty-one, fired several shots into the vehicle, striking Liuzzo in the head and killing her instantly. The Olds veered off the highway and careened through the roadside brush before skidding to a halt. "I don't think you hit them," said Gary Rowe, a low-ranking Klansman who had been working as a paid FBI informant for six years. The triggerman, beaming with satisfaction, slapped his thirty-one-year-old coconspirator on the leg and replied, "Baby brother, don't worry about it. That bitch and bastard are dead and in hell. I don't miss." Despite his certainty of the kill, they circled back and shined a light inside the wreck. Seeing blood on both bodies and movement from neither one, they drove off, back to Birmingham, congratulating each other the entire way.[28]

Miraculously, Leroy Moton was unharmed; he feigned mortal injury to deceive the gunmen. When stillness and quiet returned to the darkness, he stumbled out of the wrecked car and made his way to the highway where he stopped a pickup truck ferrying marchers to Selma. As the blood-splattered teen dove into the back of the vehicle, he shouted, "Everybody down. Quick! There are men around here with guns. A woman has been killed." Without hesitating, the driver raced to safety.[29]

Martyrs were usually made of white volunteers who lost their lives in the movement, the two most famous being Michael Schwerner and Andrew Goodman, who along with black Mississippian James Chaney had been murdered in Philadelphia, Mississippi, less than a year earlier. The FBI, however, worked hard to prevent Liuzzo's martyrdom by circulating malicious tales impugning her character and casting doubt on her competence as a mother. The bureau wanted to minimize the political fallout from having had an accomplice to her murder on its payroll. To a substantial degree, the FBI succeeded. The mainstream press published enough salacious rumors about her life for the public to question her reasons for being in Alabama. Consequently, few people other than civil rights leaders, local black residents, and Detroit politicians found meaning in her death.[30]

The Sunday after the killing, about one hundred African Americans met at Mt. Gilliard Baptist Church. New York *Times* correspondent Roy Reed, who covered the march and its aftermath, reported that they gathered to "protest the night-rider slaying." Although saddened and disturbed by Liuzzo's murder, they did not assemble solely to memorialize a white woman who most of them didn't even know. Rather, they gathered for the inaugural mass meeting of the LCCMHR.[31]

In the coming months, the LCCMHR would become a fully functioning, incorporated, movement organization with a clearly defined list of ten objectives for improving social conditions and economic opportunities for African Americans. In time, it would have an organizational structure based on a community representation model that placed community members on an executive committee that met every Wednesday. It would also have a set of decision-making rules that involved public problem solving at neighborhood and countywide mass meetings. At its inaugural meeting, however, Chairperson Hulett had very little to say about the LCCMHR's organizational structure or its purpose other than

Two Alabama state troopers, standing on the side of U.S. Route 80 in Lowndes County, guard the wreckage of the car that Viola Liuzzo, a thirty-nine-year-old homemaker from Detroit, was driving at the conclusion of the Selma to Montgomery March on March 25, 1965, when she was shot and killed by Ku Klux Klansmen. Photo by William Lovelace/Express/Getty Images.

that the group sought to coordinate a voter registration campaign and that it needed volunteers for the following week.[32]

Sidney Logan, Jr., attended the LCCMHR's initial mass meeting. The forty-two-year-old widower lived with his four children on an eighty-acre farm in Gordonsville. Listening to meeting participants sing, "Which Side Are You On?" confirmed the impulse to join the fight against white supremacy that compelled the World War II veteran to be present at the meeting in the first place. "I had to go out and show them what side I was on," he recalled. His opportunity to take a public stance came sooner than even he imagined. State troopers recorded the license plate numbers of the vehicles parked outside the church and provided whites with a list of the owners. Logan explained that the day after the meeting, "white peoples" called on him, expressed their dismay at his "messing around" with civil rights activists and advised him to stop. His refusal led to a boycott of his truck hauling business and eventually to its failure, but it did not cause him to switch sides. A year later, he ran for sheriff.[33]

LCCMHR leaders scheduled a second mass meeting for the following Sunday, the day before the registrars' office reopened. Hulett and the others understood the enormous importance of these community gatherings. Growing up in the black church taught them about the ability of spirituals and witnessing to stir people to action. Meanwhile, the positive response to the first mass meeting demonstrated the ability of freedom songs and testimonials by those who had attempted to register to inspire people who wanted to act but either did not know how or were too afraid. They also knew that they had to get the Sidney Logans of the county to side publicly with the movement, and mass meetings were an excellent way to reach this critical group. Accordingly, they spent the week after the first mass meeting trying by word-of-mouth to get as many people as possible to come to the next meeting. Their effort received an unexpected and substantial boost from SNCC organizers who entered the county the day after the Liuzzo murder.

Two years earlier, in the summer of 1963, Bernard Lafayette, a veteran of the Nashville student movement, and his wife, Colia, a Mississippi organizer who had worked closely with NAACP leader Medgar Evers, established a beachhead for SNCC in the Alabama Black Belt by organizing high school and college students in Selma. Their initial efforts, though, yielded few concrete results. "I feel that many people are afraid to identify with the Voter Registration Project, either out of fear or just plain apathy," reported Bernard Lafayette in June 1963. The Lafayettes' patience, persistence, and hard work, however, bore fruit in the form of an organized cadre of young people who marched on the Dallas County courthouse in October 1963 and tested local compliance with the 1964 Civil Rights Act the following July. Unfortunately, sheriff Jim Clark and his posse defeated both efforts by beating black protesters with cattle prods and batons, which led to a lull in direct action that lasted through the end of 1964. By the time that the Lafayettes left Selma to return to school, African Americans had secured few tangible gains. Nevertheless, by organizing Selma's young people the duo provided SNCC with a springboard from which to launch future organizing efforts in the area. "For most people, Selma, Alabama, hardly existed before the marches of 1965," recalled former SNCC executive secretary James Forman. "But people like the Lafayettes, of whom the world at large knows nothing, were there long before, turning the first stone, breaking the first earth, planting the first seed."[34]

SNCC reestablished its presence in the Alabama Black Belt in the fall of 1964 when Silas Norman, Jr., a former sit-in leader at Paine College in Augusta, Georgia, became the organization's state project director and took up residence in Selma. In the opening months of 1965, several SNCC veterans joined him. Most came from Mississippi, where they had helped the Mississippi Freedom Democratic Party (MFDP) attempt to win recognition as Mississippi's official delegation to the Democratic National Convention in August 1964 in Atlantic City. Although backroom arm-twisting by President Lyndon B. Johnson prompted Democratic Party decision makers to reject the MFDP bid, the experience provided SNCC activists with valuable insights. Among other things, it exposed the Democratic Party's lack of commitment to civil rights. Up to that point, many within the organization assumed that black and white liberals in the Democratic Party had simply been dragging their feet on civil rights, but Atlantic City demonstrated that liberals were not just slow to move—they were unwilling to move.[35] The experience also showed that the social and economic concerns of rural working-class blacks diverged at several critical points from those of the Democratic Party. It also revealed that trying to replace segregationists at the state level in order to control local political structures was not viable. "We thought we could take over the Democratic Party of Mississippi and that's a farce," recalled a SNCC activist. "Them crackers ain't never going to let us in."[36] Finally, it showed that appealing to the conscience of white northerners was as pointless as appealing to the conscience of white southerners. "The national conscience was generally unreliable," concluded the same SNCC worker.[37]

The effect of these revelations on SNCC members depended on the member's view of the movement. Although everyone found the new insights disturbing, those who believed that the freedom struggle was principally a moral crusade remained committed to direct action protest and moral suasion. Fewer and fewer SNCC members, however, saw the movement this way. With the notable exception of chairperson John Lewis, who adhered to nonviolence as a way of life, most of the organizers who subscribed to the moral perspective had defected to SCLC, which meant that the overwhelming majority of black SNCC organizers now viewed the movement primarily as a political struggle. The outcome of the challenge forced the members of this group to reconsider their tactics, beginning with working with Democrats. Robert Parris "Bob" Moses, the driving force behind the Mississippi campaign, explained that before the convention they were committed to working within the Democratic Party, but that afterward they began contemplating ways of organizing African Americans outside the party. It also prompted them to eschew moral suasion. "Never again were we lulled into believing that our task was exposing injustices so that the 'good' people of America could eliminate them," recalled former SNCC program director Cleveland Sellers. "We left Atlantic City with the knowledge that the movement had turned into something else. After Atlantic City, our struggle was not for civil rights, but for liberation."[38]

SNCC organizers mulled over the convention experience at a time when many of them were becoming interested in achieving freedom rights through black solidarity, institution building, and community control. Their interest in Black Nationalist approaches sprang from a variety of sources, but especially from their experiences in the field. Southern white hostility and northern white indifference to their struggles in Mississippi forced them to rely almost exclusively on local black communities for support. Without this assistance, SNCC projects would have failed almost as soon as they began. But the appeal of Black Nationalism was not simply a reaction to white indifference and intransigence. SNCC organizers drew equal inspiration from the self-determining cultural practices of black southerners, which gave rise to the social and economic institutions that enabled black communities to survive. Black cultural values taught the young activists the importance of community self-reliance and solidarity.[39]

Working with local people caused SNCC activists to look at Black Nationalists and Pan-Africanists, including Marcus Garvey, Kwame Nkrumah, Elijah Muhammad, and Franz Fanon, in a new light, and scrutinizing their theories and practices provided fresh insights into the advantages of Black Nationalist approaches. Studying the teachings of Malcolm X, however, encouraged their Black Nationalist sensibilities the most. In defiant tones, Malcolm gave voice to the young radicals' hopes and frustrations, and by 1965 his fiery oratory and pointed political analysis made him the unofficial voice of SNCC. Tragically, Malcolm fell to assassins' bullets before his relationship with the young activists could fully mature.[40]

The independence struggles of people of color enhanced the appeal of Black Nationalism. SNCC organizers looked to freedom movements in Africa and throughout the African Diaspora for inspiration and direction. For many, interest in these struggles was personal. A few SNCC members were from the Caribbean and learned about anticolonial struggles from family members and friends. Others had mingled with college students from Africa who were helping break the chains of colonialism. A handful had even traveled to the continent. After the 1964 Democratic convention, about a dozen SNCC members toured several independent African nations and met with prominent government leaders, student activists, and African American expatriates who delineated the connections between the liberation movements on the continent and the African American struggle in the United States.[41]

SNCC was at a crossroads at the end of 1964. It no longer had an organizing program because so many of its members were uninterested in working within the Democratic Party. Although SNCC activists remained committed to organizing around the vote, the MFDP model had lost its appeal. SNCC also lacked a primary theater of operations. Black Mississippians did not give up on the Democratic Party as had SNCC organizers. During the convention, they received more support from national delegates than many people thought was possible and generated significant local interest and media attention. As a result, they decided to keep working under the Democratic umbrella. SNCC organizers continued to assist them, but they had no heart for it.[42] "Clearly we had to provide any technical support they requested until they no longer needed us," elaborated a veteran SNCC organizer. "But doing so without pushing our ideas of what their best interests were or their programs ought to be could be tricky. The relationship was ambiguous, with real potential for tension."[43] To avoid conflict, SNCC activists began slowly withdrawing from the state.

The absence of specific organizing objectives led several battle-weary veterans to drift away from the organization. Bob Moses was the most notable activist to leave. After the convention in Atlantic City, he stopped participating in SNCC decision making, and shortly thereafter he resigned. As the catalyst for SNCC's work in Mississippi, his departure created a leadership void that everyone knew would be hard to fill. But into this space stepped executive secretary James Forman, administrative secretary and future executive secretary Ruby Doris Smith Robinson, and program secretary Cleveland Sellers. Their management skills brought order to SNCC's day-to-day operations and they reined in some of the undisciplined behavior that had begun to splinter the expanding staff. The trio also made the tough decisions about the allocation of resources that others shied away from. Their tireless work sustained SNCC. The departure of Moses and other veterans, therefore, did not leave SNCC bereft of effective leadership, nor did it deprive SNCC of expert organizers. The organization retained a core group of experienced field secretaries who had been baptized in the waters of the Mississippi.[44]

A standout in this group was twenty-three-year-old Stokely Carmichael, a tall, slender Trinidadian who attended high school in New York City and college in Washington, D.C. Carmichael was charming, witty, and blessed with a disarming smile that he knew how to use. By all accounts he was unflappable; he was as comfortable breaking bread with black sharecroppers as he was dining with the white elite. He also had a passion for politics that stemmed from his belief that the movement was a political struggle rather than a moral crusade. "I never saw my responsibility to be the moral and spiritual reclamation of some racist thug," he said. "I would settle for changing his behavior, period. Moral suasion, legal proscription, or even force of arms, whatever ultimately it took, that's what I'd be for." Carmichael was also a gifted orator whose rhetorical style drew on the rhythmic cadences of Mississippi's black Baptist preachers and the fiery exhortations of Harlem's stepladder proselytizers. His facility as a public speaker was second only to his deftness as a grassroots organizer. In addition, the former Freedom Rider, who spent his twentieth birthday in Mississippi's Parchman Penitentiary, was one of SNCC's most experienced field secretaries. During the summers of 1962 and 1963, he worked as an organizer in Greenwood, Mississippi, and during the summer of 1964, after graduating from Howard University, he served as SNCC's project director for the MFDP's Second Congressional District, which covered most of the Mississippi Delta. Although he learned how to organize in Mississippi, he perfected his craft in Alabama.[45]

Carmichael and other Mississippi veterans gravitated to Alabama because the absence of an MFDP-like organization appealed to those interested in working outside the Democratic Party. The opposition of the state project director to interracial projects also attracted those whose experiences in Mississippi taught them that working with whites was unnecessarily dangerous and weakened racial solidarity at the grassroots level.⁴⁶ Once in Selma, SNCC organizers began working closely and effectively with local youth, but soon after they arrived, SCLC field secretaries began canvassing the city in preparation for a voting rights campaign. At first, the personal relationships that existed among SNCC and SCLC workers, several of whom were former SNCC members, mitigated interorganizational conflict. Within weeks, however, irreconcilable differences surfaced over SCLC's insistence that Selma residents needed Dr. King and his lieutenants to lead them, as well as SCLC's support of a federal plan to have voter registration applicants sign an appearance book in lieu of actually registering. SCLC's proposal to march to Montgomery, which led to Bloody Sunday, and Dr. King's about-face during the second attempt to walk to the state capitol the following Tuesday, also angered SNCC organizers.⁴⁷ "Here comes SCLC talking about mobilizing another two-week campaign, using our base and the magic of Dr. King's name," recalled Carmichael. "They going to bring in the cameras, the media, prominent people, politicians, rat-tat-tat, turn the place upside down, and split. Probably leaving most of the strongest people sitting in jail. *That* was the issue, a real strategic and philosophical difference."⁴⁸

SNCC and SCLC's conflicting views over the management and direction of the Selma campaign caused their alliance to falter. "We decided that it was not productive for us to fight with SCLC," remembered Silas Norman, Jr. Consequently, SNCC withdrew from Selma, but it did not pull its field secretaries out of the Black Belt entirely. Instead, it dispatched organizers to the rural counties surrounding the city. Norman explained that SNCC simply decided to "move to places where [SCLC] would not come." At the top of this list was "Bloody Lowndes."⁴⁹

SNCC's interest in Lowndes County derived from several factors. The county's proximity to Selma meant that it was accessible: organizers could get in, and, more importantly, they could get out relatively easily. The county shared many of the same social and economic characteristics as places that SNCC had already organized, such as Leflore County, Mississippi. "Enter Lowndes County and you back in the Mississippi Delta," remembered Carmichael. "Miles of cotton plantations, a huge black majority, an aging population, serious poverty, *serious* political and economic oppression. The same Wild West ambience, whites in cowboy boots and

Stetsons wearing handguns with rifle racks in the pickup trucks."[50] These similarities gave SNCC workers an advantage in terms of knowing where to look in the black community for local leadership and, equally important, what to expect from the white community regarding resistance. In addition, neither SCLC nor any other civil rights organization had a permanent presence there. SCLC had made overtures to local activists but failed to send full-time fieldworkers to the county, meaning that SNCC could avoid the strategic disagreements that led to its withdrawal from Selma. "So as far as the movement was concerned, this was virgin territory, bro, with no organizational rivalries to deal with," explained Carmichael.[51] Moreover, Lowndes County was an extremely violent place, which meant that future competition from civil rights groups was unlikely. According to Norman, "The decision was that Lowndes County was so bad that nobody would come in there showcasing, that it was only going to be serious work there, and so we would not be bothered and would not be in conflict."[52] The county's sinister mystique also meant that if SNCC succeeded, then it would be considerably less difficult to organize black communities in neighboring counties. "SNCC people felt that if they could help crack Lowndes, other areas—with less brutal reputations—could be easier to organize," said Carmichael. "This might be considered a kind of SNCC Domino Theory"[53] In other words, the extreme nature of local oppression made organizing Lowndes County the key to reforming Alabama's Black Belt. Finally, the Selma to Montgomery March provided SNCC organizers with an excellent point of entry. In late March 1965, when the demonstration finally took place, it gave the activists an opportunity to generate a list of local contacts by talking to the people who turned out to meet the demonstrators.[54] "We trailed that march," explained Carmichael. "Every time local folks came out, we'd sit and talk with them, get their names, find out where they lived, their addresses, what church, who their ministers were, like that. So all the information, everything you'd need to organize, we got."[55]

Less than forty-eight hours after the march ended, five SNCC activists, carrying little more than the names of the Lowndes County residents they met during the march, slipped quietly into the county. Carmichael led the way. Joining him were Scott B. Smith; Willie Vaughn, a student at Tuskegee Institute; Judy Richardson, an Atlanta staffer who recently spent time setting up freedom schools in Mississippi; and Bob Mants, a twenty-year-old Atlanta native who withdrew from Morris Brown College two years earlier to work as a field secretary in southwest Georgia.[56]

The organizers wasted no time tracking down the people on their list. During the day, they visited their contacts at their homes. Their immediate goal was simple. They wanted to get to know local people, and they wanted local people to get to know them. At night, they piled into Carmichael's car, one of the few SNCC vehicles in the Alabama Black Belt, and drove to Selma, where they slept on cots crammed into the corners of SNCC's office at 31½ Franklin Street.[57] By the middle of their first week, they were in dialogue with the leaders of the LCCMHR. The discovery that African Americans had already started organizing to obtain the vote excited them because it indicated that independent politics had a strong chance of taking root. "It seemed more and more a logical place for the ideas that we were developing out of the MFDP experience," noted Carmichael.[58] Hulett and the others, however, were skeptical about the young activists' offer to help. SCLC representatives made similar overtures but failed to follow through on their promise to send personnel, and with the march over and the dignitaries and press leaving the region, it seemed increasingly unlikely that they would do anything.[59] Additionally, LCCMHR members were acutely aware of how dangerous working in the county would be and questioned the willingness of the young organizers to endure, especially when whites turned violent. Exactly what the SNCC activists said to convince the local leaders of their commitment to work in the county is unknown. By the end of the week, however, the team of organizers was distributing leaflets advertising the LCCMHR's second mass meeting.[60]

SNCC activists sought to notify as many African Americans about the April 4, 1965, meeting as possible by crisscrossing the county and handing out flyers at places where black folk congregated and white folk did not. The task was daunting given the size of the county, the limited number of organizers, and the short amount of time remaining before the event. Realizing this, the team shifted approaches. Drawing on lessons learned in Mississippi, they decided to enlist the help of local students by putting leaflets in their hands to take home to their parents. At first, the organizers attempted to reach the students as they rode the rickety school buses that the county provided. John Jackson, a sixteen-year-old student hired by the county as a school bus driver to cut costs, recalled the curious, almost comical sight of SNCC workers waving frantically at school buses, trying desperately to get them to stop. When he pulled over, the SNCC worker who boarded announced, "There's going to be a mass meeting. Ya'll come out," and then began passing back leaflets. But very few drivers were "crazy enough," as Jackson termed it, to actually stop. This prompted the team of organizers to stake out Lowndes County Training School (LCTS), the largest of the county's black high schools, and hand out flyers to students as they boarded the buses for the afternoon ride home.[61]

Recalling his first days working in Lowndes County less than a year after SNCC's project began, Carmichael said, "Whenever you work in [a] county, there's always a point where there comes a confrontation between a civil rights person and the police. A direct confrontation in front of the people. [The response of] the people will depend on how that confrontation goes. Who wins depends upon how well you handle this situation." Such a confrontation took place outside LCTS. Not long after the crew of SNCC field secretaries arrived on the scene, a jittery school official, obviously worried about the repercussions of civil rights workers being on campus, telephoned the county sheriff. The most likely culprit was the longstanding black principal, R. R. Pierce, who lorded over the school as though it was his personal fiefdom and was hostile to the movement from the beginning. Whoever the informant was, the sheriff took him or her seriously because five cars bearing fifteen deputies arrived at the school in a flash.[62]

The deputies surrounded the SNCC workers and began yelling. One officer said, "You shouldn't be here and you could be arrested." "They started talking shit," recalled Carmichael, "so I started talking shit." "If you're going to arrest me, do it," he said. "If not, don't waste my time. I got work to do. I can't be bothered listening to your lectures." The same deputy replied, "I'm just telling you for your own good . . . white people don't like this . . . and you're liable to get hurt." It was the "same old bullshit," Carmichael later said.[63]

Dumbfounded by Carmichael's audacious behavior, the deputies tried to bide time by ordering him and his comrades to stay put while they investigated, but Carmichael was relentless. He knew his refusal to back down had caught them by surprise and he was not about to give them a chance to regroup. Instead, he raised the stakes: "Look man, you been investigating long enough. I'm leaving. Either I'm under arrest or [I'm] not." "We don't know yet," said one of the deputies. Carmichael had them. With bold defiance he declared, "When you find out, you come get me." Not knowing what else to do, the deputies left.[64]

Scores of students watched the confrontation in disbelief. Never before had they seen someone stand up to the police and escape without being beaten or at least arrested. Most did not even think it was possible.

Consequently, after the deputies' ignominious retreat, they swarmed the organizers, clamoring for the flyers, which they delivered to their parents along with harrowing accounts of the encounter. A local legend was born that afternoon. Thereafter, when canvassing, black people never failed to ask SNCC workers, "Are you those civil rights fighters that cussed the cops out?" Toeing the line between humility and bravado as only Carmichael could, he typically answered, "We had a little bit of trouble and we set them straight." One can almost see the Cheshire cat grin forming on his face and the smiles that his statement must have elicited. Carmichael's direct and public challenge of the deeply ingrained culture of racial deference, which most people dared only dream of doing, left a lasting impression on the average African American. It also excited LCCMHR leaders. The potential of such displays of fearlessness to energize people thrilled Hulett and convinced him that SNCC organizers could and would help the movement.[65]

Measurable evidence of the resonance of the LCTS incident came at the LCCMHR's second mass meeting. Movement leaders hoped that a few more people would turn out for the meeting than showed up the previous Sunday but prepared for even fewer to attend. No one expected five hundred people to pack Mt. Gilliard, but at least that many were on hand.[66] "People were really swinging," remembered Carmichael, his amazement and pride still detectable many months later.[67]

The specific aim of this particular mass meeting was to recruit volunteers to go to the county jail the next day to register. Countless dozens said they would, and on Monday morning many new faces were sprinkled among the thirty-seven women and thirty-eight men who lined up, two abreast, outside the jail. Also at this meeting LCCMHR leaders formally introduced the SNCC organizers. Coming only a few days after the confrontation with the police, they received an enthusiastic welcome followed by pledges of support, including a generous offer by Emma and Mathew Jackson, Sr., to use a four-room house they owned two miles north of Mt. Gilliard as their headquarters.[68]

The Jacksons were born in White Hall, Mathew in 1910 and Emma two years later. They came from large farming families and spent their lives in the field, first as sharecroppers and later as Resettlement program landowners. They wed as teenagers and had ten children together. Although his education ended in the seventh grade and hers in the eighth, both believed strongly in formal schooling and made great sacrifices to send three of their children to St. Jude's in Montgomery and three others to

Autauga County Training School. Several Jackson children eventually matriculated at Alabama State.[69]

The Jacksons believed fervently in justice and equality, so it is no coincidence that they were among those who attempted to register on March 1, 1965. That morning, they submitted their names to the registrars, fully aware of the possible consequences. Sure enough, within days, a white merchant whose shop was no more than three or four miles from their home sent word that he would no longer extend credit to them and that he wanted the ten dollars that they owed. Mr. Jackson wrote the shopkeeper a check for the full amount and as he handed it to his daughter to deliver, he resolved never to do business with the man again—a promise he kept.[70]

The Jackson children took after their parents. Their youngest son, John, was the student school bus driver who allowed SNCC field secretaries to distribute leaflets to his passengers, an act that cost him his job. His fascination with the organizers led him to spend every free moment in their presence. At night, he discussed their activities with his father, including the fact that they had to leave the county at sundown. "Them boys are going to get killed trying to make it back to Selma, and George Wallace is going to hang them if they keep going into Montgomery," he recalled telling his father. The elder Jackson knew the point his son was trying to make. John was asking him to allow the SNCC workers to stay at the house that his brother had recently vacated. There were plenty of reasons not to permit them to move in, the foremost being that it would put the family in great danger. Universally, the people white southerners most closely associated with movement activism were those who sheltered outside organizers. As with all major decisions in the Jackson household, husband conferred with wife, and together they decided to make their oldest son's unoccupied house available to SNCC.[71]

The SNCC team visited the house the day after the mass meeting. The humble, well-built structure sat twenty-five yards or so off the main road. One of its sparsely furnished rooms had nothing more than a little couch, although the other two had a couple of beds. The kitchen had a small stove and a washtub but lacked a refrigerator and a sink. This made sense, though, because there was no indoor plumbing; fortunately, there was a water pump about a dozen paces beyond the back porch and an outhouse another dozen beyond that. Although the house lacked just about every major modern convenience, it was a godsend. The next day, the young activists moved in and transformed the dwelling into their base of operations for the next eighteen months.[72]

The Jacksons' kindness did not end with the gift of the freedom house. They embraced the organizers as sons and daughters. "I took them as my children," said Emma Jackson. "They went in and out of my house just like they did their own."[73] They also schooled them on the ways of the county. Mathew Jackson, Sr., was particularly helpful in this regard. He talked to the young activists long into the night and seemed never to tire even after laboring in his fields all day. SNCC workers respected and greatly admired the Jackson clan for their generosity and commitment. Martha Prescod Norman, a SNCC field secretary who worked in Lowndes County, said, "I don't think anybody who spent more than a second in Lowndes County didn't know the Jackson family and respect them for their courage and their tremendous dedication."[74] SNCC activists were particularly fond of the Jackson patriarch. "Strong individuals are not uncommon in the struggle. This man, however, became an image that inspired in us a new dimension of Black peoplehood," explained H. Rap Brown, a former Alabama organizer. "Here was a man who placed the good of people before personal interest and safety. His involvement in the struggle was complete. And next to his family of ten children, this struggle was his greatest concern." The affection and esteem that SNCC organizers had for the Jacksons, together with the care and concern that the Jacksons exhibited toward them, exemplified the special kind of relationship that emerged between SNCC activists and local people, a relationship that, Brown pointed out, provided organizers with their "most gratifying and rewarding experiences."[75] Fellow field secretary Gloria Larry, who also spent a considerable amount of time organizing in Lowndes County, marveled at this relationship. She explained that it was "really quite phenomenal that those of us in our twenties . . . could go and work on a daily basis with sharecroppers—communicate, build these bonds, share the love, trust each other. The generation gap was not a factor. The different cultural backgrounds were not impediments. When I look back on it I see just how amazing that whole meeting of the minds was."[76]

The Jacksons, though, paid a tremendous cost for sheltering the SNCC workers. Some family members were fired from their jobs, others could not find steady employment, and everyone lost friends. "If you were a Jackson and you were from Lowndes County you were [considered] in that mess," explained John Jackson. "Nobody [wanted] to fool with us."[77] More than that, their lives were in constant danger. Night riders targeted the movement's most public supporters, and people who housed outside organizers were extremely visible. When whites resorted to nocturnal terrorism later that year, they targeted the Jacksons repeatedly. On December 30, 1965, four men in a red pickup truck parked in front of Mathew Jackson, Sr.'s home, casually exited their vehicle, and began shooting indiscriminately into the house. "It was as though they were going hunting," reported SNCC's Fay Bellamy. Mr. Jackson, though, did not panic. Instead, he grabbed one of his guns and returned fire. Unwilling to risk their own lives, the night riders retreated, but the Jackson family was not out of danger. Mathew Jackson's daughter Dorothy, a public school teacher who lost her job because of her involvement in the movement, lived up the road and the night riders had taken off in her direction. Mr. Jackson sent John to warn his sister but by the time he arrived the four men were already shooting into her house. The headlights of his vehicle, however, drew their fire, forcing John to throw his car into reverse and speed backward along an unlit road. The gunmen gave chase, shooting from their truck the entire time before disappearing into the night. Miraculously, no one was hurt, but the bullet holes in John's car and in both residences told a story that local activists would relive often.[78]

After SNCC moved permanently into the county, LCCMHR leaders launched an ambitious campaign to recruit new members in an attempt to broaden the base of the movement. This effort had two core components. The first involved door-to-door canvassing and relied heavily on SNCC organizers, and the second entailed tapping into preexisting social networks and depended wholly on local people.[79]

Canvassing was grueling work. SNCC workers woke before dawn, partnered up, and disappeared into the morning mist. Wearing their unofficial field uniform of blue jeans and a simple work shirt they arrived at people's homes so early that they often caught families eating breakfast. This was a bonus because it was rare for a home owner not to invite the hungry activists in for hot biscuits, grits, and fried chicken no matter how many mouths were already around the table. At daybreak, the toughest part of their work began—convincing people to confront their own resignation by helping them see that they possessed the power to shape their own lives. On makeshift porches, across roughly hewn kitchen tables, or while working rows of cotton under the southern sun, they explained the reasons for the mass meetings and registration attempts. During these discussions, they carefully avoided abstractions, choosing instead to talk about politics and government in terms of local conditions and opportunities. If people wanted running water, paved roads, better schools, and a law-abiding sheriff, then they ought to attend a mass meeting and consider trying to register.[80]

People listened politely. Some asked a few questions but most remained quiet and offered only an occasional nod of agreement. In the end, almost everyone was noncommittal. Choosing to attend a mass meeting and deciding to register were neither quick nor easy decisions. People had to believe that change was possible and, equally important, that acting in these specific ways would improve their lives. They also had to decide if they could live with the consequences of white landowners, employers, and creditors finding out about their activities. SNCC canvassers appreciated the gravity of the commitments they were asking people to make and remained patient. Before they moved on to the next house, they promised to return, which they did, and sometimes, but hardly always, on the third, fourth, or maybe even fifth visit, they received a verbal commitment to attend a mass meeting or a pledge to register.[81]

Carmichael summed up their early canvassing efforts as "slow and hard work" made exponentially more difficult by the lack of cars with which to transport canvassers efficiently about the county and the absence of two-way radios and telephones for easy communication.[82] SNCC workers did have one resource that was not in short supply. As full-time organizers, they had as much time to canvass as there were hours of daylight. This was crucial because very few local people could canvass due to work and family obligations. In fact, for many months, the only two local adults who canvassed everyday were John Hulett and Lillian McGill, the former because he could not find work due to his movement activities, and the latter because her clerical job with the Department of Agriculture was seasonal and subsequently she quit.[83] Thus, SNCC's role in widening the base of the movement hinged on the ability of its organizers to bring one household into the struggle at a time through the daily grind of canvassing.

Broadening the movement's base also took place one person at a time. African Americans belonged to a wide range of social organizations, and the LCCMHR's earliest supporters accessed this extensive network to pull people into the movement. Church groups were particularly fertile ground for recruits. Josephine Waginer, an active member of Mt. Gilliard, recruited at meetings of the church usher board and senior choir. Emma Jackson talked to fellow members of the Home Mission Society at Mt. Zion Christian Church in White Hall. Sallie Steele and Mrs. C. L. Thomas did the same at missionary meetings at Mt. Sinai Baptist Church in Tyler and First Baptist Church in Hayneville. Women belonging to missionary

While canvassing in Lowndes County in July 1965, twenty-three-year-old SNCC field secretary Stokely Carmichael talks to a local resident on his front porch about the local movement. Courtesy of the Library of Congress, Prints and Photographs Division, *Look* magazine, Photograph Collection, LC Look-Job 65–2434.

societies also recruited outside the church. In fact, they ranked among the movement's most effective recruiters because of their lengthy involvement in the lives of community members, from celebrating births and providing care for the sick to consoling the bereaved. Their volunteerism earned them the trust and respect of the community, which they parlayed into audiences with people who might not otherwise have sat down with movement advocates. LCCMHR supporters also tapped into mutual aid societies like the Daylight Savings Club. Mrs. Waginer and her husband, Frank, were the secretary and treasurer of the Guys and Gals Social and Savings Club and pulled some of its members into the struggle. Mr. Waginer also recruited at meetings of the Union Burial Society, which had chapters in White Hall, Tyler, and Hayneville. Although Masonic orders abounded, none supported the movement officially. Nevertheless, they served as important recruiting conduits because quite a few Masons were active in the struggle. John Hunter, for example, drafted some of his brothers at Masonic Lodge 161 in Fort Deposit, and Arthur Jackson did the same at St. Anthony's Lodge 238 in Hayneville. Lucy Bandy promoted the movement among the Eastern Stars at Rose Beauty Chapter 176 in Hayneville, as did Mattie Lee Moorer at Chapter 73.[84]

The combined efforts of local movement supporters and SNCC activists had immediate benefits. Attendance at mass meetings skyrocketed. Whereas only one hundred people attended the LCCMHR's inaugural mass meeting on March 28, 1965, nearly one thousand turned out for two simultaneous gatherings held just two weeks later. Ramah Baptist Church also opened its doors. Like Mt. Gilliard, Ramah was the linchpin of a community of independent black farmers. Located in Calhoun, it had been the primary religious institution for African Americans in the southeastern part of the county for nearly a century. It also made significant secular contributions, including setting in motion the process that led to the founding of the Calhoun School. By hosting one of two mass meetings on April 11, 1965, the church allowed the movement to establish its presence in a community that activists had to organize if the movement were to succeed. The receptivity of Ramah, however, did not prompt other churches to open their doors; it was not until midsummer that a third church, Old Bogahoma Baptist in Gordonsville, hosted a mass meeting. Finally, the number of people who tried to register soared. On the first registration day in May 1965, some 150 people stood outside of the jail in dizzying ninety-degree heat for more than five hours to have their names added to the voter roll. The turnout tripled the number of folk who attempted to register in March, and doubled the number of people who tried to get on the books in early April.[85]

The new recruits were overwhelmingly working-class. They were homemakers like Hattie G. Lee and Gerline McWilliams, tenant farmers like Eugene Peoples, common laborers like James Brooks, and railroad workers like Sam Jones. Small farmers including Booker T. Barlow and Charles Smith joined as well, as did skilled workers such as beautician Nealie Mac Gordon and bricklayer Robert Strickland. They also came from communities scattered across the county. Hattie Lee lived in the northeast in Burkville, while Gerline McWilliams resided in the northwest in Trickem. Eugene Peoples made his home in the west in Collirene and Robert Strickland in the east in Lowndesboro. Booker T. Barlow lived south of Lowndesboro in Hayneville, while James Brooks resided in the central part of the county in Gordonsville. Charles Smith's farm was in the southeast in Calhoun not far from where Sam Jones lived in Fort Deposit. In addition, women filled their ranks. SNCC contact lists, which consisted of names taken at mass meetings and registration attempts, reveal that women joined in numbers equal to and frequently greater than those of men. These lists also show that married couples often joined together, as did entire nuclear families and even extended families, which speaks to the success that movement activists had recruiting through kin networks.[86]

The reasons folk joined the struggle varied. Many enlisted to make life better for their children, as did Ed Moore King. The cup of endurance had run over for some, as it had for Sidney Logan, Jr. For quite a few, it was a matter of faith. Emma Jackson explained her service to the movement as fulfilling her obligations as a Christian: "Your duty is to serve people and I have always wanted to do that. I was taught that."[87] For others it was a combination of these factors. According to Mattie Lee Moorer, "We were at a point that there was so much that we were tired of, and we were willing to risk our lives to get to vote and whatever else went with voting. There is a time for everything according to Ecclesiastes 3, and the time had come in Lowndes County." Regardless of their reasoning, each individual conquered the justifiable fear of challenging white power that immobilized so many for so long. When a white man who had extended a one-month loan to Mrs. Moorer, which she had repaid at 25 percent interest, admonished her to "quit going to these meetings," she flatly refused, then boldly told him, "I may be dead when I leave Lowndes County, but I am going to be the last one alive."[88] Movement participants still feared white violence, but like Mrs. Moorer, they refused to allow it to paralyze them.

As the movement gained momentum, it spread to the Lowndes Diaspora. sncc organizers were integral to this process. While canvassing, they learned about the sizeable population of Lowndes County natives living in Detroit. Realizing that this community could be a valuable source of support, they began collecting the names of sons and daughters, brothers and sisters, and cousins and classmates who had migrated north. In early June, Bob Mants traveled to Detroit where he rendezvoused with Dorothy Dewberry, a native of the city, a sometime student at the Detroit Institute of Technology and codirector of the Detroit wing of sncc's fundraising apparatus. Ahead of Mants's visit, Dewberry scheduled meetings with several local organizations with ties to Alabama, including a group from Christ Church of Conant Gardens and the Ann Arbor branch of the Alabama State University Alumni Association. Mants and James Black, a ninety-three-year-old retired preacher who accompanied him on the trip, received pledges of financial support from these groups after explaining the aims of the movement and the obstacles confronting local activists. Dewberry also arranged an audience with a group of Lowndes County expatriates who, after meeting with Mants and Black, decided to mobilize support for the movement by forming the Detroit-Lowndes County Christian Movement for Human Rights (Detroit-lccmhr). To lead them, they turned to veteran union organizer Simon Owens, one of the most politically active members of the Lowndes Diaspora.[89]

Those who joined the Detroit organization tended to have relatives who participated in the struggle back home. Will and Mary Jane Jackson, the parents of Detroit-lccmhr member Margaret Shine, for example, lived in Blackbelt and were extremely active in the county. Members also tended to belong to churches, social clubs, and civic associations that catered to people from Lowndes County. Frank Pierce, a member of the city's Calhoun School Alumni Association, joined the Detroit-lccmhr and encouraged fellow alumni, as well as his brothers and their wives, to do likewise. Up north, social networks were just as important to movement recruitment as they were down south.[90]

The principal activity of the Detroit-lccmhr was fundraising. Each month the organization sent one hundred dollars to its namesake, making it the movement's most reliable donor. Detroit activists also collected and trucked canned food and clothing to the county to help people who had been fired or evicted for supporting the movement. They launched this effort during Mants's initial visit by giving him several boxes of clothing and books to take south.[91]

Back in Lowndes County, the number of people participating in the movement increased every day, but only a small fraction of African Americans joined the fight.[92] Most working-class blacks stayed away from mass meetings and the registrars' office, unwilling to risk the little bit of economic security they had managed to eke out on the vague promise of social change. The vast majority of professionals, a group that consisted mainly of a couple hundred public school teachers, remained on the sidelines as well. Many of them also felt that they were too vulnerable economically to join the movement, especially after Hulda Coleman, the county's superintendent of education, made it known that she would fire any school employee who tried to register. Poor people tended to avoid the movement as well. The ties that bound them to whites kept them from becoming active. Sharecroppers, day laborers, and domestic workers lived on white-owned land, worked in white-owned fields and homes, borrowed white-owned money, and shopped at white-owned stores. They possessed the least but had absolutely everything to lose; living in poverty allowed no margin for error. The likelihood of violence kept people of all classes from getting involved. When asked why more people had not joined them, Mrs. Frank Miles, Jr., explained that most were simply "afraid of being killed."[93] At the same time, some stayed away because they clung tightly to the idea that progress would come in due time and that it was better to be patient than to force change. In addition, more than a few members of the social elite refused to work under the direction of less-educated nonprofessionals, to say nothing of their reluctance to mingle with common laborers and domestics. Finally, some people simply did not want to alienate whites with whom they had spent a lifetime cultivating personal relationships that helped them endure Jim Crow.[94]

Several professionals and poor people did defy conventional wisdom and join the fray. Sharecropper Amanda Glover and schoolteacher Sarah Logan publicly participated in the movement from the beginning even though it cost the former her home and the latter her job.[95] Even more participated covertly. Although schoolteachers Uralee and James Haynes stayed away from mass meetings and the registrars' office because they "didn't feel free" to support the movement openly, they communicated regularly with local leaders, giving advice when asked and donating money when they could.[96]

The general unwillingness of most people to participate in the struggle allowed nontraditional leaders to emerge. In a sense, these folk, drawn primarily from the ranks of the working class, became movement leaders by default. This did not mean that they were unqualified. On the contrary, each possessed life experiences that prepared them for these roles. A handful, such as John Hulett and Charles Smith, had gained valuable leadership experience through the civil rights organizations and unions they joined while working outside of Lowndes County. The remainder received leadership training through churches, civic groups, and social organizations. Most officers of the LCCMHR served as a deacon or church trustee, while others were either a president, vice president, secretary, or treasurer of a Sunday school, savings club, home mission society, or fraternal lodge.

The prevalence of nontraditional leaders in the movement distinguished it from similar groups in neighboring Selma and Montgomery, as well as in nearby Tuskegee, where the black elite dominated. Adding to the uniqueness of this cohort was the paucity of preachers. Not a single minister was an officer in the LCCMHR. In fact, the clergy did not have much of a presence in the movement at all. Among the 150 people who attempted to register in April 1965, only one was a minister. The irregular fellowship schedule of rural black churches was largely responsible for the poor clerical showing. Most of the county's churches, particularly those located in tenant communities, met for Sunday service only twice a month, and some just once, because their small congregations, which in many instances had fewer than two dozen members, could only afford half-time preachers. These ministers, who floated between churches and usually lacked formal theological training, typically arrived on Sunday morning, delivered a sermon, departed in the evening, and did not return for weeks. This arrangement did not give preachers and parishioners enough time together to forge reciprocal, secular obligations. Congregants looked to preachers for their Sunday lesson and little else. For guidance on social issues, financial concerns, and political matters, they turned to missionary women and church elders. Adding to the disconnect between preachers and parishioners was the impossibility of communicating with ministers during the workweek because so many lived and worked outside Lowndes County and very few African Americans had convenient access to telephones. Ministers were literally beyond the reach of congregants Monday through Saturday or for even longer stretches of time. The low profile of preachers in the movement, therefore, was a function of their limited role in the daily lives of rural people.[97]

Women were among the nontraditional leaders who filled the void created by the absence of ministers and other professionals, and they exercised their leadership in ways that tested the boundaries of standard gender conventions. Lillian McGill, for example, was at the center of the movement's leadership circle and contributed to the struggle in ways that challenged the prevailing beliefs that governed women and public leadership.

From a financial standpoint, it did not make much sense for McGill to leave her job with the Department of Agriculture, which paid seventy-seven dollars a week, to work for the LCCMHR as its secretary for ten dollars a week, especially because she was the primary caregiver for her three small children. But McGill, who was a member of the Senior Missionary Society at Unity Baptist Church and the adviser to its Junior Missionary Society, was a community activist at heart. She considered the well-being of African Americans to be as important as that of her own family. Compassion and a commitment to racial uplift were integral to her being and guided her decision to work for the LCCMHR. "It was the thing that would improve the conditions for most of the people and not leave one or two people comfortable while everybody else suffered," she explained. Fundamentally, she simply could not ignore the opportunity to help the black community that working for the movement presented.[98]

Lillian McGill's official title as secretary belies the work she actually did. Certainly, she handled the LCCMHR's correspondence and took notes at meetings, but she also managed the organization's finances and traveled inside and outside the state as its principal fundraiser. She was a full-time field worker who canvassed the county seven days a week, occasionally with friends, and frequently with SNCC organizers, but most often with Hulett. She spoke regularly at mass meetings and many considered her to be one of the movement's most dynamic orators. She was also intimately involved in every facet of executive committee decision making, from deciding what issues to discuss at mass meetings to selecting which federal programs to bring to the county. According to Hulett, she was "the brains of the movement." Yet her title never changed. In certain respects, this really did not matter. She did the work that needed doing and no one questioned her right to do it. Moreover, she never felt conflicted about the arrangement. There was so much work, so few people, and seemingly so little time that pausing to reflect on intra-organizational gender bias was an indulgence she could not afford. Nevertheless, working under an ill-fitted title did matter. Above all else, it undervalued her seminal contribution, causing people to first look elsewhere for formal leadership. When Hulett resigned as chairperson of the LCCMHR to lead the independent political party, the people overlooked McGill as his successor even though her movement resume identified her as the most qualified candidate.[99]

McGill represented a unique brand of women's leadership. She held an office with a title, albeit an ill-fitting one, at a time when women worked mostly in non-titled positions. She operated inside a leadership circle when it was more common for women to exert influence from the outside. She spoke frequently at mass meetings during an era when women's voices emanated more often from the choir loft than from the pulpit. She also worked in the field. With tremendous ease, she shifted between the roles of movement spokesperson and grassroots organizer. In these ways, she challenged the idea that women's leadership was inherently different from men's and necessarily subordinate. Despite her example, traditional gendered notions of leadership prevailed, and although this did not restrict the work that she and other women performed, it limited the positions they held and the recognition they deserved.

As spring gave way to summer, the extraordinary became the ordinary. In March 1965, it was inconceivable that hundreds of African Americans would line up voluntarily outside the county jail to register. But by May 1965, that is exactly what was happening. Twice a month, African Americans donned their best Sunday clothes and traveled to Hayneville in defiance of local custom. Unfortunately, their determination to be included in the political process did not change the registrars' low opinion of them. "These people just coming down here because they been threatened by Communists and the NAACP and those folks," said registrar Golson. "Why, they been told they going to lose their welfare and Social Security checks if they don't register. Some of them don't even know what their names is. Most of this outside agitation is just to get their money out of them."[100] The people's resolve also did not dissuade the registrars from trying to exclude them. Each registration day, the triumvirate worked hard to unnerve and intimidate black applicants. They sauntered through the crowd in the morning making a great show of the fact that they were armed. Once inside the jailhouse they placed loaded pistols on the examination table in plain view of the test takers and next to the whiskey bottles they swigged throughout the day.[101] Nevertheless, the people kept coming, which forced the registrars to administer the qualification exam, but only to as few people as possible. Of course, the test itself was a major obstacle, particularly its literacy component, which had impeded black voter registration for more than sixty years by overmatching black applicants with poor literacy skills. Elzie McGill confessed that he could not answer many of the test questions because he "quit school in the fourth grade" and "hadn't much learning."[102] One of the questions that stymied McGill and others was, "How many members of the House of Representatives did South Carolina have in the first Congress?"[103] Although the answers to such questions appeared in a paragraph printed immediately above, providing the correct response was more than a matter of merely glancing up. For many African Americans who never completed elementary school, answering constitutional trivia while sitting in the county jail in front of belligerent whites was simply overwhelming. The combined effect of the test and the registrars' antics limited the number of African Americans who registered successfully to twelve through the end of May 1965. At that rate, it would take four generations for the county's five thousand eligible African Americans to register.[104]

The snail's pace at which the county added African Americans to the voter roll prompted SNCC to prepare a lawsuit on their behalf. The goal of the suit was to secure a federal court order instructing county officials to stop using the literacy test. In mid-May 1965, Martin Berger, an attorney from New York who worked closely with SNCC in the past, began collecting evidence of local voter discrimination. The prospect of the lawsuit excited movement supporters so much that a couple hundred people volunteered to be plaintiffs.[105]

The SNCC complaint spurred the federal government to act. John Doar, the assistant attorney general of the Civil Rights Division of the Justice Department, informed the registrars that their "practices were in violation of federal law" and insisted that they "discontinue" using the literacy test and "refrain from using the application form as anything other than an information sheet" or face a Justice Department lawsuit.[106] Local officials had no choice but to take Doar seriously. The attorney general's office had already won a series of lawsuits seeking to suspend the test in Dallas, Montgomery, Macon, Bullock, and Elmore counties. Desperate to avoid federal intervention, the registrars processed roughly one hundred applications in June 1965 but added only about fifty new voters, far more than ever before but hardly enough to mask their ongoing discriminatory behavior or to dissuade the Justice Department from filing suit. Nor was it enough to win a promise from the government not to send federal registrars to the county under provisions of the Voting Rights Act, which was winding its way through Congress. Consequently, the registrars met secretly with U.S. attorney Carl Gabels and agreed to drop the literacy portion of the registration application and keep the registrars' office open

African Americans attempt to register to vote inside the Lowndes County jail in Hayneville in March 1965. © Bruce Davidson/Magnum Photos.

for four consecutive days beginning Tuesday, July 6, 1965. The agreement was made public the same day it took effect.[107]

Movement activists were excited because they understood that the pressure they put on the county and the federal government led to the concessions. "We've fought for the removal of this test for so long it's hard to believe that it's really gone," remarked Carmichael. The changes also thoroughly energized them. "Our next step must be to urge all of the people to flock to Hayneville, the county seat, to register before 4 o'clock Friday," said Carmichael.[108] With this in mind, the LCCMHR organized nightly mass meetings and SNCC workers appealed to their national headquarters to send more organizers and provide additional cars. African Americans responded enthusiastically, flocking to the old jail in unprecedented numbers. By the end of the week, some three hundred people had lined up to register and more than two hundred had managed to file applications.[109]

The abandonment of the literacy test was a real victory for the movement. Unfortunately, it was not the turning point that many hoped it would be because the registrars continued their discriminatory ways. Instead of disqualifying black applicants for answering exam questions incorrectly, they declared them ineligible to vote because of technical errors and omissions, such as writing their first name where their last name belonged or misspelling their street address. Their defiance was remarkably effective in limiting the growth of the black electorate. In July 1965 they refused to register almost half the African Americans who came before them. A Justice Department review of twenty applications revealed that the registrars discarded sixteen without reasonable cause. The registrars also refused to amend their behavior. They promised the U.S. attorneys that they would reconsider the disqualified applications, but they never did.[110]

The registrars' persistent, prejudicial behavior was tremendously disappointing. "We just couldn't keep bringing the same people down over and over," said Carmichael. "And other people would say, 'Oh, I'm not going to pass anyway, so fuck it.'"[111] Still, more than one hundred African Americans gathered regularly at the jailhouse whenever the registrars met. On August 2, 1965, at least that many people endured the heat and humidity to file registration applications.[112] Their unmistakable determination to secure the franchise, coupled with the registrars' recalcitrance, compelled U.S. attorney general Nicholas Katzenbach to assign federal registrars to Lowndes County to process qualified applicants. He did so under authority granted to him by the Voting Rights Act, which President Johnson signed into law on August 6, 1965, with great ceremony in the same room that President Lincoln inked his name to the Emancipation Proclamation.[113] Lowndes County was among the 548 counties nationwide that met the criteria for receiving registrars, but one of only nine to receive them immediately. The attorney general dispatched registrars to so few counties because the Johnson administration believed that promoting voluntary compliance would limit the president's exposure to the political fallout generated by his support of the new legislation. Rather than shelter Johnson, this policy protected the status quo.[114]

Confusion surrounded the arrival of the registrars on August 14, 1965. A spirited crowd of African Americans gathered outside of the old Hayneville jail early that Saturday morning in anticipation of the federal appointees working out of the county registrars' office, but the federal officials never showed. Instead of the county seat, they went to Fort Deposit and set up shop on federal property at the post office. By midday, they had straightened out the mix-up but the delay limited the number of people able to file registration applications to forty-nine. The next day, sixty-seven people submitted qualifying forms, and on Monday slightly more than one hundred did the same. Not surprisingly, the three-day turnout was considerably less than that in Dallas, Hale, and Marengo counties, which received federal registrars as well. The unannounced relocation of the registration site and difficulties shuttling people to the southeastern portion of the county were largely to blame, but so too was fear of reprisals. Everyone understood the message conveyed by the pickup truck parked outside of the post office each day with a rifle on full display.[115]

A simplified registration application counterbalanced the initial low turnout. The federal form had only six written questions pertaining to identity and residency, and six yes-or-no questions designed to satisfy state requirements regarding sanity and felony convictions. The straightforward application that the nondiscriminating but unfriendly federal registrars processed enabled 90 percent of the earliest applicants to become registered voters, completely reversing the pattern established under the local registrars. The number of applicants continued to grow over the next few weeks but tapered off around Labor Day, partly because of the start of the harvest season, which made it difficult for agricultural workers to steal away from the fields, but also due to a series of evictions and a wave of white violence. Although registering remained economically risky and physically dangerous, by the end of October 1965 some two thousand African Americans, or 40 percent of the black electorate, had become eligible voters.[116]

· · ·

Lowndes County was experiencing a revolution. At the beginning of 1965, there was not a single African American on the voting roll, but by the end of the year, African Americans represented almost half of all registered voters. This remarkable development began simply enough with a conversation among close friends at a benevolent society meeting about black political exclusion. It evolved slowly through chance encounters, including Hulett bumping into an acquaintance from White Hall. It grew through public displays of courage, beginning with the first group of would-be registrants who submitted their names and addresses to courthouse officials. It matured because local people such as Ed Moore King, who petitioned the leaders of Mt. Gilliard to open the doors of the church to the nascent movement, recognized the significance of the moment. It gained momentum quickly, fueled by the foresight of local activists to form an autonomous organization devoted specifically to grassroots activism, and by their willingness to collaborate with SNCC, which transformed the Selma to Montgomery March into an organizing opportunity. Collaborating with SNCC was especially significant because Carmichael and his team of organizers challenged the tradition of racial deference in ways that inspired action by people formerly frozen by fear. Equally important, they worked full-time to broaden the base of the movement through the slow and hard work of canvassing. Their role, though, was purposefully complementary, and when coupled with the absence of black professionals, created space for nontraditional leaders, particularly women, to emerge. At its core, this was a working-class revolution that succeeded in enfranchising African Americans because its supporters were prepared to take advantage of the political opportunities that they helped create.

In the end, the local voter registration campaign shined much-needed light on the structural impediments to black political participation. This compelled the Justice Department first to pressure courthouse officials to abandon the literacy test, and then eventually to send federal registrars to the county. Movement participants made the most of these developments by flocking to Hayneville after the county dropped the literacy exam, and by registering with federal officials even though signing up to vote remained extremely dangerous. Through these actions, African Americans gave meaning to the Voting Rights Act, and in the ensuing months, they broadened their struggle beyond the ballot box in ways unimaginable only a few months earlier.

3

We Ain't Going to Shed a Tear for Jon

School Desegregation, White Resistance, and the African American Response

They walked to the Cash Store to purchase snacks and cold beverages for their fellow demonstrators who waited anxiously in the blistering August sun. The mere thought of a refreshing cola and a bite to eat raised everyone's spirits. After spending a week in the county jail, they were desperate for something other than prison gruel. The store was only about fifty yards from the jail and served African Americans freely, so no one anticipated trouble, but when the four activists reached the establishment, a fifty-two-year-old police volunteer armed with a pistol and a 12-guage shotgun appeared in the doorway shouting, "Get off this property, or I'll blow your goddamn heads off, you sons of bitches."[1] Ruby Sales, the first person to reach the entrance, froze, immobilized by fear and uncertainty. "My mind kind of blanked," recalled the SNCC volunteer from Tuskegee Institute. "I wasn't processing all that was happening."[2] Behind her, Jonathan Daniels reacted swiftly. The twenty-six-year-old white student at Episcopal Theological Seminary in Massachusetts had spent much of the summer in Selma but had been volunteering in Lowndes County for several weeks, having convinced SNCC's Stokely Carmichael and his team of field secretaries that he was serious about working at the grassroots. The young seminarian shoved Sales aside, stepped in front of special deputy Tom Coleman, and in an attempt to diffuse the situation asked quickly but calmly, "Are you threatening us?" The volunteer officer did not answer. Instead, he leveled his gun and fired a load of buckshot into the cleric's chest. Daniels flew backward, hitting the ground motionless. His companion, Father Richard Morrisroe, turned instinctively to flee. The twenty-seven-year-old Catholic priest who ministered to a black congregation in Chicago came to Alabama less than three weeks earlier to attend the 1965 annual convention of SCLC. Rather than return directly to Chicago, he drove with Daniels to Lowndes County. As Morrisroe retreated, he snatched local activist Joyce Bailey by the hand, but before the pair could get away, the deputy shot him in the back. The priest collapsed instantly and would need eleven hours of emergency surgery to survive. Bailey, though, managed to scamper to safety unharmed. A moment later, Coleman approached the felled clergymen and stared at them intently. He then nonchalantly laid down his shotgun, walked calmly to his car, and drove around the corner to the county courthouse.[3]

"Jon's murder grieved us," recalled Carmichael, who lamented Daniels's death more than most activists because he permitted Daniels to join the project even though experience and instinct told him that Lowndes County was too dangerous for white workers. "His wasn't the first death we'd experienced," he said. "But it was in some ways the one closest to me as an organizer." "I had never seen my son like that," recalled Carmichael's mother, Mabel, whom he visited immediately after the shooting. "Silent, grim, like a heavy, heavy weight was pressing on him. Even when his father died, that had really hit him, but this was different."[4]

Personal grief sparked collective anger. The Sunday after the murder, some one hundred movement supporters gathered in Gordonsville and listened to Carmichael give voice to their shared outrage. "We're going to tear this county up," he said. "Then we're going to build it back, brick by brick, until it's a fit place for human beings." Drawing on Daniels's Christian devotion and the prophetic tradition of the black church, he added, "We ain't going to shed a tear for Jon, 'cause Jon is going to live in this county. We ain't going to resurrect Jon, we're going to resurrect ourselves." Anger could have destroyed the project by frustrating SNCC activists to the point of inaction, but instead it reinvigorated the endeavor by causing them to renew their commitment. "We want to show the people that we are not afraid of Lowndes County and that they can't run us out," said Carmichael. "We want them to know that if that is the price that has to be paid, there are some people willing to pay it." Toward this end, Carmichael invited ten veteran organizers from what he described as "some of the toughest counties in the South" to work with them. He wanted these organizers, all of whom he knew personally from his summers in Mississippi and college days at Howard University, to help expand the movement beyond voter registration by working to improve the quality of black schools, desegregate white schools, gain control of federal aid programs, and create an independent, countywide political party.[5]

Local activists also mourned for Daniels. In the short time that he had been in the county, they came to know him well and embraced him as they had SNCC's field secretaries. "We felt like he was one of our family," said a movement supporter. The shooting itself also surprised them, but they were not overly amazed because of the local white tradition of resorting to violence to suppress challenges to the status quo.[6] "Things were moving a little too fast for the whites," explained local leader John Hulett, "and they had to do something to stop it."[7] Lowndes County activists, however, refused to be intimidated. Through the grapevine, they sent word to whites that they were prepared to meet violence with violence. "You kill one of us," they said, and "we'll kill three of you." At the same time, they increased self-defense measures in part by providing weapons to SNCC organizers, some of whom would have rejected the guns a few months earlier but now accepted them gratefully. In addition, they began to think more seriously about alternative political approaches to change, including the possibility of forming their own political party.[8]

Local whites wrestled with their own outrage, but their equally intense feelings stemmed from empathy for Coleman rather than sympathy for Daniels. "He is respected in the community," remarked a deputy sheriff. "He laughs and jokes a lot. I'd call him a friendly person." Another associate said, "He was not the kind to lose his mind, and let things get away from him." It helped that Coleman hailed from good stock. "He is from one of our oldest and best families," said Sheriff Ryals. Indeed, his sister Hulda was the long-standing superintendent of the county board of education, having inherited the position almost thirty years earlier from their ailing father, Jesse. She was also the chief defender of the dual education system and a major architect of the plan to stop desegregation, although her efforts had not been completely successful. "She was upset," observed a family friend, "and I know it was on his mind." Also troubling him was the arrival of the federal registrars as well as the recent demonstration in Fort Deposit. According to neighbors, both events had him "worked up."[9]

Coleman drew empathy from local whites because he was not a fanatic prone to irrational behavior, but rather an upstanding member of the community from a prominent family. From their perspective, he acted just as any southern white man should whose family and way of life were under siege. For two decades, Coleman worked for the state highway department, reaching upper-level management near the end of his tenure and earning the respect of high-ranking local and state officials with whom he interacted regularly. He was different only in that he pulled the trigger. "He's like the rest of us around here," said county prosecutor Carlton Perdue. "He's strong in his feelings." "This has been expected for a good while," said a white man from Hayneville. "If they continue this thing it will happen again—maybe not here, but somewhere." Support for Coleman also grew from the thought that white activists, especially those masquerading as clergymen, were race traitors in the tradition of the abolitionists of old, and they, like Viola Liuzzo, deserved their fate. "If they'd been tending to their own business like I tend to mine, they'd be living today and enjoying themselves today," said Perdue. Given white attitudes, it is hardly surprising that a grand jury consisting of seventeen white men and a single African American refused to indict the confessed killer for first-degree murder, which carried a maximum penalty of death, and settled instead on manslaughter, which came with a sentence of only one to ten years in prison. It is also not surprising that one month after the shooting an all-white jury found Coleman not guilty.[10]

Lowndes County was a powder keg waiting to explode. "I know the white people are really worked up," said a white resident, and "I haven't seen any sign of anyone backing off since the shooting."[11] In the aftermath of the murder, whites ratcheted up the effort to maintain white supremacy. Daniels's death, coupled with Coleman's acquittal, emboldened them. The crime, however, did not happen in a vacuum. Coleman tried to thwart the movement because it was gaining momentum. In addition to voting rights, African Americans had begun fighting to improve black schools and even desegregate white schools. In this charged environment, Daniels's murder was the most dramatic expression of white resistance. The most successful expression of white resistance, however, was the creation of a private white academy one year later. Neither event, though, foiled the movement. African Americans faced white resistance head-on, with guns in hand when necessary.

Lowndes County Training School (LCTS) was a jewel in the crown of the black community. The county's oldest and largest public high school for African Americans owed its lofty status to its humble beginnings. A half century earlier, Robert McCord, a black farmer born in slavery and subsequently the owner of a nine-hundred-acre plantation in Gordonsville, sold seven acres at a modest price to four black neighbors. Volunteers eventually built a five-classroom, two-story, frame building on the land, located ten miles from Hayneville. "If one man can build a house, why not a community build a school," explained W. C. Carnes, J. H. Pugh, and R. H. Chisholm, the school's original trustees. White lack of interest in black education enabled the black community to retain significant control over the school even though the trustees deeded the property to the county in order to secure public funds to cover operating expenses. It also made it easier for African Americans to embrace the centrally located school as their own. It makes sense, then, that every time the county invested in the school, including when it built a much-needed auditorium in 1951, African Americans celebrated inching a little closer to realizing their dream of providing their children with a quality education.[12]

This precious gem, however, was far from flawless. Compared to the all-white Hayneville High, LCTS lacked much of what students needed in order to be prepared for advanced academic training or a world of work beyond menial labor. The school had a library, but not enough books; offered chemistry, but lacked adequate laboratory facilities; and provided transportation, but relied on student bus drivers. Through fundraising, volunteering, and selective lobbying, African Americans tried to eliminate the gross inequalities produced by segregation, but they simply could not. This caused them to love and loathe the school simultaneously, a schizophrenia common to the Jim Crow era.[13]

Students felt exactly the same way about LCTS as their parents did. They appreciated the school's history but detested its scarce resources and uneven academic program. There was a time when they would have dismissed complaining to white authorities as foolhardy, but that time had passed. Unlike other southern grassroots movements where local youth inspired area adults to act, in Lowndes County the opposite occurred, owing to the early emphasis on voting rights and the initial absence of outside organizers. Local youth did not become active in the struggle until April 1965, fully one month after the first voter registration attempt. At that time, a group of LCTS students led by John Jackson, who permitted SNCC workers to distribute flyers on his bus, and senior Timothy Mays, who participated in the Selma to Montgomery March from start to finish, presented superintendent Hulda Coleman with a list of grievances and demands that included increasing the library's holdings, extending the library's hours of operation, banning mandatory extracurricular activities during class hours, and adding a breakfast program. Coleman dismissed the petition without explanation, but rather than deter the students, her arbitrary decision strengthened their resolve. As soon as they realized that she did not intend to address the issues that they raised, they voted to boycott the school for the remainder of the semester. Their decision reflected their political acumen: due to Alabama's use of average daily attendance statistics to determine local funding levels, lowering the county's daily school attendance figures would substantially reduce the amount of money that the state appropriated to the county board of education.[14]

The students knew that they had to have the support of adults for the boycott to succeed, but convincing parents to allow their children to miss school for any reason is always difficult. As a result, they appealed to the leaders of the LCCMHR for help and received the support and assistance they desired. A general longing to improve black education encouraged local activists to back the boycott, but so too did personal experience. Hulett was one of several local leaders who had graduated from LCTS and among the many movement people with children enrolled there. Lowndes County activists also recognized the value of fighting to improve a segregated school. A decade had passed since the U.S. Supreme Court ruling in *Brown* and the dual education system remained intact. In fact, nothing had changed and there were absolutely no signs that anything was about to. Improving segregated schools was not simply the best hope for raising the quality of black education—it was the only hope.[15]

LCCMHR leaders added to the list of student demands. Foremost, they called for the removal of longstanding African American principal R. R. Pierce. "We have some good teachers," explained Mrs. Frank Miles, "but [we] need [a] principal."[16] For years, black parents openly criticized Pierce for his lack of leadership and poor management skills, but the board of education continually ignored their complaints. Through the boycott, movement leaders hoped to liberate the school from a man many believed was much more interested in using his position to advance his personal well-being than to educate students.[17]

SNCC organizers backed the boycott enthusiastically. They placed tremendous value in black institutions generally, and in black schools specifically, partly because almost all the organizers attended segregated grade schools and historically black colleges. "White schools are best all right [*sic*], but only because they get more money than the Negro schools," explained Carmichael. SNCC's Alabama activists also did not believe in desegregation merely for the sake of social integration. "We see integration as an insidious subterfuge for white supremacy in this country," said Carmichael. "The goal of integration is irrelevant. Political and economic power is what black people have to have."[18]

The movement's base also embraced the boycott, which local leaders and SNCC organizers discussed at mass meetings. Black parents wanted their children to be "second to none," explained local leader Lillian McGill, but they had completely lost faith in LCTS; because enrolling their children in white schools was not possible, they welcomed the chance to improve the only educational option available to them. LCCMHR leaders assumed that this group's opinion represented the views of the broader black public and launched the boycott in late April 1965, but they miscalculated. Although the movement's core supporters accurately reflected the socioeconomic profile of the African American population, their active participation in the voting rights campaign made them more willing to challenge white power and predisposed them to support the boycott. The broader black public, like the movement's base, placed a premium on education but believed that even poorly administered education was too valuable to disrupt. Consequently, they continued to send their children to LCTS. Absent widespread support, the boycott was ineffective. Movement leaders, however, refused to call it off until word spread that county officials would not register a single soul until every student returned to school. Because momentum for voting rights was building while interest in the boycott continued to lag, the decision to halt the boycott was easy. Local activists, though, remained committed to improving LCTS, so they pledged to renew the boycott in the fall after bolstering support during the summer by having voter registration workers discuss its importance as they canvassed.[19]

Superintendent Coleman was glad to see the boycott unravel but could not let down her guard even momentarily because a much greater threat to the public schools loomed large on the horizon. The Justice Department had initiated a series of school desegregation lawsuits across the South under authority granted to it by Title IV of the Civil Rights Act of 1964, and its lawyers had secured mandatory desegregation orders in cases brought against nearby Black Belt counties. Equally worrisome was the possibility that the federal government would start withholding funds from school districts guilty of racial discrimination in accordance with Title VI of the same law. Although Coleman could not have cared less about losing the $4,000 that the county received annually from the federal government for education, she was greatly concerned about missing out on a share of the $1.3 billion that Congress had made available to poor school districts through the Elementary and Secondary Education Act of 1965 (ESEA).[20]

To be eligible for ESEA monies, Coleman needed to submit a desegregation plan to the Department of Health, Education, and Welfare (HEW). Before the new legislation and the Justice Department lawsuits, she would have scoffed at the idea of voluntarily drafting such a proposal. The chance to double the county's $900,000 education budget by submitting a plan, however, and the likelihood of having a desegregation program imposed on the county by a federal court for failing to do so, compelled her to reconsider. Together with the five members of the school board, she reviewed court-ordered and voluntary plans in effect in neighboring Black Belt counties and realized immediately that it was possible to put in place a procedure that actually preserved the dual education system. The key, of course, was freedom-of-choice pupil assignments, which required students wishing to leave segregated schools to apply for transfers to attend schools previously reserved for members of the other race. This placed the burden of desegregation squarely on the shoulders of black students, because everyone knew that white students would not apply for transfers to attend black schools. Furthermore, if African Americans did not request transfers, which was a likely scenario given the high probability of reprisals, or if county officials rejected their applications, which was just as likely, then they would have to stay put, leaving the dual education system intact.[21]

Freedom-of-choice convinced Coleman and the school board to adopt a desegregation plan on June 2, 1965, based on voluntary student transfers. In a letter to officials at HEW's Office of Education, Coleman explained, "The plan is identical to those adopted in Bullock County and Macon County under a District Court order; and also identical to plans adopted by Greene, Hale, and Perry Counties since the passage of the Civil Rights Act. It is the feeling of our Board of Education that the most feasible course for us to adopt would be a plan in line with those in effect in counties with situations similar to ours," which was her genteel way of saying that the board patterned its plan after counties that also had too many black children and too few white children. Coleman further explained that only high school students would be eligible to apply for transfers in 1965. Students in the seventh and eighth grades would have to wait until the following year to apply, while those in elementary school would remain segregated for the foreseeable future. "To force us to apply the plan to elementary grades in this initial year would, in our judgment, prove disastrous": whites would abandon the public schools completely "should integration . . . proceed too rapidly." She assured the federal officials that the county's plan "would not precipitate" such an exodus.[22]

The school board placed a notice in the county weekly on June 17, 1965, announcing its decision and outlining the procedure for filing transfer applications. "Those pupils desiring to transfer from the schools they have previously attended must file in the office of the Superintendent of Education, in Hayneville, Alabama, applications for transfer on or before July 15, 1965 . . . signed by the parent or guardian of the pupil and on the form prescribed by the Lowndes County Superintendent of Education," read the announcement. The notice also informed the public that "all pupils in the Lowndes County Public School System shall attend the school they have previously attended or have made application to attend unless the parent or guardian of said pupils are advised to the contrary on or before August 1, 1965."[23] Although the announcement did not mask the obvious impediments to quick and judicious desegregation inherent in the plan, it sent shock waves of horror pulsing through the white community. White schools were sacred spaces. They were the main sites of privilege for poor and working-class whites who gained much less from Jim Crow than did their economic and social betters. Furthermore, maintaining school segregation was essential to keeping black boys away from white girls, which was a serious concern because many whites insisted that the goal of integration was miscegenation. "Niggers in our schools will ruin my children morally, scholastically, spiritually, and every other way," proclaimed one white mother.[24]

Whites were also furious at the school board. For the first time, they felt betrayed by their elected representatives, who at this critical moment proved incapable, or possibly even unwilling, to fight to preserve white supremacy. They were well aware that dual education systems elsewhere were under assault, but they sensed no immediate local threat. African Americans had not taken to the streets and the Justice Department had not filed a lawsuit. The possibility of securing more funds for public education failed to diffuse their anger; no amount of money was worth putting their children in classrooms with black brutes. White solidarity was cracking, but not because of ideological differences—everyone believed in white supremacy and segregated education—but because of conflicting approaches to maintaining dual education. This division cleared the way for nonelected officials to lead the resistance, and, unlike public office-holders, they were not nearly as constrained by federal mandates.

In the wake of the desegregation announcement, the wcc, which until that time had been quiet, immediately began to mobilize. In the same edition of the Lowndes *Signal* that carried the school board's notice, the wcc "urgently requested that every white man, woman and child in the county make a special effort to attend" an emergency meeting at the courthouse the following evening.[25] The specific purpose of the gathering was to raise awareness of the impending school crisis and to discuss forming a private white academy as a way to preserve segregated education. Whites enthusiastically embraced the idea of creating a private school but favored proceeding slowly. Launching and sustaining a white academy would be expensive and time-consuming, and they did not want to undertake the task needlessly. They decided to wait to see how many African Americans were foolish enough to apply for transfers before taking further action.[26]

African Americans were just as surprised as whites by the board's announcement. After a century of absolute segregation in education and a decade of vociferous denunciations of *Brown*, they did not expect the courthouse crowd to set the process of desegregation in motion. As a result, they possessed a deep skepticism of the board's commitment to eliminating dual education. Ongoing white opposition to voter registration reinforced this belief. The leaders of the LCCMHR shared these misgivings, but they also recognized that the desegregation plan presented African Americans with a unique chance to improve the quality of black education. Although they had not discussed mounting a challenge to segregated education before the announcement, they quickly began to rally support for school desegregation, which reflected their determination and ability to take advantage of political opportunities as they surfaced. Convincing black parents to apply for transfers to send their children to Hayneville High, however, proved even more difficult than persuading them to keep their children out of LCTS. Many feared economic reprisals for publicly supporting desegregation, while others refused to put their children directly in harm's way. In the end, forty-six parents filed transfer applications by the July 15, 1965, deadline, and not surprisingly, almost every one of them was active in the movement.[27]

LCCMHR activists wanted to involve many more people in the desegregation process. WCC leaders, on the other hand, hoped that far fewer African Americans would participate. With some four dozen transfer applications sitting on the superintendent's desk, whites imagined Hayneville High desegregating swiftly. "All deliberate speed" suddenly took on new and frightening meaning. In response, they moved forward with plans to create a private white academy. Two business days after the deadline for submitting transfer applications passed, Ray Bass, a high-ranking official in governor George Wallace's administration, a past secretary of the WCC, and the current president of the recently organized Lowndes County Private School Foundation, filed papers with the state to incorporate the foundation as a prelude to establishing a system of private white schools. "We can't wait to find out how extensive integration will be," he explained. "We must make advance preparations."[28] In line with this reasoning, the foundation held a public meeting that Friday at the Lowndesboro Recreation Center, an eight-room facility that the segregated Lowndesboro Recreation Club donated to the foundation for use as a school. The two hundred people who attended the gathering agreed to create a private white high school at that site; to begin holding classes on September 27, 1965, about one month after the start of the public school term; and to add additional grades as needed. "President Bass and staff workers urge that everyone join in and make this project a big success," reported the Lowndes *Signal*.[29]

Popular support for a private school did not mean that whites were willing to surrender Hayneville High without a fight. On the contrary, they were prepared to take extreme measures to keep the school segregated, not only to protect white privilege, but also to preserve a treasured community institution that was a source of pride and solidarity. Seemingly every white resident had a personal connection, either past or present, to the school, just as African Americans had with LCTS. Consequently, black families that sought to transfer children to Hayneville High anticipated systematic harassment. As expected, less than two weeks after the application due date, SNCC's Bob Mants reported that fifteen to twenty families had been "visited by a group of eight white people, who are mostly merchants and landowners who have Negroes in their debt or on their land," and had been told to withdraw their children's applications or face severe consequences.[30] On July 17, 1965, shortly after noon, Oliver "Buddy" Woodruff, a charter member of the WCC, called Jordan Gully, whose daughter Wilma Jean had applied for a transfer, to the door of his home. "What kind of shit [are you] trying to run over [me]?" demanded Woodruff. "I don't know what you're talking about," replied Gully. Irritated, Woodruff asked if he had a daughter named Wilma Jean. "Yes." Where is she? "In the house." "You're the head of your house, ain't you?" "Yes." "Didn't [you] know that she was going to register?" "Yes." Annoyed, Woodruff said, "Y'all paying attention to those folks running up and down the roads. We didn't bother y'all about registering, we didn't bother y'all about going to mass meetings [but] I'll be goddamn [*sic*] if this shit is going over this time. We let y'all by about registering. This shit ain't going to pass this time. We going to stop it. Don't you ask me for no damn help for nothing." Defiant, yet cautious, Gully asked, "What y'all up to? You don't want us to have any schools for our children?" Woodruff replied cryptically, "We're going to fix a way for y'all to have a school."[31] Mac Champion, Jr., a math teacher and the head football coach at Hayneville High, was much less ambiguous when he visited Eli Logan. He promised the staunch movement supporter that the Ku Klux Klan "would be through" at once if he did not remove his son's name from the list of students seeking to attend Hayneville High. He also warned Logan not to mention his visit to the "civil rights workers." Logan refused to withdraw his son's application, and he told Champion to inform the Klan "to be sure that they came during the day and not by night . . . because it won't be good for them if they come at night."[32] Despite the threats, only one family removed their child's name from the transfer list, a remarkable testament of black determination.[33]

Few parents expected county officials to accept all the transfer applications. At the same time, hardly anyone thought they would reject almost every one, but that is exactly what they did. The deadline for notifying students about the fate of their applications was Friday, July 30, 1965, and on that day, the community learned that the school board had approved only the transfer requests of John Hulett and Lillian McGill, which was a not-so-subtle attempt to placate the movement's most visible leaders in hopes of undermining the desegregation drive. The rejection notices were dismissively brief and did not explain the reason for the adverse decisions. Of course, everyone understood that a desire to preserve segregated schools prompted the judgments, but no one was willing to accept "because we said so" as an explanation for blatant discriminatory behavior anymore. Instead, they decided to go to the superintendent's office and demand a detailed explanation. On Monday morning, they gathered at the courthouse, determined to have an audience with Coleman. It was the closest thing to storming the bastille that the county ever witnessed, but if their defiance caught Coleman off guard, she did not show it. Undaunted, unsympathetic, and unrepentant, she told them that their children had been rejected because of poor attendance and because their standardized test scores demonstrated that they did not have the aptitude to share classrooms with white students. The use of attendance records was predictable; the use of standardized test results, however, was completely unexpected and left everyone baffled and angry. Not even the black teachers who administered the tests suspected that school officials would use them this way. Sarah Logan, a veteran teacher whose son's transfer request had been rejected because of his test scores, said that they had been told that the tests would be used to pinpoint students' "weak points."[34] As it stood, school desegregation was set to proceed with fewer black students than a single hand's count, just as it had in a half dozen other Black Belt counties and as it would in innumerable school districts across the South.[35]

In the absence of an appeals process, some twenty parents sent a signed letter drafted by SNCC attorney-in-residence Ruth Moskowitz to the U.S attorney general the next day. The petition detailed the prevailing condition of harassment in the county and racial discrimination in the public schools and called on the Justice Department to bring legal action against the school board. The formal complaint allowed the attorney general to launch an investigation under the provisions of Title IV of the 1964 Civil Rights Act. The probe, however, did not begin in earnest until September 1965. In the interim, movement activists prepared for token integration at Hayneville High and a renewal of their LCTS boycott.[36]

The leaders of the private school initiative spent the remaining days of summer trying to decide how to proceed. They had acquired a building, secured commitments from at least five teachers, and collected the ten-dollar membership fee to join the foundation from some 150 parents, but the scuttlebutt was that whites would not abandon Hayneville High if the number of African Americans admitted remained at or very near two.[37] "If it is the law, I guess we'll have to stomach it," said one white man with obvious sarcasm that nevertheless hinted at an acceptance of tokenism.[38] Rumors swirled, however, that many more African Americans would enroll by the first day of classes, and the approval of three additional transfer requests in early August seemed to confirm these suspicions. It was hard, therefore, to determine the precise level of support for forming an academy immediately. "We just don't know how many parents are interested," confessed Bass, "because we are all waiting to find out how extensive integration of the public schools will be."[39] Anxious yet unable to proceed without greater assurances, they marked time until the start of the public school year.

The movement's young people were equally anxious. They wanted desperately to be a part of the fight for freedom but could not find a niche. The boycott of LCTS had failed, the school board had blocked their attempt to integrate Hayneville High, and they could not participate in the registration tries because they were too young to vote. Determined to contribute to the struggle, two dozen youth decided to picket a handful of stores in Fort Deposit to protest discriminatory hiring practices, unequal and discourteous treatment, and price gouging. This was a bold decision. Fort Deposit was the most dangerous town in the county. It was "worse than anything I saw in Mississippi last summer," confessed one SNCC activist.[40] Indeed, Bob Mants and fellow SNCC organizer Jimmy Rogers, a twenty-eight-year-old air force veteran and graduate student at Tuskegee, had been trying since early summer to organize area adults but had made few inroads.[41] "The reason that they have been having such a hard time getting anything going is because the Klan has been actively intimidating people," reported Carmichael.[42]

The leaders of the LCCMHR admired the young people's enthusiasm and wanted to increase their involvement in the movement, but they staunchly opposed direct action. They were much more interested in acquiring power through the vote than drawing attention to their lack of it through picketing. Moreover, they believed that the Black Belt generally, and Lowndes County specifically, was entirely too dangerous for this form of protest. At best, demonstrators would be beaten or arrested; at worst, they would be killed. As evidence, they pointed to the spring demonstrations in neighboring Wilcox County that ended almost as soon as they began after police attacked protesters with clubs and concussion smoke bombs. SNCC organizers tended to share this perspective but they did not attempt to dissuade the upstart activists from picketing. In true SNCC fashion, once the young people insisted on carrying out the protest, the organization promised to support them.[43]

On an oppressively humid mid-August morning a score of local youth made their way to the AME church just outside of Fort Deposit to finalize strategy for the demonstration scheduled for later that day. They were energized and focused, but soon after arriving at the church they received disturbing news from a pair of FBI agents in town to observe the federal registrars' first day of work. The agents reported that the local police intended to arrest the demonstrators the instant they appeared and that a crowd of white men armed with clubs, broken bottles, and guns was assembling at the automobile dealership owned by registrar Carl Golson's brother. If the students were lucky they would be arrested before the mob had a chance to attack. Nervous energy thicker than the summer air enveloped the demonstrators, but the likelihood of arrest and the possibility of white violence were not enough to compel them to call off the protest. Instead, they steeled their nerves through prayer and song, split into three groups of eight to ten people, gathered their homemade signs, some of which read, "Wake up! This is not primitive time" and "No more back doors," and departed for Water's Dry Goods, the Community Grill, and McGruder's Grocery.[44]

Although it was not too early for Saturday shopping and socializing, the central business district was deserted except for a handful of deputies, the crowd of white men at the car dealership, and a small group of African Americans waiting for the federal registrars. When the young people arrived and saw the deputies and the armed mob, they did not balk; in solemn determination, they proceeded to form their picket lines. Surely they were afraid, but they masked their fear completely. Perhaps their poise surprised the mob because its members failed to react, which gave the deputies time to intervene and arrest all twenty-nine demonstrators. The protest lasted mere minutes, but the young people were thankful that it ended without violence.[45]

The deputies charged the students with disturbing the peace and parading without a permit and took them to Fort Deposit's tiny two-cell lockup. The students were then herded onto a flatbed truck normally used for hauling trash and transferred to the slightly larger, but no less cramped, county jail. Soon after arriving in Hayneville, Carmichael and fellow SNCC organizer Christopher Wylie joined them. The duo had been arrested not long after the demonstrators on charges of reckless driving and leaving the scene of an accident following a minor automobile collision with a carload of armed whites. Like the others, they were arrested before any harm befell them.[46]

The arrestees made it through the night, albeit uncomfortably. They received a modicum of relief the next morning when a contingent of fifty movement supporters arrived bearing hot food, cigarettes, chewing gum, and books. At daybreak, LCCMHR leaders had convened an emergency meeting in Trickem to coordinate a response to the arrests. Although they disapproved of the demonstration, they refused to abandon their children. They were worried about the safety and welfare of all the demonstrators, but in particular they were concerned about the well-being of the minors, so they insisted on and secured their immediate release. At the same time, they retained the services of Birmingham attorney Peter Hall, who filed a petition to have the remaining cases heard in federal court.[47]

The young activists understood that being in police custody was not much safer than being on a picket line, but this did not prevent them from trying to bring a measure of normalcy to their incarceration. They spent their time reading and writing, singing freedom songs, and debating the implications of the ongoing Watts uprising. Not knowing when they might be released was also frustrating. Bond was set at one hundred dollars each, a princely sum for movement activists. Indeed, SNCC had only enough cash to bond out two people, so everyone except for Carmichael and Wylie, whom the demonstrators decided should go free because they knew best how to marshal the legal and financial resources needed to get everyone else out, prepared for a lengthy stay. Early on Friday, August 20, however, the guards unlocked the cell doors and informed them that they had to leave. O. P. Edwards, the mayor of Fort Deposit, telephoned the jailhouse that morning and ordered their immediate release. Edwards had not experienced a change of heart. Rather, he had learned about the petition filed by Hall and wanted desperately to avoid additional federal meddling in county affairs.[48]

The demonstrators' sudden reversal of fortune caused more trepidation than jubilation because the deputies refused to explain the reason for their release. Moreover, no one was waiting to pick them up so it was obvious that their friends had not posted their bond. "I just did not trust that suddenly without penalty we would be allowed to go free," recalled SNCC's Ruby Sales. "It was just very incongruent with the blindness of their racism that they would release us on our word, when they didn't think we even had a word." "The other thing," said Sales, was that "I knew enough about Stokely Carmichael and also the local people, like the Jacksons, that if we were being released from jail, their commitment was such that they would be there to meet us."[49]

The demonstrators kept close to the jailhouse after they left. "We stood outside of the jail because we felt it would be safe, rather than walking all over town," said activist Jimmy Rogers.[50] But deputy sheriff Joe Jackson denied them the small measure of security that standing in the shadow of the jailhouse provided. "You'll have to get the hell off county property," he said while walking to his patrol car. Willie Vaughn, a twenty-one-year-old SNCC organizer, tried to bide time by asking, "This is federal property, isn't it?" "No it's not," snapped Jackson. "It's county property and you've been released from jail so get the hell off."[51] The students had to comply, but they made sure to keep the building within eyesight.

Vaughn, a native of Greenwood, Mississippi, and a veteran of the movement in that state, knew from experience that they had to get off the street—to remain in public view was to invite trouble. Movement supporter Fannie Robinson lived nearby and she owned a telephone, so Vaughn walked to her house and called William Cosby, the LCCMHR vice chairman, to request transportation out of Hayneville. Unfortunately, Cosby was not at home. After leaving a detailed message with Cosby's wife, Vaughn rejoined the others. While he was away Jonathan Daniels, Richard Morrisroe, Ruby Sales, and Joyce Bailey walked to the Cash Store where Tom Coleman shot the two white priests, killing Daniels.[52]

The shooting was on the mind of everyone in the black community when school opened one week later, except for Arthalise Hulett. The son of the LCCMHR chairperson had been waking up at 4:30 a.m. all summer and did so again on the last day of August 1965, but rather than reporting to his father's fields after completing his early morning chores, the fifteen-year-old rode with his parents to his aunt's house in Hayneville where he waited patiently for the start of his first day at Hayneville High. When asked by a reporter how he felt, the tenth grader replied, "I'm not nervous at all—so far, at least." Despite his calm, there was plenty to be uneasy about since Daniels's murder seemed only to fuel the bloodlust of whites. Lillian McGill, whose son joined Art that morning, recalled white people saying, "If these niggers show up over here . . . there's going to be blood in the streets." The possibility of violence was real and everyone knew it. Even Sheriff Ryals had sense enough to post fifteen special deputies outside the school. The small group of black parents, though, took their own precautions. McGill brought the gun she carried when she canvassed and kept it nearby as she and the other mothers escorted their children to the school just before the morning bell. If blood was going to be shed, it was going to be "more than black folks' blood," she later said.[53] Mercifully, the fragile peace held.

The tension was as palpable inside Hayneville High as it was outside. Throughout the day, white students harassed the African American newcomers by treating them as though their black bodies were diseased. In the hallways, they scattered and gasped whenever they approached. In the classrooms, they refused to speak to them. In the lunchroom, they made them sit by themselves. And on the school bus during the afternoon ride home, they forced them to sit in the back and jeered as they disembarked. Through it all, the black teens maintained their poise and dignity. Though young, they understood the stakes.[54]

Not surprisingly, white and black parents viewed token integration completely differently. The former embraced it quickly, which pleased the superintendent tremendously. Coleman worked hard to put together a de-segregation plan that preserved segregated education while simultaneously maintaining the county's eligibility for ESEA funds, and she exerted equal energy meeting with white parents, students, and teachers trying to allay their fears about the process. At the same time, it forced Ray Bass to shelve the WCC plan for an all-white academy, although he promised to renew the effort if the pace of integration increased. Black parents, meanwhile, found no joy in this form of desegregation primarily because it left the dual education system intact, trapping nearly every black student in the same woefully inadequate schools. Because it was obvious to everyone that the new norm would confine black children to segregated schools for the near future, movement leaders continued their efforts to improve black schools, beginning with boycotting LCTS for a second time.[55]

LCCMHR activists had been building support for a renewed boycott all summer and had been pleased with the people's response. At a mass meeting held the Sunday before the first day of school, some three hundred movement supporters reaffirmed their commitment to keep their children at home until Superintendent Coleman met their demands, which ranged from hiring adult school bus drivers to ending mandatory extracurricular activities, especially fundraising, during regular school hours. Most of all, they wanted her to remove Principal Pierce. The next day more than four hundred students, representing roughly two thirds of the student body, stayed out of school, which thrilled LCCMHR leaders, but momentum was hard to sustain. Two weeks after classes began, attendance increased threefold; even Hulett's other son, John, Jr., was back in school. Once again, Coleman had been unyielding in her opposition to the parents' demands. She was also unwavering in her support of Pierce. "We hire on the basis of ability," she said, and in her opinion the veteran administrator was "capable." In addition, parents feared that their children were missing too much school, a concern that Pierce exploited. "I think it is suicide for the child to stay out of school," he said. "With the competition and changing times and the scientific and all goings on now, I think we ought to figure more time for school instead of less." Ironically, boycott organizers had been saying exactly the same thing. Pierce also preached patience: "These improvements they want take time—they can't be done overnight. I'm open to work with all my folk—including my white friends. I'm an educator, and all I want to do is move forward."[56]

Movement supporters remained steadfast in their determination to oust Pierce. At a mass meeting in mid-September 1965, passions flared as they discussed and debated the future of the waning boycott, but they eventually agreed to continue the protest. Hulett and other movement leaders promised to lead by example by taking their children back out of school. "We will keep our children out until Pierce is removed even if it takes a whole year," declared Hulett. "This time we really mean business." They also instructed canvassers to resume discussing the protest as they moved about the county. Timothy Mays, who helped launch the spring boycott before he graduated, did just that. "Dr. Pierce is hurting your child," he said to every parent who would listen. "I know. At college, I had to get lessons I missed out here. That's a hard-test."[57]

To help sustain the boycott, SNCC activists, together with teachers dismissed by Coleman because of their involvement in the movement, organized a tutorial program for out-of-school students. Although they instructed the young people in a range of academic subjects, it was not enough to convince most black parents to set aside their fears about their children missing class time. As a result, only a few families honored the protest for an extended period, which eliminated all hope that the boycott would bring about meaningful change. The ineffectiveness of the boycott reinforced the notion that protest alone was not enough to transform society, a revelation that helped generate interest in controlling local government. After the failed boycott, "some began to think in terms of running the county themselves," recalled Hulett.[58]

For the children of the families who stayed true to the boycott, SNCC organizers created a floating freedom school that met one night a week in Lowndesboro, Trickem, Blackbelt, and Mosses in the homes of movement supporters. Field secretaries Gloria Larry and Tina Harris, along with veteran public school teachers Sarah Logan and Dorothy Hinson, taught classes on grammar, mathematics, French, and African American history. Like freedom schools elsewhere, the instructors relied on personal creativity to compensate for scarce teaching resources. During a lesson on slavery, the teachers succeeded in getting the students to think critically about the Peculiar Institution while learning about American jurisprudence by staging a mock trial in which a student, pretending to be a slave, sued his imaginary master for his freedom. Students also served as lawyers and made arguments on behalf of the plaintiff and defendant before a jury of classmates empanelled to decide the case. The popularity of the freedom school curriculum encouraged SNCC activists to host evening and weekend discussion groups on African and African American history for young people and adults at the freedom library they established in Hayneville during the summer. The library and school were the movement's first attempts at creating parallel institutions to offset deficiencies in existing structures. While never intended to replace the county's educational institutions, they did reflect SNCC organizers' understanding of, and local activists' growing appreciation for, the ability if not the necessity of parallel structures to support and sustain the struggle. This was an important insight that also sparked interest in independent politics.[59]

Pattie McDonald, a forty-four-year-old homemaker and the mother of several young children, recognized early on the value of parallel institutions, including the need for a freedom library. This prompted her to let SNCC use the small two-room house that sat unoccupied just behind her modest Hayneville home. This simple gesture carried serious consequences because it associated her family with the fight against white supremacy. From that time forward, whites made the McDonalds a target of their campaign of intimidation. The harassment started with a series of phone calls in early August 1965 from men, who identified themselves only as members of the Klan, ordering the McDonalds to leave that "civil rights mess" alone. Then word reached them by way of black cooks and housekeepers employed by whites that Leon McDonald, Pattie's husband, was the focus of an assassination plot. The two white men who stalked him every morning as he walked to catch his ride to work and every evening as he returned home lent credence to the rumors. In addition, during the middle of August, the McDonalds repeatedly spotted a pair of white men—perhaps the same duo that had been shadowing Leon—staking out the freedom library, and friends informed them that whites were planning to bomb their home. Keenly aware of how dangerous the situation had become, Mrs. McDonald wrote to Silas Norman, SNCC's Alabama project director, and advised him to instruct Scott B. Smith, the field secretary assigned to Hayneville, to be sure to "stay away for a while & if he just have to come back to be careful & watchful" because "things are still hot." "It is a shame we can't rent our own house to who we want to & stay home in peace," she wrote. "It is a miserable life to live."[60]

The tranquility of nightfall normally provided Mrs. McDonald with relief from the stress of managing a crowded household all day, but lately it offered no reprieve. Instead, it added to her anxiety and compounded her misery because darkness provided night riders with a cloak of invisibility. Her daughter Shirley Ann understood the burden she carried, so when she heard the plaintive wail of her one-year-old brother shortly before midnight on September 1, 1965, she looked in on him. Walter needed nothing more than his diaper changed, and after performing this chore, she took him to her bed rather than to his crib. This simple act saved her brother's life. As soon as they lay down, bullets tore through the house, shattering the window just above Walter's crib and ripping through the walls in several rooms, including Pattie and Leon's bedroom. Miraculously, all twelve people in the house survived the attack.[61]

The assault on the McDonalds marked the beginning of a fierce campaign of nocturnal terrorism. Until that time, whites relied primarily on economic reprisals and verbal harassment, and they operated mainly during daylight. But by late August 1965, the steady rise in the number of African Americans attempting to register to vote, the arrival of the federal registrars, the student demonstration in Fort Deposit, and the desegregation of Hayneville High had transformed what many whites perceived initially as a manageable annoyance into a serious crisis that necessitated the use of deadly force. Tom Coleman was the first to push the resistance beyond economic retaliation and verbal intimidation, but his indictment and impending trial for the midday slaying of Jonathan Daniels caused others to express their deadly rage at night to ensure anonymity. There were now consequences for killing people in broad daylight, but the social costs and legal penalties for murder, although sufficient to force violence into the shadows, were not nearly severe enough to prevent it altogether.[62]

The Klan played an active role in creating and sustaining the new level of terror. The four Birmingham men who gunned down Viola Liuzzo were Klansmen. Tom Coleman fraternized openly with known Klan members, prompting speculation that he too belonged to the organization. Hayneville High football coach Mac Champion, Jr., promised Martha Johnson, whose daughter applied for a transfer to his school, that the Klan was "going to get the leaders of these mass meetings" and identified John Hulett, Sarah Logan, Sidney Logan, Jr., William Cosby, Frank Miles, Jr., and Matthew Jackson, Sr., by name. And twice in July, the hate group held public rallies in the county seat.[63] Nevertheless, the KKK was not the main source of racial terrorism. White property owners, employers, merchants, and parents drew on the custom of ordinary people resorting to violence to suppress race-based insurgency and led the attacks on movement activists by organizing informally, as they had in days of old. Consequently, most acts of racial terrorism in Lowndes County did not involve Klansmen.

The secondary role of the Klan voided the newsworthiness of violence in Lowndes County. The major media outlets generally confined coverage of civil rights violence in the South to episodes involving the terror group and white victims. The ambush of Liuzzo and the murder of Daniels received banner headlines, while the assault on the McDonalds' home and the freedom library, and the shootings at the Jackson homestead and the freedom house, went unreported despite SNCC's publicity efforts.[64] Almost every instance of racial terrorism in the county went unnoticed by the public. As a result, violence failed to spark the moral outrage needed to force federal officials to intervene on behalf of African Americans. For those in the trenches, white violence had no upside. It simply cost lives and reinforced fear. If local activists and SNCC organizers could have avoided it, they certainly would have. Unfortunately, it could not be sidestepped.

The absence of newsworthy violence exposed movement participants to a relentless wave of terror. "The violence kept cropping up," said Carmichael in late February 1966, and federal officials did almost nothing to stop it and Alabama lawmen did even less.[65] "In Lowndes County no one will protect Negroes," observed local activist Frank Miles, Jr. Willful neglect on the part of police agencies at all levels of government compelled African Americans to institute their own safety measures. "We have to defend ourselves," said Miles.[66] Out of necessity, movement people fortified their homes. In order to be prepared when night riders called, Fort Deposit resident Bessie McMeans stacked a dozen or so guns on a mattress that she placed in her living room. Others relocated shotguns from the backs of closets to behind bedroom doors or oiled old pistols and placed them atop nightstands. While canvassing they toted weapons. Hulett always kept a shotgun in his car and shells in his pocket, and he rarely went into the field without his .38 special. The five-shot, snub-nose revolver was far from reliable—Hulett confessed that he had to aim right to hit a target on his left—but years of practice made him an expert shot with his weapon of choice. They also organized armed caravans to and from mass meetings. During the first movement gathering in Fort Deposit, local activist Robert Strickland trailed a convoy of several dozen cars that departed from White Hall with what Hulett described as something akin to a machine gun mounted on the roof of his vehicle. In addition, they posted armed sentries outside churches, leaders' homes, and the freedom house; they also provided SNCC field secretaries with armed escorts and guns of their own.[67]

Local activists did not suffer from a want of weapons. They had any number of pistols and shotguns found commonly in rural households across America, plus a few army-issue guns provided by veterans.

Ammunition was harder to come by. Every gun shop within reasonable driving distance stopped selling bullets to African Americans from Lowndes County soon after the movement started. The ban forced movement supporters to rely on members of the Lowndes Diaspora to smuggle what they needed into the county. Mathew Jackson, Sr.'s daughter routinely purchased large quantities of ammunition and more than a few weapons in Georgia, where she worked as a schoolteacher, and brought them home whenever she visited.[68]

Although heavily armed, movement people did not use guns as organizing tools. They did not drive around the county displaying rifles in automobile gun racks or parade in front of the courthouse with sidearms drawn. There was no need for suicidal displays of bravado because everyone in the black community knew of their commitment to armed self-defense, and each time they repulsed an attack they made whites aware of their pledge to meet violence with violence. Local activists also did not form a paramilitary group, although they had the ability to do so, as evidenced by the creation of a social movement organization and several auxiliary groups. Instead, they met their defensive needs as they arose. This conscious decision to decentralize armed resistance reflected the nature of the threat they faced. White violence emanated from diffuse sources, rather than from a single entity such as the Klan, or even the sheriff's office, which was better suited for regulating farm labor than controlling movement behavior. Consequently, there existed neither an easily identified terrorist group for a black paramilitary organization to defend against nor a large police force for them to combat. African Americans were most concerned about their white neighbors. Also contributing to the loosely organized character of armed resistance was the extremely high rate of gun ownership among African Americans and the strong bonds of kinship, friendship, and community around which they built the movement, which gave local activists the capacity to coordinate self-defense as needed. They could count on any number of people to guard a mass meeting because so many people possessed weapons and were willing to protect their friends and family. Consequently, armed self-defense in Lowndes County looked very different than it did in Monroe, North Carolina, where Robert F. Williams dug foxholes and built barricades at entry points to the black community. It was distinct from incarnations in Bogalusa and Jonesboro, Louisiana, where the Deacons for Defense and Justice protected civil rights demonstrators. And it was of another variety than what surfaced in Oakland, California, where the Black Panther

Party for Self-Defense used guns both to recruit black youth and to keep the police honest. Thus, the lack of public posturing and the absence of armed groups did not mean that African Americans rejected self-defense, only that local conditions necessitated, and community traditions allowed, alternative means of expression.[69]

The decision not to form an armed resistance organization also echoed African American indifference to nonviolence. In fact, for local activists, nonviolence was a nonissue. Movement supporters praised the Lord and passed the ammunition without discussion, debate, or the slightest bit of hesitancy. As a result, there was no need to create a separate organization committed explicitly to self-defense in order to protect the kind of nonviolent persona needed to win over white hearts and minds. Quite simply, the Lowndes movement was not a moral crusade, so its leaders had nothing to hide.

Local activists objected to nonviolent protest for several reasons. They opposed it because it was too dangerous. "You can't come here talking that nonviolence shit," said one resident. "You'll get yourself killed, and other people too."[70] Based on lived experience, movement leaders believed that it was safer to let white people know, without too much fanfare, that they possessed guns and were not afraid to use them. "[It's] the only thing to stop them from killing you," said local activist Lemon Johnson.[71] They also rejected nonviolence as a way of life because it contradicted local traditions, such as small-game hunting, that legitimated the use of guns. The absence of nonviolence workshops also kept the ideology from gaining a foothold. Intense instruction in nonviolence was necessary to win converts to the alien concept, but the overwhelming majority of SNCC's Alabama organizers had lost interest in teaching about the philosophical and tactical approach to change. "I have simply stopped telling people they should remain nonviolent," said Carmichael in January 1966. "This would be tantamount to suicide in the Black Belt counties where whites are shooting at Negroes and it would cost me the respect of the people."[72]

Armed self-defense negated the effectiveness of midnight marauding, frustrating the attempt by whites to defeat the movement through violence. Although whites continued to target black activists, they adjusted to their inability to neutralize local leaders and SNCC organizers by exploiting the economic vulnerability of the movement's base. As the 1965 cotton-picking season neared its end, dozens of sharecroppers received eviction notices. "I been living on this one farm since January 20, 1931, and then Wednesday a week ago—two days before Christmas—the landlord

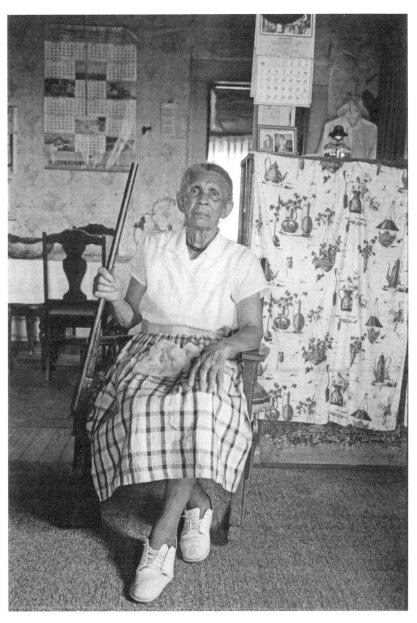

Lowndes County resident with a typical weapon found in the homes of African
Americans (1965). Courtesy of the Library of Congress, Prints and Photographs
Division, *Look* magazine, Photograph Collection, LC Look-Job 65–2434.

took and sent word by the boss of the place [that] we had to move 'cause they wanted the house," explained fifty-year-old Amanda Glover, who lived in St. Clair on land owned by E. R. Meadows. "He didn't give no other reason, and I didn't ask for none," said the mother of five. "I'm just goin' to get on like he told me." The reason she had to move, though, was obvious. "I just think he wanted his house because they found out we had registered to vote," said Glover. Meadows employed six black families and evicted only those with registered voters.[73]

Many evictees moved in with friends and family, crowding already-cramped quarters in order to remain in the county. "I registered in August and got asked to leave our house in October after we had been there for seven years," explained Annie Bell Scott. "We moved in a two-bedroom house with my sister right after that. Eleven of us been living there all together."[74] Despite the tremendous discomfort and inconvenience, Scott was fortunate. Quite a few people had neither kith nor kin to shelter them and had no choice but to leave the county. Although the wave of evictions was demoralizing, this exodus was devastating because evictees ranked among the movement's most stalwart supporters. Sharecropper Threddie Lee Stewart, for example, ran for a seat on an Agricultural Stabilization and Conservation Service committee as a movement candidate in October 1965 before losing his house and the right to work the land that his family had worked for three generations. The movement would have collapsed without farmers like him.

To keep evictees from leaving Lowndes County, SNCC organizers proposed building a tent city on six plus acres that the LCCMHR had purchased just off Route 80, less than a half mile from Mt. Gilliard Baptist Church. After receiving the approval of LCCMHR executives for the project, organizer Gloria Larry drove to Atlanta three days after Christmas and, with two thousand dollars borrowed from SNCC's emergency fund, bought ten army surplus tents, sixty cots, and a dozen stove heaters. She returned to Lowndes County immediately and, together with local activists, fellow organizers, and student volunteers from Tuskegee, closed out the year by wading through ankle-deep mud to pitch the brown-and-green tents. Among those who toiled in the muck and mire was twenty-two-year-old Tuskegee freshman Sammy Younge. Tragically, less than a week later, Marvin Segrest, a white gas station attendant in Tuskegee, shot and killed Younge following a daylong voter registration drive in Macon County that the navy veteran helped organize. Not surprisingly, an all-white jury found Segrest not guilty of murder.[75]

Woman and child living in Tent City in Lowndes County in 1966.
© John F. Phillips/johnphillipsphotography.com.

Freedom City, as some locals called it, raised people's spirits. "I feel good," said Jeff Davis, an older man who along with his wife was among the first evictees to move into the makeshift village. "I'm just my own man now."[76] But life in the refuge was hard. The first set of families, totaling fifteen people, shared a single outhouse and toted water for cooking and drinking from a well on a distant farm. On top of that, some of the tents had holes that freely admitted the wind and the rain, and only two had wood floors to trap the feeble heat emanating from the inefficient stoves. One month into its existence, the camp still needed much more than it offered its homeless occupants, including "portable refrigerators, portable toilets, firewood, wood to make floors for the tents, bunk beds, folding beds, non-perishable meats and fruits, non-prescription medical supplies, disinfectants, and toilet articles," according to a list compiled by SNCC's

Boys living in Tent City in Lowndes County display rifles used to defend the camp against night riders. © John F. Phillips/johnphillipsphotography.com.

Bill Mahoney and Dorothy Zellner.[77] This catalogue also testifies to the spartan furnishings in each tent. One item that every dwelling had, however, was a gun. Weapons were necessary because night riders took aim at the tents as soon as they appeared. "Tent City was like a shooting gallery," said SNCC field secretary C. J. Jones. "They used to come by there three or four times a week and shoot into Tent City, and you have to remember that there were women and children living in Tent City."[78]

To help alleviate the suffering of those living in the rough-and-ready camp, the Detroit-LCCMHR collected canned food and clothing in the Motor City for two months starting in February 1966 to ship to Lowndes County. Its members made formal solicitations at churches, and a sympathetic preacher who had a Sunday radio show implored his listeners to contribute to the cause. At the same time, they made informal appeals throughout the community and at their jobs by asking family, friends, and coworkers to make donations. John Stephenson, for example, collected two hundred dollars' worth of food and forty dollars in cash from fellow workers at the Chrysler Outer Drive plant. By the end of March 1966, they had amassed more than twenty tons of vital supplies. Meanwhile, Detroit-LCCMHR president Simon Owens tapped into his network of union contacts and secured the services of a truck and a driver free of charge from Teamsters Local 337 to transport the food and clothing to Alabama. Owens, along with his son and Detroit-LCCMHR members Robert Pierce, Frank Pierce, and Willie Moton, left their factory jobs early on April 5, 1966, to load the truck. SNCC organizers Ernest Hyman and Wilbert Lott joined them, as did Perry Bradley, a Teamster from Local 299. The truck arrived in Lowndes County just before Easter and movement activists distributed its contents immediately. Through this and other fundraising efforts, the Lowndes Diaspora became the lifeblood of the settlement.[79]

To provide evictees with more permanent relief, local activists sued white landowners in U.S. District Court. In *Miles v. Dixon*, attorneys representing African Americans maintained that white landowners attempted to prevent them from registering to vote and obtaining political power by "evicting them or threatening to evict them from their homes and lands, denying them credit, denying them an opportunity to continue sharecropping or tenant farming arrangements, and otherwise denying them their livelihood." The lawyers described in detail economic sanctions against twenty black farmers. They also outlined "a conspiracy to terrorize the Negro people of Lowndes County by acts of violence, including murder."

The legal team petitioned the court to enjoin white landowners from "threatening, intimidating, or coercing in any manner" people attempting to participate in the political process; to instruct the landowners to allow evictees to return to their homes; and to dispatch marshals to establish a permanent presence in the county and arrest anyone who broke laws designed to protect "franchise activities."[80]

The prospects for a favorable ruling were good. The plaintiffs marshaled a wealth of credible evidence, most notably sworn affidavits documenting the evictions of dozens of African Americans for registering to vote, in clear violation of the Voting Rights Act. At the same time, the white landowners defended their actions feebly by insisting that it was a simple coincidence that only black farmers who registered to vote had been evicted. In addition, the Justice Department sided with the plaintiffs. U.S. attorney general Nicholas Katzenbach, who authorized sending federal registrars to the county in August 1965, believed that the court should issue an injunction to halt the coercive activities of the white landowners, and he was confident that the court would provide at least a temporary order. But judge Frank M. Johnson, Jr., who presided over the Middle District Court of Alabama and whose rulings and decrees in several civil rights cases served as models for judicial remedies for racial discrimination, dismissed the case in June 1966, citing a lack of evidence in all but one instance. Judge Johnson wanted smoking gun evidence showing that white landowners conspired at some specific place and time to evict and intimidate black farmers for registering to vote and supporting the movement. The white landowners, though, did not have to hold a secret meeting to reach a consensus about using economic coercion and physical intimidation to slow the movement's momentum. They understood the stakes and knew instinctively that they needed to resort to the old way of doing things to preserve the racial caste system.[81]

In the absence of federal intervention, the evictions continued into the spring, through the summer, and beyond the fall of 1966, exacerbating fear and making organizing considerably more difficult. "With most people coming from plantation areas, it was extremely hard, after the evictions came along, to get those people registered to vote," said Lillian McGill. Indeed, the evictions and Tent City were sobering reminders of the high price of freedom. "It's a very frightening thing to have to accept the cold reality . . . that in order to exercise their rights, to get what they could get in this great Democracy in America, here in 1966, people were living in tents," observed field secretary George Green.[82] This experience, though, taught the camp's inhabitants and other movement supporters important political lessons. According to Carmichael, "[It] served to instill a sense of the tremendous need to establish an independent base of group power within the community."[83] This significant insight inched people closer to third-party politics. Meanwhile, a favorable court ruling in a school desegregation case filed on behalf of African Americans by the Justice Department in January 1966 moved people closer to obtaining quality education for black children.

In August 1965, assistant U.S. attorney general John Doar notified Hulda Coleman that he had received a written grievance from African Americans complaining of racial discrimination by the school board. If school officials did not remedy the situation, the attorney general would seek legal redress on their behalf in federal court under authority granted to him by Title IV of the 1964 Civil Rights Act. "The purpose of this letter is to provide your school board with the required statutory notice [of the complaint]," explained Doar, "and to afford the board a reasonable opportunity to correct the matters complained of."[84] School officials responded by insisting that they were already in compliance with federal law and cited as evidence the freedom-of-choice gradual desegregation plan that they adopted in June 1965.[85] Francis Keppel, the U.S. commissioner of education, found the county's plan wholly inadequate. In a letter to Coleman sent three weeks after Art Hulett's first day at Hayneville High, he explained that the plan fell well short of federal standards in several areas, including "notice to parents, the method by which choice is exercised, publication of the plan, provision for assignment of pupils in cases of overcrowding, availability of school transportation, facilities, and activities on a nondiscriminatory basis, preparations for the desegregation of the faculty, transfers of pupils into and out of the school district, and the grades to be desegregated this year." Given local officials' track record of obstinacy, he also concluded that "further efforts to secure compliance with the [Civil Rights] Act by voluntary means would not be fruitful," and informed Coleman that the county had one week to notify HEW of its intention to submit a new plan.[86] Coleman and the board gambled that the government would not pursue legal action and refused to submit a new proposal. Their decision triggered an investigation by the Justice Department and led U.S. attorneys to file a lawsuit in federal district court at the start of 1966, naming Coleman, the county board of education, the state board of education, and the state superintendent of education as the defendants.[87]

United States v. Lowndes County Board of Education et al. sought to enjoin the county from operating a dual education system based on race. "Unless restrained by this Court the defendants will continue to operate the public schools of Lowndes County on a racially segregated basis and will continue to deny to Negro children in Lowndes County educational opportunities and facilities equal to those provided to white children, in violation of the Fourteenth Amendment to the Constitution of the United States," read the plaintiffs' complaint.[88] A. R. Meadows, Alabama's superintendent of education, mapped out a defense that hinged on the county's alleged financial inability to consolidate its more than two-dozen black schools, and, by implication, its inability to provide for the immediate creation of a unitary school system. Coleman and the school board rejected this approach, realizing that pleading poverty in this manner would neither save segregated public education nor make the county eligible for ESEA funds. Instead, they capitulated. On February 8, 1966, they passed an extraordinary resolution acknowledging that the public school system "is now and has been in the past a dual school system based on race," and that African American children had been afforded educational opportunities "unequal to and inferior to" those provided white children. To make amends, they proposed desegregating the first grade in September 1966 in addition to the previously scheduled desegregation of grades seven and eight. They hoped that this change to the existing desegregation plan would be enough to keep the court from issuing a more substantial order. The resolution also authorized the superintendent to "forthwith apply for Federal funds," and within days of the declaration, she submitted a request for $1.5 million in federal assistance. "The board wants every penny it can get," confessed Maury D. Smith, the school board's attorney.[89]

The mea culpa eliminated the need for a formal court hearing, but it did not keep Judge Johnson from issuing an unprecedented desegregation order. In a consent decree handed down on February 11, 1966, he instructed the school board to desegregate every grade by September 1, 1967, starting with grades six through twelve that fall. By imposing a hard deadline, he sought to avoid the "all deliberate speed" misstep that the U.S. Supreme Court had made a decade earlier. He also called for the closure of twenty-four black schools that failed to meet the most minimum standards necessary for productive operation, "as soon as practicable" but no later than the September 1967 deadline, and outlined a new procedure for pupil transfers. "No choice will be denied for reason other than overcrowding," he declared. In addition, he ordered the creation of remedial education programs to "eliminate the effects of past discrimination" and offered guidelines for managing faculty and staff that allowed for affirmative action. "Race or color will henceforth not be a factor in the hiring, assignment, reassignment, promotion, demotion or dismissal of teachers and other professional staff, with the exception that the assignments may be made to further the process of desegregation," he wrote. "Affirmative steps," he added, "will be taken to eliminate racial assignment heretofore made."[90]

Coleman accepted the sweeping mandate grudgingly, realizing that segregated education as it existed for almost a century would not survive the summer. She did find a small measure of solace in a subsequent ruling by HEW officials that the county's acquiescence satisfied federal requirements for releasing money to local school districts.[91] But hardly anyone else in the white community found comfort in HEW's decision. For them, Judge Johnson's decree signaled the Apocalypse, and no infusion of federal funds was worth the onset of the end of days.

With desegregation imminent, Ray Bass and the leaders of the private school initiative launched an aggressive effort to open Lowndes Academy by September 1966. W. O. Crawford, the president of Southern United Life Insurance in Montgomery, spearheaded a capital campaign that raised more than one hundred thousand dollars by the start of summer to cover immediate operating expenses, create an endowment, and provide scholarships to defray the cost of tuition, which started at thirty dollars a month for families paying for only one student. A televised financial appeal in July 1966 by governor George Wallace, whose administration tried unsuccessfully to direct public money to private schools, helped the academy's finance committee climb closer to its short-term fundraising goal of five hundred thousand dollars. Meanwhile, Bass worked hard to recruit disenchanted public school teachers and by August 1966 had signed up a full complement of instructors, including Hayneville High's Mac Champion, who spent the previous summer trying to intimidate transfer applicants. Bass expended equal energy encouraging white parents to enroll their children, and they responded enthusiastically, especially those with students in grades slated for immediate desegregation. Indeed, by late summer, the push to open Lowndes Academy had become a total community effort. Two weeks before the first day of class, white women who routinely hired African Americans to clean their homes gathered at the Lowndesboro Recreation Center, the site of the new school, and scrubbed the floors and washed the windows, while their husbands plastered and painted. And one week later, they came together again for an open house, a barbecue, and to watch the school's new football team, composed almost entirely of former Hayneville High players, in a Friday night practice game.[92] These activities provided those who had pooled their resources to preserve segregated education with an opportunity to celebrate the opening of Lowndes Academy, a singular accomplishment that testified to the capacity of ordinary whites to defy the federal government and preserve a key pillar of the racial hierarchy. It was the high-water mark of white resistance.

Ray Bass welcomed more than two hundred students, fully one-third of the county's white school age population, to Lowndes Academy when it opened for classes on Monday, August 29, 1966. It was a promising beginning for segregated private education and marked the start of a process of white flight from the public schools that proceeded swiftly from that day forward. It also reflected the failure of the school board to manage desegregation in such a way as to keep whites from abandoning the public schools. "We can't compel students to attend the public schools," bemoaned board of education attorney Maury Smith, who also noted that only 9 white students enrolled in Hayneville High that fall. The previous year, 366 white students attended the school. Rather than fault whites for turning their backs on public education, Smith and others blamed African Americans. "The people in Lowndes County were so determined to overcome that they overcame too much," said Smith. "They have now converted an all-white school into an all-Negro school."[93]

While school officials lamented the end of segregated public education, movement activists hailed desegregation as an important step toward educational equity and moved quickly to take advantage of the opportunity to send their children to better-resourced schools by enrolling them in the previously all-white institutions. In late August 1966, LCCMHR leader Alice Moore happily reported that "school registering is moving on nicely at Hayneville High," meaning that those who sought to enroll in the county's flagship high school were able to do so unmolested.[94] Only about 100 black children, however, sought admittance to Hayneville High that summer, and almost all of them were the sons and daughters of movement participants. John Hulett reenrolled his son Art and registered his other son, John Edward. Local activists were not afraid to let their children plunge headlong into the still uncertain waters of desegregation. Most black parents, though, were far more cautious and did not want to risk possible reprisals or interrupt their children's education. They also found comfort in having their children taught by black teachers whom they knew cared about educating African American youngsters. As a result, when the fall term began, only about 120 black students attended the previously all-white schools.[95]

The first days of desegregation passed peacefully. "Things were quiet at all the county's schools," observed a reporter. The uneventful start to the school year was due wholly to the nonappearance of white students and to their parents' acceptance of desegregation as a fait accompli. Nevertheless, the transition to the white schools was far from seamless. At Hayneville High, in addition to the absence of white youth, all manner of school supplies and equipment, from typewriters to the football bleachers, had vanished. Their disappearance, like that of the white students, was no mystery—they too had been whisked away to Lowndes Academy.[96]

The Lowndes movement began with a voter registration drive and expanded beyond the ballot box when local leaders acted on their deeply rooted desire to improve the quality of education available to African Americans. Circumstance dictated that they first try to make segregated black schools better, which they did by boycotting LCTS. The ineffectiveness of the boycotts generated interest in controlling the local government by confirming that protest alone was incapable of creating meaningful change. The formation of the freedom schools also increased the appeal of independent politics by demonstrating the ability of parallel institutions to sustain and advance the struggle. In these ways, movement experiences began to radicalize people's politics.

Although the leaders of the movement believed that quality education was more important than school integration, they recognized the potential of the latter to spark the kind of change that African Americans wanted. Accordingly, the instant there was an opportunity to desegregate white schools they seized it and did not relent in the face of threats and school board subterfuge. Unable to dismantle the dual education system on their own, they brought the full weight of the federal government to bear on county and state officials and secured a landmark consent decree that finally ended de jure segregation in public education.

White resistance started with the efforts of elected officials to thwart black voter registration and delay school desegregation. Its leaders alternated between the courthouse crowd and private citizens depending on the ability of elected officials to maintain the status quo; no matter who stood at the helm, however, it enjoyed widespread support. It also grew in lockstep with the Lowndes movement. The success of the voter registration campaign and the expansion of the struggle beyond the ballot box intensified white resistance, resulting in the murder of Jonathan Daniels and a ferocious wave of nocturnal terrorism that the national press and federal government ignored because it involved neither the Klan nor white victims. For more than a century, whites used murder and mayhem to maintain the racial hierarchy. Consequently, when threats and economic reprisals failed to collapse the movement, they fell back on their default setting—violence. Armed self-defense, meanwhile, was the default setting for African Americans. When whites picked up weapons, they did too.[97] Their belief in self-defense also rendered nonviolence irrelevant. The absence of a formal self-defense group and the refusal to organize around the gun were not signs of a lack of commitment to self-defense, but reflections of the nature of the threat that African Americans faced and of their ability to meet violence with violence whenever necessary.

Both the Lowndes movement and the white resistance adjusted quickly and effectively to the ebb and flow of the conflict. Movement activists, for instance, responded to the flood of evictions by building a tent city. Although they failed to stop the evictions, they succeeded, with the help of the Lowndes Diaspora, in keeping dozens of movement families in the county. Whites, meanwhile, reacted to the inability of elected officials to maintain segregated public schools by establishing a private white academy. In short, neither struggle was static.

The fight to improve segregated black schools and to desegregate white schools was only the beginning of the effort to broaden the movement beyond voter registration. Soon after launching the education campaign, LCCMHR leaders, with the help of SNCC organizers, worked to increase economic opportunities for African Americans by taking advantage of various federal programs. At the same time, whites continued their highly coordinated effort to thwart the movement's growth and expansion. These endeavors yielded a mixed bag of victories and defeats for both sides. They also produced new levels of black political awareness that helped make an independent third party possible.

4

I'm Going to Try to Take Some of the Freedom Here Back Home

The Federal Government and the Fight for Freedom Rights

Everyone was upset. Four weeks simply was not enough time to organize black farmers to win control of the local Agricultural Stabilization and Conservation Service (ASCS) committees, which administered federal farm programs. Unfortunately, that was all the time the activists had. In June 1966, the U.S. Department of Agriculture voided the previous year's ASCS election in the Alabama Black Belt because wealthy white farmers used fraudulent means to stay in power. The department, however, let Alabama officials set the deadline for mailing in the ballots for the new election, and, not surprisingly, the state bureaucrats waited until mid-July 1966 before announcing that August 15, 1966, was the deadline. They did this knowing that such short notice would stymie the effort to organize African Americans.[1] "We are sick and tired of the tricks that this racist government—from the federal to local—attempts to play on black people in this country," wrote SNCC's Stokely Carmichael in a letter to ASCS administrators. In his missive, Carmichael demanded that the election be pushed back to November 1966 and be conducted by federal officials: "If the government can spend billions of dollars to kill people in Vietnam to assure free elections, then they had better spend some of those dollars to assure free elections in Lowndes County ASCS."[2]

Carmichael knew that a strongly worded letter would not be enough to change the government's position, and so did his fellow organizers. Consequently, they partnered with national advocates for small farmers and filed a lawsuit in federal district court in Washington to have the election rescheduled. "If we win the lawsuit and postpone the elections we will have enough time to raise money to make a thorough enough campaign,"

explained Mike Kenny, the field coordinator for the National Sharecroppers' Fund. Shortly before the August 1966 deadline, the court heard testimony from each side. More than two dozen black farmers from Alabama
traveled to the nation's capital for the hearing, and their presence in the
courtroom sent a powerful message. "When the people come to Washington, the government listens," said Donald Jelinek of the Lawyers' Constitutional Defense Committee. Their testimony proved just as powerful,
leaving little doubt that fraud and intimidation kept African Americans
from having a say in ASCS governance. Persuaded by their statements,
the court postponed the election until September 15, 1966, which gave the
activists less time than they wanted but more time than they had. "The
extension will allow us to combine the momentum and organization of
the November 8 [general] election with that of ASCS," said Carmichael.
For the black farmers, the ruling was a singular victory that many took to
mean that the federal government was on their side. "I like Washington,"
said Arthur Brown, one of the black farmers who made the trip north.
"I'm going to try to take some of the freedom here back home."[3]

The involvement of the federal government in the Lowndes movement
was no accident. Local activists needed federal resources to expand the
fight for freedom rights beyond voter registration to include, among other
things, economic security. So they drew Washington into the struggle by
applying for Office of Economic Opportunity (OEO) grants, organizing
black farmers, filing lawsuits in federal court, and testing local compliance with the 1964 Civil Rights Act and 1965 Voting Rights Act. Lowndes
County whites did not mind the government having a hand in county
affairs. For years, they welcomed relief, recovery, and subsidy programs
sponsored by federal agencies. At the same time, they insisted on being
able to dictate the terms of government participation. More than anything
else, they wanted to control federal money to make sure that it did not
undermine white supremacy. Accordingly, they did not stand idly by as
African Americans pulled Washington into the conflict. Instead, they defied federal mandates, defended their actions in court, fought to control
federal dollars, and conspired with Governor Wallace to mobilize state resources to protect the status quo.

Federal officials proceeded slowly and cautiously when dealing with
local matters, an approach that advanced the fight for freedom rights
in some instances and bolstered white resistance in others. The impact
of federal involvement on the movement, however, cannot be measured
solely by the success rate of lawsuits or grant applications. The grassroots

organizing activities that federal involvement generated must also be taken into account. These activities produced a wealth of experiential knowledge that helped transform black politics by making African Americans more amenable to forming their own political party. In profoundly simple ways, the organizing experiences that resulted from federal involvement elevated people's political awareness and pushed the movement in a radical new direction.

Lowndes County activists took tremendous pride in the democratic structure of the LCCMHR. The organization's members made major decisions collectively at Sunday mass meetings, while the executive committee, which consisted of LCCMHR officers and representatives from black communities across the county, made the everyday decisions during the week. This arrangement allowed marginalized African Americans to have their voices heard. It also made the LCCMHR uniquely qualified to operate a Community Action Program (CAP). CAPs were local initiatives funded by the OEO that sought to increase poor people's standard of living. CAPs differed tremendously from the usual government assistance programs because they required ordinary people to participate fully in all decision making. This unique stipulation heightened their appeal for grassroots organizers. "In the black belt," wrote activists in Lowndes County, "our history teaches us that only if Negroes participate at least equally with whites in the formation, planning, policy-making and control of a program, will that program possess the capability of producing genuine benefits for Negroes."[4] The very real possibility of creating job training, adult education, daycare, or even housing construction programs whose sole purpose was to lift poor people out of poverty added to the activists' excitement. Their enthusiasm, however, was tempered by the knowledge that CAPs could not end all economic woes. To achieve such a lofty goal, there needed to be a radical restructuring of the American economy, which was far beyond the OEO's mandate. Still, CAPs offered poor people a genuine opportunity to gain a modicum of economic justice. Realizing this, the executive committee of the LCCMHR decided in July 1965 to develop a CAP grant proposal. Through the Community Action Program, the committee hoped to move poor blacks a step closer to economic equality.[5]

The democratic ethos responsible for the progressive structure of the LCCMHR informed the way the organization's leaders created the CAP proposal. They began by holding town hall meetings in just about every black community to explain the War on Poverty. They also conducted countywide elections to select two representatives from each community to serve on an antipoverty action committee. LCCMHR officers and SNCC organizers met with the community representatives in early August 1965 and reviewed the CAP application procedure. Eager to move forward, the representatives asked local leaders John Hulett, Frank Miles, Jr., and Lillian McGill to notify OEO director Sargent Shriver of their intention to apply for a CAP. In a letter to Shriver, the three activists praised the War on Poverty for offering hope to African Americans in the Black Belt. They also explained their preference for a single countywide CAP because they knew there was a chance that they could be paired with a nearby majority white county, which would greatly reduce their ability to govern the program as they saw fit. If they had to be paired with another county, they suggested neighboring Wilcox County. "The counties are contiguous," they wrote, and, more importantly, "Negro leadership in each county has worked with and respects the leadership and citizens in the other counties. We know we can cooperate fruitfully." In addition, the local leaders noted the people's willingness to work closely with Lowndes County whites, but added that they were prepared to "move ahead" without them if they rejected their "offer to cooperate."[6]

The same democratic spirit that guided the formation of the antipoverty action committee led movement leaders to invite whites to join their grant-writing effort. They did not, however, extend the invitation immediately. "We felt we had to organize among our own people to create a united position and protect our own interest as Negroes and the majority population group," they explained. By mid-August 1965, they finally felt comfortable enough to ask whites to form a partnership. "As citizens of our community, we believe that all citizens regardless of color must work together for the economic and social betterment of our county," wrote Lillian McGill in a letter to more than a dozen white elected officials and businesspersons. The War on Poverty "presents a fine opportunity for our county to bring into its economy thousands of dollars and obtain expert skills and services to cope with problems which our disadvantaged citizens face. It is toward this [end] that we are directing this letter." If whites wished to collaborate with them, they were welcome to attend the official organizing meeting of the antipoverty action committee scheduled for August 25, 1965, at Mt. Gilliard Baptist Church. "We realize, too, that equal [participation] and sharing of responsibility by white and colored citizens working on the same committee is a departure from the past parctis [sic]," wrote McGill, acknowledging the unprecedented nature of the undertaking. "However, times are changing. An anti-poverty program is essential to our community if we wish to be a prosperous, modern county that can deal with the challenges and enjoy [the] benefits of 20th century American life."[7]

Dr. William Staggers, the mayor of Benton, the old plantation town that was the site of the brutal whipping of Joe "Buck" Seles in 1933, was the only person who bothered to respond to the invitation, and he declined to participate. "It is not possible for me to take on any more activity outside of my practice, my Church work and the duties that go along with the Mayor's job," he wrote in a kindly worded letter. He also suggested, almost as an afterthought, that they take no further action until the OEO decided the fate of the CAP application filed by Alabama Area 22, which purported to represent Lowndes, Covington, Butler, and Crenshaw counties. No one in the movement had ever heard of Alabama Area 22, so the LCCMHR immediately dispatched its legal counsel to the OEO regional office in Atlanta to obtain more information. Once there, the attorney made a startling discovery. Two weeks earlier members of the Lowndes County board of education and board of revenue formed a partnership with representatives from the three predominantly white counties that Staggers mentioned and submitted a CAP application. This was a pre-emptive move designed to block movement activists from bringing a CAP to the county. It was also an attempt to circumvent the OEO's requirement that poor people participate fully in the planning and implementation of CAPs, because collaborating with the white counties reduced African Americans to a numerical minority. The lawyer also discovered that the proposal had the blessing of regional OEO administrators, who, unlike officials in Washington, sympathized with local white power brokers. Alabama OEO bureaucrats, all of whom pledged fealty to Governor Wallace, the South's most vociferous opponent of antipoverty programs, also endorsed the proposal. Equally disturbing was the revelation that Alabama Area 22 claimed to have the full support of the movement community. As evidence, its sponsors pointed to the presence on the steering committee of a single African American—William "Sam" Bradley, a black landowner and entrepreneur from Calhoun.[8]

Bradley graduated from Tuskegee Institute during the Great Depression and parlayed his degree into a series of jobs with federal recovery agencies. He supplemented his modest income by training hunting dogs, which put him on friendly terms with quite a few prominent whites. Meanwhile, he used his savings to purchase a Calhoun Land Trust farm. Bradley did not put much stock in grassroots organizing. In 1935, when the Sharecroppers' Union began working in the county, he wanted nothing to do with it. "I didn't think they'd succeed," he recalled. "They didn't have anything to fall back on." Three decades later, he stood on the sidelines as the Lowndes movement took shape for the very same reason. His distaste for grassroots activity, which was common among members of the small black middle class, did not mean that he opposed change. On the contrary, he sincerely wanted African Americans to enjoy their freedom rights. His approach to creating change was just different. He preferred to exploit his personal relationships with whites, which he cultivated carefully over the years. For example, before the movement began, he delicately broached the subject of voter registration with several county registrars, hoping to win some concessions. "I was working with the local board of registration," he said somewhat grandiosely, "to bring it to pass that they would voluntarily register black people. And I got many promises that it was going to happen, but it never really happened. It was always something that came up and it didn't happen." Broken promises did not shake Bradley's commitment to this approach. Consequently, when school superintendent Hulda Coleman asked him to serve on the Alabama Area 22 steering committee, he saw it as an opportunity to make a real difference. Area 22's sponsors, meanwhile, viewed the offer as a chance to forestall change because they knew that Bradley was a movement outsider.[9]

McGill and Hulett filed an objection to Alabama Area 22 immediately. In their remonstration, they demanded that Washington administrators reject the group's application due to "unfair representation." Alabama Area 22, they said, simply did not represent African Americans. "[W]e checked to fine [sic] that no one who have [sic] shown any interest in the changes and conditions of the poor people seem to be on this commitee [sic]. We went even further to fine [sic] out that even though we have a county wide [sic] movement with representatives from every community in Lowndes County, none of thes [sic] people were contacted in the movement." They also noted that Sam Bradley did not speak for African Americans: "The name of the one negro [sic] whom we have been informed is on this so called bi-racial committee have [sic] never come out to see what the poor and needy people wants [sic] or think or need. We have approached him and he seems very nonchalant about the cooperation of the county poor people and county-wide togetherness." In addition, they pointed out that grouping Lowndes County with three predominantly white counties disenfranchised African Americans. Lastly, they reiterated their willingness to work with whites but also emphasized their complete lack of interest in letting whites "totally represent us": "We have never been fairly represented in our county in anything so we are anxious to help represent ourselves. We no longer wish to be spoken for without being asked what is best for poor people and how we will be governed in relation to Federal funds."[10]

Rather than wait for a reply, McGill and the others proceeded with their plans. On August 25, 1965, they gathered at Mt. Gilliard Baptist Church to organize the Lowndes County Anti-poverty Action Committee. Whites were invited but none showed up; Sam Bradley also stayed away. Their absence, though, did not keep the attendees from approving the creation of the action committee. Before the meeting adjourned, however, they revisited the issue of white participation and, after considerable discussion, agreed to allow whites to join the committee at any time. This was truly a magnanimous gesture given the underhanded way that whites created Alabama Area 22, the hostility whites displayed for efforts to improve black education, and the recent spate of white violence, which included the murder of Jonathan Daniels less than one week earlier.[11]

Once officially established, the antipoverty action committee began gathering information on local conditions. For the next three weeks, the committee met with poor blacks across the county to discuss their most pressing problems. The committee planned to meet with whites as well, but no one on that side of the color line was willing to talk on record about these matters. The committee presented its findings at a mass meeting on September 17, 1965. African Americans filled the sanctuary of Mt. Gilead Baptist Church in Trickem to listen to the report and debate the best ways to use federal money to solve local problems. By the end of the evening, a consensus emerged on several key issues. Above all else, the people agreed that a Lowndes County CAP should focus on job training and housing, two areas of desperate need. They also agreed to appoint local white power brokers to the action committee. "Although we have decided to move ahead to help ourselves, and, although we constitute over 80% of the population of our county, we believe it is in the better interest of our county and all its citizens to have whites and Negroes fighting the war against poverty," explained movement leaders. At the same time, they limited whites to no more than half the seats on the committee in order to safeguard African American interests.[12]

Movement activists worked closely with SNCC organizer Gloria Larry on the grant proposal for the next two months, using the common vision

A woman stands in front of her ramshackle house in Lowndes County in 1966, one of the many homes that the LCCMHR hoped to replace through the Community Action Program. Photo by Louis H. Anderson/Courtesy of Estizer Smith.

that emerged at the mass meeting as their guide. When they submitted the proposal in November 1965, they requested several hundred thousand dollars to develop adult education and housing construction programs. In their rationale, they emphasized the participation of poor people. "At all times," they wrote, "residents and members of target areas and groups will play active and controlling roles in program direction, policy making, decision making, and advisory functions in carrying out the programs proposed by this application and future applications." They also stressed their willingness to work with whites but stated emphatically that they could not afford to wait on them.[13]

The effort to secure funding for a Community Action Program tested the patience and democratic sensibilities of movement supporters. White opposition was not unexpected, but the extent to which whites used deception to keep African Americans from gaining even a small amount of power was surprising. The experience, though, was extremely instructive. Foremost, it gave movement supporters a much greater sense of the unwillingness of whites to share power equitably, an insight that left a lasting impression. Indeed, in the months ahead, movement supporters pointed to white opposition to the grant, and specifically to the covert creation of Alabama Area 22, as evidence of the need to chart their own course politically.

As movement activists waited for word on their proposal, they continued to look to the federal government for assistance. Even earlier, they seized on an opportunity to help black farmers created by reforms to the ASCS, the division of the Department of Agriculture that decided how many acres of cotton, tobacco, wheat, rice, and peanuts a farmer could plant and sell. The ASCS also regulated crop prices through cash payments, loans, and crop purchases. In 1964, it spent $7.2 billion on price supports, with a significant portion going directly to farmers as cash payments. If obtained, these subsidy checks could keep a farmer in the black; if not, they could push him or her into the red. In these ways, the agency controlled the fate of tens of thousands of farmers.[14]

Local farmers administered ASCS programs through county committees comprising three voting members and two alternates. Similarly structured committees at the neighborhood level elected the members of the county committee at an annual convention. Any farm owner, tenant farmer, or sharecropper over twenty-one-years-old could vote for the members of the community committees in the ASCS election or sit on an ASCS committee. The federal government purposefully configured eligibility broadly in order to encourage the participation of small farmers. Minimal federal oversight, however, enabled wealthy white farmers to dominate. In Lowndes County, not a single African American had ever sat on an ASCS committee. "I've gotten one of those ASCS ballots in the mail for over five years now," said a local black farmer. "I started voting but it was always the same kind of people on the ballot." The government's hands-off approach extended to the administration of ASCS programs. As a result, the wealthy white farmers who ran ASCS offices routinely discriminated against African Americans by assigning them much smaller acreage allotments, denying their requests to plant additional acreage, rejecting their applications for farm loans, declaring them ineligible for conservation assistance, withholding direct cash payments, and turning their checks over to white creditors. Such treatment eroded the ability of black farmers to earn a decent income, climb out of debt, and become financially independent.[15]

Two of the many black farmers in Lowndes County in 1966 who would have ben-
efitted from the election of African Americans to Agricultural Stabilization and
Conservation Service committees. © John F. Phillips/johnphillipsphotography.com.

SNCC organizers were well aware of the importance of the ASCS and familiar with the problems associated with its local administration. During
the summer of 1964, a group of field secretaries in Mississippi launched
the Federal Programs Project to familiarize black farmers with the kinds
of financial assistance available through the agency. By 1965, this project
had evolved into a statewide effort in Alabama, but the organizers there
did not just want to increase general awareness of the ASCS; they also
wanted to help African Americans win control of ASCS committees. "Ad-
mitting poor farmers on the committees—and many of these would be
Negroes—would divide the pie much differently," said SNCC's Chris Wiley.[16] Recent changes to the ASCS candidate nomination procedure gave
African Americans a real chance of winning. In previous years, the members of ASCS committees nominated their successors, and the wealthy
white farmers on these committees always nominated other wealthy white
farmers. In March 1965, however, federal officials yielded to demands to
democratize the ASCS and instructed the county committees to nominate

African Americans in proportion to their percentage of the population. They also created a provision that allowed individual farmers to submit petitions to get on the ballot.[17]

SNCC workers began discussing the importance of controlling the ASCS committees with African Americans in the Alabama Black Belt in May 1965. At a meeting held that month at SNCC's Selma office, they shared all that they knew about the federal agency. "I've broken down the laws of the ASCS [and] found out about the ASCS elections," explained SNCC's Elmo Holder at the meeting. "[I've] gone to Washington and hopefully gotten their cooperation. By [the] end of the week, I will have gotten the community boundaries for all the counties we're working in." The organizers also announced plans to hold a series of workshops in the counties surrounding Selma, including Lowndes County, to generate interest in and build momentum for the ASCS elections that fall.[18]

SNCC workers started holding local ASCS workshops in July 1965. During the height of the Lowndes County voter registration campaign, they met with groups of ten to fifteen black farmers in the county's six ASCS communities to explain the agency's programs and discuss the upcoming election.[19] The workshops revealed an astounding reality—most African Americans had been kept completely in the dark about ASCS programs, policies, and procedures "They've never heard of the ASCS committee," said SNCC's Janet Jemott. "All they see is Mr. Charlie who comes around and takes their cotton away."[20] At the same time, SNCC workers continued to seek clarity about the election. "We do not feel that the [ASCS] handbook does fully and adequately cover questions of eligibility requirements," wrote Elmo Holder in a letter to Alabama ASCS officials. "Must, for example, a candidate actually live, vote in local political elections, etc. to be eligible or is it enough that he own and operate a farm in the community? Would you also define the terms 'sharecropper' and 'tenant farmer?' How does this differ from a common 'farm laborer?'"[21] When SNCC workers felt they had a firm grasp of election details, they invited people who expressed an interest in ASCS organizing to Selma for a weekend workshop beginning on September 17, 1965. "Local people would get an opportunity to find out how the information that we already have was obtained," explained Jemott. "People who attend the workshop would then return to the counties and disseminate this knowledge, and share those skills learned by setting up and leading meetings and other workshops."[22] The start of the harvest season limited the turnout to nineteen people the first day and seven the second day. But the farmers who showed up, especially the movement participants from Lowndes County, were eager to begin ASCS organizing and started doing so as soon as they returned home.[23]

Mathew Jackson, Sr., who provided SNCC organizers with the freedom house, was one of several black farmers who worked to increase ASCS awareness by speaking at black churches during Sunday service. "I'd do it in practically every church I went to," he said. "I just explained to them as I went along . . . [that] it was time out for letting white people make a monkey out of us. In other words, use us for working tools." In addition, he led regular ASCS discussions at the LCCMHR's weekly mass meetings. African Americans responded favorably to the call for action and pledged to support black farmers in the ASCS elections. "We want someone to run who will stand up against the big boss," explained Walter Blocton of Tyler, a small community just off Route 80. "We have never had anyone on the committee who would tell the Negro farmer what the ASCS can do for him." Jackson was also one of twenty-four African Americans who submitted petitions to get on the Lowndes County ASCS ballot that fall. When asked why he ran for a seat on an ASCS committee, he said simply, "I thought probably that I knew more about these people in here, their needs, more so than the people that were already in these offices."[24]

Black candidates from Lowndes County and four other Black Belt counties gathered at SNCC's Selma office on October 24, 1965, to learn more about the rules governing the ASCS elections and to discuss campaign strategy, including how to counter the inevitable white efforts to steal the election. SNCC organizers were particularly concerned about the ASCS officials nominating African Americans en masse in an attempt to divide the black vote. "In areas where Negroes put up their own candidates there is absolutely no legitimate reason why the committees should put up additional Negro candidates," argued Elmo Holder a few months earlier in a letter to the executive director of the Alabama ASCS. "Moreover, if many Negroes are nominated and only a few whites, this will only be a device by which the Negro vote could be split and if the whites, as obviously will be the case, vote as a bloc, the whites will retain total control of the committees." Holder implored the state director to limit the total number of people that a county committee could nominate to eight, but the director took no action. As a result, when the Lowndes County ASCS ballots arrived in the mail a few days after the Selma meeting, the organizers' greatest fear came true. In addition to the 24 African Americans who filed petitions to run for office, ASCS officials put another 109 African Americans on the ballot. In Community A, where Mathew Jackson, Sr., was a candidate, they added 36 African Americans, and in Community C, they nominated an additional 68 African Americans. At the same time, they placed no more than three whites on each ballot and chose not to put a single African American up for election in Community E, which had no movement candidates. "It's clear that they used the ruling only to split the Negro vote," said SNCC's John Liutkus. "In 'E,' if they were following the ruling straight, they would have put Negroes on the ballot in proportion to whites."[25]

In addition to nominating African Americans en masse, ASCS officials sent some African Americans empty ballot envelopes and others ballots for the wrong election. On most occasions, the staff at the Hayneville ASCS office exchanged the incorrect ballots for the correct ones after verifying the person's eligibility, but on several occasions they outright refused. The movement's candidates and those who signed their nomination petitions also faced harassment and intimidation. The white farmer who owned the land that candidate Threddie Lee Stewart and his family had worked for three generations evicted him, his wife, and their three children soon after his candidacy became public.[26]

Local activists responded to attempts to influence the outcome of the election by rallying support for the movement's candidates through a word-of-mouth campaign. SNCC organizers assisted them by blanketing Lowndes County with leaflets identifying the candidates and calling attention to the dishonest practices of local officials. "The white folks are trying to trick Negro farmers in Lowndes County by putting names of many Negro farmers on the ASCS list," read one flyer. "Do not divide your vote! Do not let the white folks divide us! We must stick together!" SNCC organizers also met with members of Alabama's state ASCS committee and convinced them to bring in federal observers to ensure fair elections, but Ray Fitzgerald, the state official in charge of the elections, blocked this and similar measures.[27]

Lowndes County ASCS officials counted the mail-in ballots at the local ASCS office in Hayneville on November 15, 1965. At other ASCS headquarters in the Black Belt, the atmosphere was tense during the ballot count, but in Lowndes County, officials treated African American observers, including Stokely Carmichael, courteously. The absence of hostility pleased movement supporters, but the results of the election did not. The only movement candidates to win voting seats were Sidney Logan, Jr., Emory Ross, and Streety Reeves. Mathew Jackson, Sr., and the seven remaining movement candidates, including Threddie Lee Stewart, won seats as alternates, which carried no voting privileges. "They are rather meaningless," lamented SNCC's Doug and Tina Harris.[28]

The mass nomination of African Americans, which split the black vote, allowed white farmers, who voted as a solid racial bloc, to prevail. The disenfranchisement of eligible black voters also played a decisive role. Several white candidates won by only a few votes. In one community, the three white candidates received sixty-two, sixty-one, and sixty votes, while the five movement candidates received fifty-eight, fifty-eight, fifty-six, fifty-six, and fifty-three votes. The election would have turned out differently had every eligible black voter received his or her ballot. SNCC organizers also believed that white candidates benefited from the participation of ineligible white voters, due to the unbelievably high number of ballots submitted by whites, and possibly from the unlawful destruction of black ballots.[29]

SNCC's John Liutkus filed a grievance with the ASCS office in Washington on behalf of the movement's candidates. In the complaint, he pointed specifically to the gross manipulation of the new nomination procedure and asked federal officials to void the election results. An investigator sent to Lowndes County from Washington confirmed the veracity of the complaint. "[W]e have determined that while the number of Negroes nominated on a county basis conformed to the letter of the controlling election procedures . . . it was evident that the spirit of the procedures were not complied with," wrote William Seabron, assistant secretary of the U.S. Department of Agriculture. "The effect of the nominating procedure used was to give the white nominees an advantage over the Negro nominees, and therefore was self defeating of the Department's stated objectives concerning equal opportunity in the ASCS committee system." As relief, the department instructed the Alabama officials to conduct new elections. Unfortunately, federal authorities neither disclosed their findings nor issued their directive until June of the next year.[30]

In the absence of immediate federal action, Lowndes County activists prepared for the ASCS county convention scheduled for the end of November 1965. Usually, convention delegates elected five people from the community committees to the county committee, with the understanding that the alternates on the lower committees would fill the vacancies created by the departure of the others. At the 1965 convention, however, the white members of the community committees elected five unaffiliated white farmers to the county committee, thereby blocking the ascension of the African American alternates.[31]

Failing to win control of ASCS was tremendously disappointing. "We had big plans for those farm subsidies," said Carmichael. The defeat would have been easier to accept had whites not used deception to stay in office. "We did it fair and square," added Carmichael. "We believed in them, and they cheated us. They told us to vote and we did everything they said." The ASCS experience was so disheartening that a few local people dropped completely out of the movement. "Some of them, you know, they wasn't strong enough to just go on," said one activist. "They just decided that you can't tell [whites] nothing." Others, though, redoubled their efforts, believing that change was still possible. They did so, however, with a much greater understanding of how whites planned to deal with black voters in the post–Voting Rights Act era. They realized that winning political power required more than merely having the right to vote, or even having black candidates to vote for. It required elevating people's political awareness and mobilizing the black electorate. This knowledge pushed many squarely into the camp of independent politics. "The white folks tricked us in the ASCS elections, that's when I started to get wise to the Democratic Party," said ASCS candidate Sidney Logan, Jr., who eventually ran for sheriff on the third-party ticket. "The Democratic Party is full of tricks. White people control it." Although dispiriting, the ASCS experience proved to be a critical component of local people's political education and a defining moment in the evolution of an all-black party. "Many people in the Christian Movement and SNCC feel that Lowndes County public officials threw away their last chance to court the Negro vote in [the 1966] election," said John Hulett.[32]

The effort to use the ASCS and the OEO to improve the economic well-being of African Americans receded to the background of the Lowndes movement during the winter and spring of 1966 as local activists and SNCC organizers concentrated on building an independent political party. Federal involvement in the Lowndes movement, however, reached new heights during this period through a series of lawsuits filed in federal district court by local activists, movement sympathizers, and the Justice Department. These cases, which included the school desegregation lawsuit, produced rulings that reverberated locally and nationally, perhaps none more than the decision in *White v. Crook* regarding jury discrimination.

While movement activists organized black farmers and drafted the CAP grant proposal, the Justice Department prepared a lawsuit charging Lowndes County's jury commissioners with excluding African Americans

from jury service solely because of their race in violation of the Fourteenth Amendment, which guarantees due process and equal protection
of the laws. The commissioners kept African Americans off juries by selecting prospective jurors from the county's list of eligible male voters,
which up to that time carried the names of whites only. A joint team of
lawyers from the American Civil Liberties Union and the Episcopal Society for Cultural and Racial Unity (ESCRU) originally filed the lawsuit
on behalf of local African Americans after the murder of Jonathan Daniels, who was studying to become an Episcopal priest.[33] The class action
lawsuit, the first of its kind to seek specific remedies for systematic racial jury exclusion, sought a court order compelling the commissioners to
draft a new list of prospective jurors that included African Americans. It
also sought to have the Alabama law excluding women from jury service
declared unconstitutional.[34] The immediate goal, though, was to delay the
trial of Tom Coleman until a jury that included African Americans could
be empanelled. "To allow any jury trials in Lowndes County, Alabama to
take place until the names of Negroes have been placed on the jury roll
and in the jury box without racial discrimination will have a chilling effect
on free speech, subject other persons to killings without equal recourse to
law and irreparably hamper seriously our efforts and the efforts of others
in Negro voter registration," explained Henri Stines, the director of ES-
CRU's southern field service.[35] Although Coleman's trial proceeded without black jurors, resulting, not surprisingly, in his acquittal, the lawsuit
attracted the attention of the Justice Department, which joined the case in
October 1965 and assumed responsibility for most of the legal work under
authority granted to it by the 1964 Civil Rights Act.[36]

A three-judge panel, which included Richard T. Rives of the U.S. Court
of Appeals for the Fifth Circuit and Alabama district court judges Frank
M. Johnson and Clarence W. Allgood, rendered an opinion in *White v.
Crook* on February 5, 1966. The judges found that the jury commissioners
used procedures that "resulted in jury service in that county being limited
to a small number of adult, white male citizens, with Negro male citizens
and female citizens of both races being systematically excluded either by
practice or, in the case of the women, by statute." "It must be concluded,"
wrote the judges, "that in their action, conduct, and procedures followed,
[the defendants] not only failed to adhere to the laws of the State of Alabama relating to the selection of qualified jurors, but clearly violated the
Equal Protection and Due Process Clauses of the Fourteenth Amendment
which make unlawful the systematic exclusion of Negroes from jury service

because of their race." In addition, the judges concluded that Alabama's law barring women from jury service also violated the equal protection clause of the Fourteenth Amendment. "Women have a right not to be excluded as a class from jury service," wrote the judges. As a remedy, they ordered the defendants to compose a new jury list without regard to race or gender and to include no less than one thousand names. If they failed to comply immediately, the judges said they would appoint someone to do it for them.[37]

The ruling was a major victory for African Americans. For generations, all-white juries protected the system of white supremacy by unjustly punishing African Americans and shamelessly refusing to convict whites guilty of racially motivated crimes, including murder. Allowing African Americans to sit on juries meant balancing the scales of justice. It took some time, however, for equilibrium to be reached. When Lowndes County empanelled its first integrated jury in September 1966 for the trial of Eugene Thomas, who participated in the murder of Viola Liuzzo during the Selma to Montgomery March, the judge allowed defense attorneys to dismiss everyone affiliated with the movement, and the eight black men who were eventually seated were so afraid of what might happen if they convicted a white man that they went along with the white jurors' "not guilty" assessment. "You have to live in this area to realize the pressure Negroes are under," said Alabama attorney general Richmond Flowers, who prosecuted the case. "I don't believe they can do what they'd like to do, for fear of white people." J. L. Chestnut, Jr., one of the few practicing black attorneys in Alabama at the time, explained, "When you've grown up in an atmosphere where you could get whipped for not saying 'sir,' it's highly uncomfortable to be arguing your convictions with a white person."[38]

Federal court intervention was the key to ending the exclusion of African Americans from juries, just as it was essential to forcing the school board to desegregate the county's public schools. African Americans drew encouragement from judicial recognition of their just claims and hope from judicial action taken on their behalf. The federal courts, however, did not always take their side. In *Miles v. Dixon*, judge Frank M. Johnson dismissed a lawsuit that sought to keep white landowners from evicting African Americans who supported the movement. Such adverse decisions often exacerbated the problems that African Americans faced. Judge Johnson's ruling in *Miles v. Dixon* sent the unmistakable message to white landowners that retaliatory evictions were permissible, and as a result movement supporters continued to suffer reprisals.[39]

• • •

Local leaders turned their attention back to the War on Poverty in March 1966 as they applied for a federal grant to train fifty farm workers, many of whom lived in Tent City, in building trades so that they could construct their own homes. They also planned to help the laborers finance their new homes and sought to prepare them for future employment by offering classes on basic reading, writing, mathematics, and home economics. The LCCMHR Committee on Housing, chaired by Robert L. Strickland, a forty-two-year-old brick mason who lived in Lowndesboro but worked in Montgomery, applied for the grant under Title III (b) of the Economic Opportunity Act, which set aside funds for training seasonally employed and migrant farm workers. Although agricultural mechanization and the use of chemical pesticides had reduced the day-to-day need for black farm workers, most bureaucrats did not view these laborers as seasonally employed, which increased the likelihood that the funding request would be denied. But a Title III (b) grant was the best chance that movement activists had of bringing the War on Poverty to the county. Their proposal for a Community Action Program languished in Washington and had little chance of ever being funded as long as Lowndes County officials refused to endorse it. The problem was that the OEO required some local government involvement in CAPs. The Alabama Area 22 CAP proposal met a similar fate but for a different reason. The OEO's Washington administrators were serious about maximizing the participation of the poor, and the Area 22 CAP proposal came nowhere near this basic requirement. Later in the year, local blacks and whites would try to forge a compromise, but at the time nothing was in the offing, so the local activists applied for the single purpose grant. To everyone's surprise, the OEO approved funding for the project in the amount of $240,640. For many people, the midsummer announcement was a clear sign that Washington was on their side. It showed that "the federal government is concerned with the welfare of the people in Lowndes," said Strickland.[40]

A great many things occurred between the submission of the grant proposal in March 1966 and the OEO's announcement in July 1966. Locally, movement supporters formed the Lowndes County Freedom Organization (LCFO) and nominated a full slate of black candidates to run against the Democratic Party's white candidates in the November 1966 general election. Nationally, Stokely Carmichael became the chairperson of SNCC and introduced the world to Black Power. These developments pushed the movement in a direction that disturbed those already troubled by black protest, which helps explain why officials in the Alabama statehouse and the Lowndes County courthouse wanted desperately to block the grant.

As soon as governor George Wallace learned about the award, he directed the Alabama Legislative Commission to Preserve the Peace to investigate. The commission, along with the Alabama Sovereignty Commission and the Subversive Unit of the Alabama Department of Public Safety, formed the heart of the governor's elaborate political spy network, a system cloaked in secrecy. The state legislature, which authorized the committee's creation in 1963 in response to civil rights protests in Birmingham, instructed its five members to "study, investigate, analyze, and interrogate persons, groups, and organizations engaged in activities of an unlawful nature against the sovereignty of the State of Alabama." From the outset, the commission monitored the activities of civil rights groups and movement organizers, and provided Wallace with detailed reports. In 1965, it began watching the Lowndes movement and supplying the governor, as well as Lowndes County officials, including superintendent Hulda Coleman and sheriff Frank Ryals, with information obtained through paid informants. As the local movement gained momentum, the commission became obsessed with SNCC, which it described fantastically as "an extremely dangerous, irresponsible group, which tends to promote acts of violence to gain support for their own goals." In a report circulated among elected officials and state agencies in June 1965, the commission concluded that SNCC "must be smashed by legal action, or we will court a major disaster."[41]

Edwin Strickland, the staff director for the commission, authored the investigative report that Wallace requested. Relying heavily on newspaper clippings, Strickland pointed out that the LCCMHR was the "alter ego" of the LCFO, "which originated the call for 'Black Power,' now sweeping the nation to the accompaniment of violence." He also noted that the principal promoter of the LCFO was SNCC, and that its chief organizer was Stokely Carmichael, who "advocates the 'burning down' of courthouses in his bid for 'Black Power'" and "is planning on November 8, 1966, to create in Alabama, through the use of the 'toughest Negroes in Chicago, New York, Watts, Philadelphia and Washington,' a situation calculated to creat [*sic*] riot, lawlessness and possibly bloodshed." "The evidence is clear and undisputed," wrote Strickland, "that in making the grant of federal O.E.O. funds to the Lowndes County Christian Movement, the federal government is financing [the] 'Black Panther,' and SNCC, both forces opposed to our Vietnam policy, and revolutionary in character."[42]

Less than a week after Strickland filed his report, Wallace called a press conference to issue a statement on Black Power and the OEO grant. Standing before a throng of print and television media in the state capitol, the governor denounced the grant, which he said amounted to "financing the revolutionary 'Black Power' movement in this country." Using the information that Strickland provided, he linked the LCCMHR to the LCFO, and the LCFO to SNCC. "It is shocking to see such support given to organizations which oppose constituted authority in this country." He also connected the LCCMHR to Stokely Carmichael, whom he disparaged as the "instigator of the 'Black Power' movement." In case this was not enough to generate a public outcry, he disclosed that Robert L. Strickland, the chairperson of the LCCMHR Committee on Housing, had served several years for murder in Alabama's infamous Kilby Prison, which once held the Scottsboro Boys.[43]

In advance of the press conference, Wallace telegrammed OEO director Sargent Shriver demanding that he rescind the grant. The LCCMHR was a group that "advocates 'Black Power,' violence, turmoil and disorder, bordering on treason," he said. He also noted that the grant should have gone through the OEO office in Alabama, over which he exerted total control. "You have followed an unorthodox procedure," he wrote, "and it would appear that this action was a direct effort to circumvent a governor's power of veto of this program."[44] That same day, M. E. Marlette, Jr., the Title I director for the Lowndes County school board, telegrammed John Sparkman, Alabama's junior U.S. senator, denouncing the grant. Writing on behalf of the "responsible citizens" of the county, he insisted that funding the project meant financing a "militant Civil Rights organization." In a series of subsequent letters to Lister Hill, Alabama's senior statesman in the U.S. Congress, Marlette ratcheted up the rhetoric, calling the LCCMHR "a black-racist organization that is by no means representative of the majority of county citizens, both Negro and white." He also suggested that Robert L. Strickland possessed "the potentialities for violence and influence to violence that are more acute and dangerous in him as an adult than in him as a youthful killer. He is a 'Burn, Baby, Burn' adult." In addition, he said that Strickland lacked the educational credentials and "financial integrity" to manage a project with such a large budget.[45]

Shriver responded to the accusations immediately. In a statement released about thirty-six hours after Wallace's press conference, he said that his office contacted the governor about the grant application in April 1966 and notified him of the decision to fund the project two months later.

He explained that grants to help seasonal farm workers made under Title III (b) did not require a governor's approval. In the preceding sixteen months, his office had made 143 such grants and "none of these has been criticized by any governor." Shriver also pointed out that the LCCMHR was a nonprofit organization chartered under Alabama law, and that Robert L. Strickland was not the project director. Although Shriver was sure of the legality and appropriateness of the grant, he yielded to political pressure and withheld the funds until his office investigated "all the allegations and objections," which took several months.[46]

Shriver's decision delighted the opponents of the grant, especially Wallace, who claimed victory over those attempting to undermine the sovereignty of the state of Alabama. Wallace was not opposed to the War on Poverty, evidenced in part by his support of antipoverty programs controlled by white allies, but he politicized everything and it was to his advantage to decry the grant.[47] Movement leaders, though, were furious, especially with Wallace, whom they rightly blamed for the uproar. Charles Smith, the chairperson of the LCCMHR, explained in a public statement that once the governor realized he could not control the grant he "got on television to discredit the [Lowndes movement] in order that the people in the Poverty Office in Washington would become afraid." Dredging up Strickland's conviction, without mentioning the circumstances behind it, was a part of this effort. In 1941, Strickland killed one of four white assailants. Although he acted in self-defense, an all-white jury found him guilty of murder. He received a full pardon five years after his conviction. "It is safe to say that if Mr. Strickland had been white and his attackers black, Mr. Strickland would have no jail record today," said Smith. "Tom Coleman is still a free man."[48]

The controversy stirred up by Wallace reminded African Americans that the state government actively supported the white resistance. At the same time, it renewed fears among local whites that movement activists would succeed in using the War on Poverty to undermine the racial caste system, a concern that prompted them to rethink their approach to securing funding for a Community Action Program. It did not change their underlying motivation, however, which remained the control of federal resources. The county board of revenue spearheaded the new effort. In a special session on August 8, 1966, the board voted unanimously to abandon the multicounty Alabama Area 22 approach and to organize instead a countywide CAP action committee. The board tapped Carl Golson, the irascible voting registrar, to coordinate the effort, an odd choice to build a bridge across the racial divide given the contempt he displayed for African Americans trying to register. Golson, however, set about his task with enthusiasm, drumming up support in both the white and black community and securing commitments from representatives on either side of the color line to attend a public meeting at the courthouse on September 21, 1966.⁴⁹

Although movement leaders suspected that something other than altruism was at play, they joined more than one hundred African Americans and nearly as many whites at the courthouse. After Golson called the meeting to order, he spent several minutes reviewing the procedures for forming a CAP. Then he introduced a pair of OEO representatives from the state and regional offices, who filled in key details. After they spoke, he fielded questions from the audience. Movement activists used this time to call for a vote for a temporary committee chairperson. Whites took for granted that Golson would be the chairperson, but the activists felt that Robert L. Strickland, the movement's OEO coordinator, should serve in this capacity. A debate ensued, but the issue was resolved quickly. By a show of hands, the people chose Scott Billingsley for the position. Billingsley was the county's black agricultural extension agent. In this capacity, he worked closely with people of both races. Moreover, he supported the movement, which pleased African Americans, but was not a frontline activist, which eased white concerns. Tempers flared during the debate, but everyone settled down after the vote. Passions rose even higher, though, during the discussion of the racial composition of the proposed thirty-member CAP action committee. Although whites constituted only 20 percent of the population, they insisted that the committee have equal racial representation, a major concession from their perspective. African Americans, however, wanted the committee to reflect the racial makeup of the county. Strickland and Lillian McGill led the call for an 80/20 split and refused to accept anything less out of fear that black interests would be subordinated to white interests. Parliamentary order soon broke down, as did civil discourse. To avoid complete chaos, Golson gaveled the meeting to a close.⁵⁰

The consensus among whites was that movement activists ruined the meeting. They "deliberately sabotaged" it, said M. E. Marlette, Jr. "At no time would the black power representatives accept consideration of a ratio other than 80–20. They were so loud and demanding that the whites and other Negroes were allowed no opportunity for discussion."⁵¹ Black assertiveness was indeed upsetting because it defied long established customs of racial deference. African Americans had found their voice and refused to keep silent. They were in no mood to placate the opposition, especially after failing one week earlier to win control of additional ASCS committees in the court-ordered repetition of the 1965 ASCS election.[52]

Although movement activists mistrusted whites, they knew that they had to work with them if they wanted to bring a CAP to the county, a point that OEO officials underscored repeatedly. After considerable discussion, they agreed to approach whites with a new plan for allotting seats on the action committee. On November 2, 1966, seven members of the movement's poverty program committee, led by Ed Moore King, met with Golson at the courthouse and proposed reserving eighteen seats on the committee for African Americans and thirteen seats for whites—a 60/40 split. When Golson presented the proposal to the members of the board of revenue, they promptly rejected it, insisting that the action committee be divided evenly between the races. "The white people are prepared to accept some Human Rights people as members of the board of directors of a Community Action Program," explained M. E. Marlette, Jr. "But as for participating in, or serving in any position in, a project solely connected with the Human Rights (black power) group, no." The sticking point remained control. "It is seemingly impossible [to form a CAP] because the white people . . . will never be willing to surrender their voice in affairs to a dominant black power structure," said Marlette. The inability of the two sides to agree on a power sharing arrangement kept the OEO from ever awarding a CAP to Lowndes County.[53]

The federal government possessed the resources to help African Americans expand the fight for freedom rights beyond voter registration. Movement activists attempted to access these resources through the OEO and the ASCS. It was not enough, however, for these agencies to funnel money to Lowndes County. ASCS poured millions of dollars into the county over the years with very little positive impact on the lives of African Americans because of the discriminatory practices of local administrators. To make a difference, African Americans had to control these resources. Lowndes County whites, however, adamantly opposed African American control of federal funds because they knew that the economic independence it would engender would undermine white supremacy. Consequently, they worked hard to keep federal dollars that they could not control out of the county. Alabama officials applauded this effort and used the power and authority of the state government to support it.

The federal government had steered clear of the local conflict for nearly a century, adopting a laissez-faire approach to race relations that allowed white interests to prevail over black interests. Movement activists, however, pulled Washington into the struggle, believing that the strength of their legal and moral claims would compel federal officials to side with them. Sometimes, though, the federal government got involved by dint of circumstance, as was the case when Lowndes County residents presented the OEO with competing CAP proposals. In nearly all instances, federal authorities moved cautiously, seemingly torn between supporting the legitimate claims of African Americans and a desire not to fan the flames of revolution. This approach led Sargent Shriver to award the LCCMHR nearly $250,000 to help lift black farm workers out of poverty, only to withhold the money for several months because of scurrilous charges leveled by local and state officials. It also prompted judge Frank M. Johnson, who ruled in favor of African Americans in the jury discrimination and school desegregation cases, to rule against them in the eviction lawsuit. The federal government was caught in a political conundrum. It wanted to address the legitimate needs and demands of African Americans while simultaneously appeasing white voters and powerful white politicians like Governor Wallace. Furthermore, the federal government rarely acted with urgency on social matters, a function of a general lack of political will and the nature of an unwieldy bureaucracy. At times, it stood solidly with African Americans, recognizing past and present racial discrimination and seeking to remedy it. On other occasions, when right and wrong seemed just as stark, it sided with the white resistance.

The effect of federal intervention on the movement was mixed. In many instances, it advanced the fight for freedom rights by providing African Americans with critical resources to ameliorate the prevailing condition of poverty and by removing impediments to racial equality, such as de jure segregation in education and de facto discrimination in jury selection. The full impact of federal intervention, however, was rarely felt immediately. It took more than a decade for justice to prevail in the courtroom after *White v. Crook*. Nevertheless, the federal government made a real difference. It needed to do much more, however, to eviscerate white supremacy. Even when permitted by law, the federal government was only willing to go so far. After assuming the burden of creating change, it often shifted this responsibility back to African Americans. The Justice Department, for instance, sent federal registrars to Lowndes County, but neither it nor the federal judiciary did much of anything to protect African

Americans from reprisals, ranging from evictions to retaliatory violence. After Jim Crow crumbled, it was up to African Americans to clear the mountain of debris that remained.

Even though federal involvement was not enough to transform Lowndes County completely, it created political opportunities for African Americans to challenge white supremacy. ASCS reforms, for example, failed to eliminate racial discrimination in the administration of federal farm programs, but they provided movement activists with a chance to organize black farmers. Such opportunities were invaluable because they put African Americans in a position to agitate for the full spectrum of freedom rights. Rarely, though, did these activities immediately produce the desired results. The process of organizing, however, gave local people a wealth of experiential knowledge. Fighting for control of the ASCS, for instance, revealed the importance of political education and political mobilization, whereas the effort to bring in poverty programs exposed the unwillingness of whites to share power equitably. These insights raised people's political awareness, and in doing so helped lay the foundation for the formation of an all-black, independent, political party. It was neither apocalyptic events nor movement messiahs that set the stage for the radicalization of black politics, but rather the slow and hard work of organizing.

5

We Gonna Show
Alabama Just How Bad We Are
*The Birth of the Original Black Panther Party
and the Development of Freedom Politics*

It was a beautiful day to vote. The cloudless sky was crystal blue and the temperature had not quite reached Alabama hot. As the workday neared an end, hundreds of people made their way to First Baptist Church, the site of the LCFO candidate nomination convention. Sharply dressed in their favorite hats and finest suits and dresses, they gathered on the church lawn where third-party volunteers checked their voter registration status to confirm their eligibility. State law forbade unregistered voters from participating in the May 3, 1966, event, and LCFO officials, fearing disqualification for even the slightest transgression, adhered to the letter of the law. The volunteers directed eligible voters to a row of seven wooden tables. At each table, they handed them a slip of paper with the names of the black candidates seeking to become LCFO nominees printed on the left side, and the party's black panther logo beneath the phrase "One Man—One Vote" on the right. The candidates stood about a dozen feet behind the tables so that the voters could easily identify them, but poll watchers monitored all interaction to ensure that no one told them for whom to vote. The volunteers also assisted those unable to read and physically incapable of standing in line. After placing an "X" next to the name of the candidate of their choice, the voters slid their ballots into the cardboard boxes located beside each table and then moved on to the next station.[1]

As the people voted, SNCC field secretaries, equipped with two-way radios, patrolled the area for signs of danger. Because the sheriff refused to protect black voters, the young organizers remained vigilant. Local people were also on guard. "I remember when that minister got

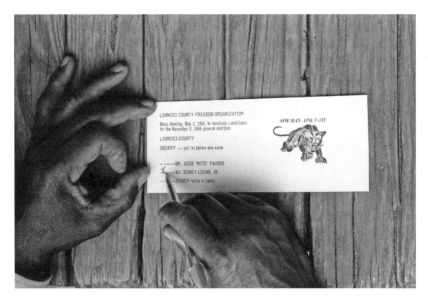

LCFO supporter casts ballot for Black Panther nominee for sheriff on May 3, 1966.
© Flip Schulke/CORBIS.

shot here," said a sixty-seven-year-old veteran of the First World War, referring to the murder of SNCC volunteer Jonathan Daniels. "He had his arms folded and just got shot down." The man then reached into the pocket of his overalls and produced three shotgun shells. "We gonna protect our friends this time," he said. Fortunately, there was no violence that day.[2]

The possibility of an attack did not dampen the spirit of the people. Children scampered about, playing their usual outdoor games, while those who had already voted lingered under shade trees talking amiably. One group even serenaded the crowd with freedom songs. "There was a festive air to the affair," wrote a reporter.[3] The enormousness of the occasion, however, was not lost on anyone, especially SNCC organizers. Near sunset, SNCC field secretary Willie Ricks ascended the steps of the church and delivered an impromptu speech that lived long in everyone's memory. Nicknamed "The Reverend" because of his country preacher oratorical style, the Chattanooga, Tennessee, native could stir the souls of black folk like few others. That evening, the high school graduate, sporting black frame spectacles and a denim jacket, reminded the crowd of the incongruity of being black and a Democrat. "Do you know George Wallace is a Democrat?" he asked rhetorically. "And the people who work you for three dollars a day—what are they? The people who wear those white sheets at night and call themselves the Ku Klux Klan—what are they? If you black in Lowndes County, you aren't no Democrat—you black!" He also praised those assembled for challenging white supremacy in ways that transformed how their neighbors thought of them. "When people talk about Selma, they tell you there's some bad white folks down there. When they talk about Wilcox County or Greene County, they tell you there's some bad white folks down there. But when you mention Lowndes County, they say, 'There's some bad niggers down there.' We gonna show Alabama just how bad we are!"[4]

The LCFO convention was a memorable event for the black community, which had not hosted such a gathering since Reconstruction. It was equally important to SNCC's Alabama organizers, who had worked tirelessly to create a grassroots third party to provide an alternative to the Democratic Party. The significance of the LCFO convention, however, transcended its local meaning. The selection of seven African Americans to run against white Democrats in November 1966 was a triumph for democracy. Although there was nothing particularly radical about the candidate selection format, the process of political education that African Americans underwent leading up to the convention cut completely against the grain of American politics. After the 1965 Voting Rights Act became law, SNCC organizers developed a unique political education program for Lowndes County residents that used workshops, mass meetings, and primers to increase general knowledge of local government and democratize political behavior. As a direct result of this effort, the emerging black electorate rejected the undemocratic traditions that defined American politics. Rather than promote the interests of the socio-economic elite, draw candidates exclusively from the ranks of the propertied and the privileged, or limit decision making to a select few individuals, they adopted a freedom rights platform, selected candidates from the poor and working class, and practiced democratic decision making. In this way, the political education process gave rise to freedom politics. This new kind of political engagement coupled the movement's egalitarian organizing methods with the people's freedom rights agenda. The embrace of freedom politics by third-party supporters made the LCFO convention the high point of the Lowndes movement.

• • •

When SNCC organizers entered Lowndes County in March 1965, they did so with an eye for establishing a grassroots, independent political party. "It is not enough to add more and more people to the voter rolls and then send them into the old 'do-nothing,' compromise-oriented political parties," explained Carmichael. "Those new voters will only become frustrated and alienated."[5] Within SNCC, Carmichael was a leading advocate of third parties. His attraction to independent politics stemmed primarily from the lessons he learned at the 1964 Democratic National Convention. These insights included the need for African Americans to refrain from entering into coalitions unless they had an equal say in the terms of the union. "It is absolutely imperative that black people strive to form an independent base of political power *first*," he argued. "When they can control their own communities—however large or small—then other groups will make overtures to them based on a wise calculation of self-interest. The blacks will have the mobilized ability to grant or withhold from coalition."[6] Carmichael imagined independent parities as the first step toward creating these bases of power.

Carmichael introduced the leaders of the Lowndes movement to the idea of creating an independent party, but he waited to do so until the end of the summer of 1965. He knew that he could not approach them until he earned their trust, which required demonstrating that neither the slow pace of progress nor white violence could chase SNCC activists away. He also had to help them build a critical mass of supporters, because a third party had to have an active and sizeable constituency. Throughout the spring and summer of 1965, SNCC helped build this constituency by canvassing the county and promoting voter registration. Carmichael also needed local leaders to generate a body of experiences capable of elevating political awareness to the point where organizing outside the two-party framework became an acceptable option. Lowndes County activists began accumulating these politicizing experiences during the middle months of 1965 as they organized to improve black public schools, desegregate all-white public schools, win control of county farm committees, bring in antipoverty programs, and respond to reprisals that ranged from mass evictions to murder. Finally, he had to wait until African Americans had the vote in hand, which did not occur until federal registrars appeared in the county in August 1965.[7]

At an executive committee meeting of the LCCMHR held two weeks after the Voting Rights Act became law, Carmichael finally suggested that African Americans form their own political party. During his pitch, he shared his distrust of the Democratic Party, which he later called "the most treacherous enemy of the Negro people on a national basis. They step on us, they take our vote for granted and we're completely irrelevant."[8] Regarding Alabama Democrats, he said, "There's no room for Negroes in the same party as Wallace."[9] He also questioned the trustworthiness of Lowndes County Democrats. Movement leaders were intrigued by Carmichael's analysis and asked for precise details about creating a third party.[10]

After the meeting, Carmichael relayed the leaders' request to SNCC's research department. The research department was a remarkably efficient unit that had grown in less than two years from a single staff member clipping newspaper articles to a team of six that conducted staff training and gathered specific intelligence for field secretaries.[11] Jack Minnis, the department's resourceful director, handled Carmichael's inquiry personally. A skilled researcher, he combed the entire twelve-volume set of the *Alabama Code of Laws* with trademark thoroughness. "Alabama law says it is possible to bring to existence a totally new political party," wrote Minnis in his report to the Lowndes Project leader. "Whether or not this is, in fact, possible is not quite so certain. But, under Alabama law, there appear to be sufficient provisions for political activity independent of existing party and power structures, that it may be worthwhile to attempt such action."[12] The specific state law that Minnis referred to was Title 17, Section 337 of the *Alabama Code*. The statute, a relic of the Reconstruction era, was written by ex-Confederates to help them retake political control of the state. The law stated that a group of qualified voters could establish a third party by forming an organization with the express purpose of running candidates for office and holding a candidate nomination convention on the first Tuesday in May, the same day as the Democratic primary. Voters could not participate, however, in both a convention and the primary.[13] "I should suppose that the proceedings of the new organization could be invalidated if it could be shown that even one of its members voted in the primary," speculated Minnis. Finally, if one or more of the organization's candidates received at least 20 percent of the total vote in the general election, then the state would recognize the organization as a political party.[14]

The long-forgotten law was exactly what Minnis had hoped to find. Still, there was a lot more to forming an independent party than the steps outlined in the obsolete statute. "There are provisions for appointment of poll watchers, vote counters, election clerks, etc., that will have to be thoroughly understood by the people," explained Minnis. "It's going to take a major educational effort, I'm sure, between now and next November." Forming a party would be a daunting task, but Minnis believed that it could be done and he looked forward to meeting with SNCC's Lowndes County staff to "discuss the whole thing in greater detail."[15]

Minnis's discovery excited Carmichael and his co-organizers, but they did not let their enthusiasm interfere with their commitment to letting the people decide the direction of the movement. Although they wanted Lowndes County residents to create an independent party, they remained true to SNCC's organizing tradition by leaving the decision to form a party to the people themselves. Thus, when Carmichael met with the LCCMHR executive committee in September 1965, he explained the procedure for establishing a third party and enumerated the benefits of political independence. Then, he stepped aside and let them determine the next move. "The SNCC workers brought the idea to us that we could organize our own political group if we wanted to," recalled Hulett, who headed the LCCMHR at the time. The decision, he added, "was left entirely to the people of Lowndes County."[16]

The prospect of forming a third party sparked a debate among the LCCMHR officers about how to maximize the voting strength of African Americans. "We thought about what we were going to do with these 2,500 registered voters in the county, whether or not we were going to join Lyndon Baines Johnson's party," explained Hulett. "Then we thought about the other people in the state of Alabama who were working in this party. We thought of the city commissioner of Birmingham, Eugene "Bull" Conner; Al Lingo, who gave orders to those who beat the people when they got ready to make the march from Selma to Montgomery; the sheriff of Dallas County, known as Jim Clark—these people control the Democratic Party in the state of Alabama." As a part of this conversation, they discussed the leaders of the Democratic Party, including Robert Dickson, Jr., the chairperson of the Lowndes County Democrats and a vocal proponent of white supremacy.[17] They quickly concluded that they should not cast their lot with such men. According to LCCMHR founding member Frank Miles, Jr., "It didn't make sense for us to go join the Democrat party, when they were the people who had done the killing in the county and had beat our heads."[18] Instead, they decided to pursue independent politics. In their view, this was the best way to give meaning to black votes. "We felt that if it was anyway possible for us to do anything, we would have to form our own party. And that was a third party," explained local activist Mathew Jackson, Sr.[19] They also decided to ask SNCC organizers to help them navigate these uncharted waters. They turned to the student activists not because the idea to form a party had come from them, but because of the personal bonds of trust and respect that existed between them. Although local leaders initially doubted the organizers' commitment to working in the county and their ability to endure white violence, fighting together in the movement's trenches demonstrated that they were sincere and that their resolve was strong.[20]

The decision by local leaders to form their own party allowed Carmichael and other advocates of independent politics to begin a serious discussion within SNCC about making third parties the focus of the organization's work. In an internal memo, political strategist Courtland Cox framed the issue brilliantly with a clever play on a familiar Biblical scripture. Revising Mark 8:36 he asked, "What would it profit a man to have the vote and not be able to control it?"[21] He added, "When you have a situation where the community is 80 percent black, why complain about police brutality when you can be the sheriff yourself? Why complain about substandard education when you could be the Board of Education? Why complain about the courthouse when you could move to take it over yourself? [In] places where you could exercise the control, why complain about it? Why protest when you can exercise power?"[22] The logic of this argument, combined with local interest in independent politics and the decline of SNCC projects in Mississippi, drew a slew of experienced organizers to Lowndes County. "A lot of folks from Mississippi had become frustrated with the Democratic Party orientation of the MFDP, and by the prevailing atmosphere of uncertainty within the organization," recalled Carmichael. "So they began to look at Lowndes County and saw that we were disciplined and had a clear program that could use their talent. In a time of transition, it seemed like one of the few viable programs with a clear focus that SNCC had."[23]

The arrival of reinforcements beginning in the fall of 1965 transformed the Lowndes Project into a laboratory for testing the feasibility of organizing independent parties, and in the process it breathed new life into SNCC. More than a year had passed since the MFDP's defeat in Atlantic City and SNCC as an organization still lacked an organizing program. Consequently, everyone in the organization paid close attention to the project's development. They were unwilling, however, to make the development of third parties the organization's primary focus—at least not yet. SNCC's operational culture dictated that actual programs, rather than theories, determine SNCC policy. This viewpoint prompted them to wait to see what became of the third party in Lowndes County before organizing independent parties elsewhere.[24]

SNCC activists wasted little time designing a political education program to help African Americans create a political party capable of spreading democracy locally. The program stressed sending canvassers "into areas where no one has bothered to go before," said SNCC's Courtland Cox. "The Democratic Party is willing to include Negroes, but not junkies, bums, workers or the dispossessed and poor." The program emphasized focusing on the problems that plagued "those who are illiterate, those who have poor educations, [and] those of low income," added Cox.[25] It recognized the right of ordinary people to make decisions about their own lives, which SNCC's Alabama organizers said was "the most fundamental right that a member of a democratic society can have."[26] It also challenged traditional leadership hierarchies. "It's not radical if SNCC people get political offices, or if M. L. King becomes President, if decisions are still made from the top down," said Carmichael. "If decisions get made from the bottom up, that's radical."[27] Finally, it stressed placing group interests ahead of personal interests.

The ideas behind the political education program sprang directly from the organizing philosophy of influential SNCC adviser Ella Baker. The veteran activist, who helped establish SNCC in 1960, believed passionately in organizing ordinary people, not just middle-class professionals. "I have never been diploma conscious," she once said. She also believed fervently in the right of ordinary people both to make the decisions that affected their lives and to develop leaders among themselves. Baker weaved a commitment to these principles into the fabric of SNCC, and the organization's Alabama organizers applied them to electoral politics. In this way, Baker left her imprint on the Lowndes movement.[28]

SNCC activists developed the political education program with local politics in mind. "Until county courthouses can be taken over, bit by bit, there is no point focusing faraway on glamorous offices which leave the local situation unchanged," explained Jack Minnis, the program's principal architect.[29] SNCC's Alabama organizers also pointed out that local politics offered African Americans an opportunity to become "the distributors of any state and federal resources, the taxers of any industry in their county, the determiners of the quality of education and the money spent for county schools."[30] The emphasis on local politics reflected SNCC's evolving understanding of the loci of power in southern politics. "If you control the county level then you're in a position to bargain," said Carmichael. "You can tell whoever you're bargaining with—this is what we want. If you go to the state and you don't have the power then you just have to get what you can. Once you have the power, I don't care whose government you're under—George Wallace or James Eastland—they have to meet your power on that level."[31] SNCC activists also believed that county politics was the best way for African Americans to retain control of their political agenda. According to Carmichael, "If you organize on a state level, things get too confused and you lose a lot, and if you organize on a national level, the same thing happens, there are too many compromises you have to make, too many of what people call 'political decisions,' and what happens is that the powerful people make those decisions and the other people just get stepped on."[32] Local leaders concurred with these basic assumptions. Hulett believed adamantly in the primacy of county politics. "The election of local officials is the most important thing for people in Lowndes County," he said.[33] The political education program, therefore, sought to instill in African Americans a commitment to democratic practice and to teach them how to gain control of the local government.

After studying Alabama election law and county government for two months, Minnis and his research team hosted four weekend workshops for Lowndes County residents at SNCC's Atlanta headquarters. "The purpose of the workshops was to help the Lowndes County people learn everything they needed to know about the political laws of Alabama as they applied to county government," explained Minnis.[34] The organizers hosted the initial retreat in early December 1965, a few weeks after black farmers failed to win control of the ASCS. At the meeting, SNCC researchers led twenty-five residents in a careful examination of the statutory and constitutional provisions for conducting elections and nominating independent party candidates. They also discussed the legal powers associated with the positions up for election in November 1966, which included sheriff, tax assessor, tax collector, coroner, and three seats on the school board. By deconstructing political power and authority in these ways, they hoped to demystify county government.[35]

During the workshops, the facilitators steered the discussions away from abstract theories until, as Minnis phrased it, "the participants had a clear idea of the statutory powers of the offices."[36] For example, analysis of the theories of arrest and habeas corpus, differences between civil and criminal procedures, and dispossession and foreclosure occurred only after everyone understood the duties of the sheriff. By grounding political theory in actual Alabama law, political power took on concrete meaning. This approach also brought into sharp relief the extent to which serious abuses of power were taking place. Minnis reported that after discussing the duties of the coroner "it became clear to everyone" that murder at the hands of persons unknown "could never have gone uninvestigated and unpunished" without the coroner's "connivance" and "collusion." What's more, this method prompted participants to think about new solutions to old problems. A conversation about the power and authority of the school board, for instance, led to a debate about physical plant necessities, curriculum shortcomings, and teacher qualifications. Minnis recalled that by the end of the weekend it was obvious to everyone that winning control of the county courthouse through independent means was "the appropriate machinery for building the kind of society in that county, which the people of that county wanted."[37]

Within days of returning from Atlanta, the leaders of the LCCMHR announced plans to form their own party. "The white folks think they can let a few of us vote and fool us," said a local movement supporter. "They just don't see that we're now startin' to see how to use the vote to help ourselves instead of helpin' them."[38] They named their party the Lowndes County Freedom Organization and planned to rename it the Lowndes County Freedom Party after the November 1966 general election, assuming they received 20 percent of the vote. In addition, they selected a snarling black panther as their ballot symbol to meet the state requirement that every political party have a logo due to the high rate of adult illiteracy. There are several conflicting stories about the origin of the symbol, including one that has SNCC activists choosing it because it reminded them of a fiercely determined local activist. In truth, the logo was the brainchild of SNCC field secretary Ruth Howard, who patterned it after the panther mascot of Clark College in Atlanta, Georgia. The panther was not her first suggestion. Initially, she proposed a white dove, but "nobody thought that worked," she later confessed. The problem was that the dove failed to capture the seriousness of purpose and the indomitable spirit of the people of the county. The black panther pleased everyone, however, because it conveyed these characteristics perfectly. "The Black Panther is an animal that when it is pressured it moves back until it is cornered, then it comes out fighting for life or death," said Hulett. "We felt we had been pushed back long enough and that it was time for Negroes to come out and take over." Moreover, everyone knew that cats preyed on roosters, and a white rooster was the symbol of the Alabama Democratic Party. "We felt that the panther could destroy the rooster," said Hulett. "That is our plan. On November 9 we feel we can destroy the rooster in Lowndes County."[39]

The logo not only energized local activists, but it also captured the imagination of African Americans nationwide. The reason for its broad appeal was obvious to Carmichael. The black panther represents the "strength and dignity of black demands today," he said. "A man needs a black panther on his side when he and his family must endure—as hundreds of Alabamians have endured—loss of job, eviction, starvation, and sometimes death, for political activity."[40] African Americans' enchantment with the LCFO symbol manifested itself most clearly in a spate of new organizations, mainly in urban areas outside the South, that adopted the symbol as their own. In California, several groups styled themselves black panthers, including the Oakland-based Black Panther Party for Self-Defense (BPP).[41] Like countless others, BPP cofounders Huey P. Newton and Bobby Seale believed that the LCFO logo accurately reflected their political attitude. The BPP experienced phenomenal growth soon after Newton and Seal secured exclusive use of the Black Panther name in California by compelling competing groups to change their names. By 1970, the organization stood at the vanguard of the Black Power movement. As a result, the black panther emblem became more closely associated with the BPP than with the rural residents of Lowndes County.[42]

The BPP and the LCFO never established formal ties, which is hardly surprising given that the two organizations shared little in common beyond the black panther symbol. During its heyday, the BPP never seriously considered independent politics. Moreover, the Alabama group was an explicitly local organization. Local activists created it and local politics was its primary focus. Thus, rather than seek alliances with outside groups, the LCFO concentrated on building a viable political party, starting with the development of a local constituency.

LCFO organizers grew the party's base one person at a time, just as they had pieced together the LCCMHR. Political education workshops played a central role in this process. Movement leaders encouraged those who learned about Alabama government and election law in Atlanta to share their new knowledge with family and friends back home, a strategy that yielded immediate dividends. "News about the new freedom organization travels fast in Lowndes County," noted an internal SNCC communiqué. "Local people who are attending the workshops speak at church services, visit in different homes and also invite people over to their homes to talk about the new party."[43] The impact of having scores of residents discuss their new political insights with people they knew was profound. "[T] here are now in Lowndes County 400 people who know what the duties of a sheriff are," said Carmichael after the final workshop. "All of those 400 people feel qualified to run for sheriff. So you will in fact not have someone running for sheriff who can out lie the other, because that's what campaigns are all about, you know." "More than that," he added, "once the sheriff is elected, he can't step out of his bounds, because everybody knows just what his duties are."[44]

Unfortunately, many of the people who wanted to participate in the workshops were unable to do so because the trip to Atlanta was either too expensive or required too much time away from work. As a remedy, SNCC's research staff began conducting biweekly workshops in the county. Like the Atlanta workshops, the Lowndes County meetings, which began at the end of February 1966, focused on the duties of the courthouse officials up for election in November. Ahead of the first workshop, the research staff circulated mimeographed descriptions of the responsibilities of elected officials "so that everyone who was interested could find out as much about each office as he felt he needed to know," explained Minnis.[45] The primers enabled workshop facilitators to center discussions on the specific questions that residents had about each office. SNCC organizers also disseminated cartoon storybooks in an effort to reach those unable to read. The storybooks used simple, hand-drawn figures to depict the responsibilities of county officeholders and to describe the potential power of African American elected officials. The cartoon about the sheriff showed a black police officer reviewing jailhouse records with the public and appointing black poll inspectors.[46]

Once workshop participants demonstrated a firm grasp of the powers associated with the positions up for election, SNCC researchers discussed the qualifications for holding public office. According to Alabama law, anyone older than twenty-one who lived in the state for at least two years, the county for at least one year, and in his or her voting precinct for three or more months could run for office. The custom in Alabama, though, as in the rest of nation, was to limit the pool of potential candidates to the wealthy and well connected. SNCC activists were aware of this tradition. "[A]nother way in which people have been prevented from practicing politics is through teaching them that there are only a few people in each community who are 'qualified' to practice politics," wrote Alabama field secretaries. "If all the people believe these teachings, they will sit back

Excerpt from SNCC Freedom Primer explaining the duties of the sheriff of Lowndes County. In possession of author.

A coroner is elected every four years.

His main duty is to hold inquests.

When a person is killed for unknown reasons, the coroner is called upon to find the cause of death.

If evidence shows that the person may have been murdered, he then calls six people from the county to serve on a jury to determine the cause of death.

The coroner can subpoena people knowing anything about the death as witnesses.

The sheriff serves the subpoena for the coroner.

If a witness does not come before the jury, the sheriff can arrest him.

Excerpt from SNCC Freedom Primer explaining the duties of the coroner of Lowndes County. In possession of author.

and leave politics to those who say they are 'qualified.' This is pretty much what has happened in the past, and we can all see what a sorry mess the 'qualified' ones have made of things." Consequently, workshop leaders de-emphasized wealth, connections, experience, and expertise as prerequisites for holding office. "It is just a simple fact, which everyone knows if he will think about it, that each and every grown man and woman is just as 'qualified' as anyone else to decide what he wants his life to be like," argued the Alabama organizers. "There may be some information that some of us need in order to decide how to go about making our lives what we want them to be, but we can get that information and we can learn it just as well as anyone else."[47]

By teaching hundreds of residents about local government, the Lowndes County workshops, together with the Atlanta workshops, dramatically increased the size of the politically educated electorate. More people than ever before now knew the responsibilities of local officials as well as the boundaries of their power. In addition, these same folk came to see themselves as capable of holding office. They no longer viewed politics as white folks' business or even as the preserve of black professionals. It had become clear to them that ordinary people could and should occupy public office. In these ways, the workshops transitioned African Americans from voter registration to voter participation, while simultaneously laying the groundwork for a new, more democratic political culture rooted in freedom politics.

SNCC organizers were certainly not the first civil rights activists to use workshops as a means of political education. In South Carolina, Septima Clark helped pioneer the use of workshops through the Citizenship Schools she coordinated in the mid-1950s under the auspices of the Highlander Folk School. These workshops helped African Americans living on the Sea Islands get ready to take the voter registration exam by teaching them the basics of reading, writing, and government. SCLC popularized workshops in the late 1950s and early 1960s through its Crusade for Citizenship, a regional voter registration campaign modeled after Clark's Citizenship Schools. SNCC organizers, though, were the first to use workshops in the post–Voting Rights Act era to prepare African Americans for what to do with the vote.[48]

LCFO organizers did not limit their effort to build the party's base to holding workshops. They also flooded the county with literature criticizing the Democratic Party. One of their earliest and most effective flyers called attention to the state party's official slogan of "White Supremacy

Movement supporter Jesse Favors holding a LCFO flyer critical of Alabama's Democratic Party and its official slogan, "White Supremacy for the Right." © Associated Press.

for the Right." In bold type above a reprint of the slogan and an image of a crowing rooster, they asked, "Is this the party you want?" At the bottom of the sheet they inquired, "Do you want this party to decide, for you, who you can vote for next year in the counties and in the state? Or do you want to start your own organization, that you will control, that will not be for white supremacy, that will put on the ballot at next year's general election the candidates of your choice for all the county and state offices?" Printed on the flip side was a description of the law that permitted county residents to form their own party. "If Alabama doesn't want to repeat what happened to the Mississippi Freedom Democratic Party then Alabama doesn't have to," announced the activists.[49]

Independent party advocates circulated another arresting leaflet in February 1966 in response to a decision by the executive committee of the Lowndes County Democratic Party to raise the cost for running in the Democratic primary. The qualification fee for candidates for sheriff, for instance, jumped from fifty dollars to five hundred dollars, or to more than half of the annual income of most black residents. News of the hike angered African Americans and solidified support for the third party. "If we were going to build up a treasury we were going to build up our own," said Hulett.[50]

As local activists and SNCC organizers laid the groundwork for an independent political party, they looked ahead to the 1966 general election and realized that a handful of key courthouse positions, including superintendent of education and probate judge, were not up for election because state law staggered four- and six-year terms of office. In an attempt to make every county government position available immediately, they filed *McGill v. Ryals* in January 1966. In the lawsuit, which took its name from plaintiff Lillian McGill, the secretary of the LCCMHR, and defendant Frank Ryals, the county sheriff, the activists argued that whites "seized and retained all political power" by "unlawful and unconstitutional means" and excluded African Americans from participating in county government in violation of the Fourteenth and Fifteenth amendments. They also pointed out that whites used "threats, terror, and violence" to keep African Americans from "even attempting to exercise their franchise." To remedy the situation, they asked the court to vacate local offices with unexpired terms so that every county government position would be up for election that year. A failure to act would deny African Americans "their fundamental and inalienable right to be governed by persons in whose election they have been permitted to participate."[51] A panel of three federal judges, however, dismissed the lawsuit on March 31, 1966, on the grounds that the relief sought would adversely effect "the orderly transaction of government." The justices also suggested that other remedies, namely the 1965 Voting Rights Act, existed "to alleviate the effects of past discrimination." But they overstated the extent to which a special election would disrupt local governance, and they also misread the main provisions of the Voting Rights Act, which were better suited to protecting black voting rights going forward than correcting the political power imbalance created by decades of disenfranchisement. Although the ruling did not keep local activists from running black candidates in the 1966 general election, it did prevent them from fielding candidates for several important positions that year.[52]

Local activists brushed aside the adverse ruling and continued distributing leaflets and conducting workshops. The first Tuesday in May was fast approaching and party advocates still needed to accomplish a lot in order to hold a nomination convention. Most importantly, they had to officially establish the LCFO, which they did at a mass meeting at Mt. Moriah Baptist Church on April 2, 1966.[53]

Soon after the sixty movement stalwarts settled into Mt. Moriah's well-worn pews they directed their attention toward Hulett, who opened the meeting by explaining the need for an independent black party. "We have to form our own power structure," he said. "If we stay within the Democratic Party the same people will still be in control." He reminded the audience that these people were the ones who increased the Democratic Party's filing fees to deter African Americans from running in the primary. He also made the point that the little bit of room set aside within the Democratic Party for African Americans had been reserved for the black elite, who tended to put personal interests ahead of the interests of the black masses. "They get into positions of power then just walk all over their black brothers and sisters." Lastly, he connected the failure of the movement to achieve its goals beyond securing the right to vote to the absence of black political power: "We boycotted the schools most of last year and got nothing. If we had the power to put some white kids into those schools, then we'd get the money." He said that the same was true of their effort to secure poverty program funding: "The federal government's been playing around with us on this poverty program. If we had the power we could get the program." Power was the key to generating the change that they wanted: "Once you get power you don't have to beg."[54]

Choosing the party's officers was the first item on the evening's agenda. Not surprisingly, the group selected people with distinguished records of leadership in the movement. For president, they turned to Hulett, who immediately resigned as the chairperson of the LCCMHR so as not to jeopardize its tax-exempt status. They named Robert L. Strickland, the chairperson of the LCCMHR Housing Committee, vice president. Sidney Logan,

Jr., a member of the LCCMHR Anti-poverty Action Committee, agreed to serve as treasurer, and Ruthie Mae Jones and Alice Moore signed on as financial secretary and recording secretary. Lastly, Frank Miles, Jr., consented to serve as chaplain. By drafting some of the most active people in the movement, LCFO supporters sought to infuse the organization with the same willingness to challenge white power, commitment to empowering poor people, and dedication to democratic practices that had become staples of the freedom struggle.[55]

Next, they discussed the rules governing the candidate nomination convention, particularly the laws that limited participation to registered voters and banned participants from also taking part in the Democratic primary. "They'll be watching for any irregularities," warned Hulett. Voluntarily opting out of the primary, however, remained a source of tremendous concern for more than a few people, and rightly so. For their entire lives, the Democratic primary had been the single most important event in Alabama politics, and not participating in it seemed like throwing away their votes. During a spirited debate, Hulett argued that taking part in the primary would be foolhardy—because white voters still outnumbered black voters, white candidates would easily defeat black candidates. He also maintained that participating in the primary would cause them to squander their first opportunity to win control of the courthouse. He conceded that because Democratic primary winners always carried the general election, following the independent-party route meant sacrificing their say in state elections, including the gubernatorial race between Lurleen Wallace, the wife of lame-duck governor George Wallace, and state attorney general Richmond Flowers, her less reactionary opponent. But he insisted that the election of local black officials was exponentially more important. A black sheriff would do more for them than a moderate white governor, who, if elected by some miracle manifestation of white moral conscience, would be, at best, only marginally less a white supremacist than Governor Wallace. The discussion continued for some time until an elderly man who had been silent up to that point stood and shared his thoughts. With regard to not participating in the primary, he said, "So what! We ain't been votin' at all 'till now." With that, the debate ended. They would move forward with the nomination convention and observe the law that prohibited convention participants from voting in the primary.[56]

Before the meeting adjourned, the party's local organizers asked Carmichael to say a few words. During his remarks, he made a keen observation.

"This meeting is very different from any other meeting taking place in the state because the candidates are not important. It is the organization that is important." He could not have been more correct. The principal concern of LCFO advocates was establishing a people's party, one in which political candidates worked toward implementing an agenda agreed on by African Americans. The interests of individual office seekers were inconsequential. The needs of the people mattered most. In a radically democratic way, candidates were irrelevant. "We feel in Lowndes County that the power does not lie in the person who runs for office but in the organization around the person," explained Hulett.[57] Indeed, LCFO supporters did not even discuss who should, or would, run for office that night even though the convention was only four weeks away.[58]

The desire to create a people's party emerged out of the political education workshops. For four months, African Americans studied the legal responsibilities of county officeholders, discussed the shortcomings of white elected officials, and debated the best ways to create lasting change. Their critical examination of local government provided them with a new framework for processing lived experiences, which helped them see exactly how whites in positions of political power protected the racial caste system. It also led them to devise creative ways to transform existing political practices. Foremost, it convinced them of the necessity of filling the courthouse with people who were responsive to their needs.

The belief that the collective interests of African Americans trumped the political aspirations of individuals kept party supporters from volunteering immediately to run for office. In fact, no one stepped forward as a candidate until the middle of April 1966. A disdain for political professionalization was not the only factor limiting the candidate pool. Fear of white retaliatory violence was equally important. Running for office challenged white power much more than registering to vote or housing outside organizers. It required extraordinary courage not only on the part of prospective candidates but also from their families because it put people's lives in extreme danger.

Hulett and his family displayed such courage continuously for more than a year. Thus, it is no surprise that he considered running for sheriff. Among the local activists, he was a logical choice for the position. No one was more closely associated with the movement and few people had been as willing to challenge white power as openly. Additionally, there was a groundswell of support for him to seek the LCFO nomination. Conversations about possible candidates were rare, but when they did occur

Hulett's name invariably surfaced. In the end, though, he chose not to run. He believed that he could do more for the movement working behind the scenes.[59]

In the wake of his decision, others stepped forward. Sidney Logan, Jr., reaffirmed which side he was on by seeking the LCFO nomination for sheriff. So too did Jesse Favors, a railroad laborer and the vice president of the usher board at Mt. Gilliard Baptist Church. Alice Moore, a forty-two-year-old mother and farmer's wife, offered herself as the LCFO nominee for tax assessor. Frank Miles, Jr., the LCFO chaplain, and Josephine Waginer, a homemaker and active member of Mt. Gilliard, volunteered to run for tax collector. For coroner, Emory Ross came forward, and for school board, Robert Logan, a Sears, Roebuck employee and the brother of Sidney Logan, Jr., volunteered. John Hinson, a bricklayer born in Montgomery who had moved to the county after marrying Mathew Jackson, Sr.'s oldest daughter, also volunteered to run for a seat on the school board. Joining them as prospective school board nominees were Bernice Kelly, Virginia White, Willie Mae Strickland, who was the wife of LCFO vice president Robert Strickland, and her sister Annie Bell Scott, a resident of Tent City.[60]

These six men and six women had much in common, not the least of which was courage. They all belonged to families that had been very active in the movement. The Logans, for example, joined the struggle en masse the previous spring, a decision that cost Robert's wife, Sarah, a veteran public school teacher, her job. Although courage and family affiliations set them apart, many other aspects of their lives made them indistinguishable from everyone else. Indeed, the biographical profiles of the candidates reflected the movement's constituency. Some were landless, but many were small landowners. A few were active in large community churches, whereas others worshipped at small family churches. Most were married and almost all had young children. Each also had some schooling, but the amount varied tremendously, from college coursework to little more than elementary school training. In short, they were ordinary, working-class, black men and women who became involved in independent politics because they happened to be born into a racially volatile situation at a unique moment in American history.[61]

The candidates made their public debut on Sunday, April 24, 1966, at a mass meeting at Mt. Moriah. About two hundred people gathered at the Beechwood church to hear what they had to say. One by one, the prospective nominees addressed the crowd from the pulpit. "We have too long waited and done nothing for ourselves," declared Jesse Favors. "Vote for me and I'll stand up for fair treatment." Sidney Logan, Jr., followed Favors to the microphone and explained that if he were sheriff African Americans would not have to fear the law. "I will not be the man to stand in the court-house door when you come to seek power," said the World War II veteran, playing on the image of Governor Wallace trying to keep black students out of the University of Alabama. Alice Moore explained that "if everyone had been taxed their share we'd have better schools and good roads today." The speeches evinced the candidates' firm grasp of the power of the offices they sought and their knowledge of the extent to which white elected officials neglected their duties. They also reflected their clear understanding of the central significance of racism and the uneven ownership of wealth to the problems plaguing the black community.[62]

With less than two weeks to go before the nomination convention, there was still a lot to do and not much time to do it. Because the candidates needed to learn more about the powers associated with the offices they hoped to occupy, SNCC activists scheduled three workshops specifically for them. "We'll talk all about the offices as they revolve around the power to tax," explained Minnis, who directed the workshops. "Taxation is a powerful weapon—it is the only weapon devised by politicians that can take money from the rich and give it to the poor."[63] LCFO organizers also had to rally support for the candidates, which they did by holding community meetings. Every night the candidates, or one of their representatives, spoke to scores of African Americans who gathered at neighborhood churches to meet and learn about the Black Panther. At the same time, they canvassed the county encouraging African Americans to register. They were not content, however, with simply mobilizing the black electorate. They also wanted to educate them. With this in mind, they organized a series of political education workshops for the public that drew thirty to forty people nightly.[64]

The efforts of SNCC activists to create a new political culture appeared to be working, but success was hard to measure. The outcome of the May 3, 1966, convention would be the most accurate indicator. A strong turnout by black voters would mean that African Americans approved of the independent party and the new political practices responsible for its emergence and growth. The convention, therefore, became a referendum on whether developing independent political parties ought to become SNCC's new organizing program.[65]

• • •

Enthusiasm for the Black Panther ran high, which gave party supporters good reason to believe that African Americans would participate in the convention in significant numbers. Indeed, Black Panther fever seemed contagious. Not only had it spread rapidly in the county, but it also swept across the Black Belt, carried by local supporters who testified personally at Sunday services and weekday mass meetings to the power and potential of independent parties. On March 20, 1966, for example, roughly sixty residents traveled to six nearby counties to explain what was happening in Lowndes County and to urge their neighbors to organize parties of their own. Such activity anchored the effort to spread the Black Panther regionally, and then, perhaps, nationally.[66] "First we're going to straighten out this county, then we're going to spread abroad . . . into the other counties of Alabama, then into the North, into Harlem, Chicago, Watts," said Frank Miles, Jr.[67] Although the Black Panther never made it out of Dixie, at least not in the form of the LCFO, it did find a home in several Black Belt counties. In Dallas County, African Americans formed the Dallas County Independent Free Voters Organization; in Wilcox County, they established the Wilcox County Freedom Organization; and in Greene County, they formed the Greene County Freedom Organization.[68]

Not everyone caught Black Panther fever. Alabama whites proved universally immune to it, and the black middle class exhibited their own stubborn resistance. "If it is evil to have all-white government, it is also evil to have all-Negro government," mused Stanley Smith, a sociology professor at Tuskegee Institute and one of two African Americans elected to the five-member Tuskegee City Council in 1964.[69] The black middle class in Lowndes County was extremely small. It consisted mainly of a couple hundred public school employees. It was also not politically active. Even those who opposed the movement rarely acted on their opposition. There was no middle-class political organization, for instance, that challenged the LCFO's pursuit of power. Instead, middle-class blacks tended to watch from the sidelines and usually voiced their criticism in private. But the potential for organized opposition existed, and this possibility worried movement organizers tremendously. The response of Tuskegee's black professionals to the Black Panther, therefore, is extremely instructive because it illuminates the less-than-democratic black political traditions that SNCC activists wanted desperately to avoid, and it exposes the motives behind that group's general hostility for the LCFO.

Since the early 1940s, African Americans employed at Tuskegee Institute and at the city's segregated Veterans Administration hospital, worked through the Tuskegee Civic Association (TCA) to promote civil rights. In 1960, a favorable Supreme Court ruling in *Gomillion v. Lightfoot*, which effectively overturned a discriminatory state law that neutralized the voting strength of African Americans in Tuskegee by gerrymandering them out of the city, set the stage for a climactic electoral showdown four years later. The leaders of the TCA and the Macon County Democratic Club (MCDC), the political arm of the local movement, however, shied away from the face-off. Rather than sponsor black candidates for a majority of the seats on the city council and the board of revenue, they decided among themselves that the ruling white minority should retain control of the local government; consequently, they backed only a few carefully selected African Americans for office. Charles Gomillion, the dean of the school of arts and sciences at Tuskegee and the chairperson of both the TCA and the MCDC, explained, "We will try to support white candidates who seem to be in a position to render the best service for the total community."[70] An unrepentant gradualist, Gomillion believed that too many black faces in the courthouse would scare whites, which would make the formidable task of dismantling Jim Crow and achieving racial equality that much more difficult. For Gomillion, gradualism was appropriately accommodating, and many black professionals, including those outside the Black Belt, agreed. In Birmingham, for instance, the black elite spent several generations cultivating personal relationships with white powerbrokers and did not wish to lose the precious little political capital they had accumulated by appearing to favor a government takeover. This possibility truly frightened whites because of the century-old fear that African Americans, once in power, would treat them just as they had been treated. Thus, black professionals in the Magic City praised the Tuskegee model of black political participation, and after the Voting Rights Act became law, they urged black Alabamians to support the Democratic Party. The Alabama Democratic Conference Inc. (ADCI), a statewide political advocacy group established by black Birmingham's movers and shakers in 1960 to support the presidential bid of John F. Kennedy, led the way by working hard to deliver black votes for white gubernatorial candidate Richmond Flowers in the 1966 Democratic primary.[71] The LCFO, therefore, represented an approach to politics that ran counter to that of most black professionals, and its rising popularity promised to undermine the standing of this group by reducing the influence that its members had over the broader black electorate.

National civil rights organizations were no less hostile to the Black Panther. Although Charles Evers, the NAACP's Mississippi field director and the self-anointed heir to the legacy of his brother Medgar, did not speak for the NAACP as a whole, he reflected the views of the national office when he said that the organization would never support the push for "all-black government." "We want Negroes in all departments of government," he explained, "but we don't want to go from white supremacy to black supremacy."[72] The NAACP, however, had only a handful of political organizers on the ground in Alabama, which limited its ability to influence the state's black citizens. SCLC, on the other hand, had a strong presence in Alabama, and like the NAACP and countless black professionals, found the LCFO extremely problematic.

Before the ink dried on the press release announcing the formation of the independent party, SCLC's Alabama organizers called a meeting of state leaders and grassroots activists to encourage them to support the Democrats. "This meeting came about when we first heard talk of a black panther party," said Hosea Williams, SCLC's Alabama director of voter registration and political education. At the meeting, Williams made no effort to mask his disdain for the LCFO. In a lengthy diatribe, he stated that it possessed all the markings of reverse racism and demanded to know if its advocates planned to "treat white folks like the white folks treated them? Will they hate the white folks like the white folks hate them?" Beyond that he warned, "We may mess around here and create a monster in Alabama [that] will be detrimental to generations of Negroes unborn." He laid blame for the third party idea squarely at the feet of SNCC and accused its field secretaries of deliberately duping naive African Americans. "There ain't no Negro in Alabama including ourselves that knows one iota about politics. Politics is a science," he said, and black folk had neither the opportunity nor the time to study it properly. "This is why I think SNCC is taking advantage of the Negroes." The Georgia native ended his rant by saying that independent politics was bad mathematics. "We are only 35 percent of the people in Alabama, and 10 percent in the nation. We can't go pitting race against race."[73]

Like the black elite, political interests fueled Williams's contempt for the Black Panther. SCLC activists aspired to dictate the course of black politics in the post–Voting Rights Act era. They wanted African Americans to join the Democratic Party and support southern white moderates for office, believing that this was the only way for them to realize the full potential of re-enfranchisement. "We must let the Negro vote hang there like a ripe fruit, and whoever is willing to give the Negro the most free-dom can pick it," said Williams. "We may not be able to elect a black man, but God knows we can say what white man."[74]

From the outset, SCLC decision makers looked to Alabama as the place to popularize their political vision. The reason for their interest in the state had everything to do with the timing of Alabama's Democratic primary. Set for May 3, 1966, it was the first election in the Deep South since the passage of the Voting Rights Act. Committed to working in Alabama, they launched a statewide voter registration drive in October 1965. The thinking behind this stratagem was neither altruistic nor demo-cratic. Speaking of the state's black voters, Williams said, "The person who register[s] them controls them." To oversee black voting behavior, SCLC formed the Confederation of Alabama Political Organizations (COAPO). Williams marketed the COAPO as the voice of Alabama's black electorate and insisted that it was capable of delivering black votes to white candi-dates in exchange for political spoils that could be redistributed to loyal-ists at the county level. "We've got to say, 'White folks, what you going to give us?' We've been selling our vote all along. Now we've got to sell it for freedom."[75]

The COAPO had two immediate goals. First, it sought to deliver the black vote for Attorney General Flowers in the gubernatorial race. "For all of these years whites have bloc-voted to keep us down," said Dr. King of COAPO's call for a "united Negro vote" in support of Flowers. "Now we got to bloc-vote to get ourselves out of this dilemma."[76] Williams was confident that they would make good on their promise given the time they had spent registering black voters, particularly in the Black Belt. Sec-ond, COAPO wanted to sponsor black candidates for local offices in ma-jority black counties where SCLC maintained a strong presence, such as Wilcox and Perry. Like the Tuskegee Civic Association, however, COAPO chose not to back African Americans for every available office. "We don't want to look like we're taking over," explained Albert Turner, director of SCLC's operations in Alabama. "But we do want to elect enough Negroes so it will do some good."[77] To reach its goals, the COAPO applied strategies that SCLC used to mobilize African Americans for civil rights demonstra-tions—methods that had little to do with political education and every-thing to do with garnering media attention. In late April 1966, the COAPO arranged for Dr. King and a half dozen of his advisers to take a six-day, seventeen-stop tour of the state. From George Wallace's hometown in Bar-bour County to Brown AME Chapel in Selma, Dr. King and his entourage instructed African Americans to vote for Flowers and the local black candidates they named. Not surprisingly, they avoided Lowndes County. "We don't want Dr. King picketed or booed or anything like that," said Williams.[78] Bypassing Lowndes County was easier than ignoring the success of SNCC's political education program. Borrowing from SNCC's playbook, SCLC hosted a weekend workshop at Ebenezer Baptist Church in Atlanta for the black candidates they had picked to run for office. Approximately fifty of the sixty Democratic primary hopefuls attended. Their experience, though, differed substantially from that of the Lowndes County residents who attended SNCC's Atlanta workshops. Among other things, there was very little dialogue between them and retreat organizers. The latter invited them to Atlanta to learn what to expect in the coming days by listening rather than asking questions and sharing concerns. Except for the preponderance of black faces, typical American politics was the order of the day.[79]

The mainstream liberal media was well aware of the controversy swirling around the LCFO and unapologetically opposed the Alabama organizers. Rather than form independent parties, the press believed that African Americans ought to align with Democrats. "If they fuse their strength with liberal white voters they can achieve tangible gains in fairer administration of justice and better treatment from state and local government," wrote the editors of the New York *Times* shortly before primary day. The editors also blamed SNCC for the political shortsightedness of Alabama's black voters. "[The] Student Nonviolent Coordinating Committee's call for Negro voters to boycott the primary is destructive mischief-making" and "can only produce frustration and defeat for the state's Negroes," they lamented. To them, SNCC's "rule-or-ruin attitude" derived from the same mind-set of "extremism for the sake of extremism" that "prevailed in the refusal of the Mississippi Freedom Democrats to accept a generous compromise worked out in their behalf at the 1964 Democratic National Convention." Like Williams and his fellow SCLC organizers, the press was sure that SNCC had hoodwinked black voters by exploiting their political immaturity to advance a reckless "revolutionary posture toward all society and Government."[80]

Public criticism of the LCFO deeply disturbed the party's backers. SNCC organizers were especially concerned about the effect that it would have on future projects. They were confident that African Americans in Lowndes County would be able to decipher the truth about the LCFO given their nearness to the organization but were less sure that those living outside the county would be able to sift through the misinformation and see the LCFO for what it truly was. Their worries led them to make plain the purpose and goals of the LCFO through a series of speeches, letters to editors, interviews, and position papers. In a letter to the *Times*, SNCC executive secretary James Forman responded to the accusation that his organization's call for African Americans to participate in third-party conventions rather than the Democratic primary was not only extremist but also a willful attempt to deceive unsuspecting black voters. "If, as is true, SNCC workers in Alabama have expressed the opinion that the outcome of the Democratic primary has little relevance in terms of the needs of the majority of Negroes in certain counties, it is because the people themselves feel this way," he wrote. "If, as is true, SNCC workers have advised Negroes not to vote in the Democratic primary, it is because of this feeling but also because of a law which could be used to invalidate the independent nominating conventions on the grounds that voters had also participated in the Democratic primary." He ended by asking, "Does all this sound like 'extremism for the sake of extremism' as your editorial states?"[81]

To the charge that the LCFO was a manifestation of reverse racism, Carmichael answered, "There is nothing wrong with anything all black. There is nothing wrong with anything all white. What is wrong with either of those things is when force is used to keep somebody else out based on color. That's what is happening in this country."[82] SNCC political strategist Courtland Cox added in a position paper that the LCFO's "major emphasis is to bring political power at the county level to the poor and excluded—the color of skin is incidental. The extent to which blackness is seen as a 'problem' is one of the manifestations of a segregated and racist society."[83]

SNCC activists also dismissed the notion that political compromise was in the best interests of African Americans. "What kind of compromises can we make with these guys that been beating us over the head all these years?" Carmichael asked a *Newsweek* reporter.[84] A SNCC essay on Alabama laid bare the issue: "From the viewpoint of a tent city resident sleeping with a gun in a freezing tent there can be no middle ground. Who can ask a tent city resident to forget that he lost his home because he tried to act like a good citizen and vote? Who can blame the dispossessed for asking if the vote of a landless person is equal to the vote of a landowner?"[85] This is why SNCC activists refused to tell black voters to support white candidates. "What you have in this country is that Negroes are always told to vote for someone who is less of a racist instead of more for Negroes," said Carmichael. At a mass meeting attended by the press, Carmichael clarified this point by calling attention to Flowers's record as attorney general. "When Jonathan Daniels was killed, Richmond Flowers said he was for justice. He didn't say he was for Negroes. He said he was for justice. When Sammy Younge was killed that cracker didn't say anything. When a white man is killed, he says he is for justice and when a Negro is killed, he doesn't say anything . . . He's never said he's for us, and there's a big difference."[86]

Finally, the organizers explained away attacks from "middle class leaders" as a function of their not having had "the SNCC experience." "They have not watched their friends beaten and killed while the federal government stood sterilly [*sic*] by taking notes," read the SNCC essay on Alabama. "They have not organized people to vote in mock elections proving that hundreds of thousands of Negroes in the black belt are disenfranchised and then find that neither the Democratic Party, nor the United States Congress will deal with that fact. The men in a comfortable position in life will not understand SNCC unless they know what it is to live with the pervading fear of violence from creditors, sheriffs, hostile whites, and the 'boss man.'"[87]

Despite their best efforts, the organizers were unable to stem the tide of negativity emanating from friends and foes alike. SCLC's Albert Turner, for example, continued to lambast SNCC and the LCFO. At a Perry County mass meeting on April 17, 1966, he said, "SNCC doesn't register voters, [and] doesn't care about registering voters." He also said that the organization was trying to split the black vote.[88] As primary day approached, the chasm separating independent-party advocates from SCLC and the black elite remained as wide as ever.

In preparation for the nomination convention, Hulett asked sheriff Frank Ryals for permission to hold the election on the courthouse lawn. "We are trying to obey the law set by Alabamians," he explained in a letter to Ryals. "We hope that you do the same."[89] Sheriff Ryals, however, refused to allow them to use the public square. When pressed for an explanation, he said that he could not protect African Americans from angry whites, but movement activists disputed this claim. Everyone knew that the sheriff could keep whites from attacking them if he wanted to.[90]

In response to the sheriff's decision, LCFO leaders convened an emergency mass meeting during which a consensus emerged for proceeding with plans to hold the convention at the courthouse. The prospect of white violence no longer paralyzed frontline activists. "We been walkin' with dropped down heads, with a scrunched-up heart, and a timid body in the bushes," explained an older man a few months later. "But we ain't scared any more. Don't meddle, don't pick a fight, but fight back! If you have to die, die for something, and take somebody before you."[91] Ever since the murder of Jonathan Daniels, local organizers had waged an armed defensive struggle against their white opponents that had kept the movement afloat. To exercise the franchise as they saw fit, they resolved to continue to meet violence with violence. "If the sheriff cannot protect us, then we are going to protect ourselves," declared Hulett.[92]

The willingness of movement activists to defend black voters did not keep them from seeking a peaceful resolution to the dispute. To avoid bloodshed, Carmichael wrote to U.S. assistant attorney general John Doar and explained that the LCFO had "no choice" but to hold its convention at the courthouse. State law required that such events take place at an official polling place, and the courthouse was the only voting site in the county that was not a white-owned business or a private white residence. Carmichael insisted that the Justice Department had an obligation to protect black voters because the county sheriff had abdicated his duty: "Since Sheriff Ryals has put the LCFO on notice that he will not permit holding the mass meeting, we feel the responsibility for providing such protection as will permit the orderly and uninterrupted conduct of the mass meeting without undue physical danger for the participants [falls to] the U.S. Justice Department." Carmichael also alluded to the willingness of African Americans to defend themselves in the absence of federal intervention: "If we do not hear from you, or if the U.S. Government does not find itself able to protect the participants in the mass meeting we shall be forced to look to such resources as we can muster on our own to provide such protection."[93]

The Justice Department was much more concerned about blacks killing whites than about the illegality of the sheriff's actions. To avoid a race war, the department dispatched investigator Charles Nessem to the county. The Saturday before the convention, Nessem met with Hulett and asked what African Americans intended to do if whites began shooting. "We are going to stay out there," replied Hulett. Blacks and whites will "die together." Nessem implored Hulett to call off the event, but the local leader refused. "We are going to have it," he said, and "we are going to protect ourselves." Nessem met with Hulett for a second time Sunday afternoon, but once again failed to persuade him to cancel the convention. Hulett's resolve prompted Nessem to ask the state attorney general to allow the LCFO to hold its convention at an alternate site. After some cajoling, Richmond Flowers agreed to permit the LCFO to meet at First Baptist Church, an African American church located a half mile from the courthouse. When Nessem relayed this information to Hulett, the local activist asked, "Do you have any papers that say that's true, that are signed by the Governor or the Attorney General?" "No," answered Nessem. "Go back and get it legalized," said Hulett, "and bring it back here to us and we will accept it." "And sure enough," recalled Hulett, "Monday at 3 o'clock I went to the courthouse and there in the sheriff's office were the papers all legalized and fixed up, saying that we could go to the church to have our mass meeting."[94]

The peaceful end to the courthouse dispute did more than just allow the convention to take place. By not balking at the prospect of a bloody confrontation with whites, African Americans demonstrated the value of collective determination and spirited defiance. "When people are together, they can do a lot of things, but when you are alone you cannot do anything," observed Hulett.[95] From that moment forward, African Americans embraced racial solidarity more explicitly. In fact, this incident was one of the key movement experiences that led many people to embrace Black Power later that summer.

On Tuesday, May 3, 1966, some nine hundred registered black voters descended on First Baptist Church and cast ballots in the LCFO convention. After party officials tallied their votes, Hulett announced the winners. Sidney Logan, Jr., won the nomination for sheriff, and Frank Miles, Jr., received the nod for tax collector. Alice Moore and Emory Ross would represent the LCFO as the candidates for tax assessor and coroner, and Robert Logan, John Hinson, and Willie Mae Strickland would be the school board nominees.[96] The results pleased party supporters. "We have our candidates," said Carmichael in an interview late that evening. "Their names will be on the ballot November 8 along with our symbol, the Black Panther. All the people have to do is pull the lever under the panther. November 8 we vote. November 9 we take over the courthouse."[97] The nominees shared Carmichael's enthusiasm. When a reporter asked Sidney Logan, Jr., about his chances for victory in the fall, he answered, "I don't go out to lose."[98] What excited people the most was the strong turnout. Nearly half the county's registered black voters participated in the election. "The movement had opened the eyes of many Negroes," said White Hall shopkeeper William Cosby.[99] "We must use the vote to get out of the cotton fields and we can't do that by voting for the boss man," explained a local black farmer.[100]

Of course, not every African American who voted on May 3 cast ballots in the LCFO convention. Some seven hundred black voters took part in the Democratic primary.[101] Their experience was relatively uneventful. "It wasn't nothing bad," said sixty-four-year-old Iona Morgan, who mustered the courage to vote at the courthouse. The pedestrian nature of their experience reflected a level of white tolerance for black political participation that had not existed locally in nearly a century. "'Course, we'd rather it wasn't this way," said L. W. Crocker, a white voting inspector assigned to the courthouse on Election Day. "But it is, and we have to accept it." There were limits, of course, to how far whites would acquiesce to the new order. They stomached African Americans participating in the primary because it meant that they were not taking part in the Black Panther convention. Voting for white candidates was one thing, but voting for African Americans was entirely different. Nevertheless, African Americans who participated in the primary found their first voting experience personally fulfilling. "It felt good to me," said eighty-one-year-old Willie Bolden. "It made me think I was sort of somebody."[102]

Lowndes County residents dressed in Sunday finery and work clothes participate in the LCFO nomination convention held on the grounds of First Baptist Church in Hayneville on May 3, 1966. © Flip Schulke/CORBIS.

LCFO chairperson John Hulett making the rounds during the LCFO nomination convention on May 3, 1966. © Jim Peppler.

It is not hard to imagine why African Americans took part in the Democratic primary given the gravity of the event and the tangle of socio-economic ties that bound blacks and whites. Economic vulnerability, interracial friendships, fear of provoking white violence (especially by electing a black sheriff), and a belief in the inability of poor and working-class people to fulfill the obligations of elected office were among the factors that prompted black voters to go to the courthouse rather than to First Baptist Church on Election Day. Testimony from African Americans who voted for white incumbents in neighboring Wilcox County illuminates some of these motivations. Leo Taylor, a fifty-four-year-old house painter, voted against the black candidate for sheriff in the Wilcox primary. "It was too early for us to have a colored sheriff," said Taylor, who supplemented his income by driving a school bus for the county. "The white folks wouldn't have liked that a bit and it would have caused some trouble." Buster Lawrence, a fifty-eight-year-old farmer, said he voted for the white candidate for tax assessor because the two men had known each other their entire lives. "I lived across the road a ways from him when he was little," explained Lawrence. "He's loaned me his car before to go to Birmingham, and when I need to borrow a little money, I can get it from him and his family. He helped me so I helped him."[103]

·   The willingness of black voters to support white incumbents helps explain the defeat of black candidates in Democratic primaries across the Black Belt. Ahead of the election, political observers speculated that African Americans could win as many as twenty contests in six Black Belt counties given the twofold increase in black registered voters since the Voting Rights Act became law. Black candidates, however, failed to win a single race outright even though black voters turned out in record numbers; they did force runoffs in five elections, including the race for sheriff in Macon County, where black voters rallied behind Lucius Amerson rather than the white candidate favored by black professionals. The willingness of white officials to resort to electoral fraud also worked against African Americans. Across the state, they disqualified black ballots, switched polling sites without prior notification, allowed ineligible whites to vote, counted illegal absentee ballots, and marked ballots for illiterate black voters. White bloc voting was equally responsible for the outcome. Quite simply, white Alabamians refused en masse to vote for African Americans. They also chose not to vote for white candidates who failed to pledge allegiance to white supremacy. The principal beneficiary of these voting tendencies was Lurleen Wallace, who won the gubernatorial race with more votes than her nine opponents combined and almost three times as many votes as Flowers. Despite all the talk about a white moderate vote, it never materialized.[104]

Local activists viewed the poor showing by Flowers, the failure of black primary candidates to win simple majorities, and Lucius Amerson's strong performance in Macon County as validation of their political project.[105] But rather than dwell on the ill fortune of others, they began strategizing for the November 1966 election. Defeating white candidates would not be easy, especially because local whites would undoubtedly vote as a bloc and resort to electoral fraud as had their neighbors. Moreover, there was little expectation that the black elite would rally behind the Black Panther. "Our biggest fight now is among our own people, like the professional people, school teachers and preachers who don't want any part in it because once the common Negro moves up he will become equal with him," said Hulett.[106] To win, they would have to organize those African Americans who remained on the sidelines, the majority of whom were unemployed and underemployed agricultural workers living on white folks' land.

For SNCC, the poor showing by black primary candidates coupled with the strong convention turnout demonstrated that independent county-wide politics offered African Americans their best opportunity to secure political power. Moreover, it confirmed the feasibility and practicality of developing all-black parties. Almost two years after the MFDP defeat in Atlantic City, SNCC had finally found a new organizing program.

The creation of the LCFO reflected the desire of African Americans to use the ballot to secure their freedom rights. This foray into electoral politics was an integral part of the Lowndes movement. It was inseparable from the voter registration drives that marked the beginning of local civil rights protest, intertwined with the fight to improve segregated black schools and desegregate white schools, and interwoven with the effort to increase economic opportunities for black farmers. Not surprisingly, local activists' movement experiences, filtered through a prism of pre-movement memories, played a critical role in the development of the LCFO by predisposing them to promoting democratic practices and a populist agenda. The political education workshops created by SNCC organizers standardized these practices by providing African Americans with the interpretative tools they needed to apply insights gained from organizing to electoral politics.

The LCFO enabled people whose views had been suppressed since Reconstruction to express them publicly. This alone was a remarkable accomplishment. The party, however, did more than give a voice to the voiceless. It also introduced freedom politics, which offered its adherents a more democratic way of doing things. Instead of privileging the interests of the social and economic elite, it made the needs of the poor and working class a top priority. Rather than limiting leadership to a handful of people, it democratized decision making. It also rejected wealth, whiteness, and previous political experience as prerequisites for holding office. The LCFO's most significant achievement, therefore, was its ability to elevate the political awareness of African Americans to levels seldom achieved by others in the movement. In the process, it made freedom politics synonymous with black politics. The party's supporters, however, wanted to do more than just transform black politics. They wanted to replace the undemocratic traditions that defined American politics with more democratic practices. The LCFO convention was a significant step in this direction, but to normalize freedom politics African Americans had to unseat white office holders in the November 1966 general election.

6

Tax the Rich to Feed the Poor
Black Power and the Election of 1966

It was nearly impossible to hear over the clamor they created as they finalized plans for the election scheduled for the next day. But a Sunday morning quiet seized them the moment that the Black Panther candidates began assembling near the pulpit. Alice Moore, the forty-two-year-old nominee for tax assessor, stood proudly among the group as each addressed the crowded sanctuary of Mt. Moriah Baptist Church. The Lowndes County native was a dedicated servant of the people. She was active in several clubs at Mt. Elam Baptist Church and a member of numerous community organizations, including Union Burial Society No. 9. She had also joined the movement as soon as it began. As an LCFO nominee, she was accustomed to addressing mass meetings, but she tended to shy away from theatrical speechifying. This evening was no different. When her turn came to speak, she chose her words carefully. In a calm yet commanding voice, she said, "My platform is tax the rich to feed the poor." Then, without uttering another word, she sat down. Nothing else needed to be said.[1]

Moore's platform reflected her core political beliefs. It also reflected the guiding principles of the LCFO. Local activists and SNCC organizers formed the independent party to oust whites from the county courthouse and replace them with African Americans committed to extending freedom rights to everyone. For more than a year, they organized with an eye toward taking over the local government, and as the 1966 general election approached they stood on the cusp of realizing this goal. The very real possibility that African Americans would gain political power in 1966 made that year's vote the climatic event of the Lowndes movement.

The election of 1966 was also an important moment for SNCC as an organization. During the summer of 1966, SNCC adopted a new organizing program, which it dubbed Black Power. The program involved sending

African American organizers into black communities to cultivate ra-cial consciousness and build independent political parties. The Lowndes movement played a leading role in the development of this program. Or-ganizing in Lowndes County reinforced SNCC activists' appreciation of rural black southerners' cultural values and reconfirmed the significance of community controlled institutions. Working with the LCFO was par-ticularly important. The formation of the party convinced SNCC activists to make building grassroots third parties the centerpiece of their work. It also provided them with a blueprint for establishing these parties. As a result, the election of 1966 was the first major test of SNCC's most signifi-cant Black Power project.

The selection of a full slate of LCFO candidates during the party's conven-tion on May 3, 1966, thrilled SNCC organizers. SNCC had operated with-out a central organizing program ever since the MFDP failed to unseat Mississippi segregationists at the 1964 Democratic National Convention. The success of the LCFO nomination convention, however, provided the organization with programmatic direction by demonstrating the grass-roots appeal of independent political parties. "We were convinced that we had found *the* Lever we had been searching for," recalled SNCC program director Cleveland Sellers.[1]

Less than one week after the convention, some one hundred SNCC ac-tivists descended on Kingston Springs, Tennessee, for a staff retreat. Their primary goal was to reach a consensus on an organizing program. With this in mind, they made three major policy decisions. First, they voted to make the development of third parties the focus of SNCC fieldwork. Sell-ers explained that they believed that "such organizations working together could end racial oppression once and for all."[3] Second, they decided to pro-mote black consciousness, which they defined as ideas and behaviors that affirmed "the beauty of blackness" and dispelled white supremacist con-structions of race. "We have to stop being ashamed of being black," said Stokely Carmichael. "They oppress us because we are black and we are go-ing to use that blackness to get out of the trick bag they put us in."[4] Third, they agreed to limit organizing in black communities to African Ameri-cans. "It seemed to us a major contradiction to ask white secretaries to go among black sharecroppers and convince them of their power to be self-determining and independent," explained Gloria Larry, a veteran of the Lowndes Project.[5] "We will not fire any of our white organizers," said Car-michael, "but if they want to organize, they can organize white people."[6]

The Lowndes Project played a decisive role in these decisions. In addition to persuading SNCC members to build third parties outside of Alabama, it convinced them to promote black consciousness. Appeals to black pride in Lowndes County were less overt than later manifestations. "We've done it without talking about 'Whitey' and 'getting rid of 'Whitey' and that shit," said Carmichael.[7] Nevertheless, they were plain to see. The play to black solidarity inherent in the black panther ballot symbol was unmistakable. The Lowndes Project also influenced the decision to prohibit white volunteers from organizing in black communities. Restricting the activities of whites had become increasingly common on SNCC projects, but the Lowndes Project was the most glaring example of this trend.[8] In Lowndes County, SNCC organizers refused to allow whites to work in the field mainly because they believed that it was needlessly dangerous. As evidence, they pointed to the senseless murder of white volunteer Jonathan Daniels in August 1965. "A few whites were working in Selma and some of the other counties, but not in Lowndes," said Carmichael. "This was not because we had any formal policy of excluding them, we simply did not encourage them . . . The general feeling was that we couldn't, on principle, exclude anyone who genuinely wanted to struggle against racism. On principle. But as a practical matter, under the objective conditions, we found it would have been foolhardy, even irresponsible, to bring in whites."[9]

The decisions made at the Kingston Springs meeting formed the basis of SNCC's new organizing program. Going forward, SNCC would send African American activists into black communities to develop black consciousness and build independent political parties. In essence, they would do what Carmichael had done in Lowndes County. Thus, the inspiration for SNCC's new program was not what anyone had said or wrote, but what field secretaries in Alabama had actually accomplished. Very soon, SNCC members began calling the new program Black Power, an abbreviated version of the slogan "Black Power for Black People" that Lowndes County organizers helped popularize. For SNCC activists, Black Power meant celebrating blackness, cultivating racial solidarity, and building black institutions, and the catchphrase described their new program perfectly. "[Black Power] was a more specific way of saying what we mean," said field secretary Willie Ricks.[10] It was also a way to link SNCC to its organizing roots.

To implement Black Power, SNCC activists turned immediately to Carmichael, whom they elected chairperson of the organization during a contentious election at the end of the retreat. Many believed that having the architect of the Lowndes Project oversee the process of spreading black consciousness and building third parties was necessary for the program's success. In addition, John Lewis, the incumbent chairperson, had alienated many field secretaries, especially those working in Alabama and Mississippi, and had fallen out of favor with some of the Atlanta staff, particularly those with connections to Howard University. Lewis viewed the movement as a moral crusade, which conflicted with the dominant belief within the organization that the movement was a political struggle. This ideological difference, however, was nothing new, and most people probably could have continued to live with it. What troubled SNCC members the most was Lewis's growing opposition to independent third parties, which became clear during the run-up to the LCFO convention when he encouraged African Americans in Alabama to vote in the Democratic primary while touring the state with Dr. King.[11]

In the weeks following his election, Carmichael moved quickly to export the organizing approach that his team perfected in Lowndes County to other rural southern communities, starting with the counties surrounding Lowndes. His duties as chairperson, however, involved endless fundraising trips, which prevented him from spending much time in Alabama. If it were up to local activists, Carmichael would have remained in the county. "Yes[,] we are all looking for your return home (smile)," wrote LCFO candidate Alice Moore late that summer. "Here is where *Stokely* belong. We will loan you to other places, but they will have to return you safely home."[12] His absence, though, did not create a leadership vacuum. SNCC field secretary Bob Mants, who had worked in the county for more than a year, coordinated the Lowndes Project in his place.[13] A skilled organizer and able leader, he worked well with local activists. Although the people missed Carmichael, they were happy to have Mants. With his help, preparation for the November 1966 election proceeded seamlessly.

To win the general election, the LCFO needed twice as many people to vote for Black Panther candidates than the nine hundred people who participated in the party's nomination convention. Realizing this, local leaders focused on increasing the party's base of support. As summer began, they sent movement volunteers back into the field to talk to African Americans, but unlike earlier efforts, they focused squarely on the poorest black communities. "We go into the worst areas where people are still afraid and shaky, people who live on plantations," explained LCFO chairperson John Hulett. "We go in and talk with these people and let them know that they can live without these landowners . . . Once you start telling people

SNCC field secretary Stokely Carmichael playing with a local child during the
LCFO nomination convention on May 3, 1966. Two weeks later, he was elected
the chairperson of SNCC. © John F. Phillips/johnphillipsphotography.com.

this they start thinking about it. You may have to leave them for a day or two, but you keep going back to them and finally you're able to pull most of those people in."[14] Andrew Kopkind, a writer for the *New Republic*, witnessed this process up close when he shadowed Hulett as he canvassed the "least organized" black community in the county. Kopkind's account of their visit to one household captures the canvassers' deft dance:

> The people were "shaky," Hulett said. They were wary of "that mess" and of the white Northerner. But Hulett approached briskly and confidently. "Baby," he told a child, "tell your mother to step to the door." He introduced himself, and asked the woman whether she had heard of the Freedom Organization—"with the emblem of the black panther"—whether she would register to vote when the federal registrars came to town. She was unresponsive. "We got to do something," he went on. "You know it, we need good schools and running water for our houses. We been pushed around too long." The woman nodded perfunctorily; "uh huh," she answered, in the way the people do in Baptist church services, but now with less faith. "You don't need to be afraid," Hulett said. "If we all stand together, there ain't nobody can turn us 'round." Hulett talked a while longer, then asked if she and her family would come to a community meeting at the church two nights later. The woman was noncommittal.
>
> "They'll come, I think," he said as we left. "You got to go back to these people and talk to them about their problems. They know what can be done." Two nights later, at a ramshackle church in a stand of pine trees, the meeting had just begun when the woman and her husband—dressed in their Sunday finery—walked in.[15]

Hulett and his fellow canvassers had tremendous success piquing people's interest in the LCFO. The key was their ability to talk about change in concrete terms. If African Americans supported the LCFO candidates, then once they were in office they would be able to improve black schools, secure financial assistance for farmers, curb white violence, halt unlawful evictions, and tax wealthy landowners. It also helped that the Black Panther candidates were the only alternatives to the Democrats. "The Democratic Party was still the party of white supremacy," explained SNCC's Gloria Larry. "People knew that that wasn't something that they wanted to be involved in, so it wasn't difficult for us to talk about independent organizing."[16]

Political education was an integral part of the process of building popular support for the party. "Educating the population, not just manipulating them, was very important to us," recalled snc c political strategist Courtland Cox.[17] Accordingly, lc fo organizers held workshops at which they discussed the powers associated with the offices up for election. They also invited the public to attend workshops designed specifically for lc fo candidates. At these gatherings, they scrutinized the pitfalls of holding positions of power. "These workshops dealt with the ways in which people with money pay off elected officials and get them to sell-out ordinary folks," explained Jack Minnis, the director of sncc's research department. After several sessions, the participants "began to see what they had to watch for in a candidate they elected to public office. More important, they began to see that the people do not have to put up with such sellouts. They began to see that officials whom they elect to office, when they sell out this way, can be removed by impeachment, prosecution for not doing their jobs properly, special elections, and so forth."[18]

Although boosting attendance at the workshops and mass meetings was essential to expanding the party's base, movement activists still had to get people in front of a registrar before the September deadline for qualifying to vote in the 1966 election passed. To meet this challenge, they launched a countywide voter registration drive that netted hundreds of new black voters. By Election Day, they had raised the total number of registered African Americans to 2,800, which was 400 more than the total number of registered whites. Still, it was only half the county's eligible black voters.[19]

As Lowndes County activists galvanized local support for the lc fo, Carmichael rallied national support for Black Power. He launched this initiative in Mississippi in June 1966 during James Meredith's March against Fear. After a white Mississippian shot Meredith at the beginning of his solo demonstration, Carmichael persuaded sncc's executive committee to allow him and a handful of veteran field secretaries to join those planning to resume the march on Meredith's behalf. Carmichael wanted to organize African Americans as the march wound its way through Mississippi, just as he had done in Lowndes County the year before during the Selma to Montgomery March. In the best tradition of sncc, he aimed to transform a mobilizing event into an organizing opportunity. "We wouldn't just talk about empowerment, about black communities controlling their political destiny, and overcoming fear. We would demonstrate it," he explained.[20]

Civil rights demonstrator wears placard featuring LCFO black panther and the popular LCFO saying, "Move on over or we'll move on over you," during James Meredith's March against Fear in Mississippi in June 1966.
© Flip Schulke/CORBIS.

As the march entered the Mississippi Delta, local African Americans welcomed the SNCC organizers cheerfully. It was a homecoming of sorts because several SNCC workers, including Carmichael, had spent many months over several years organizing in that part of the state. The admiration that the student activists and local people shared for one another convinced Carmichael that the Delta was the place to introduce black Mississippians and the nation to Black Power.

Carmichael's familiarity with the Delta extended to its jails. Like so many other grassroots organizers, he had been arrested several times on trumped up charges stemming from civil rights–related activities. But he never got used to the local lockups, nor did he ever grow accustomed to having sheriffs trample on his civil rights. So when the public safety commissioner of Greenwood, Mississippi, arrested him for trying to help a group of marchers pitch tents outside of a Leflore County public school, he was livid. That night, following his release from jail, he returned to the schoolyard and addressed some six hundred marchers and march supporters. As he spoke, his high tenor voice pierced the darkness of the night like a bolt of lightning before a fierce summer storm. "This is the twenty-seventh time I have been arrested," he said. "I ain't going to jail no more." The crowd applauded feverishly. They were as fed up with white rule as he was. Sensing their mood, he decided to invoke SNCC's new rallying cry, but he harbored a small measure of doubt about how the crowd would respond. SNCC advance man Willie Ricks had advised him a few nights earlier that the people were ready for the new slogan, but he found his friend's report of sharecroppers joining the movement at the first mention of Black Power hard to believe. Nevertheless, he felt the time was right. After reiterating his unwillingness to return to jail, he shouted, "We want Black Power!" The crowd exploded. "What do we want?" cried Carmichael. "Black Power!" the people thundered. Carmichael repeated the question several times, and each time the crowd roared, "Black Power." Ricks was right—the people were ready for Black Power.[21]

Carmichael's June 16, 1966, speech was the most significant event of the Meredith march. It introduced a more radical slogan into the protest lexicon of African Americans. From that day forward, Black Power became a rallying cry for African Americans nationwide, from the cotton fields of the rural South to the assembly lines of the urban North. It ushered in a new phase of the African American freedom struggle. Starting that summer, the movement emphasized racial consciousness and solidarity much more explicitly. And it marked the beginning of SNCC's effort to develop independent political parties outside Alabama.

In every town the marchers entered, African Americans reacted to the call for Black Power in much the same way that the crowd in Greenwood did. The slogan resonated with them because it captured their feelings about the status quo in non-deferential tones that few had ever heard expressed publicly. The slogan, however, did more than just excite people. It also got them interested in voting, racial solidarity, and independent political parties because it referred to a plan for black political empowerment that made sense. Once ordinary African Americans became interested in Black Power, SNCC organizers were able to get them to register and to begin discussing the process of forming third parties. In this way, Black Power transcended simple rabble-rousing rhetoric and moved people to act.[22]

The response of national civil rights leaders to the call for Black Power was manifestly different. Floyd McKissick and the activists in charge of the Congress of Racial Equality (CORE) were among the few who applauded it. "Black Power is no mere slogan," said Don Smith, CORE's director of public relations. "It is a movement dedicated to the exercise of American democracy in its highest tradition; it is a drive to mobilize the black communities of this country in a monumental effort to remove the basic causes of alienation, frustration, despair, low self-esteem and hopelessness."[23] Dr. King and his ministerial aides at SCLC, however, criticized it as a poor choice of words. "It is absolutely necessary for the Negro to gain power, but the term 'black power' is unfortunate because it tends to give the impression of black nationalism," stated SCLC's president. "We must never seek power exclusively for the Negro but the sharing of power with the white people . . . Any other course is exchanging one form of tyranny for another."[24] Unlike Dr. King, whose objection to Black Power was primarily philosophical, Roy Wilkins, the executive secretary of the NAACP, disapproved of Black Power for personal and political reasons. Moreover, he denounced it vociferously in public. In fact, Wilkins led the charge against Black Power and attacked it and its advocates in much the same manner that his predecessor, Walter White, damned communism and condemned African Americans such as singer and actor Paul Robeson for speaking out in favor of it in the late 1940s and early 1950s. "Ideologically it dictates 'up with black and down with white' in precisely the same manner that South Africa reverses the slogan," declared Wilkins during the keynote address at the NAACP's annual convention in July 1966. "It is a reverse Mississippi, a reverse Hitler, a reverse Ku Klux Klan. Though it be clarified and clarified again, 'black power' in the quick, uncritical and highly emotional adoption it has received from some segments of a beleaguered people can mean in the end only black death."[25]

Fear motivated Wilkins. The civil rights moderate was genuinely afraid that white perceptions of Black Power would lead to violence against African Americans and have an adverse effect on NAACP fundraising. He also worried that it would jeopardize the organization's access to national politicians. His concerns had merit. Not long after the Meredith march, police repression directed at black militants increased. Liberal whites also began using Black Power as a litmus test for determining black militancy and stopped funding those groups, most notably SNCC and CORE, that failed the test.[26]

Liberal whites were skeptical of Black Power from the beginning. "We are not interested in black power and we're not interested in white power," declared president Lyndon Johnson at the NAACP convention, "but we are interested in American democratic power, with a small d."[27] Vice president Hubert Humphrey added, "Racism is racism—and there is no room in America for racism of any color. And we must reject calls for racism, whether they come from a throat that is white or one that is black."[28] Their skepticism stemmed from their belief that the freedom struggle had to be nonviolent and that black political interests were fundamentally aligned with their interests. These views led liberal whites to dismiss Carmichael's explanations of the ideology as ambiguous at best and unfathomable at worst. "There clearly seems to be more involved here than simple bloc voting in order to achieve equality of treatment," claimed the editors at the New York *Times*. Condemnation of Black Power by Wilkins and other civil rights moderates added to their doubt. "Nobody knows what the phrase 'black power' really means, neither those who oppose it nor those who have given it currency," wrote the *Times* editors.[29] The confusion surrounding Black Power's meaning, however, had less to do with what Carmichael said and more to do with how skeptics and critics interpreted what he said. In fact, Carmichael's explanation of Black Power as it applied to the rural South was unmistakably clear largely because he used Lowndes County as an example. And although his early explanations of what Black Power would look like in the urban North suffered from some ambiguity, by the time that his book *Black Power: The Politics of Liberation* appeared in print the next year, he had significantly clarified and complicated its northern applicability.[30]

Any doubt that liberal whites harbored about the meaning of Black Power evaporated later that summer when a position paper written in March 1966 by members of SNCC's Atlanta Project surfaced. On August 5, 1966, the New York *Times* published excerpts from the statement, which discussed ousting whites from SNCC, increasing black consciousness among organizers and black southerners, and building independent economic and political structures.[31] The *Times* presented the essay as SNCC's definitive statement on Black Power and mistakenly (or perhaps purposefully) credited Carmichael with coauthorship. For liberal whites, SNCC's brand of Black Power was no longer ambiguous—it meant exactly what Wilkins and other black moderates had alleged. "Regardless of other interpretations that could reasonably be offered of the term 'black power,' Mr. Carmichael and his SNCC associates clearly intended to mean Negro nationalism and separatism along racial lines—a hopeless, futile, destructive course expressive merely of a sense of black importance," declared the editors of the *Times*. "As a practical program, it has nothing more to recommend it than the wretched violence that some Chicago whites have been using in recent days against the Rev. Dr. Martin Luther King and his Negro followers."[32] Black moderates reinforced these claims by excoriating SNCC. Veteran activist Bayard Rustin declared, "Nothing creative can come out of SNCC."[33]

The Atlanta Project position paper, however, was not SNCC policy. The members of the project were mostly organizational outsiders who had joined SNCC only recently—they did not speak for the group. Moreover, their political beliefs more closely reflected earlier affiliations with more radically nationalistic, northern-based groups, including the Nation of Islam (NOI). One of the authors of the paper, Rolland Snellings, was actually still a member of the Revolutionary Action Movement (RAM) and had been assigned to SNCC to secretly push the vanguard group in a more militant direction. Moreover, many of the Atlanta Project activists, with the notable exception of the two project leaders, had spent relatively little time engaged in grassroots organizing. Finally, the project's members did not provide a viable organizing program to go along with their demand that SNCC emphasize black pride and build black economic and political institutions. The lack of an organizing plan kept SNCC's executive committee from endorsing the paper as policy when the project's members presented it in spring 1966. Veteran Lowndes County organizer Willie Ricks explained, "We would always say, 'Mr. Say ain't the man, Mr. Do is the man.' They talked about nationalism and that kind of thing inside

SNCC, but they did not have an organization in the community."³⁴ Programs rather than rhetoric always carried the day within SNCC, and when given the choice between the pontifications of the Atlanta activists and the political program of the Lowndes County organizers, SNCC members chose the latter.³⁵

The negative media portrayals of Black Power worried local activists in Lowndes County. "Stokely we have been reading some of your articles in the news paper and *we* know you mean good, and *we* do think what you are doing is *alright*, but you will have to be more careful, you must do more work and lest [*sic*] talk," wrote LCFO candidate Alice Moore in a letter to Carmichael. She also advised him to plan his speeches "before your whole SNCC staff and let them be satisfied too. For you can hurt yourself, SNCC, and also Lowndes County."³⁶ Carmichael wrote back immediately, assuring Moore of his good intentions. He noted, however, that "now I speak for SNCC and the tone has to be different." He hoped, though, that "the members of the L.C.F.O. will not become upset by what is said in the newspaper, because most of the times I haven't said that."³⁷ Carmichael's note pleased the local leaders. "Yes we understand why you speak as you do, but just remember that we understand, but maybe some do not. (smile)," responded Moore. "Yes the LCFO understand that most things that have been said is not true but we are just concerned about you and you know that. (smile)."³⁸

Carmichael's assurances cleared the way for local movement supporters to fully embrace Black Power. After visiting the county that summer, Margaret Long, a freelance journalist and novelist, wrote that everyone she talked to "smiled approvingly at the slogan 'Black Power' and SNCC's democratic, if fierce, incitements in the majority black counties."³⁹ "Ain't nothin' the matter with us!" declared a black resident at a movement meeting she attended. "We don't hate nobody for the color of their skin. We ain't shootin' nobody or th'owin' bombs in their house at their women and children. But we ain't gonna no more take it. They shoot in our house and we shoot back. We aims to get Black Power."⁴⁰

African Americans in Lowndes County grasped the fundamental meaning of Black Power better than most people. "This was a group of black people who were out to right centuries of wrong in their own little corner of the world," explained Carmichael. "These people did not have to argue Black Power; they understood Black Power."⁴¹ Local people embraced the ideology as their own partly because it resonated with their movement experiences. The preceding two years made it abundantly clear that they needed to control the local government to create lasting change. "Once we've got Black Power, we've got something going," said Alice Moore. "Our schools are cold in the winter and our children have to run out and get trash and wood to build a fire and keep warm before they can study and learn. We'll get our children in a place that's already comfortable."[42] Local people also responded favorably to Black Power because its core tenets corresponded with the ways they fought for freedom rights over the years. Most significantly, it spoke directly to their practice of using social networks to marshal community resources to challenge white supremacy. When the local and state government failed to provide African Americans with adequate public education, they supported their own schools, most notably the Calhoun Colored School, founded in 1892. To secure land, they pooled their meager savings and formed the Calhoun Land Trust, which helped hundreds of black farmers escape debt-based farm tenancy early in the twentieth century. To improve working conditions for sharecroppers, they tapped into church and fraternal networks and organized a sharecroppers' strike in 1935. To help meet the material needs of impoverished African Americans, they formed benevolent societies, such as the Daylight Savings Club, whose dozen or so members purchased essential household items for the elderly and indigent in the 1950s and early 1960s. Local people not only understood Black Power, they welcomed it, because it echoed their cultural values, social experiences, and organizing tradition.[43]

As summer neared an end, activists in Lowndes County looked past the national controversy surrounding Black Power and concentrated on mobilizing the local black electorate for the November election. Toward this end, Bob Mants sent LCFO volunteers, many of whom were students from Tuskegee Institute and Alabama State University, into the field to campaign for the party's candidates. The volunteers plastered the roadways with posters urging African Americans to "Pull the lever for the Panther." They handed out leaflets explaining the importance of voting for the LCFO ticket. "Now is the time!" heralded one flyer. "If ever we had a chance to do something about the years of low pay, beatings, burnings of homes, denial of the right to vote, bad education and washed-out roads—Now is the time!" They distributed palm cards. "Negro voting power is 4 times greater in Lowndes County," read a card featuring a quartet of snarling black panthers staring intently at a solitary white rooster. Another card invoked the wisdom of Malcolm X. It read simply, "The Ballot or the Bullet."

LCFO canvasser discusses the November 8, 1966, general election with a Lowndes County resident outside his home. © Jim Peppler.

The volunteers also circulated literature on electoral procedure, including instructions on the proper way to read and mark ballots, and for the first time they passed out material promoting the party's candidates and their platforms. A leaflet about Sidney Logan, Jr., the candidate for sheriff, quoted him as saying, "I feel that the time has come for us, who have not been protected by the law, but brutalized by it, [to] begin to take action to see that justice is done without fear or favor." A flyer for school board candidate Willie Mae Strickland credited her with saying, "For changes in our children's education there must be some changes made in the board of education and how taxpayers' money is used."⁴⁴ Most importantly, the volunteers knocked on doors and engaged people in conversation in order to explain the candidates' positions, discuss their qualifications, and talk about the problems afflicting the black community.

Lowndes County whites united in opposition to the LCFO mobilization effort. Some harassed LCFO volunteers by chasing them away, usually at gunpoint, whenever they found them talking to their employees or tenants. Others threatened Black Panther candidates. According to one widely circulated rumor that emanated from the white community, black voters had "better elect fifty-two sheriffs" because whites planned to "kill one every week." The reason for the hostility was no mystery. "They don't want us to come together 'cause we get too much strength," said Sidney Logan, Jr. "Once we get together we can move them out. That's the reason for all those shootings. They think [if] they get one afraid that'll frighten a lot of them." Times, however, had changed. White harassment neither stopped campaign workers from canvassing nor caused the candidates to drop out. The determination of movement activists stemmed from their willingness to make the ultimate sacrifice for this cause. "If I [have] to lose my life for what I think is right, I ain't backing down, cause I done made up [my mind]," declared Logan. Local activist Frank Miles, Jr., said, "If they kill one, we gonna put another one in. One day somebody's gonna get tired of killing, or else we're gonna start killing too. If trouble get in our way, we're gonna walk through it."[45]

Months of exhausting preparation gave rise to high hopes for victory. "I been moving night and day, talking to my friends and getting my friends to talk to their neighbors," said Logan. "I feel very strongly we will win." Logan's brother Robert concurred. "I feel the people of Lowndes County will stand behind their candidates 100% on November 8" because the movement had "opened the eyes of all the people." "I'm sure they'll win," said a resident of Tent City who had been evicted from her home for registering to vote. "All of the people out here are registered voters, and we plan to vote for the freedom organization candidates."[46]

Not everyone believed that total victory was possible. LCFO leaders harbored some doubts partly because of Election Day logistics. "We have never tried to get out the vote so we don't know what we can do," said Hulett.[47] He also knew that some African Americans intended to split their vote between black and white candidates. R. C. May, a black landowner who farmed 148 acres of cotton and corn, said that he and his family were "with the Black Panthers" but added that he doubted that he would vote for "all-Negro office-holders" because he did not believe that African Americans should "take over." "I've made up my mind to vote for Negro candidates I feel are able to do the job, and I may not vote for some who don't meet the qualifications. I feel like treating white people like I'd like to be treated myself. And I believe that if some few colored people win in the November election, the intelligent white people will fall in line."[48] Another black landowner dismissed the LCFO candidates outright. "The people that John Hulett has running are unqualified anyway," he said.[49]

The cocksure attitude of white officials who acted as though the defeat of the black candidates was a foregone conclusion also caused trepidation. Their arrogance stemmed in part from white solidarity. There was little doubt that whites would vote as a racial bloc just as they had done during the Democratic primary. As a precaution, though, the Lowndes County Committee for Good Government, an ad-hoc, bipartisan group of local white power brokers, placed an advertisement in the county weekly identifying the candidates whom they wanted people to support. Of course, the candidates were all white, but the list also included two Republicans, which reflected a political compromise cemented during the summer, designed to preserve racial unity. But in the post–Voting Rights Act era, white solidarity was no longer enough to carry elections in the Black Belt. White candidates needed black votes, and because whites controlled the ballot box, regulated the political behavior of many African Americans living and working on their land, and knew that some African Americans, particularly schoolteachers, would vote for Democrats, they felt that victory was a fait accompli.[50] Sitting outside the courthouse the week before the election, county clerk Mac Champion interrupted his game of dominoes with Tom Coleman, the part-time deputy who had murdered SNCC volunteer Jonathan Daniels, to explain to a reporter that the "good Negroes in the county would help elect the white ticket."[51] Carlton Perdue, the county solicitor, added, "Some of the nigras who come in here seem to be pleased with their life and treatment" and would "vote the straight Democratic ticket."[52] Not unlike post-Reconstruction politics, whites pinned their expectation of victory partly to black ballots.

There was not enough time before the election for LCFO organizers to try to win over people who dismissed black candidates out of hand, or to convince those African Americans planning to split their votes to support the entire Black Panther ticket. Consequently, party officials concentrated on getting core supporters to the polls. Transportation had always been a problem for African Americans. Most people were too poor to own a car and the county did not provide public buses. Although the nation was preparing to send a man to the moon, mule-drawn carts remained the primary mode of transport for quite a few people. Fearful that LCFO candidates might lose simply because their supporters could not get to the polls, party organizers devised a free, countywide carpool system complete with predetermined stations. They told those who wanted a lift to the polls but who could not make it to a station to carry a piece of white paper to the highway and use it as a flag to hail the shuttles. The volunteer drivers would be looking for them, they said.[53]

LCFO leaders also focused on curbing ballot fraud. The Sunday before the election, they gathered at the decaying, one-room building that served as the party's headquarters and spent five and a half hours briefing the dozens of volunteers who agreed to spend Tuesday at the polls. They instructed the poll watchers to keep a careful record of the day's events, including lists of people who voted, people prevented from voting, people who asked for help, people who provided help, and people who intimidated voters. "Let's keep writing," said one party leader. "There's nothing like a pencil and paper to keep the other man honest."[54] They also prepped the volunteers on provisional ballot procedure because they expected white officials to challenge the eligibility of black voters. State law allowed voters who had been challenged to file provisional ballots after a qualified property owner witnessed them sign an oath attesting to their right to vote. LCFO organizers explained the statute and reviewed the list of nearly forty African American property owners who had agreed to serve as witnesses. Beyond that, they decided that poll watchers should challenge white voters as soon as whites began challenging black voters. "In fact, I think we ought to just challenge for the heck of it every two hours or so, just to let those crackers know that we are on our toes and they'd better not try anything," said one party supporter.[55] Everyone responded to this suggestion with great enthusiasm. They understood the irony and symbolism of challenging the right of white people to vote.

Although state law permitted poll watchers to assist voters whose eligibility had been questioned, it forbade them from aiding illiterate or disabled voters. Persons unaffiliated with a political party, however, could help anyone, opening the door for whites to steal countless black ballots. "The big point for us to make is that no black people should ask any white man for help," said a meeting participant. "We'll help each other."[56] This line of thinking prompted party leaders to instruct the volunteers to spread the word that black voters ought not return home immediately after casting their ballots as they had been advised previously because of the likelihood of white violence. Rather, they should stay at the polls as long as possible to help those in need. "Instead of pulling the black panther lever and going on home, we tell our people to pull the lever and back up fifty feet and stand by ready to help our brother if he needs it," declared Emory Ross, the candidate for coroner.[57]

LCFO leaders also urged the volunteers to be on the lookout for whites casting ballots in the name of people who had long ago left the county or had died. To combat the graveyard vote, the volunteers needed a copy of the most recent voter registration roll. Unfortunately, the list of registered voters that the party possessed was several months old. To obtain the current list someone had to go to the probate judge's office. John Hulett and Sidney Logan, Jr., volunteered to make the trip Monday morning so that the volunteers would be able to review the list that night at the final mass meeting before the election.[58]

Monday evening, several hundred movement supporters from every corner of the county gathered at Mt. Moriah Baptist Church for last-minute instructions. They also came to draw strength from one another, as well as from the divine. "God, go with us to the polls tomorrow," implored a preacher in an opening prayer. "Be there with us in the morning." After the invocation, Hulett addressed the crowd. He used his time to express his pride in all that African Americans had accomplished. "No matter what happens, tomorrow night I will hold my head as high as I have ever done. It is a victory to get the Black Panther on the ballot." The ultimate goal, though, was gaining control of the county courthouse so that they could bring about the kind of change that people wanted. To make this happen, they had to be better organized. "All we have is our organization," lamented Hulett. "In the next two years we ought to know where every house in this county is. We need the help of every Negro in our community."[59] Although they had traveled a great distance, Hulett understood that their journey was far from complete.

The church-like service quickly gave way to a political workshop during which the LCFO leaders spent a considerable amount of time explaining the carpool system and even more time reviewing the list of registered voters that Hulett and Logan obtained without hassle that morning. The list was supposed to be arranged according to voting precinct and voting box, but of course it was not. Nor did it include the race and sex of each voter—nothing was ever as it should have been in Lowndes County. Consequently, LCFO organizers asked the audience members to reseat themselves according to their voting precinct and to identify from memory the race and sex of every voter on the list. This tedious task took hours, but there was no way to avoid it.[60]

Near the end of the meeting, the candidates addressed the crowd. When Alice Moore spoke, she fired up the people simply by repeating her campaign slogan—"Tax the rich to feed the poor." After the last speech,

LCFO officials handed the microphone to Carmichael, whose presence was a joyous surprise to everyone. SNCC's chairperson had returned to the area a few days earlier, but police in Selma had arrested him for campaigning for Dallas County's independent black candidates, and no one knew if they would release him before the election. "All that day where I had canvassed people had asked about Stokely, was he out of jail, would he be at the meeting?" reported SNCC volunteer Terence Cannon. Fortunately, SNCC attorneys secured his release just in time for him to attend the event.[61]

"It is so good to be home," said Carmichael, who was genuinely happy to be back. "We have worked so long for this. We have worked so hard for the right to come together and organize. We have been beaten, killed and forced out of our houses. But tonight says that we were right!" They had accomplished what everyone had assumed was impossible, he said. "Colored people have come together tonight. They said that niggers can't come together. Tonight says that we can come together, and we can rock this whole country from California to New York City!" Sensing the irony of their unique political situation, he pointed out that the "big shot Negroes" didn't have "anybody to vote for," but that they had "somebody." "We told them we knew what we were doing. We told them we were smart enough to do for ourselves. And all those school teachers in Lowndes County who told us we were stupid and uneducated, who are they going to vote for tomorrow?" He reminded them that more was at stake than simply having their own candidates: "When we pull that lever we pull it for all the blood of Negroes that the whites have spilled. We will pull that lever to stop the beating of Negroes by whites. We will pull that lever for all the black people who have been killed. We are going to resurrect them tomorrow. We will pull that lever so that our children will never go through what we have gone through. We don't need education—all we need is the will, the courage, and the love in our hearts." Their struggle had transformed the county, he explained. "Lowndes County used to be called the Devil's Backyard. Now it's God's Little Acre." It was a source of inspiration for the entire Black Belt: "We will open the eyes of all the black people in Alabama. We're saying to them, come to Lowndes County and we will show you how! We are telling them—you don't have to depend on a cracker like Wallace. We are not non-violent. We are not saying to whites—we are going to hit you over the head. We are saying—you stop hitting us." Absolute racial solidarity was important but not essential: "There are some who are not with us. When Moses crossed the Red Sea he left some people behind.

We are going to leave some Uncle Toms behind." Carmichael was in classic form. He was awash in the energy of the moment, but his excitement about the present did not cause him to lose sight of the past:

> We have a lot to remember when we pull that lever. We remember when we paid ten dollars for a schoolbook for our children. We remember all the dust we ate. We are pulling the lever to stop that! When we pull that lever we remember the buckets of water we pulled, because we have no running water. We are pulling the lever so people can live in some fine brick homes. We are going to say goodbye to shacks, dirt roads, poor schools. We say to those who don't remember—you better remember, because if you don't, move on over, [or] we are going to move on over you![62]

The crowd cheered and showered Carmichael with handshakes and hugs as he made his way through the sanctuary. He had given voice to their passion, anger, fear, and determination as only he could. More than that, his words bolstered their courage. The day of reckoning was on them, not just for the previous year's work, but also for several generations of struggle, and he had just made plain what was at stake. Hulett understood this and brought the meeting to a close, but not before issuing a final set of instructions. He told the volunteers to arrive at the polls one hour before they opened. "We'll be there at seven," he said. He also instructed them to dress their best: "Let's dress up and look like people when we go to the polls tomorrow." "Only a John Hulett could have said that and not been misunderstood," said Carmichael.[63]

LCFO supporters could not have asked for a more pleasant day to vote, a sign perhaps that the Lord walked with them. As instructed by Hulett, the volunteers began making their way to the polls soon after sunrise, as did scores of black voters who either wanted to vote before going to work or simply were too anxious to wait. The latter arrived in pairs, small groups, or alone. Some even came with children in tow. Those who owned cars drove, while those who did not walked at least far enough to flag down a carpool shuttle or to hitch a ride with a passing black motorist. Underneath the ordinary sweaters and overcoats that they wore to ward off the crisp morning air, they sported their sharpest dresses and finest suits, having taken to heart the charge to look their best. Once at the polls they instinctively lined up. Although they did not know what to expect, almost everyone stayed in line. At this point, there was no turning back.[64]

African Americans in Lowndes County line up to vote, many for the first time, in the November 8, 1966, general election. © Jim Peppler.

The morning belonged to the LCFO as African Americans flocked to the polls in numbers far greater than whites. The favorable early turnout coupled with the absence of violence buoyed people's spirits and steeled their resolve. "I don't know if we'll win, [but] I know we will keep on fighting," said an eighty-five-year-old woman after pulling the lever for the Black Panther. "If I'm beaten I'll know I was whipped fighting."[65] The promising beginning did not cause party organizers to lower their guard. Carmichael, for one, remained in the field. He spent the entire day criss-crossing the county in his car, shouting, "Did you vote right?" to the black people he came across, and no doubt flashing his trademark toothy grin every time someone hollered back, "Sure did!" For his trouble, he was shot at as he left a service station in Fort Deposit.[66]

Around midday, the tide started to turn. Suddenly, more and more whites began appearing at the polls, spurred by news of the strong African American turnout. At the same time, plantation owners began hauling black workers to the polls with instructions to vote for the white candidates marked on the sample ballots that they had given them. Outside several voting sites, white loiterers started threatening African Americans, while inside they began "helping" them. Reports of these and other irregularities began flowing back to LCFO headquarters at an alarming rate. "Get over to Precinct 7, trouble there. Not letting our poll-watchers observe everything. Whites going in booths with Negroes," read one report. "Get up to Hayneville right away. Intimidating our people outside," read another. Still another said, "Precinct 5 needs more 'helpers' badly. See what can be done."[67] Though losing ground quickly, a remarkable number of poll watchers chose not to retreat. In the smoky backroom of the Jack Portis Store, which doubled as the Burkeville polling site, three black women, armed only with pads and clipboards, refused to abandon their post even after a white official threw out a movement lawyer. It must have taken every ounce of courage they could muster not to turn and run. By staying put, they cast a long shadow of doubt on the legitimacy of white authority. "[By] their mere presence they were challenging the very foundations of white power," observed Carmichael.[68]

Most polls opened and closed without serious incident. "Lowndes whites 'played it cool' and abstained from excessive violence [to] avoid investigation by outsiders," reported SNCC's Cleveland Sellers.[69] In Fort Deposit, however, things turned violent just before the end of the day. Whites had been intimidating African Americans and harassing LCFO monitors all afternoon, but they had not assaulted anyone until Andrew Jones, a fifty-two-year-old resident of Fort Deposit, arrived to pick up black poll watchers Clara McMeans and Bobbie Jean Goldsmith. As he stepped out of his station wagon, he heard someone say, "Andrew, what the hell are you doing here?" Before he could respond, a savage blow to the back of his head buckled his knees. As he fell, he grabbed one of the white men who had surrounded him, but he lost his grip after being clubbed a second time. Semiconscious and defenseless, his assailants began beating him with pistol handles, rifle butts, and a tire chain. Jones's sixteen-year-old daughter, Annie, witnessed the attack, and her cries caught the attention of a nearby group of SNCC volunteers who knew instantly that one of their own was in trouble. Without hesitating, they threw open the trunk of their car, divvied up a stash of handguns, and hustled to the scene, but they quickly realized that they were grossly outmanned and outgunned, so they kept their weapons out of sight. Fortunately, a newly appointed, non-movement, black deputy who observed the assault from a distance approached the mob just as someone raised a rifle to Jones's head. The deputy did not attempt to arrest anyone but his presence caused the hostile crowd to pause just long enough for the SNCC workers to retrieve Jones's limp body and hurry out of town.[70] "Mr. Jones was the last person I thought they'd try to get," said Carmichael after learning of the attack. "He's one of the toughest men in the county."[71] Indeed, Jones had chosen to remain in Fort Deposit even after receiving death threats for refusing to campaign for white Democrats. If whites were bold enough to go after him, then no one was safe. Realizing this, the party sent armed guards to the homes of LCFO activists, a show of force that very likely deterred additional violence that night.

Voting ended at six o'clock, and shortly thereafter fatigued poll watchers began trickling into party headquarters with harrowing accounts of the day's events and with precinct totals. As they submitted their numbers, office workers kept a tally on the chalkboard that occupied most of one wall. Despite reports of fraud and a late surge in white voter participation, many people clung to the thin thread of hope that the party would still win. But it did not take long for everyone to realize that victory was not to be. In the end, the chalkboard showed that the black candidates had lost to their white rivals by margins ranging from three hundred to six hundred votes.[72]

The reasons for the LCFO's defeat are clear. Although black registered voters outnumbered white registered voters, about 20 percent of the black electorate, or roughly six hundred African Americans, stayed home on Election Day, negating African Americans' numerical advantage. A great many people avoided the polls out of fear of white violence. Even those who contained their concerns about racial terrorism long enough to make the trip to the polls sometimes fled after seeing gun-toting whites congregated outside. "In one area we had a large number of people who walked

around with guns on their sides, who wasn't deputies, who wasn't [offi-
cially authorized] to carry these guns, some even had shotguns who stood
there by the polls," recalled Hulett. "When the people turned out to the
polls and seeing these people standing by, they returned to their homes,
did not vote at all."[73] Quite a few people stayed away because they feared
eviction. "Most people who live on the white people's land were afraid to
vote for the freedom organization's candidates because they'd get thrown
off their land," explained Alice Moore.[74] Those who worried about eviction did so with good reason. Hundreds of people had lost their homes
since the movement started, and after the election white property owners evicted scores more. Still others feared economic retaliation. A retired
teacher abstained from voting after school officials told her that she would
forfeit her pension if she did. There were also those who feared having
their votes stolen. "Many people stayed away from the polls because they
could not vote freely," said movement leader Lillian McGill. Rather than
"vote against themselves," they opted not to vote at all.[75]

White chicanery also reduced the number of black ballots cast. Election officials assigned half the county's black voters to polling places in
precincts far from their homes. Many occupants of the same household
had to vote at sites at opposite ends of the county, while others had to
check voter lists at several polling places before finding their assigned site;
quite a few never did figure out where they were supposed to go. The situation caused great confusion.[76]

Black nonparticipation, though, was not enough to seal the fate of the
Black Panther. As expected, whites voted as a solid racial bloc, but this
still did not give them enough votes to carry the election. White candidates needed black votes, and they received a fair share. Election returns
indicate that some four hundred African Americans voted against the
third-party candidates.[77] Many of these voters, particularly those who
were black professionals, did so willingly. Maggie Connors was not one
of them—she supported the LCFO. "I pulled the lever 'till the black cat
howled," she said to a reporter on Election Day. But Mrs. Connors knew
several people who opposed the party. When she spotted a teacher whom
she suspected of voting against the Black Panther, she quipped, "I'll bet
the rooster crowed when she voted."[78] The black elite had not supported
the LCFO before the election and made no secret afterward that they had
not experienced a last-minute change of heart. "I don't believe in going
the third-party route," said a local black landowner. "It's a foolish thing
to do."[79]

Anecdotal evidence suggests that an even greater number of African Americans cast ballots for white candidates unwillingly. Coercion was partly implicit; African Americans understood white expectations and for many people meeting these expectations was critical to their survival. They neither had to be told to vote for white candidates nor physically compelled. The U.S. Civil Rights Commission concluded in a report about the election that the totality of white "economic domination in the region, together with a history of racial violence, infects the entire political process . . . There is no need for the white landowner or the white employer to direct the Negro sharecropper or worker not to run for office, not to vote, or to vote only for the white candidates favored by the landowner. In many cases, the Negro worker knows what his white landlord or boss wants him to do and naturally conforms." Speaking for rural black people across the South, an African American brick mason from North Carolina said, "You just know what you are supposed to do and what you are not supposed to do."[80]

Even more African Americans voted for white candidates as a direct result of physical intimidation. In Fort Deposit, Sandy Ridge, and Braggs, plantation owners ordered black workers into trucks, drove them to the polls, hurried them inside, handed them completed sample ballots, and told them to vote for the white candidates marked on the sheets. Some who arrived on their own were given no choice but to accept "help" from white election officials. Others struggled to keep their ballot selections a secret. "Some white men would open the curtains with their hand, and look into the booth while the Negroes were voting," explained one black voter.[81]

Organizing shortcomings also contributed to the party's defeat. Several polling sites, including Sandy Ridge where sheriff Frank Ryals made his home, did not have any black poll watchers. At other locations, LCFO workers left early, failed to challenge white voters, or stopped taking notes when ordered to do so by whites. The carpool worked well, but there was neither enough time, nor enough cars, to transport everyone who needed a ride. In addition, the political education program, as innovative and dynamic as it was, did not reach every black voter. Having to vote twice, first in the nomination convention and again in the general election, confused some people, while voting protocol and voting machines baffled others. "We weren't really prepared," said Hulett. "We thought we was but we wasn't."[82]

The defeat was tremendously disappointing. Party supporter James Jones, who lived in Lowndesboro, captured the prevailing sentiment when he told a reporter that losing to whites made him "sick."[83] Nevertheless,

African Americans retained their fighting spirit. "Even though we lost, the people have strong confidence," said Hulett.[84] Their resolve stemmed from the LCFO's impressive showing. The upstart party received 80 percent of the black vote and 42 percent of the total vote, a remarkable achievement considering the degree of black political exclusion that had existed locally and the willingness of whites to use intimidation and fraud to stay in power. Moreover, this was not just a moral victory. The strong showing meant that the state would recognize the LCFO as an official political party. The Black Panther was here to stay.

The election of 1966 revealed the potential of freedom politics to supplant the usual undemocratic politics. The vast majority of black voters embraced the new political culture that the party represented. They welcomed the LCFO's commitment to democratic decision making and its de-emphasis on professional qualifications as prerequisites for running for office. They also approved of its populist platform. They rallied behind the idea that they could tax the rich to feed the poor. African Americans now had a blueprint for future political practice. They had a way to achieve political power without compromising their commitment to freedom rights.

The significance of the LCFO's impressive performance was not lost on SNCC organizers. "November 8, 1966, made one thing clear: some day black people will control the government of Lowndes County," said Carmichael. They also understood that the election's significance extended far beyond the county line. "Lowndes is not merely a section of land and a group of people, but an idea whose time has come," explained Carmichael.[85] That idea—the development of independent political parties to enable African Americans to engage in electoral politics in ways that placed the people's interests ahead of everything else—was one of the key political developments of the post–Voting Rights Act era. It sparked the push to develop a national network of independent black parties that resulted in the formation of a statewide third party in Alabama and inspired a series of national black political conventions in the early 1970s.

The election's broader significance also relates to its influence on Black Power. SNCC's version of Black Power was not an empty slogan devoid of programmatic meaning that surfaced spontaneously during the Meredith march. On the contrary, it referred to a concrete organizing program for black political empowerment that grew out of the joint efforts of rural black southerners and SNCC organizers to democratize the South. It was a product of "the ferment of agitation and activity by different people and organizers in black communities over the years," said Carmichael. The freedom struggle in Lowndes County was particularly influential. "SNCC's Alabama experience was the immediate genesis of the concept of Black Power," wrote Invanhoe Donaldson, director of SNCC's New York office.[86] Indeed, the Lowndes Project gave final form and full meaning to Black Power. Moreover, the permanent establishment of an independent political party made the Lowndes Project SNCC's most successful Black Power undertaking. Unfortunately, the web of misinformation that black moderates and white liberals spun about Black Power became a part of the standard civil rights narrative and caused most people to lose sight of the organizing experiences that led SNCC to demand Black Power. It also led people to overlook the connection between Black Power and SNCC's third-party program.

Black Power was just as important to the forward progress of the Lowndes movement as the local struggle was to the development of the ideology. Had SNCC organizers never introduced Black Power—with its emphasis on third-party politics and black consciousness—there never would have been an LCFO. Undoubtedly, African Americans would have continued to fight for freedom rights, but the ways in which they agitated and organized would have been noticeably different. It is also unlikely that they would have attained the same degree of political sophistication. Thus, neither the Lowndes movement nor Black Power can be fully understood outside of the symbiotic relationship that existed between them, which reached full maturity during the turbulent summer of 1966.

After the election, local leaders continued to organize. Although the defeat was a sobering reminder of who still held the reins of power, it also underscored the need to carry on. In the coming years, African Americans enjoyed their greatest success in electoral politics. But electing their own to public office did not mean that the movement had succeeded. There was a very real difference between black political visibility and black political power. For African Americans to reap the benefits of controlling the local government, black elected officials had to fight effectively for freedom rights.

7

Now Is the Time for Work to Begin
Black Politics in the Post–Civil Rights Era

They started arriving in Hayneville early that morning and they never stopped coming. As many as two thousand people from every corner of Lowndes County and from as far away as Detroit converged on the county seat. By noon, they had taken over the town square, which proudly displayed a stone memorial to the fallen heroes of the Confederacy. As they waited for the swearing-in ceremony to begin, they reminisced with friends and family about the struggles of the past and discussed the future, which looked considerably brighter in the wake of the election of the county's first black sheriff a few months earlier in November 1970. Perhaps the next time they gathered in Hayneville for an inauguration they would not need armed black men to guard them as they did that afternoon.

The ceremony began promptly at 1:30 p.m. inside the courthouse. More than four hundred people squeezed into the upper level of the century-old building to witness history, but hardly any white people were among them. Local whites avoided Hayneville completely that Saturday. The lone exception was probate judge Harrell Hammonds, who agreed to administer the oath of office as a gesture of gratitude for the support he received from African Americans during the recent election. After a succession of activists addressed the crowd, John Hulett placed his hand on a Bible and swore to enforce and uphold the law as the county sheriff. Hulett had been on the front line of the freedom struggle for six years and understood better than most the significance of the moment. His victory was not the end of the fight for freedom rights—rather, it was the start of an important new phase. "Now is the time for work to begin," he told the jubilant crowd.[1]

Hulett's election raised the expectations of the county's black residents, and their heightened hopes prompted them to make electoral politics their chief concern. This decision also reflected their faith in black elected officials. But in order for black officeholders to make a difference, they had to find a way to undue deeply embedded structural impediments to racial equality. White supremacy was not merely a manifestation of racist attitudes and discriminatory behavior. It was also a product of long-standing institutional arrangements that generally fell beyond the control of local officials. Alabama law, for instance, made it virtually impossible for local officials to raise property taxes to increase county school board budgets. Yet local officials were not completely powerless. By allocating their limited resources judiciously, they could keep some conditions from becoming worse and even improve others. Whether they would do so, however, was an entirely different matter.

OEO director Sargent Shriver finally released the funds for the Lowndes County Self-Help Housing and Job Training Program in November 1966. His decision came only a few weeks after the defeat of the Black Panther candidates and energized local activists. The leaders of the LCCMHR quickly hired thirty-four-year-old D. Robert Smith, a Connecticut native who worked for the Tuskegee Institute Community Education Program (TICEP), to serve as the program's director. They turned to Smith in large part because he met the strict educational requirements that the OEO had set for the position. Movement leaders also leased an old Episcopal church on the outskirts of Hayneville to serve as the program's headquarters. The abandoned church was in pitiful shape, but it was the best that they could do. Coley Coleman, the white shopkeeper who owned the building, was the only property owner in town willing to rent to them. Volunteers began renovating the church in January 1967. At the same time, adult education classes began in Ash Creek and Calhoun. More than one hundred people, all of whom lived below the poverty line (earning less than one thousand dollars annually) and tested at or below a sixth-grade literacy level, enrolled in the classes. This was their first chance to get ahead in life. "I am taking the courses so that I can do better by my children—get a better job," said Bessie McMeans. "I have nine children. Maybe at the end there will be something better for me." Nothing was guaranteed, but everyone was hopeful.[2]

The participants made tremendous progress during the first few months of 1967, and so did the volunteers working on the church. By early March, the renovation was nearly complete. But the volunteers did not get to enjoy the fruit of their labor. Just before dawn on Sunday, March 12, an

Man sifts through the ruins of the LCCMHR poverty program headquarters in Hayneville, which was destroyed by an arsonist on March 12, 1967. Photo by Louis H. Anderson/Courtesy of Estizer Smith.

arsonist set the old church ablaze. The fire burned for half the day, reducing the building to a smoldering heap of rubble. That evening, the LCC- MHR held a mass meeting at Macedonia Baptist Church in Fort Deposit. Everyone was upset, including Robert L. Strickland, chairperson of the LCCMHR Poverty Program Committee. When he addressed the crowd, he reassured the people that the program would continue. His words buoyed their spirits and strengthened their resolve. They left the meeting believing that tomorrow would be better, but it wasn't. Macedonia Baptist Church burned early the next morning.[3]

SNCC chairperson Stokely Carmichael put the attacks into context. "The bombing and burning of black churches in the American south has become one of the traditional methods used by white racists to show their contempt and hatred of black people who dare to protest the inhuman degradation and humiliation to which we have been constantly subjected for the past 400 years," he wrote. "That this method has the approval of white America and its power structure is best exemplified by

the continued refusal of the federal government, FBI, and state and local police authorities to deal with this situation and make even minimal
efforts to apprehend the perpetrators of such atrocities and bring them
to justice."[4] No one was ever arrested for torching the churches. Nor was
anyone ever arrested for setting fire to Good Hope Presbyterian Church,
an all-white church in Benton, which went up in flames one week after
the black churches burned. The state fire marshal identified arson as the
likely cause, but movement people insisted that lightning was to blame,
a thinly veiled but unsubstantiated claim of responsibility. Who or what
started the fire remained a mystery. But no more churches burned.[5]

People filled every pew of Gordonsville's Mt. Moriah Baptist Church
on Sunday, March 19, 1967, the day after the fire at Good Hope, to com-
memorate the second anniversary of the LCCMHR's founding. It was supposed to be a joyous occasion, and to a certain extent it was. The people
had a lot to celebrate, including the creation of the Black Panther Party.
But the recent fires were on everyone's mind. Since the attacks, the county
had become much more dangerous. Among other things, there had been
a spike in police harassment. The people, however, refused to be intimidated. "There's going to be some trouble if people keep up that kind of
stuff," said Strickland. They also remained focused. That afternoon, they
recommitted themselves to fighting for freedom rights.[6]

Local activists fought on several fronts in 1967. Foremost, they held
their ground on the poverty program. Less than two weeks after the headquarters burned, they moved a fifty-foot trailer onto the site to serve as
a temporary operations center. Unlike before, armed guards stood sen-
try at night. They also launched a campaign to raise twenty-five thousand
dollars to construct a permanent building. Soon they expanded the adult
education offerings, adding classes on home economics and housing construction. The classes ran through the end of the summer and made a real
difference in people's lives. "When I first came here, I couldn't do no good
writing at all," said Joe Frank Taylor. "Now I can do a lot." The classes
have "benefited everybody out here," said another program participant.[7]

Those who participated in the housing construction classes put their
new skills to work immediately by building new homes for the residents
of Tent City, many of whom had lived in the makeshift camp for a full
year. They built the homes on one-acre plots that the evictees had purchased with the help of one-hundred-dollar grants from the LCCMHR.
With the residents of Tent City resettled, the construction class participants, along with other movement supporters, began clearing the site to

build a cooperative grocery store and service station. The Lowndes County Co-op, a black economic development group started by local movement leader Elzie McGill, sponsored the venture. "Our plans are large, but we have to start small for financial reasons," said William Cosby, the co-op's treasurer. To finance the new businesses, the co-op sold common stock at twenty-five dollars a share and preferred stock, with a guaranteed higher dividend, for slightly more. Although fundraising was slow, movement leaders expected to break ground by the end of the year.[8]

Local activists also rallied around black students to ensure that whites treated them fairly at their new schools. At Hayneville High School, which used to be the county's flagship white high school, black students found classroom equality elusive. In June 1967, the school's white administrators held back sixty black students, fully half the black student population. "We went to see Hulda Coleman and asked why our kids aren't passing," explained Frank Miles, Jr., at a mass meeting. "Mrs. Coleman said that Hayneville High School kids are 'not interested in going on.' Mrs. Coleman told us that some kind of achievement tests were given, and the kids didn't pass them. But what I want to know is how a kid who was making A's and B's until last week comes up flunking. I know lots of kids worked hard." Someone else said, "I think these white people are trying to get the high school back for themselves, so they won't need a private school. That private school is costing somebody money."[9] Conflict between black students and white teachers continued in the fall, prompting Hulett and several others to pen an open letter to Superintendent Coleman documenting, among other things, beatings with switches. Coleman responded by inviting movement leaders to discuss the issues raised in the letter. "We'll be glad to send someone up there to talk with her," said Hulett. "But it doesn't do any good. We've been up there on other things, and nothing was ever done."[10]

The year ended sourly with a leadership struggle within the poverty program. Internal conflict first surfaced during the summer when director D. Robert Smith agreed to build the new headquarters on land owned by Coley Coleman and to deed the building to him after a few years. Smith made the deal without consulting the poverty program board, whose members wanted to rebuild in the black community. "Don't think that Mr. Coleman is our friend just because he rented the building to us," said board member Frank Miles, Jr. "We know how white people in Hayneville treat us."[11] The board eventually voided the contract. A second dustup occurred over the proposal for the 1968 program. The board invited local activists to help draft the document, but Smith objected to their participation, believing that a hard line should be drawn between the poverty program and political activism. He said as much to W. P. Painter, an Alabama state trooper assigned to investigate the poverty program, when the two met privately to discuss local happenings. "There are some people in the county who have a difficult time distinguishing between civil rights and a poverty program, but we have come to an agreement," he told the state investigator.¹² Smith's decision to meet with Painter cost him the trust of movement people, and eventually cost him his job. In September 1967, the board asked him to resign, citing a loss of confidence in his leadership. Smith refused to step down, and some within the movement supported him. Alice Moore, the former LCFO candidate for tax assessor and the director of the Calhoun poverty center, found no fault with Smith's leadership. "So far as I'm concerned, due to Mr. Smith's administration, seems like the program's moving on," she said. "He runs it like he has the trainees at heart."¹³ Smith, though, resigned in November. Louis H. Anderson, the poverty program's finance officer, replaced him. Anderson worked closely with the board, and during the next year he managed an expanded program effectively.¹⁴

Local activists turned their attention back to politics at the beginning of 1968. Hulett led the way, crisscrossing the county, usually by himself but often with a partner, encouraging African Americans to register. He logged so many hours knocking on doors and driving people to the courthouse that a close associate joked that his wife "doesn't know him" anymore. Some three thousand African Americans remained unregistered, and getting them on the voter rolls was critical. The LCFP planned to run candidates for the school board, the county commission, and the justice of the peace in 1968. To have a chance at victory, they needed several hundred more votes than their predecessors received, and these votes had to come from African Americans because whites remained firm in their opposition to the party. With this in mind, Hulett and LCFP leaders ratcheted up the canvassing effort by sending more volunteers into the field.¹⁵

The voter registration campaign mirrored earlier efforts. Elzie McGill explained that local leaders instructed the canvassers to encourage people to register and "get them to understand what the vote means." There was, however, one glaring difference—the absence of SNCC field secretaries. SNCC as an organization withdrew from Lowndes County shortly after the 1966 general election. The decision to leave was not easy. SNCC field secretaries had become webbed into the black community. For activists such as Bob Mants, the fate of local people was inextricably linked to their own. At the same time, they had accomplished what they had set out to do—they had organized "Bloody Lowndes." African Americans now had an effective social movement organization dedicated specifically to fighting for freedom rights, and an independent political party recognized by the state. "Our way is to live in the community, find, train, or develop representative leadership within strong, accountable local organizations or coalitions that did not exist before, and that are capable of carrying on the struggle after we leave," explained Carmichael. "When we succeed in this, we will work ourselves out of a job. Which is our goal."[16] Having achieved their primary aim, it was time to move on.

There was also a very practical reason for sncc's departure. The organization wanted to expand its third party–organizing program beyond Lowndes County, but it did not have enough experienced field secretaries to shepherd multiple communities through the long process of party building. Its staff had shrunk to about one hundred people, less than half the size it was two years earlier. People left for a variety of reasons. Some drifted away, victims of battle fatigue; some were pulled into other struggles, both inside and outside of the movement; and some were forced out. Whites are often lumped into the last group, but far more faded from sight for personal reasons or voluntarily joined the student and antiwar movements than were ever asked to leave. sncc's dwindling numbers made it impractical, if not impossible, for the organization to maintain its presence in Lowndes County and develop a national network of grassroots third parties. And soon it became hard for sncc to do anything. In the wake of its public opposition to the Vietnam War and its call for Black Power, financial donations slowed to a trickle, making it extremely difficult for the organization to cover its operating expenses. Simultaneously, both the federal government, through the fbi's domestic counterintelligence program, and several state governments, through their various police agencies, sought to destroy the organization. Local law enforcement, for instance, repeatedly arrested sncc organizers on trumped-up charges such as conspiracy to incite riot or provoke insurrection. The sharp increase in government repression, combined with the rapid evaporation of sncc's meager resources, stripped the organization of its capacity to grow and slowly robbed it of its ability to organize. Although its members never lost the will to organize, by 1968 sncc was a shell of its former self in terms of staff size and viable projects.[17]

Local movement activists owed SNCC organizers a tremendous debt. "Nobody ever [came] to us and done for us what Snick workers done," said Hulett. "And people was afraid to let 'em come in their homes, so they walked the streets. This is the first time in our history Negroes can go to the courthouse and talk loud. And when we got scared and talked real weak, the Snick boys with us took it up and talked real loud."[18] Although indebted to SNCC organizers, local activists were not dependent on them. "Stokely came down and told us how to do good," said Frank Miles, Jr. "He didn't want to take over or run us. We're independent. He told us to take what we could use from what he gave us, and leave the rest."[19] This did not mean that African Americans wanted to proceed without SNCC's help. "If we had an opportunity to have a SNCC crew like we once had, I'd be welcoming them back," said local leader Lillian McGill.[20] But they understood why SNCC organizers, particularly Carmichael, moved on. "It was just like Moses left Egypt. He had to go somewhere else," said student activist John Jackson. "They say [Carmichael's] a God-sent man and there's other work for him to do, and that he's opened our eyes and now it's time for us to do something for ourselves."[21] Mathew Jackson, Sr., John's father, said "the people really felt like he had a bigger job to do, a bigger job somewhere else; and he felt like, after hearing our people discuss this thing . . . that we'd be able to go on out on our own. Then he could go some other place and help those people."[22]

The absence of SNCC organizers did not reduce the people's commitment to freedom politics. Educating eligible voters, a hallmark of freedom politics, remained as important to LCFP leaders as registering them. Throughout 1967, they discussed the responsibilities of local officials at weekly mass meetings and made a special point of de-emphasizing political experience, wealth, and whiteness as prerequisites for holding office. They also conducted political education workshops patterned after the sessions that SNCC activists once organized. They placed a greater emphasis on the duties of poll watchers and election clerks, however, in order to guard against the kind of Election Day fraud that contributed to the defeat of black candidates in 1966. "If [African Americans] are going to be using somebody to assist them, they [will know to] use some of their own people [or to] use the officials who definitely don't go along with the [Democratic] party," said Hulett. They also took care to explain how to cast a split-ticket ballot so that movement supporters could vote for LCFP nominees in local contests and for moderate white Democrats in state races. "Most people were confused about this," said Hulett. "There were many people who thought that they could go out and just vote for one [party. Now] they won't be confused when they go to the polls on Election Day."²³

Victory, however, was far from a sure thing. The outcome of the 1967 ASCS election underscored the difficulty of winning public office. Despite a spirited effort, African Americans managed to elect just three black farmers to ASCS community committees that fall, all from the same neighborhood. "In this community, most of us own our own farms," said R. C. Mays, one of the farmers who prevailed. "In other communities, they are tenants—the man says, 'vote for me or you're off the land.'" It was the same old problem—the immobilizing effect of fear.²⁴

Despite the disappointing showing in the ASCS contest, several people stepped forward in the early months of 1968 to run as LCFP candidates in that year's general election. All of them were veteran activists, folk willing to do what others were still too afraid to do. Jesse Favors, who participated in the first voter registration attempt in March 1965, decided to run for justice of the peace. Charles Smith, who succeeded Hulett as the chairperson of the LCCMHR in December 1965, accepted the nomination to run for county commission. And John Hinson, who ran for office in 1966, chose to run again for the school board. Each candidate's distinguished record of challenging white supremacy earned him the support of the movement community.²⁵

In the spring of 1968, party officials submitted the names of the nominees to probate judge Harrell Hammonds in accordance with state law. When they delivered the list, however, they made an unusual request: they asked the judge to refrain from publishing the names until the fall, hoping that this would limit their exposure to reprisals. "Our people have been subjected to a great deal of intimidation," explained Hulett.²⁶ Although Alabama law required the judge to identify those running for office immediately, Hammonds honored the request, a decision that pleased the black community but infuriated the white community.

Hammonds was one of the wealthiest people in Lowndes County, but that had not always been the case. The fifty-one-year-old judge was born "a poor country boy," as he liked to say. His luck changed when he met and married Mary Dora Norman, whose father, a large landowner in the Fort Deposit area, started him in ranching and plantation farming. By 1950, Hammonds was a successful businessperson with a countywide reputation for industriousness. That same year, governor James "Big Jim" Folsom appointed him probate judge to complete the unexpired term of the recently deceased Robert Woodruff, the former sheriff who led the bloody suppression of the sharecroppers' strike in 1935. The appointment was Hammonds's reward for supporting "Big Jim" in the governor's race.[27]

As probate judge, Hammonds occupied the most lucrative office in county government. Probate judges had a long history of manipulating public records and exploiting privileged information to accumulate wealth. When they purchased land, they sometimes neglected to transfer the deeds, which allowed them to avoid paying taxes on their acquisitions. On other occasions, they failed to advertise public auctions and bought land that had been confiscated for delinquent taxes at below-market rates. A review of local tax records dating back to mid-century conducted by the Lowndes County tax assessor in the 1980s revealed that Judge Hammonds, after several decades in office, benefited tremendously from such schemes.[28]

Many members of the white elite resented Hammonds for holding the county's most profitable public office for so long, and their envy prompted them to keep him at arm's length. The fact that he did not descend from old money, but instead married into his wealth, provided a socially acceptable justification for snubbing him. Hammonds was well aware of his outsider status and knew that others coveted his job. "There's a privileged few down here that think they ought to rule the world," he said.[29] So he built a base of support among working-class whites by using his wealth and authority as probate judge to secure their votes. He routinely paid county and state permit fees for people short on cash and made sure to remind them of such favors before each election. He was an astute politician who mastered the art of turning the personal into the political. Nevertheless, his hold on the judgeship was tenuous. Every six years the white elite trotted out someone else for the county's top spot. In 1964, they rallied behind Republican Tommy Coleman. Although Hammonds defeated his opponent by a margin of two to one, he was growing increasingly concerned about his ability to stay in office. His worries opened his eyes to the potential of the emerging black electorate and prompted him to begin courting this new voting bloc. His decision to withhold the list of Black Panther candidates was his attempt at bridge building.[30]

The white elite viewed the judge's refusal to release the names of the LCFP nominees completely differently. To them, it was an unconscionable act of racial disloyalty, and they pilloried him for his lack of white solidarity. The editor of the county weekly initiated the assault by publishing a derisive column impugning his character. Others harassed him and his wife with threatening telephone calls. The war of words reached new heights when twenty-two of his cattle turned up dead. "Somebody put enough poison in six troughs to kill six hundred head," said Hammonds. To make matters worse, the white elite renewed plans to dethrone him in 1970.[31]

Despite pressure from local whites and the Alabama attorney general, Hammonds refused to disclose the names of the LCFP nominees until late August 1968. The delay prevented whites from harassing the black candidates during the summer, but it did not change the outcome of the fall election. In November 1968, the LCFP candidates lost to their Democratic rivals by some six hundred votes, roughly the same margin as in 1966. The reasons for the defeat were similar to those that caused the party to lose two years earlier. Although there was no violence on Election Day, white officials harassed many black voters, and white landowners and bosses threatened others.[32] The leaders of the LCFP also identified an additional factor—a black backlash against the Black Panther symbol. "The people were afraid [of] the idea of the black panther," said Hulett. They thought that as an all-black party "we were going to be detrimental to people."[33] Many movement outsiders associated the Black Panther with violence. Third-party advocate Alma Miller traced the source of this misperception to negative press coverage of the Oakland-based Black Panther Party for Self-Defense. The national media generally depicted the BPP as a violent band of mischief makers. The local and regional press not only echoed this perspective, but also insisted that the BPP and the LCFP were essentially the same. For those who failed to separate rumor from reality, the roar of the Black Panther sounded like trouble.[34]

Soon after the election, the party's leaders gathered to discuss what they needed to do differently to win in 1970. In addition to voter registration and political education work, they decided to soften the image of the party to appeal to African Americans who remained on the sidelines. Many believed that the only way to do this was to drop the black panther logo, while others argued that simply discarding the ballot symbol was not enough. They maintained that the link between the black panther and the LCFP was so deeply ingrained in people's minds that disassociating the two was impossible. With or without the black panther symbol, African Americans who had not gotten involved in the movement would still view the party as too radical.[35]

The desire to soften the image of the LCFP led the party's leaders to consider merging with the National Democratic Party of Alabama (NDPA). The NDPA was a mostly black, statewide alternative to the Democratic Party that John Cashin, an African American dentist from Huntsville, cofounded with two white activists in 1967. Although the NDPA drew its inspiration from the LCFO, it more closely resembled the MFDP. Not only was its membership interracial, but it officially supported the Democratic Party's national candidates. In 1968, the NDPA ran nearly one hundred people for local, state, and federal office, but without much success. The poor showing convinced Cashin that the party needed to harness the voting strength of the rural Black Belt, so he invited the most celebrated political group in the region to merge with his organization.[36]

Cashin's offer intrigued Lowndes County activists, partly because the leaders of the NDPA shared a commitment to freedom rights. In addition, movement outsiders considered the NDPA less radical than the LCFP because of its interracial membership and its support of the national Democratic Party. Joining the NDPA would also allow local people to become part of a statewide network of political activists, further breaking the isolation of the rural Black Belt. Nevertheless, LCFP officials balked at the overture, fearing that the party would lose its autonomy. Cashin, though, allayed their fears by explaining that he was uninterested in curtailing their independence. "[He] had a tremendous amount of respect for people like Charles Smith [and] John Hulett because [they] were the pioneers in terms of a separate party in the state," said Bill Edwards, the NDPA's executive director.[37] Satisfied with Cashin's assurances, LCFP leaders invited him to address party supporters at a mass meeting. Although Hulett and the others favored a merger, they understood that the decision to join the statewide party was not theirs to make. After Cashin's presentation, the people debated the merits of his proposal and, in the end, decided that joining the NDPA was the right thing to do.[38]

The coming together of the two parties signaled the beginning of a new chapter in local black politics. Never again would a snarling black panther appear on a ballot in Alabama. Joining the NDPA, however, did not guarantee victory in the 1970 election, and no one was more aware of this fact than Hulett. He was sure that the merger would attract more black voters, but he doubted that it would bring in enough people to defeat the Democratic nominees. Hulett's skepticism, combined with his eagerness to elect African Americans to public office, prompted him to make a series of decisions that led him and the movement away from freedom politics.

No incumbent was safe in 1970, especially not Judge Hammonds. That year, his Democratic primary opponent was former sheriff Frank Ryals. Ryals had resigned in 1967 after twelve years in office. The job simply did not pay as well as it used to since the movement curtailed his ability to shakedown African Americans and collect the fees that came with arresting people on bogus charges. As probate judge, however, he could earn a substantial income. Yet he probably would not have challenged Hammonds had the white elite not encouraged him to run. Although Ryals did not come from old money, he was preferable to Hammonds because as sheriff he demonstrated a willingness to defer to his social betters. Ryals was also electable. Support for Hammonds among working-class whites waned considerably following the judge's decision to withhold the names of the Black Panther candidates. At the same time, working-class whites were extremely fond of the former sheriff because of his unwavering commitment to white supremacy.[39]

Hammonds realized that he needed black votes to stave off defeat, so he sought out John Hulett, figuring that the movement's most visible leader would be able to persuade African Americans to participate in the Democratic primary and vote for him. He was also hopeful that Hulett would be able to keep the third party from running a black candidate against him in the general election. In exchange for Hulett's support, Hammonds was prepared to deliver enough white votes in November 1970 for Hulett to become the county's first black sheriff and for African Americans to become circuit clerk and coroner.[40]

The scheme was pure politics designed not only to allow Hammonds to keep his job, but also to increase his power within the local government by providing him with allies in key courthouse positions. Although the judge would not be able to dictate completely the actions of black elected officials, he would have much more influence over them, having helped them win office, than over the white Democratic nominees who opposed his reelection. Among other things, such influence would give him control of the ballot box since the probate judge, the circuit clerk, and the sheriff (or the coroner if the sheriff's office was vacant) supervised local elections. In a county with a long history of Election Day fraud, whoever controlled the ballot box could determine the outcome of almost any election.

Hammonds shared the details of his plan with Hulett during a private meeting at the courthouse. The judge kept the get-together a secret to avoid further eroding his base of white support, and he asked Hulett to do the same. Hulett respected the judge's request and told only his close friend, James Haynes, a vocational education teacher at Lowndes County Training School. Haynes accompanied Hulett to the courthouse and afterward the two men discussed the judge's proposal, deciding whether to accept it.[41]

The judge's plan had pragmatic appeal. They still did not have enough black votes to defeat white candidates, so they needed the white votes that Hammonds offered. They also had too few black votes to unseat the judge in the general election. Even with diminishing white support, Hammonds controlled enough white votes to beat a black challenger because of the sizeable number of black votes he was sure to receive from the hundreds of newly enfranchised tenant farmers living on his land. "Even though he doesn't give them anything they feel that they are kind of dedicated to [him] or they owe him something," said Hulett. Thus, it did not matter who won the Democratic primary for probate judge because a black candidate was unlikely to defeat that person. At the same time, African Americans cared very little for Frank Ryals because of the way he treated people while in office; Hammonds was no saint, but neither was he the devil that many people considered Ryals to be. African Americans, therefore, would presumably vote for Hammonds over Ryals in the primary. They also could do so without jeopardizing the third party's candidate selection process. Unlike 1966, third-party supporters were free to cast crossover ballots because Alabama recognized the NDPA as an official political party. This meant that the NDPA did not have to hold a nomination convention on the same day as the Democratic primary in order for its candidates to qualify for the general election. Finally, the judge's suggestion that Hulett run for sheriff was worth pursuing because Hammonds believed that he could convince his white supporters to vote for him. Although Hulett showed no previous interest in running for public office, he reasoned that if he was the best chance the people had of electing a black sheriff, then it made sense for him to run.

Although pragmatic, the judge's proposal violated a core principle of freedom politics—transparency in the decision-making process. Heeding the judge's call for discretion, Hulett kept the meeting a secret. He also did not disclose the terms of the proposal, perhaps out of deference to Hammonds, but possibly because of objections that other activists might have raised. Either way, his decision not to tell movement people about the meeting or to brief them on the proposal precluded important discussion and debate. The judge's plan also undermined the practice of selecting candidates democratically. Hammonds was willing to back Hulett for sheriff but unwilling to support anyone else, particularly Sidney Logan,

Jr., the Black Panther candidate in 1966 and the people's choice in 1970. By surreptitiously narrowing the third party's electoral options, the judge's scheme allowed exclusivity to seep into black politics.

Hulett was fully aware of the ways in which the judge's proposal contradicted freedom politics, but he decided to accept it anyway, believing that its pragmatic value offset its democratic shortcomings. There is nothing to suggest that Hulett had anything but the best interests of the people in mind when he made his decision. Nevertheless, by accepting the judge's proposal, he set in motion a series of events that caused the movement to unravel.

To uphold his end of the bargain, Hulett began drumming up support for Hammonds' reelection bid. Convincing African Americans to vote for the judge in the Democratic primary was not difficult. Frank Ryals had done nothing since leaving the sheriff's office to change black people's low opinion of him. At the same time, the judge's refusal to release the names of the Black Panther candidates in 1968, coupled with his decision not to evict tenant farmers for registering to vote and his practice of allowing poor people to live in the sharecroppers' shacks on his land rent-free, caused many African Americans to look favorably on him. In fact, these token gestures of human decency earned him a reputation as the "fairest white man in the county," said Lillian McGill.[42]

Some 2,500 African Americans participated in the Democratic primary on May 5, 1970, an unprecedented turnout. As expected, they cast ballots mainly in the race for probate judge, and their participation decided that contest. Whites favored Ryals by more than 500 votes, but African Americans gave Hammonds a landslide victory. When election officials tabulated the results, the judge had defeated the former sheriff by 2,000 votes.[43]

The strong black turnout convinced many within the movement that an African American could unseat Hammonds in November 1970, which made sustaining support for him quite difficult. Nevertheless, Hulett succeeded in persuading third-party supporters not to run a black candidate for probate judge by arguing that despite the impressive primary turnout, the third party still did not have enough black votes to defeat Hammonds. As evidence, he pointed to the sizeable number of non-movement African Americans who voted for the judge in May and who were sure to vote for him again in November. He also argued that supporting the judge would help black candidates in other races secure desperately needed white votes by demonstrating that African Americans were not plotting a revolution.

Ironically, local activists and SNCC organizers criticized this strategy when black professionals in Tuskegee used it several years earlier.[44]

After thwarting the push for a black probate judge, Hulett began hand-picking candidates to run for the other major offices up for election. He convinced Willie Ed McGhee, a member of the board of directors of the poverty program, to run for coroner, and Alma Miller, a recent graduate of Alabama State University, to run for circuit clerk. He turned to them because their movement participation made them electable and because he believed that they would defer to his judgment. He also persuaded Sidney Logan, Jr., not to run for sheriff, but instead to support his own candidacy for that office. He told the World War II veteran that white people would never allow him to win because they were afraid of him—Judge Hammonds had made this point clear. Although Logan wanted to serve, he stepped aside because he wanted African Americans to have a black sheriff even more than he wanted run. Political compromise disguised as political expediency carried the day once again.[45]

As the general election neared, Hammonds quietly encouraged his white supporters to vote for the three black candidates. Meanwhile, his wife, Mary, convinced many of her white friends to do the same by stressing that black elected officials, particularly a black sheriff, would curb their husbands' nefarious sexual escapades in the black community. The whisper campaign worked. On Election Day, about two hundred whites voted for Hulett, McGhee, and Miller. Their votes helped the trio beat the Democratic nominees by margins ranging from 140 to 307 votes. For the first time since Reconstruction, African Americans won prominent government positions.[46]

The 1970 election marked a critical juncture in the African American freedom struggle. Since 1965, movement supporters had worked hard to elect African Americans to public office, believing that this was essential to reducing the gap between the haves and the have-nots. Defeats in 1966 and 1968 tempered their enthusiasm for electoral politics. The outcome of the 1970 contest, however, rekindled their passion and prompted them to make electoral politics their primary focus. It also led them to look to black elected officials to lead the fight for freedom rights. But the inaugural class of black officeholders was not nearly large enough to enact sweeping change. Realizing this, local activists renewed the effort to elect African Americans to every office in the county government.

The push to take over the courthouse began in earnest in 1972. That year, the tax assessor's office, the tax collector's office, and the school superintendent's office were up for grabs. So too were all five seats on the county commission and three of five seats on the school board. The plum prize, though, was the superintendent's office, which Hulda Coleman had held for three decades. The superintendent controlled a multimillion-dollar budget, the largest of any local official, and, under Coleman, enjoyed final say on all policy and personnel matters. For African Americans, controlling the superintendent's office was the best way to ensure that their children received fair treatment and desperately needed educational resources. For whites, controlling the office was the only way to preserve segregation in public education. Although court-ordered desegregation had prompted a couple hundred white children to leave the public schools, more than four hundred, or about two-thirds of the county's white school-age population, remained. Nearly all of them, though, attended a single K-12 school, Lowndes County High School in Fort Deposit, which also employed nearly all the county's white teachers. A handful of black students attended the school, and some black teachers worked there as well, but only enough to keep the county in technical compliance with federal law.[47]

When the 1972 Democratic primary came around, movement activists urged black voters to participate, but this time they asked them to cast their ballots for the white challengers. They believed that black candidates stood a better chance of defeating white opponents who owed their primary win to black votes. The strategy succeeded in eliminating several white incumbents and cleared the way for the third party to field a full slate of black candidates in the general election. But the NDPA's Lowndes County Executive Committee chose to nominate only a partial ticket. The group decided not to run anyone for the third seat on the school board or for the final two seats on the county commission. Hulett was behind this decision. He wielded tremendous influence over the committee and persuaded its members not to field a full slate in order to preserve a second secret agreement with Hammonds. In an attempt to consolidate power, the judge sponsored several of the primary challengers. This group included his wife Mary, who sought one of the school board nominations. None of his candidates, though, could win without black votes, so he promised Hulett that he would finance the campaign of Hulett's choice for superintendent if Hulett convinced African Americans to support his people in the upcoming election.[48]

The executive committee's decision infuriated veteran activists. The third party's main political objective had always been to control the courthouse. The exigencies of 1970 caused the party to set aside this goal in that year's election, but now there was no need to concede anything. By all estimates, the party had enough black votes to win every contest outright. For the sake of unity, the activists acquiesced to the committee's decision. They refused, however, to go along with a second committee recommendation to change the party's candidate selection process. Instead of conducting the usual runoff, the committee wanted to appoint the party's nominees. Once again, Hulett was behind the suggestion. He lobbied for the procedural change in order to guarantee that Uralee Haynes, his choice for superintendent, secured the party's nomination.[49]

Uralee Haynes possessed the professional prerequisites to serve as superintendent, having worked in the county's public schools for twenty-nine years, mostly as an instructor of home economics and English at LCTS. The fifty-year-old teacher was Hulett's choice, however, because of his relationship with her husband, James, his close friend and political confidant. Hulett would have chosen James to run for the office but conventional wisdom suggested that a woman ought to challenge a woman. Besides, James's penchant for strong drink cast doubt on his electability. "Haynes was a night man," recalled his wife, and he made no secret of it.[50]

Although well known and well liked within the black community, Uralee Haynes lacked the movement credentials to ensure a third-party nomination. Like most teachers, she remained on the sidelines when the movement began. She and her husband participated surreptitiously by advising Hulett and making cash donations, but her absence from the front line made her a suspect choice in the eyes of many people, especially because there were plenty of folk, including some teachers, who had been much more visible in the fight for freedom rights. Hulett knew that her candidacy would face stiff opposition, so he tried to subvert the established process for selecting candidates. But his end run failed, blocked by activists whose commitment to democratic decision making remained as strong as ever. It even prompted veteran activists, including William Cosby, a cofounder of the LCCMHR, and John Jackson, the former leader of the student protests at LCTS, to run for office. Three others also challenged Haynes, but Hulett's organizing skills and Hammonds's deep pockets gave her the victory.[51]

Discord over the candidate selection process changed the way that black candidates prepared for the 1972 general election. Instead of campaigning for the third party, many embarked on personal crusades. "They campaigned like white folks," said NDPA executive director Bill Edwards.

"You'd go in that county and out of these eight candidates it seemed like about five or six of them had printed their own bumper stickers, had their own posters."[52] This approach hinted at the emergence of a new kind of black politics, one that placed the interests of individuals ahead of the interests of the people. The controversy also revealed simmering class tension. The merger between the LCFP and the NDPA, combined with Hulett's election as sheriff, led black professionals to increase their involvement in the freedom struggle. At first, veteran activists welcomed their participation, but feelings of goodwill began to evaporate when some of the newcomers started questioning the decision-making ability of poor and working-class people. "They said they had the brains and the know-how to lead the Black masses to complete victory and began calling the shots," explained veteran Detroit organizer Simon Owens.[53] The controversy also unearthed a generational divide. A couple hundred black youth had registered to vote following the ratification of the Twenty-sixth Amendment to the U.S. Constitution in 1971, which lowered the voting age to eighteen, and they were eager to participate in the party. Several even sought third-party nominations. The executive committee, however, was more interested in their votes than in their opinions, a misguided sense of entitlement that cost the party dearly.[54]

Although conflict over the candidate selection process exposed major fault lines within the movement, most people still expected third-party candidates to ride a wave of black votes into office, but only Charles Smith, the former chairperson of the LCCMHR, prevailed. Smith narrowly won a seat on the county commission, beating his Democratic opponent by a mere eighteen votes. Had a white Republican not split the white vote, he too would have lost by a couple hundred votes.[55]

Low black voter turnout was largely responsible for the party's poor showing. Alienation kept countless young people away from the polls. They were "so fed up with the mess that they did not vote," said activist Simon Owens. Frustration stemming from the candidate selection uproar prompted working-class African Americans to avoid the voting booths. "The grass roots people stayed home in disgust," explained Owens.[56] In addition, traditional campaigning failed to energize the party's base. The emphasis on individual candidates rather than on the people, the platform, and the party left many people uninterested in the election. Meanwhile, the absence of political education workshops and regular mass meetings left others unprepared. Voting fraud also contributed to the disappointing outcome. Party leaders dropped their guard on Election Day, thinking that the black poll workers appointed by Judge Hammonds, Sheriff Hulett, and Circuit Clerk Miller could manage the situation, but "quite a bit of shit" occurred, said party leader Bill Edwards, including the dismissal of black poll watchers by the white people they had replaced.[57] Black support for white candidates played an equally important role in the party's dismal performance. Some African Americans voted for white candidates purely out of fear. Public school employees, for instance, knew that they could lose their jobs if they did not support Superintendent Coleman. Others voted for whites for the same reasons that led many to spurn Black Panther candidates in earlier elections, including their lack of faith in the ability of African Americans to fulfill the duties of elected office.[58]

Infighting and overconfidence caused the third party to squander an excellent opportunity. "We had the ball and sure were moving downfield, deep in their territory. But we fumbled it away and [whites] have recovered it," said a local activist.[59] Statewide returns confirmed the lost opportunity. The NDPA won more than thirty elections across Alabama and did particularly well in the Black Belt.[60] The misstep was unfortunate, but at least it made the way forward clear. "The only thing left for us to do is to go back and try to organize all over again," said the same local activist. "We have to bury ourselves in the grass roots people, and let them and the youth take the lead, because I do not think they will trust us again."[61]

While most people looked to regroup, Hulett looked to move on. Prior to running for sheriff, his dedication to the third party and to freedom politics had been undeniable. No one had done more to build the party or to promote freedom rights and democratic decision making than he had. But once in office, his interest in the party and in freedom politics began to fade. Almost imperceptibly, he started to put his political career ahead of the people he served, and at some point during his first term he decided to direct his energy toward building a black political machine. A commitment to freedom politics, however, still permeated the third party, so he turned to the Democratic Party to realize his goal.

Not long after the 1972 general election, Hulett joined the Democratic Party. On his way out, he persuaded several movement activists to accompany him. With their help, he intended to take over the Democratic Party and fill the county courthouse with loyal black Democrats. In 1974, he ran for reelection as a Democrat and convinced coroner Willie McGhee to do the same. He also talked Elder Fletcher Fountain and Willie Wilson, Jr., into seeking Democratic nominations for the school board. In addition, he worked to pack the Lowndes County Democratic Executive

Committee—the local party's governing body—with his friends. In the upcoming election, Uralee Haynes, Charles Smith, Sarah Logan, Charlie Whiting, Jr., and Joe Frank Brown all sought seats on the committee. On his own, Hulett sought to strengthen his alliance with Hammonds by rallying black support for the judge's white candidates and involving Hammonds in the effort to elect two African Americans to the school board. Hammonds wanted these particular black candidates to prevail because their success would make his wife, whose term in office did not expire until 1976, the pivotal swing vote on a racially divided five-member board. Hulett even tried to broaden his support among white voters by endorsing George Wallace for governor. Wallace had toned down his race baiting considerably and had even started courting black elected officials by privately granting them personal favors and publicly channeling federal dollars their way. Hulett justified his endorsement by pointing to the governor's acceptance of a grassroots takeover of the Lowndes County Community Health Clinic in Hayneville.[62]

Hulett's jump to the Democratic Party confounded countless movement activists, the majority of whom still believed that independent politics offered African Americans their best chance for political empowerment. Equally perplexing was Hulett's support of Wallace, a man dubbed the "arch enemy of desegregation" by activist Simon Owens. "We were sad to hear someone like John Hulett, who had been such a strong fighter against Wallace, trying to explain his actions by saying Nixon had made it impossible to get funds for Black clinics without having to go begging to Wallace," said Owens.[63] For many people, the endorsement was a disappointing act of political opportunism that portended real trouble.

Hulett's actions transformed local black politics by causing the third party to collapse. The party survived the disastrous 1972 election, but the frustration and alienation that surfaced among key constituencies had weakened it severely. To remain effective, the party needed to concentrate its resources on strengthening its base. Hulett's defection, however, precipitated an exodus of personnel that robbed the party of veteran activists at the precise moment that it desperately needed experienced organizers to canvass and conduct political education workshops. By preventing the party from engaging in sustained organizing, the mass departure precluded a grassroots revival from occurring. Simultaneously, it signaled to African Americans that they no longer needed a third party to fight for freedom rights because there was room for them within the Democratic Party.[64]

The demise of the third party did not eliminate interest in freedom politics. Movement activists, including some of those who switched parties with Hulett, continued to value freedom rights and democratic decision making. Hulett's new brand of politics, however, threatened to undermine the political culture that so many people, including Hulett, labored so hard to create. To preserve the movement way of doing things, a small group of veteran activists organized to remove the black sheriff from office. The disintegration of the third party, however, meant that they had to challenge him in the Democratic primary. J. C. Coleman, a retired civil servant and Korean War veteran, volunteered to run against Hulett and in February 1974 announced his candidacy for the Democratic nomination for sheriff. Publicly, Coleman spoke about promoting intraracial unity and interracial harmony. "I feel that I can be of some help to the county in trying to re-unite the people—both black and white," he told a local reporter.[65] Privately, he talked about beating Hulett. But Coleman's chances for victory were slim because he lacked Hulett's resources and name recognition. In addition, most black voters were not privy to the movement's internal dynamics. As far as they knew, Hulett's political commitments had not changed. His endorsement of Wallace raised some eyebrows, but most people dismissed it as politics. Hulett was neither the first nor the last black politician to embrace Wallace. Besides, the sheriff's race was not a referendum on Wallace. African Americans had an opportunity to express their displeasure with the governor in the gubernatorial contest, which they did by voting overwhelmingly against him. Instead, it was a referendum on Hulett's performance as sheriff.

"Bloody Lowndes" had always been a dangerous place for African Americans, but during Hulett's first term in office he improved conditions considerably. As chief law enforcement officer, he not only ended police brutality, but also stopped random acts of racial violence perpetrated by ordinary white citizens. The key to his success was his willingness to arrest whites for breaking the law, something many people believed a black person would be too afraid to do. African Americans were grateful for these reforms, and to preserve them they voted ten to one in favor of Hulett in the 1974 primary.[66]

Hulett's victory over Coleman was just one of several primary wins for his group of new black Democrats. Those who sought seats on the Democratic Executive Committee also prevailed, as did the candidates for coroner and school board. Their success all but guaranteed victory in the 1974 general election. As expected, all the new black Democrats won even

though whites crossed party lines and voted for the Alabama Conservative Party's local ticket, which included two of the white candidates who
lost in the Democratic primary. The November 1974 sweep enabled African Americans generally, and Hulett and his people specifically, to retain
control of the sheriff's office and the coroner's office, and to gain control
of two seats on the school board. It also moved the struggle for political
power inside the courthouse.[67]

After the 1974 election, the reconfigured board of education, which consisted of the school superintendent and the five members of the school
board, became the primary battleground in the fight for control of the
government. Black board members Elder Fletcher Fountain and Willie
Wilson, Jr., together with Mary Dora Hammonds, wasted little time establishing the school board's authority over personnel matters. Against the
wishes of Superintendent Coleman, they suspended R. R. Pierce, the long-
standing black principal of Lowndes County Training School (soon to be
renamed Central High School), pending the outcome of an investigation
into charges of behavioral misconduct and fiscal mismanagement. Concerned Parents and Students for Quality Education in Lowndes County,
a local advocacy group cofounded by J. C. Coleman and his wife in the
early 1970s, gathered much of the evidence used against Principal Pierce.
The board eventually fired Pierce for mishandling several thousand dollars in school money.[68]

The three board members also integrated Coleman's administrative staff
by replacing several white employees with black educators. One of the
new black hires was Eli Seaborn, a junior high school principal and Hulett protégé, who came on as assistant superintendent. The board's actions
infuriated Coleman, who said they "served only to create disunity, distrust
and a sense of job insecurity among capable and dedicated employees."
She added, "Never in my 36 years as Superintendent has employee mo-
rale been as low as it is now," a remarkable statement given the hundreds
of black teachers who over the years kept silent about poor school conditions and poor pay for fear of losing their jobs. Coleman's assessment
of the future under the reconfigured board was bleak. "Until the Board
of Education in Lowndes County realizes that they are a policy-making
body and not an administrative body, there will be nothing but chaos and
confusion." Given the three board members' "obvious lack of knowledge
and understanding of proper Board function," Coleman believed she had
only one of two choices. "I can continue in office and watch them destroy

all we have worked a life-time to build, or I can resign with the earnest desire that a Superintendent will be appointed who will be allowed to administer the school program without so much unnecessary interference." Coleman chose to resign on August 31, 1975.[69]

After Coleman stepped down, conflict on the board subsided noticeably. In fact, the board managed to reach a consensus on several important issues, including naming a new superintendent. By a unanimous vote, the board appointed Uralee Haynes to complete Coleman's unexpired term. Despite the new spirit of cooperation, disagreements about policy and personnel continued. Most notably, the board could not agree on a timetable to implement a consent order to integrate the public school faculty. The black board members and Mary Dora Hammonds wanted to break up the cluster of white teachers at Lowndes County High School immediately, but the remaining white board members insisted on delaying the teacher transfers. A divided board eventually voted three to two to proceed with the transfers.[70]

The board's decision prompted Warren McLelland, the white principal of Lowndes County High, and several of the school's seventeen white teachers to resign in protest. McLelland spoke for the disgruntled employees when he said that the transfers would jeopardize the quality of the school's education program. White parents who sent their children to Lowndes County High agreed and began withdrawing their children from the school. At the time, the school enrolled all 204 white children remaining in the school system. Within five years, fewer than a dozen white children attended the public schools.[71]

Most of the white parents sent their children to private white academies. Many enrolled them in Fort Deposit Academy, a private white school that white parents and businesspeople in the Fort Deposit area opened in 1974 in anticipation of losing control of Lowndes County High. A few who did not mind the cross-county commute sent their youngsters to Lowndes Academy, which by the mid-1970s was a model private white academy in the Alabama Black Belt, drawing students from throughout the county and from Montgomery, Dallas, and Crenshaw counties. Although principal Mac Champion admitted that the sole purpose of Lowndes Academy was to separate white children from black children, he insisted that the school's supporters "don't hate Negroes. There's a difference between segregation and discrimination. We get along fine with them. Only we believe we should have the right to socialize and study the way we please and with whom we please." He added that the decision to segregate "doesn't mean we are not Americans. We are, and good ones down here. But America means freedom to choose what school you want to attend."[72]

The white elite blamed African Americans for the upheaval at Lowndes County High. They also blamed Judge Hammonds because his wife voted consistently with the black school board members. In retaliation, they conspired to oust the judge in the 1976 election by sponsoring their own black candidate in the Democratic primary. Their choice to face Hammonds was William "Sam" Bradley, who worked closely with white power brokers over the years. In the mid-1960s, Bradley lent his name to the effort by white officials to wrest control of War on Poverty initiatives away from movement activists. More recently, he helped Coleman oversee the county Head Start program, which tended to exclude teachers and families with movement connections. By backing an African American, the white elite wagered that black solidarity would trump the ties that bound black voters to the judge. This was shrewd politics, but Hammonds was equally cunning. To shore up support in the black community, he visited a prominent black church, thanked African Americans for their past support, and asked for their votes in the future. This simple gesture of appreciation and respect paid tremendous dividends in the primary. White candidates rarely acknowledged black support and never solicited black votes openly. By reaching out to African Americans publicly, Hammonds reminded black voters why he deserved the label "the fairest white man in the county."[73]

A lot was at stake in the 1976 primary. In addition to the probate judgeship and the superintendent's office, all five seats on the county commission were up for grabs. As the local governing body, the county commission possessed tremendous power. Its members also enjoyed significant extralegal benefits, including access to public money to construct and maintain roads and buildings on private property, and the use of county vehicles for personal business.[74] The white elite had already lost one seat on the county commission to former LCCMHR chairperson Charles Smith and were loath to lose anymore. A new district judgeship was also on the line. District judges handled most of the cases that brought people to court, from traffic violations to misdemeanors. Rose Sanders, a black organizer and civil rights attorney with a law degree from Harvard University, was a candidate for the position. Although the thirty-year-old native of North Carolina practiced in Selma, she established residency in Lowndes County in order to run. The legal activist enjoyed the support of Hulett and his people, which gave her a marked advantage over white candidate Ted Bozeman, the county solicitor.[75]

As the primary approached, the white candidates grew more confident about their prospects for victory, while the black candidates grew more distrustful of their opponents. The mood of both groups turned on absentee ballots. By late April 1976, Lowndes County voters had submitted some 350 absentee ballots, nearly twice as many as any previous election, and second only to Jefferson County, which had fifty times as many people. "It really looks suspicious," said Hulett. "Some of these people are getting them because they say they will be out of town on election day. I know that's not so in some of the cases." Hulett added that many of the applicants were black senior citizens with poor reading skills. "A white person is picking them up and taking them to the registrar's home to vote." "White people have never tried to help blacks vote before," he said. "You have to wonder why they're taking this effort to provide free transportation now for blacks." African Americans had real cause for concern because "elections in the Black Belt can be swung by a few votes," said state legislator Alvin Holmes.[76]

As expected, many of the 1976 primary races were extremely close, but not the race for probate judge. Harrell Hammonds trounced Sam Bradley by three thousand votes. The judge's public appeal for black support contributed significantly to the lopsided victory, but it was not the sole determinant. African Americans had long memories. They had not forgotten that Bradley worked with whites to take War on Poverty programs away from movement activists. Nor had they forgotten that he opposed the LCFP. Thus, they did not simply vote for Hammonds—they also voted against Bradley, whose politics were out of step with their own. To the dismay of the white elite, African Americans considered a vote for Bradley an act of racial disloyalty, not solidarity.[77]

The race for superintendent was also not particularly close: Uralee Haynes defeated her opponent decisively. Every other contest, however, was decided by a narrow margin, and absentee ballots figured prominently in the outcomes. Circuit clerk Alma Miller fell to her white challenger by only thirty-two votes, and Rose Sanders, the people's choice for district judge, loss to Ted Bozeman by fewer than two hundred votes. Two black candidates did prevail in the hotly contested elections for the county commission. Charles Smith retained his seat and Frank Miles, Jr., upset C. A. Day by a single vote. America Daney, meanwhile, managed to force a runoff with C. Raymond Dean by receiving more votes than the white incumbent and a second white candidate. Unlike previous years, the 1976 primary did not automatically decide the outcome of the November general election. African Americans complained bitterly about irregularities to the state Democratic Executive Committee hoping for new elections in several races, and whites protested Frank Miles's single-vote victory. Runoffs, recounts, and special elections left everyone guessing about the Democratic nominees in key contests for a couple of months, but by the end of the summer everything had been settled. In the runoff for the fifth seat on the county commission, the white incumbent defeated Daney, and in a new election for circuit clerk, Miller fell 328 votes shy of victory. Miles, though, held on to his county commission nomination after state officials dismissed his white opponent's petition for a recount.[78]

Four of the black candidates who failed to secure a nomination ran as independents in the 1976 general election, and a white candidate in the same situation ran on an alternative ticket. Each received more than two thousand votes, but none beat their Democratic opponent.[79] The courthouse remained divided. Hulett and Hammonds controlled the sheriff's office, the probate judge's office, the coroner's office, and the school board, while the white elite controlled the circuit clerk's office, the tax offices, the new district judgeship, and the county commission. The battle for the courthouse would be decided conclusively during the next two elections, as would the fate of freedom politics.

Although very few people realized the depth of the alliance between Hulett and Hammonds, it was clear to everyone that it was the key to the political insurgency. To drive a wedge between the two men, the white elite persuaded George Hammonds, the judge's brother and an original member of the board of directors of Fort Deposit Academy, to run for sheriff in the 1978 Democratic primary. It was a move as clever as any they tried previously. George Hammonds's candidacy created considerable problems for the political partners because the judge needed Hulett to marshal black votes, and Hulett needed the judge to control the courthouse. To preserve the alliance, the judge agreed not to endorse anyone for sheriff, and Hulett consented to mobilize black support for Virginia Crook, the judge's white clerk and choice for tax assessor. Hulett, though, could not endorse a white candidate publicly because African Americans were determined to field a full slate of black candidates in the primary. Consequently, he campaigned secretly for Virginia Crook for tax assessor and publicly for Elbert Means, a thirty-three-year-old African American from Fort Deposit.[80]

Elbert Means had a passion for black economic self-determination that he traced to a childhood incident involving his parents. One summer, W. E. Pritchett, the white man who owned the land his parents worked, demanded that they sell a considerable portion of their cattle because they owned too much livestock for a black family. Rather than accede to Pritchett's request, his parents exhausted their meager savings and purchased a one-mule farm in Calhoun. Their determination to live autonomous lives also inspired Means to agitate for racial equality. As a high school student in neighboring Selma, he participated in the desegregation campaign that SNCC field secretaries Bernard and Colia Lafayette organized in 1963. He continued his activism at Alabama State University in Montgomery in the mid-1960s until a draft notice sent him to Southeast Asia. The Vietnam War did not extinguish his desire for freedom rights, and, after his discharge in 1968, he reenrolled at Alabama State hoping to pick up where he left off. But money was short, so he withdrew from school after a year and, like thousands before him, moved to Detroit in search of work. While there, he met his wife, Harriet, who not only shared his commitment to freedom rights but also his willingness to agitate for racial equality. Harriet's views and activist spirit stemmed from her father, an official with the United Auto Workers who worked closely with Coleman Young, Detroit's first African American mayor. In 1975, Elbert returned to Lowndes County with Harriet to care for his aging father; after a short while, he became involved in the local struggle.[81]

Harriet and Elbert believed deeply in the county's black elected officials, and like most African Americans they held Hulett in especially high regard. But a chance encounter with former student organizer John Jackson shook their faith in Hulett and the others. Jackson distanced himself from Hulett around the time the sheriff abandoned the independent party. Having grown up in the movement, he wanted nothing to do with Hulett's new brand of politics. Jackson was brutally honest with Harriet and Elbert when they met while canvassing in White Hall, telling them that Hulett no longer had the people's interests at heart; he pointed to Hulett's deals with Judge Hammonds as evidence. The pair dismissed the disclosures as malicious gossip, not wanting to believe that Hulett could have drifted so far from the movement's center, but as Election Day approached, the rumors began resembling reality. While knocking on doors in Hope Hull, Harriet learned that Hulett had been campaigning for the white candidate for tax assessor. "We're going for Virginia Crook now," people reported him saying before handing them her campaign card. Hulett purposefully waited until the end of the primary season to rally black voters for Crook to avoid debating the issue publicly. But Elbert drew attention to the matter immediately. At one of the few mass meetings held in 1978, he confronted Hulett and demanded to know why he was soliciting votes for the other candidate. Hulett's dissembling infuriated Elbert, and only a calming word from Harriet kept the Vietnam veteran from knocking the truth out of him.[82]

Hulett's double-dealing shattered Harriet and Elbert's faith in him. Nevertheless, they continued campaigning, trying to get people to stick with Elbert. On Election Day, their perseverance paid off. Elbert received nearly two thousand votes in the primary, twice as many as Virginia Crook and almost five hundred more than the white incumbent. Meanwhile, Hulett defeated the judge's brother, who received virtually no votes from African Americans. Black incumbent Willie McGhee also won the nomination for coroner, and black candidates Percy Bell and Andrew McCall defeated the white tax collector and a white school board member. For the first time in a local election, not a single white candidate prevailed, not even one backed by Hulett and Hammonds.[83]

Means's victory lifted his spirits, and as soon as he took office he looked for ways to provide poor and working-class blacks with tax relief and make wealthy whites shoulder a fair share of the local tax burden. He began by carefully reviewing the property evaluations and tax assessments of everyone in the county, which revealed egregious errors that universally advantaged whites and disadvantaged African Americans. He found that large landowning whites rarely paid taxes on all they owned. Judge Hammonds was a principal beneficiary of this tendency. Although he owned some fifty thousand acres, he paid taxes on only a fraction of it. After Means recalculated the judge's tax bill, he owed an additional forty thousand dollars. Accurate accounting produced a cash windfall for the county. Means also found that his white predecessors typically assessed property owned by African Americans at the highest allowable rate. In many instances, African Americans paid thirty cents on the dollar in property tax when they should have paid only ten cents. At the same time, whites routinely paid the lowest possible rate. Means corrected the unfair assessments immediately. To provide black senior citizens with additional tax relief, he publicized Alabama's homestead exemption, which excused homeowners older than sixty from having to pay taxes on their houses and lots. At the start of his first term, the single binder that listed the people who received the exemption contained only four black names, but within a few years the names of black claimants filled four binders. He also expended considerable energy helping African Americans retain possession of their land. Rather than take kickbacks offered by whites for advance notice of land to be sold for back taxes, he reached into his own pocket to cover the cost of locating delinquent landowners, most of whom were African Americans who no longer lived in the county.[84]

Not surprisingly, Means's equal application of the tax code irritated and angered wealthy whites, including Hammonds. After so many years in control, they grew accustomed to reaping the rewards of discriminatory tax policies. Hulett, though, could not have cared less because he gained very little from the traditional way of doing things, though he was bothered by Means's independence and clear sense of right and wrong. Lowndes County sheriffs seemingly always turned a blind eye and extended an upturned palm toward those engaged in illegal moneymaking activities. For a fee, they allowed bootleggers to make and sell hooch and local hustlers to operate gaming dens and prostitution houses. Many people suspected that Hulett continued this practice because illegal businesses remained open even though everyone knew the locations of these enterprises and the identities of the petty criminals who ran them. Others speculated that he made similar arrangements with marijuana growers who in the mid-1980s planted scores of fields with thousands of marijuana plants. Three raids by state narcotics agents in 1986 alone netted a crop worth more than one million dollars.[85] Means, though, refused to participate in unlawful activities and declined to cover them up. His willingness to assist state auditors investigating major discrepancies in black tax collector Percy Bell's accounting books, which eventually led to Bell's arrest for embezzling almost forty thousand dollars, infuriated Hulett, as did his cooperation with the FBI following Bell's conviction for knowingly registering cars stolen in Detroit.[86]

By 1980, a small group of loosely connected black activists who shared a dislike for Hulett's politics began to coalesce around Means, whose commitment to freedom politics encouraged them. The group consisted of activists like Abdullah Shabazz of Hayneville, who were too young to have participated in the struggles of the 1960s, and grassroots organizers like John Jackson, who took part in the movement as teenagers and remained politically active. Some older movement organizers were also involved, including Ed Moore King, the White Hall resident who convinced the deacons at Mt. Gilliard Baptist to open the doors of the church to the LCCMHR in 1965. In the 1980 Democratic primary, Shabazz ran for county commission against machine candidate Thomas Pringle and received 25 percent of the black vote—a strong showing for an anti-machine black candidate, but not nearly enough to win. Ed Moore King, who ran for school superintendent against Uralee Haynes, also collected about a quarter of the black vote in a losing effort.[87]

The conflict between black opposition candidates and those aligned with Hulett and Hammonds was much less important to black voters than electing a full contingent of African Americans to the county commission. Consequently, black voters rallied behind commissioners Frank Miles, Jr., and Charles Smith, who retained their seats on the board, and William Cosby and Joe Frank Brown, who defeated the white commissioners who beat them four years earlier. They also supported Thomas Pringle, who completed the electoral sweep by beating black opposition candidate Abdullah Shabazz and three white contenders. After more than a decade of trying, African Americans finally controlled the county commission.[88]

Expectations were high for the black commissioners because conditions for African Americans remained deplorable. The black unemployment rate was 15.8 percent and rising. For the county as a whole, it jumped from 4.7 percent in 1970 to 12.1 percent in 1980. Poverty remained exceedingly high. In 1979, 45 percent of Lowndes County residents lived in poverty, whereas the national average was 11.7 percent. The Reagan administration exacerbated the situation by drastically reducing direct payments to individuals. Food stamp assistance and aid for dependent children declined 31 percent locally between 1985 and 1986. These cuts affected some 5,600 people, almost half the county's total population. The public schools also continued to under-perform. "The main problem confronting the school system is money," said Uralee Haynes. State allocations, which were based on average daily student attendance, declined precipitously when whites abandoned Lowndes County High. Around the same time, federal allocations decreased. Between 1980 and 1982, the Reagan administration cut Title I funds, which the county used for nutrition and education programs, by nearly one hundred thousand dollars, forcing the school board to eliminate several programs and dismiss thirty-six teachers' aides.[89]

The black commissioners lacked the resources to make a real difference in the lives of poor people. In fact, they barely had enough money to meet the operating expenses of the county government. In 1983, they slashed the payroll of every department by 60 percent just to avoid shutting down. Debt inherited from the previous commissioners was a major part of the problem. Equally troublesome was the lack of access to capital because the only bank in the county refused to extend loans to the board once African Americans controlled it.[90]

In an effort to provide poor people with some relief, the commissioners attempted to work with public agencies and private industrial development groups to bring companies into the county to bolster the local economy. But partners were hard to find. In 1981, when the state convinced General Electric to build a $1.5 billion plastics production plant in the county, it never consulted the black commissioners. They had no input into the incentives package used to lure the *Fortune* 500 company, which included a state sales tax exemption on all expenses related to the construction of the chemical plant, and a total property tax exemption on the six thousand acres that GE bought in Burkeville, seventeen miles west of Montgomery. The sweetheart deal meant that the county government depended on GE philanthropy to realize a financial gain from the placement of the plant in Burkeville. It also meant that the sole benefit for Lowndes County residents was jobs, but even that proved elusive because GE tended to hire better-educated white workers from Montgomery to meet its labor needs.[91]

GE was not the only company interested in Lowndes County. The same year the company announced its plans to construct the Burkeville plant, a waste management firm petitioned the state to put a hazardous waste dump in nearby Lowndesboro. Companies involved in the production and disposal of materials that posed risks to the environment and public health looked to establish sites in poor rural counties, especially those with black majorities, because they tended to lack the political clout to block them. As with GE, no one ever consulted the black commissioners about the dump. But the waste management firm underestimated the resolve of Lowndes County residents, both black and white, rich and poor, to fight the landfill. In a rare display of cooperation across the color line, four hundred residents packed the gymnasium at Hayneville High on October 5, 1981, and formed Lowndes Citizens to Fight Deadly Dumping in Alabama. To chair the organization, they turned to Sam Bradley, the black director of the county's Head Start program. Ted Lingham, the white mayor of Lowndesboro, served as vice chair. That afternoon, Commissioner Thomas Pringle announced that the commissioners had passed a resolution declaring the county's intention to refuse outside hazardous waste. Within two weeks, the group had raised enough money to hire an attorney to fight the landfill in state and federal court and had launched a campaign to pressure Black Belt legislators to oppose the project. By the end of the year, a bill to block the proposed dump, sponsored by several state representatives from the region, sat on the governor's desk awaiting his signature.⁹²

The successful effort to block the landfill did not deter other companies from trying to locate waste disposal sites in the county, forcing locals to fight attempts to place dumps in the county for a quarter century. The interracial nature of the first anti-landfill campaign, however, did not lead automatically to local organizing across the color line on other issues. It was even hard to sustain interracial organizing around opposition to landfills, evidenced in part by the creation of the mostly black Lowndes County Concerned Citizens Group, chaired by Harriet Means, in the late 1980s.⁹³ Interracial organizing did occur, however, and, like the earlier effort, it was effective.⁹⁴ The initial grassroots campaign also failed to ease conflict within the courthouse. As the 1984 election approached, the tension between Hulett and those who opposed his brand of politics was palpable.

Elbert Means was the most visible and vocal member of the black opposition, and Hulett longed to be rid of him. But ousting Means proved more difficult than he imagined because of the tremendous grassroots support that the tax assessor enjoyed, especially among older African Americans who tended to vote in greater numbers than other segments of the population. To unseat Means in 1984, Hulett turned to his son John Edward Hulett, one of the first African Americans to graduate from Hayneville High School. The younger Hulett returned to the county after receiving a political science degree from Miles College in Birmingham and serving four years in the air force. On the campaign trail, he promised to work closely with his father and others in the courthouse. "I want to establish a harmonious working relationship with all elected officials and agencies," he said. "I believe this is necessary in order to project a positive image of our county to our local residents, as well as throughout the country. Such a relationship is the key to industrial growth."⁹⁵

Anticipating a close race, Hulett dipped into the bag of dirty tricks that the white elite used to steal elections in the 1970s. As soon as the circuit clerk posted the names of those requesting absentee ballots, he and others began visiting them to make sure they voted their way. Means suspected that Hulett would try to manipulate the outcome of the election, but he was still surprised to receive a telephone call from a supporter at the New Hope Seniors' Center urging him to come immediately because Hulett

and school board member Elder Fletcher Fountain were filling out absentee ballots for the center's patrons. When Means arrived, he caught the
pair completing the mail-in forms, and "they were not marking those ballots for me," he later quipped. Although the incumbent tax assessor succeeded in having these particular votes disqualified, he remained gravely
concerned about fraud.[96]

On Election Day, Means received ninety-one more votes than John Edward Hulett, but after election officials appointed by Sheriff Hulett and Judge
Hammonds counted the absentee ballots, which they did behind closed
doors, Means lost the primary by four votes. Dismayed, he immediately filed
a grievance with the Lowndes County Democratic Committee, but chairperson Eli Seaborn, who also happened to be Hulett's choice to succeed retiring
school superintendent Uralee Haynes, upheld the dubious count. Means appealed Seaborn's ruling to the Democratic Party's statewide governing body,
which found sufficient evidence of ballot tampering to order a new election.
Means prevailed in the closely monitored special election, but the cost of
prosecuting the challenge nearly bankrupted his family.[97]

Means was not the only black opposition candidate to win in 1984. Bob
Mants, the former SNCC organizer, also won a seat on the board of commissioners. Mants returned to Lowndes County to work with local activists not long after SNCC left. He supported Hulett for several years until
he became disillusioned with his politics. Mants's service to the movement
and commitment to freedom politics made him extremely popular among
working-class blacks, who cast more votes for him in 1984 than they did
for anyone else.[98]

Black opposition candidates were gaining momentum by the mid-
1980s. With each election, more and more African Americans turned to
them, hoping that they could produce better results than did Hulett and
his people. But Hulett's extensive personal contacts, along with his organizing expertise, allowed him to marshal sufficient black votes to keep the
opposition from stringing together enough victories to dismantle his machine. When Means and Mants won in 1984, Ed Moore King lost to Eli
Seaborn in the race for school superintendent, and two years later Abdullah Shabazz failed to unseat Hulett's choice for the school board. Hulett
was also willing to use voting fraud to stay in power. In 1990, he helped
Willie Ruth Myrick defeat Means in the primary for tax assessor by pad-
ding her vote total with absentee ballots. Means again gathered compelling evidence of electoral misconduct, but with two daughters about to
enter college he and his wife could not afford another costly challenge.[99]

The black opposition did not let themselves be discouraged by losses to Hulett and those loyal to him. They continued to seek public office throughout the 1980s and 1990s, but instead of running exclusively for positions in the county government they branched out and ran for positions in several of the county's municipal governments. John Jackson, the former student organizer, led the way. In 1979, the two hundred residents of the newly incorporated municipality of White Hall elected him mayor. In this capacity, he did more for the black landowning community than the county ever did. Under his leadership, the municipal government used local tax revenue and federal, state, and private development grants to complete a $340,000 water system; establish twenty-four-hour ambulance, fire, and police service; start a day care program; and launch an emergency medical technician training program. Jackson credited these first-term accomplishments to lessons learned from SNCC organizers. "SNCC challenged us to dream in Lowndes County, to dream of lawyers who were concerned about justice and not a judgeship," he said. "To dream of county elected officials who would become public servants and not politicians."[100] Jackson's advocacy of freedom rights and democratic governance transformed White Hall. By 1990, the tiny town boasted nearly one thousand residents and once again was a beacon of hope in Lowndes County.[101]

The success of Jackson and other black opposition candidates at the municipal level had remarkably little effect on Hulett's popularity. Throughout the 1980s and 1990s, African Americans continued to elect him to office. In 1982 and 1990, he received more than 75 percent of the total ballots cast when he ran for reelection as sheriff, and in 1994 he beat a field of four when he ran for probate judge (Harrell Hammonds resigned as probate judge in 1984 due to poor health).[102] Initially, African Americans supported Hulett because of his impeccable movement credentials. He was a civil rights hero whose record of activism before becoming sheriff gave them no reason to doubt his willingness or ability to lead the fight for freedom rights. Once in office, they rewarded him for fulfilling his charge as the county's chief law enforcement officer. Ending white lawlessness was no minor feat given the history of local violence. It was especially meaningful to African Americans old enough to recall life before a black sheriff. These core black voters were haunted by indelible memories of racial terrorism. They remembered shakedowns by sheriff Frank Ryals in the sixties, beatings at the hands of sheriff Otto Moorer in the forties and fifties, plantation owners running amuck during sheriff

Robert Woodruff's tenure in the twenties and thirties, and the stories their parents told about sheriff J. W. Dickson terrorizing African Americans at the turn of the century. By ushering in the era of personal safety, Hulett earned the respect, gratitude, and votes of African Americans.[103] "Black folk were glad to see that Negro with a badge," said John Jackson.[104] Mattie Lee Moorer explained that "he does not kill. He does not shoot. He doesn't beat prisoners," which made him "the best high sheriff" the county had "ever known."[105] Hulett's performance as sheriff took on even greater meaning in the late 1970s and early 1980s when sharp spikes in police brutality occurred in urban areas across the state, most notably in Birmingham, and throughout the rural South.[106] If nothing else, it was safe to travel the roads of Lowndes County. Hulett's popularity, therefore, was not a product of black naivety; African Americans were not simply duped by his charisma and civil rights record. Instead, it stemmed from their long memories and Hulett's actual accomplishments.

Although political fissures within the black community did not substantially lessen Hulett's popularity, they did enable whites to regain a fair amount of power within the local government. White candidates had the upper hand in elections involving more than one black candidate, especially after Judge Hammonds stepped down and whites resumed voting as a solid racial bloc. The advantage was plain to see in 1980 when O. P. Woodruff, the white candidate for probate judge, beat black machine candidate Thomas Pringle and black opposition candidate Ben Davis after they split the black vote.[107] Black political divisions also contributed to a drastic decline in black voter participation. The effectiveness of Hulett's machine at the county level gave African Americans very few electoral alternatives, and rather than vote for white candidates, many people opted not to vote at all, which helped negate their numerical edge. Indeed, by the early 1990s, the majority of African Americans simply stopped voting. In the 1994 Democratic primary, only 34 percent of the voters in Gordonsville and Mosses, two overwhelmingly black precincts, took part in the election.[108] The undemocratic exercise of black political power, which caused black disunity, disillusionment, and disengagement, made the revival of white political power possible.

The political renaissance that whites enjoyed in the late 1980s and early 1990s weakened Hulett's machine considerably. He was still the most popular politician in the county, but he no longer wielded the same degree of influence inside the courthouse that he once enjoyed. With his power fading, he decided not to run for a second term as probate judge in 2000.

His absence from the courthouse after thirty years in office ended black boss politics. He remained relevant, however, through his political heirs, the foremost being his son John Edward Hulett, who succeeded him as probate judge. In 2006, Hulett's son began his second term in office. That same year the venerable civil rights leader and the county's first black sheriff died quietly at his home at age seventy-eight.[109]

Movement activists believed that obtaining political power was the key to reducing racial disparities and improving local conditions. It was also a way for African Americans to have a full say in the decisions that affected their lives. Electing African Americans to public office, however, failed to create the kind of sweeping change that movement activists hoped. Although it ended racial terrorism, it did not produce equality of opportunity or outcome. Twenty years after African Americans gained control of the courthouse, the public schools continued to under-perform. In fact, they were in jeopardy of being taken over by the state. Segregation in education also endured. The public schools were 99 percent black, while Lowndes Academy, the original private white academy, was 100 percent white. In addition, glaring wealth disparities persisted. The per capita income for African Americans was $8,763, while for whites it was $23,236.[110]

Despite a keen understanding of county government, movement activists underestimated the strength of structural impediments to racial equality. Black elected officials could only do so much given the limits of their authority. There was no way for them to restructure society to provide the least among them with the means to get ahead. It simply was not possible under existing state and federal law to tax the rich to feed the poor. African Americans also came to power at a time when federal resources were dwindling. By the 1980s, considerably less was trickling down from Washington. The cumulative effect of structural arrangements made it difficult for even the most well-intentioned black officeholders to generate lasting change.

Movement activists also overestimated the sustainability of freedom politics. They assumed that people would continue to adhere to its tenets once African Americans gained power because SNCC's political education program made freedom politics synonymous with black politics. But popular interest in freedom politics waned as soon as movement activists stopped doing political education work. Without the workshops and mass meetings, people lost sight of the importance of grassroots agitation and democratic decision making. This created an opening for those who rejected freedom politics to introduce a new kind of black politics, one that privileged mobilizing voters over educating them, ranked individual interests higher than group interests, and placed winning reelection above fighting for freedom rights.

The decline in interest in freedom politics was not inevitable. It occurred because of decisions made by a handful of influential people who preferred undemocratic politics. Hulett set the process in motion by agreeing to Hammonds's plan in 1970, which robbed people of the right to select their own candidates. He accelerated it by joining the Democratic Party in 1974, which destabilized the third party. Losing the third party prevented those who still believed in freedom politics from having the organizational infrastructure they needed to conduct political education work. He completed the process by using coercive and fraudulent means to defeat black opposition candidates. This prevented advocates of freedom politics from gaining the visibility they needed to renew popular interest in the movement way of doing things. The demise of freedom politics also occurred because of decisions made by the black electorate. By the mid-1980s, it was quite clear that Hulett preferred boss politics to freedom politics, yet African Americans continued to elect him to office. Although their reasons for supporting him reflected his accomplishments as sheriff, they did so knowing that his politics had changed considerably since the 1960s.

Like most democratic projects, freedom politics was hard to keep alive. Although its supporters did not realize how difficult maintaining it would be, they were well aware of the perils of power. The entire enterprise was born of SNCC organizers' awareness of the pitfalls of existing political practices and structures. As SNCC laid the groundwork for freedom politics, they cautioned against replicating the old way of doing things. "Black visibility is not Black Power," wrote Carmichael. "Most black politicians around the country today are not examples of Black Power. The power must be that of a community, and emanate from there. The black politicians must stop being representatives of 'downtown' machines, whatever the cost might be in terms of lost patronage and holiday handouts."[111] The proponents of freedom politics did not think that simply putting African Americans in public office would change the world. Instead, they believed that electing people committed to freedom politics, regardless of their race, was the way to make a difference in the lives of ordinary people. Interracial coalitions were not a problem, but the kind of interracial coalitions that emerged locally were. Ironically, the person who worked the hardest to spread freedom politics during the movement's heyday was the catalyst behind its demise. But there was no way anyone could predict in 1965 that Hulett would become a political boss more than a decade later. There were no obvious signs that he would drift away from the movement's democratic principles and practices. The fact that he did, therefore, is not evidence of some inherent flaw in freedom politics. Instead, it represents a failure on the part of the advocates of freedom politics to execute the viable political program that they had devised.

The African American freedom struggle did not end when freedom politics ceased being the dominant mode of black politics. Throughout the post–civil rights era, African Americans, including some elected officials, continued agitating for basic civil and human rights. Elbert Means fought admirably and effectively as the county tax assessor; so did John Jackson as the mayor of White Hall. But when African Americans started looking exclusively to politicians to lead the fight for freedom rights and made the Democratic Party their primary vehicle for advancing the struggle, collective action stopped almost completely. Over-investing in elected officials and the Democratic Party kept African Americans from developing new grassroots leaders, which eventually created a leadership vacuum. It also caused them to marginalize the LCCMHR, which resulted in the loss of vital organizing capacity. As a result, African Americans were not in a position to resume collective action when their investment in electoral politics yielded a poor return.

During the post–civil rights era, black elected officials squandered the chance to normalize freedom politics, which could have transformed local government and made life a bit more bearable for poor and working-class people. Their failure to take advantage of this opportunity, along with the existence of major structural impediments, allowed poorly performing schools, high unemployment, inadequate housing, and poverty to persist. Consequently, a century after W. E. B. Du Bois visited the county, conditions there remain "unfavorable to the rise of the Negro."

Epilogue:
That Black Dirt Gets in Your Soul
The Fight for Freedom Rights in
the Days Ahead

Catherine Coleman Flowers came of age in Lowndes County, having moved there from Birmingham in 1968 when she was ten years old. Although the Lowndes movement had already peaked, there was still a great deal of organizing taking place, and she watched the revolution unfold up close. Her father, J. C. Coleman, had been active in the movement almost from the start, driving from Birmingham to his hometown of White Hall every chance he got. After relocating his family to Blackbelt, a tiny village near White Hall that rarely appears on maps, he became more intimately involved in the local struggle. The cinder-block house that he built for his wife, Mattie, and their five children was a regular meeting place for movement leaders, including John Hulett, whom Coleman helped protect during his first term as sheriff. It was also the place where Flowers learned about community organizing.[1]

It was impossible to guess who would drop by the Coleman home next—John Jackson, Sidney Logan, Jr., Willie "Mukassa" Ricks, or maybe even Kwame Ture, who changed his name from Stokely Carmichael in 1969. Seemingly everyone made their way there at some point to strategize with the Colemans, and before they left, they always managed to share a bit of movement wisdom with the Coleman children. Flowers looked forward to these special moments, which never became routine. They reinforced what her parents taught her about serving the black community, something that her mother did as an organizer for the National Welfare Rights Organization. They helped her appreciate her parents' commitment to freedom politics, which had led her father to run for sheriff against Hulett in 1974. They underscored her parents' admonition to fight for racial justice, which her mother did as a spokesperson for black women like herself who had been forcibly sterilized. They also illuminated what she learned about the Lowndes movement at White Hall Elementary School from her teacher Ed Moore King, who in 1965 convinced the leaders of Mt. Gilliard Baptist Church to allow the LCCMHR to hold its meetings there.[2]

Flowers did not wait until adulthood to begin agitating for freedom rights. As a junior at Lowndes County Training School in 1974, she worked closely with her father, the vice president of Concerned Parents and Students for Quality Education in Lowndes County, to document violations of state law at the school. Black school board members Elder Fletcher Fountain and Willie Wilson, Jr., together with Mary Dora Hammonds, used their findings to bring about major reforms, including removing principal R. R. Pierce and extending classes beyond the noon hour in order to provide students with a complete academic day. As a senior, she lent her voice to the effort to replace school superintendent Hulda Coleman with an African American and spearheaded the student campaign to change the name of Lowndes County Training School to the more dignified Central High School. Like many of her classmates, she did not want to carry the stigma of having graduated from a "training school" rather than from a high school.[3]

With her diploma from Central High, Flowers enrolled at Alabama State University. She envisioned becoming a lawyer and helping poor people navigate the complicated terrain of the law, much as her parents had done informally for years. Unable to find her niche within the student activist community, she left Alabama State in 1977 and, like her father before her, joined the U.S. Air Force. The military, however, was an even worse fit. She quickly realized that the armed service was no place for a black woman accustomed to questioning authority. After securing an early discharge in 1980, she returned to Alabama State and soon became involved in student protests that sought to prevent the state government from transforming the university into something other than a historically black college. In the process, she gained valuable political experience consulting with lobbyists and lawyers from Washington and acquired important organizing experience working with activists from SCLC.[4]

With an eye toward becoming a full-time organizer, she relocated to Atlanta where she worked as an intern at the Martin Luther King, Jr., Center for Nonviolent Social Change. Her tenure there exposed her further to movement politics and culture, not all of which she found as enriching and rewarding as working at the grassroots. Atlanta, though, was very much to her liking, so after her stint at the King Center she enrolled at Georgia State University, a commuter school located in the heart of downtown. It was not long before she became active locally, this time through the Nation of Islam, whose brand of Black Nationalism impressed her. A patriarchal subculture within the NOI, however, eventually caused her to leave the organization.[5]

Marriage took Flowers to southwest Oklahoma where she completed her undergraduate education at Cameron University, earning a degree in history in 1985. An opportunity to work in Washington, D.C., in the office of U.S. congressman Robert Garcia, who represented the South Bronx in New York, brought her back east. This was not, however, her first time on Capitol Hill. In high school her activism caught the attention of the Robert F. Kennedy Memorial Foundation, which brought her to Washington for several weeks during the summer before her senior year. Both experiences, but especially the latter, helped demystify the federal government, exposing the realpolitik of Washington. Coleman worked for Congressman Garcia for six months and then took a teaching position in the D.C. public schools. Lacking seniority, she was assigned to classes with students deemed chronic underperformers, but she was able to capture the interest of many of these young people by bringing movement activists to speak to them, such as the MFDP's Lawrence Guyot. She wanted the students to benefit from interacting with grassroots organizers just as she had at their age. She also raised money to take several students south to participate in commemorative marches in Alabama and Freedom Summer celebrations in Mississippi, which added an important new dimension to what the students learned in the classroom.[6]

Flowers relocated to North Carolina in the early 1990s to help care for her father-in-law. A few years later, she moved to Detroit, following in the footsteps of the thousands of Lowndes County residents who had migrated to the Motor City since the First World War. As a social studies teacher in the Detroit public schools, she continued to expose her students to living history. In 2000 she took a group of young people to Selma to take part in the thirty-fifth anniversary celebration of the Selma to Montgomery March. While there, veteran activists encouraged her to return to the city to help unseat white mayor Joe Smitherman, who had been in office since 1965. Accepting the challenge, she relocated to the area at the end of the school year and joined the successful effort to elect African American James Perkins mayor. While working in Selma she became acutely aware of how desperate conditions still were for poor people in Lowndes County. Intent on making a difference, she reached out to Washington insiders whom she had met over the years. Her inquiries led to a collaboration with black conservative Robert Woodson, the president of the National Center for Neighborhood Enterprise (NCNE). Together, they developed a pilot project to aid the county's most impoverished residents, many of whom faced arrest and eviction because they could not afford to fix or install septic systems to properly dispose of household waste. Behind several homes, raw sewage collected in open pools and spilled into creeks.[7]

Working closely with Woodson and the NCNE from 2002 to 2005, Flowers helped keep people who could not pay for septic tanks out of jail; helped secure new waste removal systems for about a dozen families; and helped broker a deal with CitiFinancial to provide mobile homes for several others. She also played a role in the lobbying effort that secured $4.7 million in federal funds for the development of an industrial site in Lowndes County for companies supplying parts to the Hyundai automotive plant in Montgomery, which opened in 2005.[8] Flowers partnered with Woodson and other political conservatives, both black and white, elected and unelected, because she believed in working with whomever was willing to work for the people of Lowndes County. The partnership produced results, but only enough to ameliorate the desperate living conditions of a handful of families. To transform the county, a much greater influx of private and public capital was needed.

Woodson and the NCNE have moved on, but Flowers remains, working through her own nonprofit organization, the Alabama Center for Rural Enterprise (ACRE), based in White Hall, to develop best practices for addressing the root causes of rural poverty. By necessity, her programmatic agenda for improving the lives of local people is broad. A "holistic approach" has to be used to help these families, she says. People need decent housing, job training, and affordable and accessible health care. Children need better schools to prepare them for college and to compete in the knowledge economy. Her agenda also involves creating a regional economic development strategy to link the county to nearby metropolitan areas, which is essential for sustainable growth.[9]

Finding lasting solutions to the prevailing condition of poverty is Flowers's top priority. This concern has led her to partner most recently with the Equal Justice Initiative of Alabama, a nonprofit organization that has expanded its traditional focus beyond legal representation for indigent defenders and prisoners denied fair legal treatment, including death row inmates, to fundamental issues surrounding race and poverty in the Black Belt. But there are so many people in desperate need of immediate assistance that helping them often takes precedence over long-range planning. Locating a new home for eighty-eight-year-old Alberta Turner, for instance, has occupied much of her time of late. Turner's single-wide mobile home, her primary residence for the last thirty years, was severely damaged during a storm in January 2008 when a tree crashed through her bedroom. Sheets of plastic weighted down by several tires cover the yawning hole left in the roof. "It's not nearly waterproof," said her grandson. "When it rains, we have to get up there and sweep off the water, so most of it won't spill inside." The accident exacerbated damage caused three years earlier by Hurricane Katrina. At that time, Turner received $128 from the Federal Emergency Management Agency (FEMA) to make repairs, but the check was not nearly enough to complete the task and she had neither savings nor insurance to cover the difference. To make matters worse, the septic system no longer works, so raw sewage from the house empties directly into the backyard. Despite the deteriorating conditions, Turner prefers to remain where she is. "It may not be much, but it's my house," she said. "If they can get it fixed, that's fine. If they can get me a new house, well, that's fine too. But I want to stay here. I've been here an awful long time." Flowers understands Turner's desire to stay put. "I grew up in the Black Belt," she explained. "There's something about that black dirt that gets in your soul."[10]

People like Catherine Coleman Flowers are the key to carrying on the fight for freedom rights. As a part of the growing wave of African Americans returning to the southern countryside, they bring to the local struggle new energy born of not having shouldered the weight of rural poverty their entire lives, as well as fresh perspectives derived from observing local conditions from afar. They also bring important professional skills acquired while working outside of the county. In addition, they provide access to new political networks through which local people can tap into vital resources controlled by the government and nonprofit organizations.[11]

To be most effective, those who have answered the call to reclaim their rural homes have to work closely with the people who never left. Like SNCC field secretaries, they have to organize at the grassroots. Having grown up in the shadow of the movement, Flowers is uniquely positioned to fulfill this charge. She has already forged partnerships with a wide variety of local people that cross racial, class, and party lines. She has also engaged elected officials, raising the prospect of a revival of freedom politics.

The snaillike pace of progress in Lowndes County makes it hard for local people to be hopeful. Yet many lifelong residents such as Alberta Turner hold fast to the belief that better days are coming. Theirs is not a blind faith, but an optimism born of deep religious convictions. Their positive outlook is also tied to the work of people like Flowers. "I want to thank God for getting me this far," said Turner in August 2008 as she sat for the first time in her new mobile home, a gift from a coalition of people brought together by Flowers. "And I want to thank everybody that did anything to help me. I might not even know who they are, but I want them to know that I thank them and I really appreciate what they did for me."[12] Although change happens slowly in Lowndes County, it does happen because people like Flowers are committed to fighting for freedom rights.

Notes

In citing manuscript collections and interviews in the notes, shorted abbreviations and dates have been used. Please refer to the bibliography for their full identifications.

INTRODUCTION

1. In 1960, there were 12,439 African Americans living in Lowndes County, Alabama, including 5,122 of voting age, out of a total population of 15,417. There were 2,240 white registered voters, but only 1,900 of voting age. U.S. Bureau of the Census, *Eighteenth Census of the United States, 1960, Vol. 1, Pt. 2* (Washington, D.C.: Government Printing Office, 1963), 193.

2. Moss in "Candidates lose," *The Movement* (December 1966).

3. Logan, Jr. (also the black farmer) in "Lowndes County Freedom Organization leaders," *The Movement* (June 1966).

4. For a glimpse at early black protest in Lowndes County see Robin D. G. Kelley, *Hammer and Hoe: Alabama Communists during the Great Depression* (Chapel Hill: University of North Carolina Press, 1990). For general treatments of African Americans' pursuit of civil and human rights in the post-emancipation era see V. P. Franklin, *Black Self-Determination: A Cultural History of African-American Resistance* (New York: Lawrence Hill, 1984, 1992); Elsa Barkley Brown, "Negotiating and Transforming the Public Sphere: African American Political Life in the Transition from Slavery to Freedom," in *The Black Public Sphere: A Public Culture Book*, ed. Black Public Sphere Collective (Chicago: University of Chicago Press, 1995), 111–150; Michael Dawson, *Black Visions: The Roots of Contemporary African-American Political Ideologies* (Chicago: University of Chicago Press, 2001); Steven Hahn, *A Nation under Our Feet: Black Political Struggles in the Rural South from Slavery to the Great Migration* (Cambridge, Mass.: Harvard University Press, 2003); Heather Andrea Williams, *Self-Taught: African American Education in Slavery and Freedom* (Chapel Hill: University of North Carolina Press, 2005).

5. Noteworthy studies of southern black protest and white violence during the late nineteenth and early twentieth centuries include Neil R. McMillen, *Dark

Journey: Black Mississippians in the Age of Jim Crow (Urbana: University of Illinois Press, 1989); Robin D. G. Kelley, *Race Rebels: Culture, Politics, and the Black Working Class* (New York: Free Press, 1994); Rod Bush, *We Are Not What We Seem: Black Nationalism and Class Struggle in the American Century* (New York: New York University Press, 1999); Nan Elizabeth Woodruff, *American Congo: The African American Freedom Struggle in the Delta* (Cambridge, Mass.: Harvard University Press, 2003); Paul Ortiz, *Emancipation Betrayed: The Hidden History of Black Organizing and White Violence in Florida from Reconstruction to the Bloody Election of 1920* (Berkeley and Los Angeles: University of California Press, 2005).

6. There are only a couple of book-length treatments on the movement in Lowndes County. These are Charles Eagles, *Outside Agitator: Jon Daniels and the Civil Rights Movement in Alabama* (Chapel Hill: University of North Carolina Press, 1993); Mary Stanton, *From Selma to Sorrow: The Life and Death of Viola Liuzzo* (Athens: University of Georgia Press, 1998); Gary May, *The Informant: The FBI, the Ku Klux Klan, and the Murder of Viola Liuzzo* (New Haven, Conn.: Yale University Press, 2005). Although the county's black residents and SNCC organizers are discussed in each of these works, they are not the primary focus of study. Instead, these books revolve around the lives and legacies of the white victims of white violence. Two works that examine the Lowndes movement in the context of the larger African American freedom struggle are Taylor Branch, *At Canaan's Edge: America in the King Years, 1965–68* (New York: Simon & Schuster, 2006); Frye Gaillard, *Cradle of Freedom: Alabama and the Movement That Changed America* (Tuscaloosa: University of Alabama Press, 2004). Susan Youngblood Ashmore weaves an excellent discussion of the Lowndes movement into *Carry It On: The War on Poverty and the Civil Rights Movement in Alabama, 1964–1972* (Athens: University of Georgia Press, 2008). Richard Couto also incorporates an insightful analysis of grassroots organizing in Lowndes County in *Ain't Gonna Let Nobody Turn Me Round: The Pursuit of Racial Justice in the Rural South* (Philadelphia: Temple University Press, 1991). Several former SNCC activists have written about the Lowndes movement. See Stokely Carmichael and Charles V. Hamilton, *Black Power: The Politics of Black Liberation in America* (New York: Vintage, 1967); Stokely Carmichael with Ekwueme Michael Thelwell, *Ready for Revolution: The Life and Struggles of Stokely Carmichael (Kwame Ture)* (New York: Scribner, 2003); Cleveland Sellers with Robert Terrell, *The River of No Return: The Autobiography of a Black Militant and the Life and Death of SNCC* (New York: Morrow, 1973). A perceptive master's thesis on the Lowndes movement is David Campbell, "The Lowndes County (Alabama) Freedom Organization: The First Black Panther Party, 1965–1968," (M.A. Thesis, Florida State University, 1970).

7. For general treatments of SNCC see Clayborne Carson, *In Struggle: SNCC and the Black Awakening of the 1960s* (Cambridge, Mass.: Harvard University Press, 1981); John Dittmer, *Local People: The Struggle for Civil Rights in Mississippi* (Urbana: University of Illinois Press, 1994); Charles M. Payne, *I've Got the*

Light of Freedom: The Organizing Tradition and the Mississippi Freedom Struggle (Berkeley and Los Angeles: University of California Press, 1995). For an excellent analysis of SNCC's organizing philosophy and democratic practices see Wesley C. Hogan, *Many Minds, One Heart: SNCC's Dream for A New America* (Chapel Hill: University of North Carolina Press, 2007). See also Barbara Ransby, *Ella Baker and the Black Freedom Movement: A Radical Democratic Vision* (Chapel Hill: University of North Carolina Press, 2003); Carol Mueller, "Ella Baker and the Origins of 'Participatory Democracy,'" in *Women in the Civil Rights Movement: Trailblazers and Torchbearers, 1941–1965*, eds. Vicki L. Crawford, Jacqueline Anne Rouse, and Barbara Woods (Bloomington: Indiana University Press, 1990, 1993), 51–70. Insightful organizational histories written by SNCC activists include Sellers, *The River of No Return*; Carmichael, *Ready for Revolution*; James Forman, *The Making of Black Revolutionaries* (Seattle: University of Washington Press, 1972, 1997).

8. A number of studies have been published in recent years that provide valuable new perspectives on Black Power. These include Komozi Woodard, *A Nation within a Nation: Amiri Baraka (LeRoi Jones) and Black Power Politics* (Chapel Hill: University of North Carolina Press, 1999); Timothy B. Tyson, *Radio Free Dixie: Robert F. Williams and the Roots of Black Power* (Chapel Hill: University of North Carolina Press, 1999); Jeffrey O. G. Ogbar, *Black Power: Radical Politics and African American Identity* (Baltimore: Johns Hopkins University Press, 2004); Scot Brown, *Fighting for US: Maulana Karenga, the US Organization, and Black Cultural Nationalism* (New York: New York University Press, 2005); James Edward Smethurst, *The Black Arts Movement: Literary Nationalism in the 1960s and 1970s* (Chapel Hill: University of North Carolina Press, 2005); Matthew Countryman, *Up South: Civil Rights and Black Power in Philadelphia* (Philadelphia: University of Pennsylvania Press, 2006); Peniel E. Joseph, ed., *The Black Power Movement: Rethinking the Civil Rights–Black Power Era* (New York: Routledge, 2006), and *Waiting 'Til the Midnight Hour: A Narrative History of Black Power in America* (New York: Henry Holt, 2006); Judson L. Jeffries, ed., *Black Power in the Belly of the Beast* (Urbana: University of Illinois Press, 2006). An important predecessor to the new scholarship on Black Power is William Van Deburg, *New Day in Babylon: The Black Power Movement and American Culture, 1965–1975* (Chicago: University of Chicago Press, 1992).

9. Scholarly interest in civil rights organizing after 1965 has surged of late. Among the important works that examine events after 1965 are J. Todd Moye, *Let the People Decide: Black Freedom and White Resistance in Sunflower County, Mississippi, 1945–1986* (Chapel Hill: University of North Carolina Press, 2004); Timothy B. Tyson, *Blood Done Sign My Name: A True Story* (New York: Crown, 2004); Ashmore, *Carry It On*; Emilye Crosby, *A Little Taste of Freedom: The Black Freedom Struggle in Claiborne County, Mississippi* (Chapel Hill: University of North Carolina Press, 2005); Christina Greene, *Our Separate Ways: Women and the Black*

Freedom Movement in Durham, North Carolina (Chapel Hill: University of North Carolina Press, 2005); Kent B. Germany, *New Orleans after the Promises: Poverty, Citizenship, and the Search for the Great Society* (Athens: University of Georgia Press, 2007); Timothy J. Minchin, *From Rights to Economics: The Ongoing Struggle for Black Equality in the U.S. South* (Gainesville: University Press of Florida, 2007); Cynthia Griggs Fleming, *In the Shadow of Selma: The Continuing Struggle for Civil Rights in the Rural South* (Lanham, Md.: Rowman and Littlefield, 2004).

10. For more on the links between black political empowerment and the decline of movement organizing see Steven F. Lawson, *In Pursuit of Power: Southern Blacks and Electoral Politics, 1965–1982* (New York: Columbia University Press, 1985); John Rozier, *Black Boss: Political Revolution in a Georgia County* (Athens: University of Georgia Press, 1982); Frank R. Parker, *Black Votes Count: Political Empowerment in Mississippi after 1965* (Chapel Hill: University of North Carolina Press, 1990); Melissa Fay Greene, *Praying for Sheetrock* (New York: Fawcett Columbine, 1992); Katherine Tate, *From Protest to Politics: The New Black Voters in American Elections* (Cambridge, Mass.: Harvard University Press, 1994); Cedric Johnson, *Revolutionaries to Race Leaders: Black Power and the Making of African American Politics* (Minneapolis: University of Minnesota Press, 2007).

11. U.S. Bureau of the Census, *Eighteenth Census of the United States, 1960*, 59–107.

12. Ibid., 193; SNCC, "The General Condition of the Alabama Negro," (Atlanta: SNCC, 1965).

13. The most famous freedom struggles to take place in the Alabama Black Belt occurred in Dallas, Montgomery, and Macon counties, but these were also the most unusual. Their distinctiveness stemmed from the increased political maneuverability that African Americans enjoyed because of the special character of these counties. The city of Montgomery in Montgomery County is the state capital, and the city of Selma in Dallas County is second in size in the region behind Montgomery. As urban centers, African Americans enjoyed a greater degree of social and economic autonomy, created much larger black middle classes, and developed a different set of political relationships with white power brokers. As a result, African Americans had more space to organize. They also had unique organizing opportunities. For example, only in Montgomery could African Americans challenge Jim Crow through a bus boycott, because Montgomery was the only place in the region with a mass transit system. Although Macon County did not have a city the size of either Montgomery or Selma, its largest town, Tuskegee, which was the center of local black protest, was the home of Tuskegee Institute, a historically black college, and a Veterans Administration hospital that employed African Americans. Both institutions created an uncommon degree of black independence and spurred the development of a black middle class. The only other places in the Black Belt that had black institutions of higher education were Montgomery, home of Alabama State University, and Selma, home of

tiny Selma University. And no other place had a federally operated enterprise for African Americans like the VA hospital. Not surprisingly, Macon County had the highest percentage of registered African Americans in the state in 1960 at 23 percent. Only six other counties had double-digit percentages, and the only other Black Belt county was Sumter County at 15 percent. See SNCC, "The General Condition of the Alabama Negro," 24–26. For more on civil rights in Montgomery see David Garrow, *Bearing the Cross: Martin Luther King, Jr., and the Southern Christian Leadership Conference* (New York: Morrow, 1986); Stewart Burns, ed., *Daybreak of Freedom: The Montgomery Bus Boycott* (Chapel Hill: University of North Carolina Press, 1997). For more on the struggle in Selma see David Garrow, *Protest at Selma: Martin Luther King, Jr., and the Voting Rights Act of 1965* (New Haven, Conn.: Yale University Press, 1978). For a comparative look at black protest in Montgomery and Selma see J. Mills Thornton, *Dividing Lines: Municipal Politics and the Struggle for Civil Rights in Montgomery, Birmingham, and Selma* (Tuscaloosa: University of Alabama Press, 2002). The definitive work on Tuskegee remains Robert J. Norrell, *Reaping the Whirlwind: The Civil Rights Movement in Tuskegee* (New York: Vintage, 1986).

14. For more on African American organizing in the rural Black Belt see Ashmore, *Carry It On*; Fleming, *In the Shadow of Selma*; Branch, *At Canaan's Edge*; Gaillard, *Cradle of Freedom*. For a general treatment of the African American organizing tradition see Payne, *I've Got the Light of Freedom*; Ortiz, *Emancipation Betrayed*. Excellent works that probe white resistance in the rural South include Moye, *Let the People Decide*; Joseph Crespino, *In Search of Another Country: Mississippi and the Conservative Counterrevolution* (Princeton, N.J.: Princeton University Press, 2007).

15. In recent years, scholars have advanced the idea of a Long Civil Rights Movement, which revises the movement's beginning by locating its origin in the New Deal and World War II eras rather than in the mid-1950s with the U.S. Supreme Court's *Brown* ruling and the Montgomery bus boycott. While this framework correctly places the roots of 1960s black protest before the 1950s, it has its limits. It does not provide for the absence of civil rights activism during the middle decades of the twentieth century in places with rich traditions of black protest, such as the rural Black Belt. At the same time, it fails to connect civil rights activism in the places where it did occur to the forms of black protest that came before it, such as the streetcar boycotts in southern cities at the turn of the twentieth century, or to the forms of black protest that came after it, particularly Black Power protest. Thus, a significant shortcoming of the Long Civil Rights Movement thesis is that it is not long enough. It ought to extend further, both forward and backward in time. Simply lengthening the period to which it refers is insufficient, however, because the term "civil rights" does not adequately describe the wide range of protest activities that African Americans engaged in before and after the conventional civil rights era. African Americans

agitated for more than the privileges conferred by the state. The term also does not accurately reflect the types of black protest that did not rise to the level of a social movement. It is more useful to frame black protest as a part of an African American freedom struggle, with emancipation as a critical turning point in its evolution. Before emancipation, African Americans focused on obtaining their freedom, in a literal sense, by ending slavery. After emancipation, they concentrated on securing their freedom rights. In the post-emancipation era, black protest was constant, but it manifested itself differently depending on time and place. Black protest also evolved into locally oriented social movements at very specific moments, and only at certain times were these movements linked through national networks. For more on the Long Civil Rights Movement see Jacquelyn Dowd Hall, "The Long Civil Rights Movement and the Political Uses of the Past," *Journal of American History* Vol. 91, Issue 4 (March 2005), 1233–1263; Robert Rodgers Korstad, *Civil Rights Unionism: Tobacco Workers and the Struggle for Democracy in the Mid-Twentieth-Century South* (Chapel Hill: University of North Carolina Press, 2003); Nikhil Pal Singh, *Black Is a Country: Race and the Unfinished Struggle for Democracy* (Cambridge, Mass.: Harvard University Press, 2004). For a provocative critique of the Long Civil Rights Movement thesis see Sundiata Keita Cha-Jua and Clarence Lang, "The 'Long Movement' as Vampire: Temporal and Spatial Fallacies in Recent Black Freedom Studies," *Journal of African American History* Vol. 92, Issue 4 (Fall 2007), 265–288. See also Peter F. Lau, *Democracy Rising: South Carolina and the Fight for Black Equality since 1865* (Lexington: University Press of Kentucky, 2006), 1–14.

16. Most examinations of civil rights in Alabama focus on Birmingham, Montgomery, and Selma. J. Mills Thornton treats all three in *Dividing Lines*. For more on civil rights in Birmingham see Glenn T. Eskew, *But for Birmingham: The Local and National Movements in the Civil Rights Struggle* (Chapel Hill: University of North Carolina Press, 1997); Andrew Mannis, *A Fire You Can't Put Out: The Civil Rights Life of Birmingham's Reverend Fred Shuttlesworth* (Tuscaloosa: University of Alabama Press, 1999); Diane McWhorter, *Carry Me Home: Birmingham, Alabama, the Climatic Battle of the Civil Rights Revolution* (New York: Simon & Schuster, 2001). See also Robert W. Widell, Jr., "'To Stay and Fight': Birmingham, Alabama, and the Modern Black Freedom Struggle" (Ph.D. Dissertation, Emory University, 2007). For an overview of civil rights protest statewide see Gaillard, *Cradle of Freedom*. A model statewide study of rural black protest is Greta de Jong, *A Different Day: African American Struggles for Justice in Rural Louisiana, 1900–1970* (Chapel Hill: University of North Carolina Press, 2002).

17. Popular narratives of the civil rights movement continue to use 1965 as an end date and tend to ignore black protest beyond that time. See, for example, Fred Powledge, *Free at Last? The Civil Rights Movement and the People Who Made It* (Boston: Little, Brown, 1991); Juan Williams, *Eyes on the Prize: America's Civil Rights Years, 1954–1965* (New York: Penguin, 1987).

18. The meaning that SNCC attached to Black Power, as well as Black Power's experiential origin, have been lost over time, replaced by the mistaken belief that Black Power was simpleminded rhetoric inspired by the violence of urban rebellions, a view made popular by African American moderates and white liberals who objected to SNCC's approach to change. Although Carson, Dittmer, and Payne demonstrate that SNCC's version of Black Power neither was the product of urban uprisings nor meant using violence to realize impossible dreams, distortions persist. See, for example, Alan J. Matusow, *The Unraveling of America: A History of Liberalism in the 1960s* (New York: Harper & Row, 1984); Todd Gitlin, *The Sixties: Years of Hope, Days of Rage* (New York: Bantam, 1989). For variations of the usual interpretations of SNCC's decline see Belinda Robnett, *How Long? How Long? African-American Women in the Struggle for Civil Rights* (New York: Oxford University Press 1997); Lynn Olson, *Freedom's Daughters: The Unsung Heroines of the Civil Rights Movement from 1830 to 1970* (New York: Scribner, 2001); David Halberstam, *The Children* (New York: Random House, 1998).

CHAPTER 1

1. "Negro credulity," Hayneville *Examiner* (10 May 1882).
2. Ibid.
3. Historian Laurie Green refers to these antebellum attitudes as a "plantation mentality." See *Memphis and the Black Freedom Struggle* (Chapel Hill: University of North Carolina Press, 2007), 1–14.
4. W. E. B. Du Bois completed *The Economics of Emancipation: A Social Study of the Alabama Black Belt* in May 1908 but the Labor Department deemed it too political to publish. W. E. B. Du Bois to Charles P. Neill, (24 September 1906), DP, Reel 3, Frame 402; Du Bois to Neill, (7 November 1908), DP, Reel 3, Frame 461; Du Bois, *Dusk of Dawn: Toward an Autobiography of a Race Concept* (New Brunswick, N.J.: Transaction, 1940), 86.
5. Du Bois offered his assessment of Lowndes County in an essay based on his preliminary findings that he presented at the American Economic Association annual meeting in 1906. W. E. B. Du Bois, "The Economic Future of the Negro," in *W. E. B. Du Bois Speaks: Speeches and Addresses, 1890–1919*, ed. Philip S. Foner (New York: Pathfinder, 1970), 163.
6. Ibid., 163.
7. R. Russell to William Hall, (12 March 1866), WBHP, Box 1, Folder 16.
8. Poillon in John B. Myers, "Reaction and Adjustment: The Struggle of Alabama Freedmen in Post-bellum Alabama, 1865—1867," *Alabama Historical Quarterly* Vol. 32, Nos. 1 and 2 (Spring and Summer 1970), 14; Myers, "The Alabama Freedmen and Economic Adjustments during Presidential Reconstruction," *Alabama Review* Vol. 26, No. 4 (October 1973), 259–260, 262; Myers, "The Freedmen and the Labor Supply: The Economic Adjustments in Post-bellum

Alabama, 1865–1867," *Alabama Historical Quarterly* Vol. 32, Nos. 3 and 4 (Fall and Winter 1970), 164; Meyers, "The Freedmen and the Law in Post-bellum Alabama, 1865–1863," *Alabama Review* Vol. 23, No. 1 (January 1970), 60–61; Roger Ransom and Richard Sutch, *One Kind of Freedom: The Economic Consequences of Emancipation* (Cambridge: Cambridge University Press, 1977), 60; Leon Litwack, *Been in the Storm So Long: The Aftermath of Slavery* (New York: Knopf, 1979), 322–323.

   9. *Book of Marriage Licenses for Colored Persons* (1863), Lowndes County Courthouse; Hahn, *A Nation under Our Feet*, 166; Couto, *Ain't Gonna Let Noboby Turn Me Round*, 86.

   10. "Narrative of Emma L. Howard," (circa 1930s), WPA, SG 22774, Folder "Dekalb Co., #2"; James William Shores, "Reminiscence," (1851–1861), SPR 214, ADAH.

   11. "History of Bethany Baptist Church," (31 July 1950), *Alabama Church Records*, Coley 7S, Box 7, Folder 57, ADAH; June Albaugh, *Collirene: The Queen Hill* (Montgomery, Ala.: Herff Jones—Paragon, 1977), 99; Peter Kolchin, *First Freedom: The Response of Alabama's Blacks to Emancipation and Reconstruction* (Westport, Conn.: Greenwood, 1972), 107.

   12. Fort Deposit *Vindicator* (18 November 1898); Charles Denby, *Indignant Heart: A Black Worker's Journal* (Boston: South End, 1978), 11–14; "Historical Persons, Events, Data, Etc . . . " (15 September 1938), WPA, SG 22779, Folder A.

   13. Hayneville *Examiner* (4 August 1881) and (22 October 1884); Fort Deposit *Vindicator* (18 November 1898); Glen Sisk, "Alabama Black Belt: A Social History, 1875–1917," (Ph.D. Dissertation, Duke University, 1951), 384–389. For more on the role of fraternal orders in the post-emancipation era see Ortiz, *Emancipation Betrayed*.

   14. "Annual Report on the Condition of Education in Each County Board of Education," (1871), ADEP, SG 23760.

   15. Richard Bailey, *Neither Carpetbaggers nor Scalawags: Black Officeholders during the Reconstruction of Alabama, 1867–1878* (Montgomery: R. Bailey, 1993), 11–14; Walter L. Fleming, *Civil War and Reconstruction in Alabama* (Spartanburg, S.C.: Reprint Co., 1978), 387–388, 660, 671, 684; Kolchin, *First Freedom*, 151, 154; Meyers, "The Freedmen and the Law," 58–62; Horace M. Bond, *Negro Education in Alabama: A Study of Cotton and Steel* (Washington, D.C.: Associated, 1939), 64; "Interesting Points and Personages, Lowndes County," (17 June 1937), and "Historical Persons, Dates and Points: Lowndes County," (15 July 1938), WPA, SG 22779, Folder A; "Historical Persons, Facts, Dates, etc.," (n.d.), WPA, SG 22779, Folder B. For an excellent analysis of the ramifications of the paramilitary traditions of southern whites see Hahn, *A Nation under Our Feet*, 265–314.

   16. Loren Schweninger, "Alabama Blacks and the Congressional Reconstruction Acts of 1867," *Alabama Review* Vol. 31, No. 3 (July 1978), 185; Registered Voters List, Lowndes County, Alabama, (1867), *Alabama Secretary of State Papers*, SG 2702, ADAH.

17. "Colored subscribers," Hayneville *Examiner* (14 February 1883); Bailey, *Neither Carpetbaggers nor Scalawags*, 73, 79, 241; "Interesting Points and Personages," (17 June 1937), and "Lowndesboro," (15 April 1938), WPA, SG 22779, Folder A and Folder B.

18. Ben DeLemos to Editor, Hayneville *Examiner* (19 April 1882). Black voters elected John McDuffie probate judge in 1868 in an uncontested election. In 1874, McDuffie defeated his Democratic opponent by 3,151 votes. He chaired the county Republican Party executive committee for twelve years between 1868 and 1882. Hayneville *Examiner* (5 April 1882).

19. Bailey, *Neither Carpetbaggers nor Scalawags*, 207.

20. Bragg in Mildred Brewer Russell, *Lowndes Court House: A Chronicle of Hayneville, an Alabama Black Belt Village, 1820–1900* (Montgomery, Ala.: Paragon, 1951), 132; John Pritchett to Doctor, (26 November 1880), *Alabama Department of Public Health Papers*, SG 7055, Folder "Lowndes Co. Correspondence, 1885," ADAH; Hayneville *Examiner* (19 May 1881), (2 August 1881), and (19 April 1882).

21. Hayneville *Examiner* (21 June 1882), (12 July 1882), (9 August 1882), (16 August 1882), (23 July 1884), and (22 October 1884); Leah R. Atkins, "Populism in Alabama: Reuben F. Kolb and the Appeals to Minority Groups," *Alabama Historical Quarterly* Vol. 32, Nos. 3 and 4 (Fall and Winter 1970), 167–180.

22. U.S. Commission on Civil Rights, *The Voting Rights Act . . . The First Months* (Washington, D.C.: Government Printing Office, 1965), 1–7; Couto, *Ain't Gonna Let Nobody Turn Me Round*, 232; Eagles, *Outside Agitator*, 99; Fleming, *Civil War and Reconstruction in Alabama*, 807.

23. Montgomery *Advertiser* (31 March 1888), (5 April 1888), and (5 May 1888).

24. "Negro put to death for attack on girl," Atlanta *Constitution* (19 December 1914).

25. "Two Negroes said to have held up man," Montgomery *Advertiser* (24 July 1917); "Two Negroes caught," Montgomery *Advertiser* (25 July 1917); Eagles, *Outside Agitator*, 101.

26. Warren Stone Reese, Jr. (1866–1935) was the U.S. district attorney in charge of the Middle District of Alabama from 1897 to 1905 and 1909 to 1913. Warren Reese to Attorney General, (10 June 1903), and Reese to Attorney General, [Field Report] (15 June 1903), PF, File 5280-03. See also Reese to Booker T. Washington, (1 February 1905), in *The Booker T. Washington Papers, Vol. 8*, ed. Louis Harlan (Urbana: University of Illinois Press, 1972–1984), 185–187n1. For more on peonage see Pete Daniels's definitive study *The Shadow of Slavery: Peonage in the South, 1901—1969* (Urbana: University of Illinois Press, 1972, 1990).

27. Reese described Sheriff J. W. Dickson (1854–1929) and his five brothers as "men of the highest political and financial influence not only in Lowndes county [*sic*] but in the State of Alabama." They were affluent planters and controlled "a great deal of labor." Reese misspelled their last name "Dixon" Reese to Attorney General [Field Report], (15 June 1903), PF, File 5280-03.

28. After one of the Dickson brothers followed him into the grand jury room, Dillard Freeman refused to testify without assurances that he did not have to return to Lowndes County. The Freeman case was the only local peonage case that the Justice Department pursued. It did not result in any indictments. Reese to Attorney General [Field Report], (15 June 1903), and Reese to Attorney General, (27 July 1903), PF, File 5280-03.

29. Ransom and Sutch, *One Kind of Freedom*, 24; Bond, *Negro Education in Alabama*, 81; "Annual Report on the Condition of Education in Each County Board of Education," (1871), ADEP, SG 23760; Kolchin, *First Freedom*, 180.

30. Kenneth B. White, "Alabama Freedmen's Bureau and Black Education: The Myth of Opportunity," *Alabama Review* Vol. 34, No. 2 (April 1981), 108, 120.

31. Sisk, "Alabama Black Belt," 197; Bond, *Negro Education in Alabama*, 163; Harlan, *Washington Papers, Vol. 3*, 263n1; Couto, *Ain't Gonna Let Nobody Turn Me Round*, 200.

32. Calhoun Colored School Annual Reports, (1899–1900), (1904–1905), and (1908–1909), ADEP, LPR 139, Box 8.

33. "Lowndes Training School auditorium," Montgomery *Advertiser* (25 March 1951); "Historical Points, Persons, Dates," (n.d.), and "'Central' or Lowndes Co. Training School," (12 July 1939), WPA, SG 22779, Folder A; Negro Extension Agent Annual Report, (1933), ACES.

34. A few weeks after the lynching of Theo Calloway, a sheriff's posse encountered armed resistance on an N. J. Bell plantation outside of Calhoun. The next morning one hundred local whites joined thirty-eight state militiamen to "hunt down the disturbers of the peace." Forty African Americans died during the week. Montgomery *Advertiser* (8 April 1888), (5 May 1888), (6 May 1888), and (7 May 1888); Couto, *Ain't Gonna Let Nobody Turn Me Round*, 204.

35. Calhoun Colored School Annual Report (1915–1916), ADEP, LPR 139, Box 8; Booker T. Washington, "An Address at the Funeral of Mabel Wilhemina Dillingham," (17 October 1894), in *Washington Papers, Vol. 3*, 481–482; Couto, *Ain't Gonna Let Nobody Turn Me Round*, 204, 236.

36. *1901 Assessment of Taxes on Real Estate and Property in the County of Lowndes, for the Year 1902*, (1902), Lowndes County Courthouse; Washington to Dillingham, (15 August 1891), in *Washington Papers, Vol. 3*, 163–164.

37. Washington, "An Address at the Funeral of Mabel Wilhemina Dillingham," (17 October 1894), in *Washington Papers, Vol. 3*, 481–482; Rose Herlong Ellis, "The Calhoun School, Miss Charlotte Thorn's 'Lighthouse on the Hill' in Lowndes County Alabama," *Alabama Review* Vol. 32, No. 3 (July 1984), 186; Calhoun Colored School Annual Report (1915–1916), ADEP, LPR 139, Box 8.

38. Calhoun Colored School Annual Reports, (1896), (1897), (1897–1898), (1901–1902), (1927–1928), ADEP, LPR 139, Box 8; "National Register of Historic Places Nomination Form: Calhoun School," (22 July 1975), *Public Information Subject Files*, SG 6880, Folder 2, ADAH; "Confidential Memorandum to Miss

Thorn and Mr. Dickinson," (24 December 1931), PSC, MG 162, Box 25, Folder 16; "Calhoun Colored School," Lowndes *Signal*, (9 March 1933).

39. Calhoun Colored School Annual Report, (1896), ADEP, LPR 139, Box 8.

40. Calhoun Colored School Annual Reports (1897), (1897–1898), (1910–1911), (1928–1929), ADEP, LPR 139, Box 8; Butler R. Wilson, "What I Saw at Calhoun," (15 July 1931), PSC, MG 162, Box 25, Folder 16.

41. Couto, *Ain't Gonna Let Nobody Turn Me Round*, 177; Charles S. Johnson, Edwin R. Embree, and W. W. Alexander, *The Collapse of Cotton Tenancy: Summary of Field Studies and Statistical Surveys, 1933–35* (Chapel Hill: University of North Carolina Press, 1937), 1–33; Sisk, "Alabama Black Belt," 29–32.

42. W. E. B. Du Bois, *The Souls of Black Folk* (New York: Vintage, 1903, 1990), 96.

43. Du Bois, "Memorandum for U.S. Labor Bureau on Lowndes County Schedules," (16 February 1907), dp, Reel 3, Frame 431; Du Bois to Neill, (3 March 1907), dp, Reel 3, Frame 438; "South's tenant farmers given government aid," Lowndes *Signal* (9 August 1940); Denby, *Indignant Heart*, 10–11; *1901 Assessment of Taxes on Real Estate and Personal Property for Lowndes County* (1902), Lowndes County Courthouse.

44. Calhoun Colored School Annual Reports (1897), (1897–1898), (1899–1900), (1905–1906), (1929–1930), ADEP, LPR 139, Box 8; "Calhoun School, 1937–1938," 9, ADEP, LPR 139, Box 8, Folder "Calhoun Misc., 1920–1938"; Joseph P. Loud to Land Trust Subscribers, (31 January 1931), PSC, MG 162, Box 25, Folder 16; "Calhoun Colored School," Lowndes *Signal* (9 March 1933); Du Bois, "The Economic Future of the Negro," in *Du Bois Speaks*, 164.

45. Calhoun Colored School Annual Report (1932–1933), ADEP, LPR 139, Box 8; "The Resettlement Program functions in Lowndes County," Lowndes *Signal* (27 November 1935); Negro Extension Agent Annual Report (1937), ACES; "South's tenant farmers given government aid," Lowndes *Signal* (9 August 1940); Donald Holly, "The Negro in the New Deal Resettlement Program," *Agricultural History* Vol. 45, No. 3 (July 1971), 179–193; Elisabeth Lash-Quinn, *Black Neighbors: Race and the Limits of Reform in the American Settlement House Movement, 1890–1945* (Chapel Hill: University of North Carolina Press, 1993), 97–98.

46. Mays in Leon Litwack, *Trouble in Mind: Black Southerners in the Age of Jim Crow* (New York: Knopf, 1998), 321.

47. Wesley Smith Affidavit (1935), NAACP, RG II, Box C-348.

48. William P. Browne, "Benign Public Policies, Malignant Consequences, and the Demise of African American Agriculture," and Jeannie Whayne, "'I've Have Been through Fire': Black Agricultural Extension Agents and the Politics of Negotiation," in *African American Life in the Rural South, 1900–1950*, ed. R. Douglas Hart (Columbia: University of Missouri Press, 2003), 138, 143, 178. See also Woodruff, *American Congo*, 152–190.

49. Jessie Ames to J. H. McCoy (6 August 1931), ASWPL, Reel 5, No. 97, Frame 974.

50. "We the Negroes of Gary Place, Benton, Churchill Beat and Gordonsville, Ala." to B. M. Miller, (15 August 1933); Miller to A. E. Gamble, (21 August 1933); Miller to H. P. Rogers, (21 August 1933); Gamble to Miller (24 August 1933), AGP, SG 19940, Folder 9.

51. Denby, *Indignant Heart*, 11.

52. Smith Affidavit (1935), NAACP, RG II, Box C-348. The Sharecroppers' Union was a labor association organized by members of the Communist Party that sought to improve the wages and work environment of black farmers. For more see Kelley, *Hammer and Hoe*; Theodore Rosengarten, *All God's Dangers: The Life of Nate Shaw* (New York: Knopf, 1974).

53. Annie May Meriwether, Henry Roberts, and Wesley Smith Affidavits (1935), NAACP, RG II, Box C-348; "Lowndes farm hands shot by Red organizers," Montgomery *Advertiser* (23 August 1935); Albert Jackson to Bibb Graves, (25 August 1935), AGP, SG 12165, Folder 1; Kelly, *Hammer and Hoe*, 165–168.

54. Rather than spark black protest, the New Deal tended to impede it in the rural South by propping up wealthy white landowners through policies and programs implemented and administered on a racially discriminatory basis. World War II also failed to create the space that African Americans, including veterans, needed in order to challenge white supremacy publicly, even though it served as a catalyst for black protest in the urban South and North. In places like Lowndes County, the war created no new opportunities for workers to organize because industrialization never occurred. In fact, the war reduced the bargaining power of African Americans by accelerating agricultural mechanization. Much like the New Deal, the war also failed to liberalize white attitudes. During and after the conflict, Lowndes County whites remained steadfast in their commitment to white supremacy. The contradictions inherent in fighting fascism abroad and maintaining segregation at home had little affect on them. With the exception of the weeklong sharecroppers' strike in 1935, the 1930s and 1940s were a fallow period for public protest, which limits the explanatory power of the New Deal and World War II as the starting point of movement activism. This does not mean, however, that African Americans did not organize and agitate for change either before or during this period in ways that directly influenced later protest. But it does mean that the question of movement origins has to be recast to account for both the absence of public protest in rural counties like Lowndes, and for the long history of race consciousness and less visible activism in these very same places. See Richard Dalfiume, "The 'Forgotten Years' of the Negro Revolution," *Journal of American History* Vol. 55, No. 1 (June 1968), 90–160; Harvard Sitkoff, "African American Militancy in the World War II South: Another Perspective," in *Remaking Dixie: The Impact of World War II on the American South*, ed. Neil R. McMillen (Jackson: University of Mississippi Press, 1997), 70–92; Patricia Sullivan, *Days of Hope: Race and Democracy in the New Deal Era* (Chapel Hill: University of North Carolina Press, 1996).

55. In 1940, there were 19,204 African Americans living in Lowndes County, but a decade later the county's black population had fallen to 14,796. Eagles, *Outside Agitator*, 109; "Negro Exodus Cuts Lowndes' Population," Birmingham *News* (19 July 1931).

56. Bruce Nelson, "Organized Labor and the Struggle for Black Equality in Mobile during World War II," *Journal of American History* Vol. 80, No. 3 (December 1993), 956; Eagles, *Outside Agitator*, 123; Gaillard, *Cradle of Freedom*, 285–286; Charles Smith Interview (14 September 1998).

57. Smith Interview (14 September 1998).

58. Ibid.

59. Ibid.

60. John Hulett Interview (1973), (9 September 1998), and (2 August 2000); "Lowndes County Freedom Organization leaders," *The Movement* (June 1966); Gaillard, *Cradle of Freedom*, 287; Eagles, *Outside Agitator*, 122–123.

61. Paul Geib, "From Mississippi to Milwaukee: A Case Study of Southern Black Migration to Milwaukee, 1940–1970," *Journal of Negro History* Vol. 83, No. 4 (Autumn 1998), 229–248.

62. Denby, *Indignant Heart*, 29, 54–88.

63. Ibid., 89–94.

64. Ibid., 103, 96, 120, 161, 179.

65. Ibid., 175–177.

66. Dorothy Dewberry Aldridge Interview (13 June 2000).

67. SNCC, "The General Condition of the Alabama Negro," 25. For more on *Smith v. Allwright* see Peter F. Lau, *From the Grassroots to the Supreme Court: Brown v. Board of Education and American Democracy* (Durham, N.C.: Duke University Press, 2004).

68. NAACP Legal Department Press Release, (28 April 1948), NAACP, Part 4, Reel 5; Robert J. Norrell, "Labor at the Ballot Box: Alabama Politics from the New Deal to the Dixiecrat Movement," *Journal of Southern History* Vol. 57, No. 2 (May 1991), 201–234.

69. "Boswell Amendment in right direction," Lowndes *Signal* (18 October 1946).

70. The vote in Lowndes County was 581 to 104 in favor of adopting the amendment. "Boswell vote," Birmingham *Age* (6 November 1946); "State press on the Boswell Amendment," Birmingham *News* (16 October 1946).

71. NAACP Press Release, (31 March 1949), NAACP, Part 4, Reel 5; "Alabama applies stiff voter test," New York *Times* (31 January 1965); SNCC, "The General Condition of the Alabama Negro," 28; Alabama Application for Registration, Questionnaire, and Oaths, NAACP, Part 4 Supplement, Reel 4, Frame 549.

72. In 1910, four years before the boll weevil arrived in Lowndes County, local farmers planted 123,000 acres of cotton. In 1928, they planted only 60,000 acres of cotton. Increasingly, large landowners converted their cotton fields to pasture land. By 1928, the value of the county's dairy products had reached $762,000, up

from $76,000 in 1910. Tractors, mechanical cotton pickers, and other forms of mechanized farm equipment, which began appearing on county plantations in the years leading up to and immediately after World War II, completed the transformation of the agricultural economy. By 1960, half of the farms in the county used tractors. Negro Extension Agent Annual Reports (1923), (1929), (1932), ACES; Eagles, *Outside Agitator*, 105–111.

73. According to an investigator for Governor Frank Dixon, Hartsell "set a trap for Thompson." "Report on Lownes [*sic*] County Investigation," (23 June 1942), ASWPL, Reel 2, No. 19, Frame 838; Dixon to Ames, (5 June 1942), ASWPL, Reel 2, No. 19, Frame 832; "Report of Private Investigation; Lowndes County Lynching," (20 June 1942), ASWPL, Reel 2, No. 19, Frame 837.

74. Josephine McCall Interview, (21 May 2008); "Negro killed," Montgomery *Advertiser* (7 December 1941); NAACP Division of Research and Information, "A Record of Mob Violence and Race Clashes in the United States, 1947," (January 1948), NAACP, Part 17, Reel 2, Frame 344.

75. For more on the intersection of the Cold War and civil rights politics see Singh, *Black Is a Country*; Carol Anderson, *Eyes Off the Prize: The United Nations and the African American Struggle for Human Rights, 1944–1955* (Cambridge: Cambridge University Press, 2003); Mary L. Dudziak, *Cold War Civil Rights: Race and the Image of American Democracy* (Princeton, N.J.: Princeton University Press, 2000); Penny Von Eschen, *Race against Empire: Black Americans and Anticolonialism, 1937–1957* (Ithaca, N.Y.: Cornell University Press, 1997); Brenda Gayle Plummer, *Rising Wind: Black Americans and U.S. Foreign Affairs, 1935–1960* (Chapel Hill: University of North Carolina Press, 1996).

76. William G. Porter to Thurgood Marshall, (9 December 1947), copy obtained from Josephine McCall.

77. Willie Brown Affidavit, (6 October 1947); E. D. Nixon to Thurgood Marshall, (10 October 1947); T. Vincent Quinn to Franklin H. Williams, (18 November 1947), NAACP, Part 8, Reel 18, Frames 864–868.

78. Eagles, *Outside Agitator*, 111–112.

79. Hulett in Gaillard, *Cradle of Freedom*, 287.

80. "Yours for Investigation" to NAACP New York office, (5 July 1944), NAACP, Part 8, Reel 20, Frame 284.

81. "Chartered Alabama Branches as of June 1, 1956," NAACP, Part 20, Reel 4, Frame 579; "Alabama State Activities Report," (circa 1955), NAACP, Part 3, Reel 1, Frame 15–16.

82. Eagles, *Outside Agitator*, 120–125; Campbell, "The Lowndes County Freedom Organization," 16; "A worker hits freedom road," *Look* (16 November 1965); Elzie McGill Interview, (4 August 1968); Lillian McGill Interview, (2 August 2000).

83. "Mississippi White Citizen Council head spoke at Hayneville meeting Friday," and "Selma attorney talks at WCC rally," Lowndes *Signal* (24 February 1956);

"Citizens council to hold mass meeting," Lowndes *Signal* (17 June 1965). For more on the origins and the development of the Citizens' Council see Moye, *Let the People Decide*, 64–87.

1. Eagles, *Outside Agitator*, 112; "Black Power in the Black Belt," *The Progressive* (October 1966).
2. Hulett Interview, (30 May 1968) and (17 July 2000); "Lowndes County Freedom Organization leaders," *The Movement* (June 1966); Eagles, *Outside Agitator*, 120–123.
3. J. L. Chestnut, Jr., and Julia Cass, *Black in Selma: The Uncommon Life of J. L. Chestnut, Jr.* (New York: Farrar, Straus and Giroux, 1990), 120, 131.
4. Campbell, "The Lowndes County Freedom Organization," 34; Hulett Interview, (30 May 1968) and (17 July 2000).
5. "The Black Panther Party," *Young Socialist* (May–June–July 1966); Gaillard, *Cradle of Freedom*, 287–288.
6. "The Black Panther Party," *Young Socialist* (May–June–July 1966); Lillian McGill Interview, (2 August 2000).
7. Hulett Interview, (30 May 1968) and (17 July 2000); "A new freedom party," *The Militant* (2 May 1966); *The Black Panther Party* (New York: Merit, 1966), 19; Mathew Jackson, Sr., Interview, (4 August 1968); "Sheriff Hulett honored at reception," Lowndes *Signal* (4 March 1993).
8. "Negro minister says white threats cost him," New York *Times* (1 March 1965).
9. Ibid.
10. Emma Lee Jackson Interview, (4 August 1968).
11. For more on Bloody Sunday see Branch, *At Canaan's Edge*, 44–57.
12. "Victims of 'White Supremacy,' 1951–1965," NAACP, Part 22, Reel 26, Frame 945; "Woman is shot to death on Lowndes County roads," New York *Times* (26 March 1965).
13. "A new freedom party," *The Militant* (2 May 1966); "Alabama Negroes press voting drive," New York *Times* (4 May 1965); Elzie McGill Interview, (4 August 1968); Eagles, *Outside Agitator*, 121.
14. "Alabama Negroes press voting drive," New York *Times* (4 May 1965); Elzie McGill Interview, (4 August 1968); Eagles, *Outside Agitator*, 121.
15. Lillian McGill Interview, (29 May 1968); "Lowndes marks a year," *Southern Courier* (2–3 April 1966); Eagles, *Outside Agitator*, 122.
16. Lillian McGill Interview, (29 May 1968); "Lowndes marks a year"; SNCC and SCLC staff meeting minutes, (10 February 1965), SNCC, Box 7, Folder "Staff Meetings, Jan–Mar 1965"; "SCLC Organizing in Lowndes County, Alabama,"

(February 1965), SNCC, Box 94, Folder 9; "Negroes suspend Selma protests," New York *Times* (7 February 1965); CAP Application, (1966), SCLC, Box 148, Folder 2; Eagles, *Outside Agitator*, 122; Garrow, *Bearing the Cross*, 384; Branch, *At Canaan's Edge*, 21–22.

17. Lillian McGill Interview, (29 May 1968) and (2 August 2000); "Lowndes marks a year," *Southern Courier* (2–3 April 1966); Eagles, *Outside Agitator*, 125–126.

18. "Lowndes marks a year," *Southern Courier* (April 2–3, 1966); Elzie McGill Interview, (4 August 1968); Gaillard, *Cradle of Freedom*, 288; Adam Fairclough, "The Preachers and the People: The Origins and Early Years of the Southern Christian Leadership Conference, 1955–1959," *Journal of Southern History* Vol. 52, No. 3 (August 1986), 403–440.

19. Ed Moore King Interview, (17 July 2000).

20. Ibid.

21. Ibid.

22. "Rights marchers push into region called hostile," New York *Times* (23 March 1965).

23. Ryals in Eagles, *Outside Agitator*, 114.

24. Eagles, *Outside Agitator*, 125; CAP Application, (1966), SCLC, Box 148, Folder 2.

25. Wide Area Telephone Service (WATS) Report, (10 April 1965), SNCC, Box 39, Folder 5; Elzie McGill Interview, (4 August 1968); King Interview, (17 July 2000); "Alabama march passes midpoint," New York *Times* (24 March 1965); Garrow, *Bearing the Cross*, 411–412.

26. Clayborne Carson and Kris Shepard, eds., *A Call to Conscience: The Landmark Speeches of Dr. Martin Luther King, Jr.* (New York: Warner, 2001), 119–132; "Woman is shot to death on Lowndes County roads," New York *Times* (26 March 1965).

27. Stanton, *From Selma to Sorrow*, 60–64; "Praised by ex-neighbor," New York *Times* (26 March 1965); "Woman is shot to death on Lowndes County roads," New York *Times* (26 March 1965); "Mrs. Liuzzo 'felt' she had to help," New York *Times* (27 March 1965); "Dr. King to step up drive," New York *Times* (28 March 1965); WATS Report, (26 March 1965), SNCC, Box 39, Folder 3; "The White House statement by the president," New York *Times* (27 March 1965).

28. Stanton, *From Selma to Sorrow*, 47–51.

29. "Witness to slaying cites harassment," New York *Times* (27 March 1965).

30. Stanton, *From Selma to Sorrow*, 52–55.

31. "Selma Protestant church integrated," New York *Times* (29 March 1965); "Dr. King to step up drive," New York *Times* (28 March 1965).

32. "Lowndes marks a year," *Southern Courier* (2–3 April 1966); "LCCMHR Certificate of Incorporation," (2 November 1965), SCLC, Box 148, Folder 2; WATS Report, (24 October 1965), SNCC, Box 41, Folder 2.

33. "Lowndes County Freedom Organization leaders," *The Movement* (June 1966).

34. "Selma Workshop Report," (13–16 December 1963), SNCC, Box 20, Folder 5; Silas Norman and John Love, "Selma, Alabama," (March 1965), SNCC, Box 149, Folder 18; "'Snick' in Alabama," (1966), SNCC, Box 47, Folder 73; Field Report by Bernard Lafayette in Forman, *The Making of Black Revolutionaries*, 318–320, 326; SNCC, "Special Report," (February 1965), SNCC, Box 35, Folder 5; "Black Belt, Alabama," *The Commonweal* (7 August 1964); "SNCC Special Report," (February 1965), SNCC, Box 149, Folder 1; Silas Norman, Jr. Interview, (30 June 2000); Halberstam, *The Children*, 415–416.

35. "SNCC's path? Carmichael answers," *National Guardian* (4 June 1966).

36. Stokely Carmichael in "Integration is completely irrelevant to us," *The Movement* (June 1966); "Ready for the revolution," *Emerge* (June 1997).

37. Carmichael and Hamilton, *Black Power*, 96.

38. Sellers, *River of No Return*, 111; "Interview with new SNCC chairman," *The Militant* (23 May 1966); Dittmer, *Local People*, 302

39. Stokely Carmichael discusses the value and importance of community control in *Black Power*. See also Wilson Jeremiah Moses, *The Golden Age of Black Nationalism, 1850–1925* (Oxford: Oxford University Press, 1978); Van Deburg, *New Day in Babylon*. For the mechanics of how local people supported SNCC, see Payne, *I've Got the Light of Freedom*.

40. Norman Interview, (30 June 2000); WATS Report (4 February 1965), SNCC, Box 39, Folder 2; John Lewis telegram, (21 February 1965), SNCC, Box 2, Folder 7; Bruce Perry, ed., *Malcolm X: The Last Speeches* (New York: Pathfinder, 1989), 145; Joyce Ladner, "What 'Black Power' Means to Negroes in Mississippi: The New Negro Ideology," *Trans-Action* Vol. 5 (November 1967), 8–11; Carson, *In Struggle*, 135.

41. "Assumptions Made by SNCC," (11 May 1966), SNCC, Box 7, Folder "Staff Meetings, Jan–Dec., 1966"; Forman, *The Making of Black Revolutionaries*, 408; "Ready for the revolution," *Emerge* (June 1997); Carson, *In Struggle*, 134; Fanon Che Wilkins, "The Making of Black Internationalists: SNCC and Africa before the Launching of Black Power, 1960–1965," *Journal of African American History* Vol. 92, Issue 4 (Fall 2007), 467–468.

42. Dittmer, *Local People*, 320–321, 340.

43. Carmichael, *Ready for Revolution*, 437.

44. Sellers, *River of No Return*, 130–147; Cynthia Griggs Fleming, *Soon We Will Not Cry: The Liberation of Ruby Doris Smith Robinson* (Lanham, Md.: Rowman and Littlefield, 1998); Carmichael, *Ready for Revolution*, 210, 338.

45. Carmichael, *Ready for Revolution*, 172, 210, 338.

46. SNCC, "Special Report," (February 1962), SNCC, Box 35, Folder 5; Norman and Love, "Selma, Alabama," (March 1965), SNCC, Box 149, Folder 18; "Selma Workshop Report," (13–16 December 1963), SNCC, Box 20, Folder 5; "'Snick' in Alabama," (1966), SNCC, Box 47, Folder 73.

47. Atlanta SNCC Office, "Report on Selma," (7 March 1965), SNCC, Box 39, Folder 3; John Lewis to Dr. Martin Luther King, Jr., (7 March 1965), SNCC, Box 2, Folder 7; Norman Interview, (30 June 2000); SNCC and SCLC staff meeting minutes, (10 February 1965), SNCC, Box 7, Folder "Staff Meetings, Jan–Mar, 1965"; Garrow, *Bearing the Cross*, 387; Norman in Cheryl Lynn Greenberg, ed., *A Circle of Trust: Remembering* SNCC (New Brunswick, N.J.: Rutgers University Press, 1998), 97.

48. Carmichael, *Ready for Revolution*, 445.

49. Norman in Greenberg, *Circle of Trust*, 97.

50. Carmichael, *Ready for Revolution*, 442.

51. Ibid., 457.

52. Norman in Greenberg, *Circle of Trust*, 97.

53. Carmichael and Hamilton, *Black Power*, 101.

54. Norman Interview, (30 June 2000); Garrow, *Bearing the Cross*, 387; "Ready for the revolution," *Emerge* (June 1997).

55. Carmichael, *Ready for Revolution*, 458.

56. Carmichael Transcript, (19 February 1966), SNCC, Box 94, Folder 9.

57. Carmichael Affidavit, (11 March 1966), SNCC, Box 51, Folder 3; Norman Interview, (30 June 2000).

58. Carmichael, *Ready for Revolution*, 457.

59. As the local movement gained momentum, SCLC announced that it was moving north. By July 1965, Dr. King was in Illinois leading more than ten thousand people through the streets of Chicago. Garrow, *Bearing the Cross*, 415–416, 428, 441, 446; "Dr. King to press new voter drive," New York *Times* (2 April 1965); "Dr. King opens rights drive Tuesday," New York *Times* (20 June 1965); "King leads 10,000 Chicago marchers," *Southern Courier* (30 July 1965); SCLC Annual Report, (August 1965), NAACP, Part 21, Reel 17, Frame 613.

60. Jackson in Greenberg, *Circle of Trust*, 101; Mants in Greenberg, *Circle of Trust*, 98.

61. Jackson in Greenberg, *Circle of Trust*, 101; John Jackson Interview, (3 August 1968).

62. Carmichael Transcript, (19 February 1966), SNCC, Box 94, Folder 9; Mants in Greenberg, *Circle of Trust*, 99; Eagles, *Outside Agitator*, 129–130.

63. Carmichael Transcript, (19 February 1966), SNCC, Box 94, Folder 9.

64. Ibid.

65. Carmichael Transcript, (19 February 1966), SNCC, Box 94, Folder 9; Mants in Greenberg, *Circle of Trust*, 99.

66. "Lowndes County, Alabama," (10 April 1965), SNCC, Box 94, Folder 9.

67. Carmichael Transcript (19 February 1966), SNCC, Box 94, Folder 9.

68. WATS Report, (10 April 1965), SNCC, Box 94, Folder 9; "Contact List, April 5 [1965]," SNCC, Box 16, Folder 5; "Integration is completely irrelevant," *The Movement* (June 1966); WATS Report, (10 April 1965), SNCC, Box 94, Folder 9;

Mathew Jackson, Sr., Interview, (4 August 1968); John Jackson Interview, (14 July 2000); Carmichael Transcript, (19 February 1966), SNCC, Box 94, Folder 9; Hulett Interview, (17 July 2000) and (30 May 1968); Eagles, *Outside Agitator*, 130.

69. Mathew Jackson, Sr., Interview, and Emma Lee Jackson Interview, (4 August 1968).

70. Emma Lee Jackson Interview, (4 August 1968).

71. John Jackson Interview, (14 July 2000); Annie Bell Jackson Interview, (21 July 2000).

72. Gloria Larry House Interview, (28 June 2000).

73. Emma Lee Jackson Interview, (4 August 1968).

74. Martha Prescod Norman in Greenberg, *Circle of Trust*, 109.

75. H. Rap Brown, *Die Nigger Die! A Political Autobiography* (Chicago: Lawrence Hill, 1969, 2002), 92–95.

76. House Interview, (28 June 2000).

77. John Jackson Interview, (14 July 2000).

78. WATS Report, (4 January 1966), SNCC, Box 41, Folder 6; Emma Lee Jackson Interview, (4 August 1968); WATS Report, (18 February 1966), SNCC, Box 41, Folder 9.

79. "A new freedom party," *The Militant* (2 May 1966); *The Black Panther Party*, 19.

80. House Interview, (28 June 2000); "Interview with Alabama Black Panther Party organizer," *The Movement* (February 1966); Eagles, *Outside Agitator*, 128–129.

81. Aldridge Interview, (13 June 2000); House Interview, (28 June 2000); Carmichael Transcript, (19 February 1966), SNCC, Box 94, Folder 9; Eagles, *Outside Agitator*, 129, 137.

82. Carmichael Transcript, (19 February 1966), SNCC, Box 94, Folder 9; John Lewis to Mrs. Marcus I. Tucker, (22 July 1965), SNCC, Box 2, Folder 8; Detroit Area SNCC, *Freedom Voice* (1 April 1965), SNCC, Box 79, Folder 7; Jennifer Lawson Interview, (3 June 2000); "Mosses Negroes want telephones," *Southern Courier* (23 July 1965).

83. Lillian McGill Interview, (29 May 1968); Hulett Interview, (30 May 1968).

84. List of Masonic lodges and contact persons, (n.d.) RMP, Box 1, Folder "List of Masonic Lodges in Lowndes Co."; List of County Churches, (1966) RMP, Box 1, Folder "List of Churches and Meeting Days"; CAP Application, (November 1965), SCLC, Box 148, Folder 2; Hulett Interview, (17 July 2000); Lois E. Myers and Rebecca Sharpless, "'Of the Least and the Most': The African American Rural Church," 55–75, in Hurt, *African American Life in the Rural South, 1900–1950*.

85. "Alabama Negroes press vote drive," New York *Times* (4 May 1965); "Lowndes marks a year," *Southern Courier* (2–3 April 1966); WATS Report, (10 April 1965), SNCC, Box 39, Folder 5; Hulett Interview, (30 May 1968); Elzie McGill Interview, (4 August 1968).

86. CAP Application, (1966), SCLC, Box 148, Folder 2.

87. Emma Lee Jackson Interview, (4 August 1968).

88. Moorer in Couto, *Ain't Gonna Let Nobody Turn Me Round*, 87.

89. "Simon Owens dies in Detroit," Lowndes *Signal* (3 November 1983).

90. Aldridge Interview, (13 June 2000).

91. Sarah Carolyn Reese to John Lewis, (21 June 1965), SNCC, Box 84, Folder 11.

92. [Minutes of] Staff-People's Meeting, (25 May 1965), SNCC, Box 94, Folder 22.

93. Ibid.

94. Uralee Haynes Interview, (23 September 1998).

95. Sarah Logan Interview, (15 September 1998).

96. Haynes in Couto, *Ain't Gonna Let Nobody Turn Me Round*, 89.

97. "Contact List, April 5 [1965]," SNCC, Box 16, Folder 5; Myers and Sharpless, "'Of the Least and the Most': The African American Rural Church," 56–67, in Hurt, *African American Life in the Rural South, 1900–1950*. For more on leadership in Montgomery, Selma, and Tuskegee see Garrow, *Bearing the Cross*; Burns, *Daybreak of Freedom*; Norrell, *Reaping the Whirlwind*.

98. Lillian McGill Interview, (29 May 1968) and (2 August 2000); CAP Application, (1966), SCLC, Box 148, Folder 2.

99. Lillian McGill Interview, (29 May 1968) and (2 August 2000); Hulett Interview, (17 July 2000) and (2 August 2000); CAP Application, (1966), SCLC, Box 148, Folder 2; "2 rights groups," New York *Times* (23 January 1966). For more on black women's leadership see Robnett, *How Long? How Long?*

100. "Alabama Negroes press vote drive," New York *Times* (4 May 1965).

101. WATS Report, (10 April 1965), SNCC, Box 94, Folder 9; Hulett Interview, (30 May 1968).

102. Elzie McGill Interview, (4 August 1968).

103. South Carolina had five members in the U.S. House of Representatives in the first Congress. "Alabama Application for Registration, Questionnaire, and Oaths," NAACP, Part 4 Supplement, Reel 4, Frame 549.

104. WATS Report, (20 April 1965), SNCC, Box 39, Folder 5; WATS Report, (20 May 1965), SNCC, Box 40, Folder 1; "Alabama gains seen by Dr. King," New York *Times* (20 April 1965); "Alabama Negroes press vote drive," New York *Times* (4 May 1965).

105. WATS Report, (20 May 1965), SNCC, Box 40, Folder 1; Eagles, *Outside Agitator*, 132.

106. John Doar to Joseph A. Califano, Jr., (9 August 1965), in Michael Belknap, ed., *Civil Rights, the White House, and the Justice Department: 1945–1968* (New York: Barland, 1991), 196, 210–212.

107. "County in Alabama drops voting test called harsh," New York *Times* (9 July 1965); Doar to Califano (9 August 1965), in Belknap, *Civil Rights, the White House, and the Justice Department*, 196, 210–212; "A letter to Mr. Katzenback," Lowndes *Signal* (26 August 1965); Selma WATS Report, (6 July 1965), SNCC, Box 40, Folder 5.

108. Carmichael in SNCC Press Release, (8 July 1965), SNCC, Box 35, Folder 7.

109. Selma Daily Report, (6 July 1965), SNCC, Box 45, Folder 3; "9 counties to get vote aides today," New York *Times* (10 August 1965); WATS Report, (9 July 1965), SNCC, Box 40, Folder 5.

110. Doar to Califano (9 August 1965), in Belknap, *Civil Rights, the White House, and the Justice Department*, 196, 210–212.

111. Carmichael Transcript, (19 February 1966), SNCC, Box 94, Folder 9.

112. WATS Report, (3 August 1965), SNCC, Box 40, Folder 7; "Lowndes County weekly report," (5 August 1965), SNCC, Box 45, Folder 3.

113. Nicholas Katzenbach to Alabama Boards of Registrars, (8 January 1966), AGP, SG 22435, Folder 7. The 1965 Voting Rights Act authorized the Justice Department to send registrars to counties where less than 50 percent of the voting age population was registered or less than 50 percent of the voting age population participated in the 1964 presidential election. It also suspended the literacy test and similar discriminatory devices in the seven states that still used them; mandated federal oversight of local elections in places covered by the law; and required preclearance of electoral changes by the Justice Department. Commission on Civil Rights, *The Voting Rights Act*, 48–49; "Capitol is scene," New York *Times*, (7 August 1965).

114. In Alabama, Lowndes, Dallas, Hale, and Marengo counties were among the first counties designated by the Justice Department to receive federal registrars. "9 counties to get vote aides today," New York *Times* (10 August 1965); Neil R. McMillen, "Black enfranchisement in Mississippi: Federal enforcement and black protest in the 1960s," *Journal of Southern History* Vol. 43, No. 3 (August 1977), 351–372.

115. "Voting officials sign 1,444 Negroes first day," New York *Times* (11 August 1965); WATS Report, (13 August 1965), SNCC, Box 40, Folder 7; Eagles, *Outside Agitator*, 164.

116. "9 counties to get vote aides today," New York *Times* (10 August 1965); "New federal examiners," *Southern Courier* (13 August 1965); WATS Report, (13 August 1965), SNCC, Box 40, Folder 7; House Interview, (28 June 2000); Commission on Civil Rights, *The Voting Rights Act*, 2, 16, 35; WATS Report, (24 October 1965), SNCC, Box 41, Folder 2.

CHAPTER 3

1. Coleman in Ruby Sales Affidavit, (August 1965), SNCC, Box 45, Folder 12.

2. Sales in Hampton and Fayer, *Voices of Freedom*, 275.

3. "Voter drive," New York *Times* (23 August 1965); "White seminarian slain," New York *Times* (21 August 1965); SNCC Press Release, (21 August 1965), (27 August 1965), (28 August 1965), SNCC, Box 35, Folder 7; "News from the Field," (circa August 1965) SNCC, Box 40, Folder 7; "Daniels in South," *Southern Courier*

(28–29 August 1965); "Cold-blooded bigots'" *Jet* (9 September 1965); Gaillard, *Cradle of Freedom*, 279; Eagles, *Outside Agitator*, 166–179; Branch, *At Canaan's Edge*, 287–288, 305.

4. Carmichael, *Ready for Revolution*, 466–467, 470.

5. Carmichael in WATS Report, (28 August 1965), SNCC, Box 40, Folder 7; "Tense Lowndes erupts," *Southern Courier* (28–29 August 1965); "Voter drive," New York *Times* (23 August 1965); "News from the Field," (n.d.), SNCC, Box 40, Folder 7.

6. Teacher in "Daniels in South to battle hatred," *Southern Courier* (28–29 August 1965).

7. Hulett in Campbell, "The Lowndes County Freedom Organization," 36.

8. Gaillard, *Cradle of Freedom*, 289–290; "Voter drive," New York *Times* (23 August 1965).

9. Deputy sheriff and friend in "Daniels in South to battle hatred," *Southern Courier* (28–29 August 1965); Ryals in "High Alabama aide lays death to Klan," New York *Times* (22 August 1965); friend in "Tense Lowndes erupts," *Southern Courier* (28–29 August 1965); "White seminarian slain," New York *Times* (21 August 1965); "Miss Coleman is named county superintendent," Lowndes *Signal* (7 April 1939).

10. For more on Coleman's background, see Eagles, *Outside Agitator*, 185–193. Perdue in "High Alabama aide lays death to Klan," New York *Times* (22 August 1965), and "Cold-blooded bigots," *Jet* (9 September 1965); resident in "Tense Lowndes erupts," *Southern Courier* (28–29 August 1965); "Grand jury chosen," New York *Times* (14 September 1965); "Alabamian indicted," New York *Times* (10 September 1965); "All or nothing," *Southern Courier* (25–26 September 1965); "Prosecution is replaced," New York *Times* (29 September 1965); "Alabama sheriff's aide acquitted," New York *Times* (1 October 1965); "Lowndes County justice," *Southern Courier* (9–10 October 1965). The charge for shooting Morrisroe was eventually dismissed with prejudice by judge T. Werth Thagard. Coleman never stood trial for the crime. " . . . And Thomas Coleman goes free," *Southern Courier* (1–2 October 1966); "Indictment refused," New York *Times* (14 September 1966).

11. Resident in "Tense Lowndes erupts," *Southern Courier* (28–29 August 1965).

12. Trustees in "'Central' or Lowndes County Training School," (12 July 1939), and "Historical Points, Persons, Dates," (n.d.), WPA, SG 22779, Folder A; "Lowndes Training School auditorium to be dedicated," Montgomery *Advertiser* (25 March 1951); "Lowndes school dedication," Alabama *Journal* (30 April 1951).

13. "Portrait of a county with problems," *Southern Courier* (2–3 April 1966); *United States v. Lowndes County Board of Education et al.*, (11 January 1966), AGP, SG 20061, Folder 22; Alabama Department of Education, "Lowndes County Survey, 182," (1964), ADEP, SG 22324; "Negro, white Lowndes parents wonder about school integration," *Southern Courier* (13 August 1965); Lillian McGill

Interview, (29 May 1968); "'Central' or Lowndes County Training School," (12 July 1939), WPA, SG 22779, Folder A.

14. Timothy Mays Interview, (27 July 2000); "Negro, white Lowndes parents wonder," *Southern Courier* (13 August 1965); "A new freedom party," *The Militant* (2 May 1966); Hulett in *The Black Panther Party*, 19; Fleming, *In the Shadow of Selma*, 229.

15. Lillian McGill Interview, (29 May 1968); Hulett Interview, (1973); Eagles, *Outside Agitator*, 122–123; "First day of integration," *Southern Courier* (4–5 September 1966).

16. Mrs. Frank Miles, Jr., in "[Minutes] Staff—People's Meeting [at Selma, Alabama SNCC office]," (24 May 1965), SNCC, Box 94, Folder 22.

17. "Lowndes renews boycott," *Southern Courier* (25–26 September 1965); Lillian McGill Interview, (29 May 1968).

18. Carmichael in "New leaders and new course for 'Snick,'" New York *Times* (22 May 1966), and "Dr. King disputes Negro separatist," New York *Times* (28 May 1966).

19. Lillian McGill Interview, (29 May 1968); "Lowndes County Freedom Organization leaders," *The Movement* (June 1960).

20. Charles Bolton, *The Hardest Deal of All: The Battle over School Integration in Mississippi, 1870–1980* (Jackson: University Press of Mississippi, 2005), 117–125. The U.S. Justice Department had already won school desegregation cases involving Bullock and Macon counties. Hulda Coleman to Dr. Karl Burns, (7 June 1965), AGP, SG 20061, Folder 22. In 1965, Lowndes County's education budget was nine hundred thousand dollars. "4 Negroes enter Alabama school," New York *Times* (1 September 1965).

21. Hulda Coleman to Dr. Karl Burns, (7 June 1965), AGP, SG 20061, Folder 22; Bolton, *The Hardest Deal of All*, 117–166.

22. Hulda Coleman to Dr. Karl Burns, (7 June 1965), AGP, SG 20061, Folder 22; Lowndes County Board of Education, "resolution," (2 June 1965), AGP, SG 20061, Folder 22.

23. Lowndes County Board of Education, "Notice to Parents, Pupils and Teachers in the Lowndes County Public School System," AGP, SG 20061, Folder 22.

24. Resident in "Parents wonder," *Southern Courier* (13 August 1965).

25. "Citizens Council to hold mass meeting," Lowndes *Signal* (17 June 1965).

26. "Lowndes County citizens plan private school," Lowndes *Signal* (29 July 1965).

27. Coleman to Hugh Maddox, (28 October 1966), AGP, SG 20061, Folder 22; "First day of integration," *Southern Courier* (4–5 September 1965); Complaint, *United States v. Lowndes County Board of Education et al.*, (11 January 1966), AGP, SG 20061, Folder 22.

28. Bass in "Negro, white Lowndes parents wonder," *Southern Courier* (13 August 1965).

29. Bass in "Lowndes County Citizens plan private school," Lowndes *Signal* (29 July 1965); "Lowndes files private school system papers," Alabama *Journal* (20 July 1965).

30. WATS Report, (26 July 1965), SNCC, Box 40, Folder 5. See also affidavits of Martha Johnson, Robert Harris, Cato Lee, Willie Joe White, and John Hunter, SNCC, Box 45, Folder 11.

31. Jordan Gully Affidavit, SNCC, Box 45, Folder 11.

32. Eli Logan Affidavit in ibid.

33. WATS Report, (26 July 1965), SNCC, Box 40, Folder 5.

34. Logan in "Parents wonder," *Southern Courier* (13 August 1965).

35. Coleman to Maddox, (28 October 1966), AGP, SG 20061, Folder 22; WATS Report, (3 August 1965), SNCC, Box 40, Folder 7; Lowndes County Weekly Report, (5 August 1965), SNCC, Box 45, Folder 3; Eagles, *Outside Agitator*, 139–140; Bolton, *The Hardest Deal of All*, 141–166.

36. Lowndes County Weekly Report, (5 August 1965), SNCC, Box 45, Folder 3; Doar to Coleman, (16 August 1965), and Francis Keppel to Coleman, (20 September 1965), AGP, SG 20061, Folder 22.

37. "Parents wonder," *Southern Courier* (13 August 1965).

38. Resident in ibid.

39. Bass in "Alabama integrates its schools," *Southern Courier* (4–5 September 1965).

40. SNCC activist in "Tense Lowndes erupts," *Southern Courier* (28–29 August 1965).

41. WATS Report, (12 July 1965), SNCC, Box 40, Folder 5; Eagles, *Outside Agitator*, 167–168; SNCC Press Release, (28 August 1965), SNCC, Box 35, Folder 7.

42. Carmichael in WATS Report, (12 July 1965), SNCC, Box 40, Folder 5.

43. "Negroes routed in Camden, Ala.," New York *Times* (6 April 1965); Eagles, *Outside Agitator*, 167–168. For more on Wilcox County see Fleming, *In the Shadow of Selma.*

44. Eagles, *Outside Agitator*, 169–170; "48 picketers," *Southern Courier* (20 August 1965).

45. Sales in Hampton and Fayer, *Voices of Freedom*, 273–274; SNCC Press Release, (27 August 1965), SNCC, Box 35, Folder 7.

46. Eagles, *Outside Agitator*, 171; "48 picketers," *Southern Courier* (20 August 1965); Deposition of Henri A. Stines, *White et al. v Crook et al.* (23 September 1965), Alabama Attorney General's Office, SG 20170, Folder "Lowndes County Jury Commission"; WATS Report, (14 August 1965), SNCC, Box 40, Folder 7.

47. SNCC Press Release, (21 August 1965), SNCC, Box 35, Folder 7; "August 20th [Report]" (n.d.), SNCC, Box 45, Folder 3; Carmichael, *Ready for Revolution*, 467–468; Eagles, *Outside Agitator*, 173–175.

48. House Interview, (28 June 2000); SNCC Press Release, (27 August 1965), SNCC, Box 35, Folder 7; Carmichael, *Ready for Revolution*, 467–468; Sales in

Hampton and Fayer, *Voices of Freedom*, 273–275; Gaillard, *Cradle of Freedom*, 281; Eagles, *Outside Agitator*, 177.

49. Sales in Hampton and Fayer, *Voices of Freedom*, 274.

50. Jimmy Rogers Affidavit, SNCC, Box 45, Folder 12.

51. "White seminarian slain," New York *Times* (21 August 1965); SNCC Press Release, (28 August 1965), SNCC, Box 35, Folder 7; Jackson and Vaughn in Rogers affidavit, SNCC, Box 45, Folder 12.

52. "Alabama SNCC Daily Report," (20 August 1965), SNCC, Box 45, Folder 3; Sales in Hampton and Fayer, *Voices of Freedom,* 274.

53. Arthalise Hulett in "First day of integration," *Southern Courier* (4–5 September 1965); Lillian McGill Interview, (2 August 2000).

54. "First day of integration," *Southern Courier* (4–5 September 1965).

55. Counsel for the Lowndes County Board of Education to Doar, (25 August 1965), AGP, SG 20061, Folder 22; "Alabama integrates," *Southern Courier* (4–5 September 1965).

56. Pierce in "Lowndes renews boycott," *Southern Courier* (25–26 September 1965).

57. Quotes from "Lowndes renews boycott," *Southern Courier* (25–26 September 1965); Lowndes County Weekly Report, (5 August 1965), SNCC, Box 45, Folder 3; Coleman to Maddox, (28 October 1966), AGP, SG 20061, Folder 22.

58. Hulett in *The Black Panther Party*, 19; WATS Report, (24 October 1965), SNCC, Box 41, Folder 2.

59. "Friends of SNCC Newsletter No. 1," (13 November 1965), SNCC, Box 51, Folder 3; Selma Office to Personnel Committee, (circa March 1966), SNCC, Box 45, Folder 14, and Box 35, Folder 1; Tina to Janet, Bob, and Dona, (n.d.), SNCC, Box 45, Folder 14; "News of the Field No. 2," (3 March 1966), SNCC, Box 35, Folder 8; Hulett Interview, (2 August 2000).

60. Pattie McDonald affidavit, (3 August 1965), SNCC, Box 45, Folder 12; Pattie McDonald to Silas Norman, (17 August 1965) and (19 August 1965), SNCC, Box 94, Folder 4.

61. WATS Report, (1 September 1965), SNCC, Box 41, Folder 1; Alabama SNCC Daily Report, (1 September 1965), SNCC, Box 45, Folder 3; "Baby narrowly escapes Ala. nightriders shots," *Jet* (23 September 1965); Pattie Mae McDonald Interview (24 September 1998).

62. Lee Affidavit, (July 1965), SNCC, Box 45, Folder 11; Complaint, *Muffin Miles et al. v. Robert Dixon, Jr., et al.*, (10 January 1966), SNCC, Box 60, Folder 17.

63. Johnson Affidavit, SNCC, Box 45, Folder 11; Branch, *At Canaan's Edge*, 260, 280.

64. "White seminarian slain in Alabama," New York *Times*, (21 August, 1965).

65. Stokely Carmichael Transcript, (19 February 1966), SNCC, Box 94, Folder 9.

66. "Lowndes County Freedom Organization leaders," *The Movement* (June 1960).

67. Bessie McMeans Interview, (13 October 1998); John Hulett Interview, (2 August 2000); Branch, *At Canaan's Edge*, 279; Denby, *Indignant Heart*, 208.

68. Annie Bell Jackson Interview, (21 July 2000).

69. For a discussion of general disinterest in nonviolence see Akinyele O. Umoja, "The Beginning of the End of Nonviolence in the Mississippi Freedom Movement," *Radical History Review* Vol. 85 (2003), 201–226. For more on armed resistance see Tyson, *Radio Free Dixie*; Lance Hill, *Deacons for Defense: Armed Resistance and the Civil Rights Movement* (Chapel Hill: University of North Carolina Press, 2004); Christopher B. Strain, *Pure Fire: Armed Self-Defense as Activism in the Civil Rights Era* (Athens: University of Georgia Press, 2005); Emilye Crosby, *A Little Taste of Freedom: The Black Freedom Struggle in Claiborne County, Mississippi* (Chapel Hill: University of North Carolina Press, 2005); Simon Wendt, *The Spirit and the Shotgun: Armed Resistance and the Struggle for Civil Rights* (Gainesville: University of Florida Press, 2007).

70. Resident in Gaillard, *Cradle of Freedom*, 289; John Hulett Interview, (2 August 2000).

71. Johnson in Gaillard, *Cradle of Freedom*, 285.

72. Carmichael in "Fund lag plagues rights movement," New York *Times* (10 January 1966). For an example of the intergenerational transmission of the tradition of armed resistance see Denby, *Indignant Heart*, 6, 8–10, 38–39.

73. Glover in "'Tent City' rising in Alabama field," New York *Times*, (1 January 1966), and "Freedom City, Alabama," *Southern Courier*, (8–9 January 1966). Complaint, *Miles v. Dixon*, (10 January 1966), SNCC, Box 60, Folder 17; SNCC News Release, (28 December 1965), SNCC, Box 35, Folder 5; "Tent City," (5 February 1966), SNCC, Box 46, Folder 11.

74. Scott in "'Tent City' rising in Alabama field," New York *Times*, (1 January 1966).

75. SNCC News Release, (28 December 1965) and (29 December 1965), SNCC, Box 35, Folder 5; Lillian McGill Interview, (29 May 1968); Elzie McGill Interview, (4 August 1968); "Selma Negroes stripped of all but their names," Michigan *Chronicle* (19 April 1966); "Snick in Alabama," SNCC, Box 47, Folder 7; "'Tent City' rising in Alabama Field," New York *Times* (1 January 1966); "A Negro student slain in Alabama," New York *Times* (5 January 1966); "Killing of rights worker jolts Tuskegee students," *Southern Courier* (8–9 January 1966); WATS Report, (4 January 1966), SNCC, Box 41, Folder 6.

76. Davis in "Freedom City, Alabama," *Southern Courier*, (8–9 January 1966).

77. "Lowndes County, Alabama Tent City," (5 February 1966), SNCC, Box 46, Folder 11.

78. Cornelius (C. J.) Jones Interview, (25 July 1973); WATS Report, (19 September 1966), SNCC, Box 41, Folder 10.

79. "Truck to Tent City, Ala.," Michigan *Chronicle*, (16 April 1966); "Alabama Bound," Detroit *News*, (6 April 1966); "Former Lowndes residents send food," *Southern Courier*, (16–17 April 1966); Lillian McGill Interview, (29 May 1968).

80. Complaint, *Miles et al. v. Dixon et al.* (1966), SNCC, Box 60, Folder 17.

81. "U.S. will fight Lowndes evictions," *Southern Courier* (8–9 January 1966); "No proof," *Southern Courier* (18–19 June 1966). For an insightful assessment of Judge Johnson's contribution to the voting rights struggle see Brian K. Landsberg, *Free at Last to Vote: The Alabama Origins of the 1965 Voting Rights Act* (Lawrence: University Press of Kansas, 2007).

82. Green in Carmichael Transcript, (19 February 1966), SNCC, Box 94, Folder 9.

83. Carmichael and Hamilton, *Black Power*, 107.

84. Doar to Coleman, (16 August 1965), AGP, SG 20061, Folder 22.

85. Goodwyn and Smith to Doar, (25 August 1965), AGP, SG 20061, Folder 22.

86. Keppel to Coleman, (20 September 1965), AGP, SG 20061, Folder 22.

87. "U.S. sues schools," New York *Times* (12 January 1966); Complaint, *United States v. Lowndes County Board of Education et al.*, (11 January 1966), AGP, SG 20061, Folder 22.

88. Ibid.

89. A. R. Meadows to Richmond Flowers, (17 January 1966) and Lowndes County Board of Education Resolution, (8 February 1966), AGP, SG 20061, Folder 22; Smith in "Lowndes ordered to end separate schools by 1967," *Southern Courier* (19–20 February 1966).

90. "Lowndes schools told to integrate," New York *Times* (12 February 1966); "Lowndes ordered to end separate schools by 1967," *Southern Courier* (19–20 February 1966); "US backs pupil choice schools," New York *Times* (16 February 1966).

91. David S. Seeley to Meadows, (7 March 1966), AGP, SG 20061, Folder 22.

92. "Lowndes launches search for private school finances," Birmingham *News* (27 May 1966); W. O. Crawford to George C. Wallace, (27 July 1966), AGP, SG 22460, Folder 15; "Lowndes private school sets $500,000 goal," Alabama *Journal* (27 July 1966); "Lowndes Academy names final faculty members," Lowndes *Signal* (18 August 1966); "80 Negroes at Hayneville school," *Southern Courier* (10–11 September 1966); "Group prepared to run private school unaided," Birmingham *Herald* (19 August 1966); "Lowndes Academy names final faculty members," Lowndes *Signal* (18 August 1966).

93. Smith in "80 Negroes at Hayneville school," *Southern Courier* (10–11 September 1966); Coleman to Maddox, (28 October 1966), AGP, SG 20061, Folder 22.

94. Alice Moore to Carmichael, (29 August 1966), SNCC, Box 4, Folder 2.

95. "80 Negroes at Hayneville school," *Southern Courier* (10–11 September 1966).

96. Ibid.; Hulett Interview, (2 August 2000).

97. I borrow the phrase "default setting" from Angela Ryan, who applied it in a similar way in a paper she wrote for a graduate seminar I taught at Ohio State University in 2006 on the African American freedom struggle.

CHAPTER 4

1. William M. Seabron to Carmichael, (10 June 1966), SNCC, Box 4, Folder 1; "ASCS," *Southern Courier* (30–31 July 1966).

2. Carmichael to Seabron, (25 July 1966), SNCC, Box 4, Folder 2.

3. Kenny in "ASCS," *Southern Courier* (30–31 July 1966); Jelinek, Carmichael, and Brown in "Court extends ASCS elections," *Southern Courier* (13–14 August 1966); "Farm fraud charged in state," *Alabama Journal* (28 July 1966).

4. "Anti-poverty programs offer many chances for progress," *Southern Courier* (16–17 October 1965); CAP Application, (November 1965), SCLC, Box 148, Folder 2; Ashmore, *Carry It On*, 29–30.

5. Ashmore, *Carry It On*, 53, 63, 85.

6. Hulett, Miles, and McGill to Shriver, (8 August 1965), CAP Application Exhibit A, (November 1965), SCLC, Box 148, Folder 2.

7. McGill to Harold Hammond [*sic*], (14 August 1965), CAP Application Exhibit B, (November 1965), SCLC, Box 148, Folder 2.

8. William L. Staggers to Lowndes County Citizens, (19 August 1965), CAP Application Exhibit C, (November 1965), SCLC, Box 148, Folder 2; M. E. Marlette, Jr., to John Sparkman, (18 July 1966), AGP, SG 22400, Folder 21; Ashmore, *Carry It On*, 118, 150, 254, 258, 269.

9. Bradley in Couto, *Ain't Gonna Let Nobody Turn Me Round*, 83, 93, 102, 208.

10. Hulett to Community Action Program, (22 August 1965), CAP Application Exhibit E, (November 1965), SCLC, Box 148, Folder 2.

11. CAP Application, (November 1965), SCLC, Box 148, Folder 2.

12. Ibid.

13. Ibid.

14. Department of Agriculture, "ASCS Background Information," (February 1965), and SNCC, "ASCS Organizers Handbook," (1965), SNCC, Box 51, Folder 2; Eagles, *Outside Agitator*, 135; "ASCS," *Southern Courier* (30–31 July 1966); "Negro farmers must use the vote well," *Southern Courier* (25–26 September 1965).

15. Black farmer in "Negro farmers must use the vote well," *Southern Courier* (25–26 September 1965); Memo to Friends of SNCC, (5 November 1965), SNCC, Box 51, Folder 3; "Farm talk," *Southern Courier* (20 August 1965); "Discrimination in ASCS," (1965), SNCC, Box 51, Folder 2; "USDA discrimination," *Southern Courier* (2–3 December 1967).

16. "Negro farmers must use the vote well," *Southern Courier* (25–26 September 1965).

17. Alabama SNCC Staff Report, (August 1965), SNCC, Box 94, Folder 21; "Farm talk," *Southern Courier* (20 August 1965); SNCC, "ASCS Organizers Handbook," (1965), SNCC, Box 51, Folder 2; Eagles, *Outside Agitator*, 136.

18. Holder in Staff Meeting Minutes, (24 May 1965), SNCC, Box 94, Folder 22.

19. WATS Report, (19 July 1965), SNCC, Box 40, Folder 5; Lowndes Weekly Report, (5 August 1965), SNCC, Box 45, Folder 3; "Farm talk," *Southern Courier* (20 August 1965).

20. Jemott in "Farmers plan ASCS races," *Southern Courier* (30–31 October 1965).

21. Elmo Holder to B. L. Collins, (18 July 1965), SNCC, Box 51, Folder 1.

22. Janet Jemott, "Alabama SNCC Staff Report," (August 1965), SNCC, Box 94, Folder 21.

23. Janet, Tina, to Silas, Muriel (September–October 1965), SNCC, Box 94, Folder 21.

24. Mathew Jackson, Sr., Interview, (4 August 1968); Blocton in "ASCS," *Southern Courier* (30–31 July 1966); WATS Report, (24 October 1965), SNCC, Box 41, Folder 2; Carmichael Affidavit, (11 March 1966), and "SNCC Program," (1965), SNCC, Box 51, Folder 3.

25. Holder to Collins, (18 July 1965), SNCC, Box 51, Folder 1; Liutkus in "Moves hurt Negroes in ASCS campaign," *Southern Courier* (13–15 November 1965); Carmichael Affidavit, (11 March 1966), SNCC, Box 51, Folder 3; SNCC Press Release, (15 November 1965), BMP, Box 1, Folder "ASCS Community Committee Election, 1965."

26. Norman, "Summary of Incidents and Irregularities," (1965), SNCC, Box 44, Folder 15; Carmichael Affidavit, (11 March 1966), and "SNCC Program," (1965), SNCC, Box 51, Folder 3; SNCC Press Release, (28 December 1965), SNCC, Box 35, Folder 5.

27. ASCS Flyer (1965) and SNCC Press Release, (15 November 1965), BMP, Box 1, Folder "ASCS . . . 1965"; SNCC Press Release, (5 November 1965), SNCC, Box 35, Folder 7.

28. John Lewis to Orville Freeman, (30 November 1965), SNCC, Box 2, Folder 10; "New ASC Community Committee elected," Lowndes *Signal* (9 December 1965); "No Negroes elected," *Southern Courier* (8–9 October 1966); Doug and Tina Harris to Kenneth K. Marshall, (2 December 1965), SNCC, Box 149, Folder 1B; Carmichael Affidavit, (11 March 1966), SNCC, Box 51, Folder 3.

29. Carmichael Affidavit, (11 March 1966), SNCC, Box 51, Folder 3; Doug and Tina Harris to Marshall, (2 December 1965), SNCC, Box 149, Folder 1B.

30. SNCC Press Release, (19 November 1865), SNCC, Box 35, Folder 7; "Negroes win ASCS post, but irregularities charged," *Student Voice* (20 December 1965), SNCC, Box 51, Folder 3; Seabron to Carmichael, (10 June 1966), SNCC, Box 4, Folder 1.

31. "New ASC community committee elected," Lowndes *Signal* (9 December 1965); "SNCC Program," (5 November 1965), SNCC, Box 51, Folder 3; Doug and Tina Harris to Marshall, (2 December 1965), SNCC, Box 149, Folder 1B.

32. Carmichael in "Freedom City, Alabama," *Southern Courier* (8–9 January 1966); Carmichael and Hulett in "New political group," *Southern Courier* (1–2 January 1966); Mrs. Elzie McGill Interview, (4 August 1968); Logan in "Lowndes County Freedom Organization leaders," *The Movement* (June 1966).

33. Renaissance woman Pauli Murray helped write the ACLU-ESCRU brief and was instrumental in making the exclusion of women an issue. Eagles, *Outside Agitator*, 199–200; Pauli Murray, *Pauli Murray: The Autobiography of a Black Activist, Feminist, Lawyer, Priest, and Poet* (Knoxville: University of Tennessee Press, 1989), 363–364; "Negroes may sit on Liuzzo juries," New York *Times* (13 February 1966); Justice Department Press Release, (25 October 1965), SNCC, Box 175, Folder 8; "U.S. aids Negroes, fights jury bar," New York *Times* (26 October 1965); Memorandum, Opinion, and Order, *White v. Crook*, (1966), U.S. District Court for the Middle District of Alabama, AGP, SG 19969, Folder 14.

34. For nearly a century, lawyers filed federal lawsuits challenging the constitutionality of jury restrictions based on race. See, for example, *Strauder v. West Virginia* (1880) and *Virginia v. Rives* (1880). None of these cases, however, sought or proposed specific systematic remedies. Instead, they asked for rulings of constitutionality so that individual convictions could be overturned. They also did not seek rulings on the constitutionality of the statutory exclusion of women from jury service. Plaintiff's Brief: Volume 1, *White v. Crook* (1966), AGP, SG 19969, Folder 14; "Supreme Court hasn't ruled that juries must be integrated," *Southern Courier* (20–21 November 1965); Litwack, *Trouble in Mind*, 254–255.

35. Henri A. Stines Deposition, *White v. Crook* (23 September 1965), AGP, SG 20170, Folder "Lowndes County Jury Commission."

36. "Alabama sheriff's aide is acquitted," New York *Times* (1 October 1965); Justice Department Press Release, (25 October 1965), SNCC, Box 175, Folder 8; "U.S. aids Negroes, fights jury bar," New York *Times* (26 October 1965); "Johnson pledges Negroes jury aid," New York *Times* (17 November 1965); "US joins two suits," New York *Times* (11 November 1965).

37. Memorandum, Opinion, and Order, *White v. Crook*, (1966), AGP, SG 19969, Folder 14; "Lowndes County must mix juries," *Southern Courier* (12–13 February 1966).

38. "Eight Negro jurors, but same verdict in Lowndes," *Southern Courier* (1–2 October 1966); Flowers in "Jury with Negroes acquits Klansman in Liuzzo slaying," New York *Times* (28 September 1966). A decade passed before African Americans felt safe enough to render honest verdicts in racially charged cases. Chestnut, *Black in Selma*, 255.

39. Complaint, *Miles et al. v. Dixon et al.* (1966), SNCC, Box 60, Folder 17; "No proof Lowndes Negroes evicted for registering," *Southern Courier* (18–19 June 1966).

40. R. L. Strickland to Shriver, (22 March 1966), SNCC, Box 46, Folder 15; "Freedom City, Alabama," *Southern Courier* (8–9 January 1966); OEO Grant Application, (22 March 1966), SNCC, Box 46, Folder 15; Strickland in "$500,000 to CR groups," *Southern Courier* (16–17 July 1966). The OEO also awarded $302,081 to activists in Wilcox County. Ashmore, *Carry It On*, 40, 123, 150, 155.

41. "Alabama compiling file on civil rights advocates," New York *Times* (17 February 1964); Commission to Preserve the Peace, "Special Report," (June 1965), and "Biennial Report to the Alabama Legislature," (1965), AGP, SG 22449, Folder 6; Edwin Strickland to Wallace, (3 October 1967), AGP, SG 22449, Folder 2; John H. Hawkins to Albert P. Brewer, (13 May 1968), AGP, SG 22449, Folder 12; King Interview, (17 July 2000).

42. Edwin Strickland, "Report of the Alabama Legislative Commission to Preserve the Peace Requested by Governor George C. Wallace," (14 July 1966), AGP, SG 22401, Folder 5.

43. "Statement of Governor George C. Wallace," (19 July 1966), and "Black Power," WSFA-TV (19 July 1966), AGP, SG 22401, Folder 5.

44. Wallace to Shriver, (18 July 1966), AGP, SG 22401, Folder 5.

45. Marlette to Sparkman, (18 July 1966), and Marlette to Hill, (5 December 1966) and (23 January 1967), AGP, SG 22400, Folder 31.

46. "Statement by Sargent Shriver," (20 July 1966), AGP, SG 22401, Folder 5.

47. Ashmore, *Carry It On*, 87–116.

48. Chairman's Letter, (n.d.), SNCC, Box 94, Folder 9; Eagles, *Outside Agitator*, 124–125.

49. Marlette, "Report of attempts in Lowndes County, Alabama to organize an interracial Community Action Program," (18 November 1966), AGP, SG 22400, Folder 31.

50. Ibid.; Lillian McGill Interview, (2 August 2000).

51. Marlette, "Report of attempts in Lowndes County, Alabama to organize an interracial Community Action Program," (18 November 1966), AGP, SG 22400, Folder 31.

52. "No Negroes elected," *Southern Courier* (8–9 October 1966).

53. Marlette, "Report of attempts in Lowndes County, Alabama to organize an interracial Community Action Program," (18 November 1966); Marlette to Hill, (5 December 1966) and (23 January 1967); and Shriver to Hill, (17 January 1967), AGP, SG 22400, Folder 31.

CHAPTER 5

1. "Lowndes third party attracts 900," *Southern Courier* (7–8 May 1966); "Racists sweep Alabama primaries," *National Guardian* (14 May 1966); LCFO Convention Results, (n.d.), SNCC, Box 4, Folder 13.

2. Veteran in "Lowndes third party attracts 900," *Southern Courier* (7–8 May 1966).

3. "Alabama Negro candidates lead," New York *Times* (4 May 1966).

4. Ricks in "Challenging the sheriff," *Newsweek* (16 May 1966), and "Lowndes third party attracts 900," *Southern Courier* (7–8 May 1966); SNCC Press Release, (6 May 1966), SNCC, Box 35, Folder 9; Profile of Willie Floyd Ricks, (n.d.), SNCC, Box 28, Folder 3; Carson, *In Struggle*, 208–209; "The story of Snick," New York *Times* (25 September 1966).

5. Carmichael and Hamilton, *Black Power*, 181–182.

6. Ibid., 96.

7. WATS Report, (26 July 1965) and (13 August 1965), SNCC, Box 40, Folder 7; WATS Report, (24 October 1965), SNCC, Box 41, Folder 2; "Voting officials sign 1,444 Negroes first day of drive," New York *Times* (11 August 1965); Commission on Civil Rights, *The Voting Rights Act*, 16, 35; "New Federal examiners register Negro voters," *Southern Courier* (13 August 1965); Eagles, *Outside Agitator*, 197.

8. "Integration is completely irrelevant," *The Movement*, (June 1966).

9. "Interview with new SNCC chairman," *The Militant* (23 May 1966).

10. SNCC Press Release (27 August 1965), SNCC, Box 35, Folder 7; "Lowndes County Freedom Organization leaders," *The Movement* (June 1966); "2 rights groups," New York *Times* (23 January 1966); "New political group," *Southern Courier* (1–2 January 1966).

11. SNCC Press Release, (23 February 1965), SNCC, Box 6, Folder "Executive Committee, Mar—Aug, 1965."

12. Minnis to Carmichael, (4 September 1965), SNCC, Box 94, Folder 26.

13. Jack Minnis, Background on the Development of Political Strategy and Political Education in Lowndes County, Alabama," (Atlanta: SNCC, 1966).

14. Minnis to Carmichael, (4 September 1965), SNCC, Box 94, Folder 26.

15. Ibid.

16. "Lowndes County Freedom Organization leaders," *The Movement* (June 1966).

17. Hulett in *The Black Panther Party*, 8.

18. "Lowndes County Freedom Organization leaders," *The Movement* (June 1966).

19. Mathew Jackson, Sr., Interview, (4 August 1968).

20. Hulett in *The Black Panther Party*, 8; "New political group," *Southern Courier* (1–2 January 1966).

21. Courtland Cox, "What Would It Profit a Man . . . ? A Report on Alabama," SNCC, Box 46, Folder 14.

22. Cox in Greenberg, *Circle of Trust*, 108.

23. Carmichael, *Ready for Revolution*, 465.

24. "Voter drive is spurred in Alabama," New York *Times* (23 August 1965); SNCC Press Release, (27 August 1965), SNCC, Box 35, Folder 7; SNCC, "Background Information on Freedom Elections in Alabama," (1966), SNCC, Box 45, Folder 12; "Hopefuls seek 'Panther' nods," *Southern Courier* (23–24 April 1966);

Selma Office to Bill Mahoney, (April 1966), SNCC, Box 45, Folder 14; News of the
Field #4, (April 1966), and Harris to Staff, (21 April 1966), SNCC, Box 35, Folder 9.
   25. Courtland Cox, "What Would It Profit a Man . . . ? A Report on Alabama,"
SNCC, Box 46, Folder 14.
   26. "Snick in Alabama," SNCC, Box 47, Folder 73.
   27. Carmichael Transcript, (19 February 1966), SNCC, Box 94, Folder 9.
   28. Baker in Ransby, *Ella Baker and the Black Freedom Movement*, 363. For
more on SNCC's organizing philosophy and Ella Baker see Hogan, *Many Minds,
One Heart*.
   29. Jack to Bill Strickland, (21 October 1965), SNCC, Box 45, Folder 1.
   30. "Snick in Alabama," SNCC, Box 47, Folder 73.
   31. "Interview with the Black Panther Party organizer," *The Movement* (February 1966).
   32. Ibid.
   33. Carmichael in "New political group," *Southern Courier* (1–2 January 1966).
   34. Jack Minnis, "Lowndes County Freedom Organization: The Story of the
Development of an Independent Political Movement on the County Level," (Louisville, Ky.: Southern Conference Educational Fund, 1967), 1.
   35. WATS report, (6 December 1965), SNCC, Box 41, Folder 5; Minnis, "Background on the development of political strategy," SNCC, Box 46, Folder 11.
   36. Ibid., 4.
   37. Ibid., 4.
   38. Local supporter in "Lowndes County form local political group," *The Student Voice* (20 December 1965), SNCC, Box 51, Folder 3.
   39. Hulett in "Lowndes County Freedom Organization leaders," *The Movement*
(June 1966); Minnis to Carmichael and Hamilton, (4 September 1965), SNCC,
Box 94, Folder 26; "Interview with the Alabama Black Panther Party organizer,"
The Movement (February 1966); Willie Ricks Interview, (13 September 1998);
"Ready for the revolution," *Emerge* (June 1997); Jennifer Lawson Interview, (3
June 2000); Couto, *Ain't Gonna Let Nobody Turn Me Round*, 104; "The lair of the
Black Panther," *New Republic* (13 August 1966).
   40. "SNCC chairman talks about Black Power," *The Movement* (November
1966).
   41. In addition to the Black Panther Party for Self-Defense, there was the
Black Panther Party of Northern California, founded by Ken Freeman and Ernie
Allen, and the Black Panther Political Party, founded by John Floyd. Maulana
Karenga, the cofounder of the black cultural nationalist organization US, was
also inspired and deeply influenced by the black panther symbol and the LCFO.
Brown, *Fighting for US*, 28–29, 50–51, 80. The scholarship on the Black Panther
Party for Self-Defense has grown tremendously during the last decade. See
Charles Jones, ed., *The Black Panther Party [Reconsidered]* (Baltimore: Black
Classic Press, 1998); Yohuru Williams, *Black Politics/White Power: Civil Rights,*

Black Power, and the Black Panthers in New Haven (New York: Brandywine, 2000); Jama Lazerow and Yohuru Williams, eds., *In Search of the Black Panther Party: New Perspectives on a Revolutionary Movement* (Durham, N.C.: Duke University Press, 2006); Curtis J. Austin, *Up Against the Wall: Violence in the Making and Unmaking of the Black Panther Party* (Fayetteville: University of Arkansas Press, 2006); Judson L. Jeffries, ed., *Comrades: A Local History of the Black Panther Party* (Bloomington: Indiana University Press, 2007).

42. Ogbar, *Black Power*, 89; Carmichael, *Ready for Revolution*, 474–476.

43. WATS Report, (6 December 1965), SNCC, Box 41, Folder 5.

44. "Interview with the Black Panther Party organizer," *The Movement* (February 1966).

45. Minnis, "Lowndes County Freedom Organization," 2.

46. Ibid., 2–5.

47. SNCC, "Working Sheet for Alabama Party and Election Handbook," (1966), RMP, Box 1, Folder "Election Work and Materials—1966."

48. Jacqueline A. Rouse, "'We Seek to Know . . . in Order to Speak the Truth': Nurturing the Seeds of Discontent—Septima Clark and Participatory Leadership," in *Sisters in the Struggle: African American Women in the Civil Rights–Black Power Movement*, ed. Bettye Collier-Thomas and V. P. Franklin (New York: New York University Press, 2001), 95–120.

49. "Is This the Party You Want?" (December 1965), RMP, Box 1, Folder "Campaign Lit."

50. Hulett in "Lowndes County Freedom Organization leaders," *The Movement* (June 1966); House Interview, (28 June 2000); *The Black Panther Party*, 9–10; "Democrats raise Alabama filing fee," New York *Times* (5 February 1966); Hulett Interview, (20 May 1968); Minnis, "Background on the Development of Political Strategy," SNCC, Box 46, Folder 11; "New political group," *Southern Courier* (1–2 January 1966); Mathew Jackson, Sr., Interview, (4 August 1968); Gaillard, *Cradle of Freedom*, 291.

51. Complaint, *McGill et al. v. Ryals et al.*, (1966), U.S. District Court for the Middle District of Alabama, AGP, SG 19969, Folder 13.

52. "Negroes lose fight to oust all offices in Lowndes County," New York *Times* (1 April 1966); "Voter drive is spurred in Alabama," New York *Times* (23 August 1965).

53. "Lowndes party elects officers," *Southern Courier* (9–10 April 1966).

54. Hulett in ibid.

55. Ibid.

56. Hulett and unnamed speaker in ibid.

57. Ibid.

58. "Lowndes County Freedom Organization leaders," *The Movement* (June 1966).

59. SNCC, "County Reports: Lowndes County," (March 1966), SNCC, Box 45, Folder 2.

60. "Lowndes third party attracts 900," *Southern Courier* (7–8 May 1966); SNCC Press Release, (6 May 1966), SNCC, Box 35, Folder 9; "Candidate Profiles," RMP, Box 1, Folder "LCFO, Profile of Candidates"; and "1966 LCFO Convention Results," SNCC, Box 47, Folder 13.

61. "Candidate Profiles," RMP, Box 1, Folder "LCFO, Profile of Candidates."

62. "Mass meeting day Tuesday," *Southern Courier* (30 April–1 May 1966); Logan in "Lowndes County Freedom Organization leaders" *The Movement* (June 1966).

63. Minnis in "Hopefuls seek 'Panther' nods," *Southern Courier* (23–24 April 1966).

64. Ibid.; Selma Office to Bill Mahoney, (April 1966), SNCC, Box 45, Folder 14; News of the Field #4, (April 1966), SNCC, Box 35, Folder 9; Tina Harris to Staff, (21 April 1966), SNCC, Box 35, Folder 9; "A new freedom party," *The Militant* (2 May 1966).

65. "Lowndes County forms local political group," *The Student Voice*, (20 December 1965), SNCC, Box 51, Folder 3; "Student rights group lacks money and help but not projects," New York *Times*, (10 December 1965).

66. Carmichael to Hewlett [*sic*], (n.d.), SNCC, Box 45, Folder 12; "Negro candidates plan races in many counties," *Southern Courier* (19–20 February 1966); "Interview with the Alabama Black Panther Party organizer," *The Movement* (February 1966); "Student rights group lacks money and help but not projects," New York *Times* (10 December 1965).

67. Miles in "A new freedom party," *The Militant* (2 May 1966).

68. SNCC Press Release, (6 May 1966), SNCC, Box 35, Folder 6; "Lowndes third party attracts 900," *Southern Courier* (7–8 May 1966); "Racists sweep Alabama primaries," *National Guardian* (14 May 1966); "Interview with new SNCC chairman," *The Militant* (23 May 1966); "Samson Crum withdraws from Dallas sheriff race," *Southern Courier* (8–9 October 1966).

69. Smith in "2 rights groups," New York *Times* (23 January 1966).

70. Gomillion in "Whites outvoted in Alabama area," New York *Times* (24 May 1964).

71. Norrell, *Reaping the Whirlwind*, 41–42, 118, 123–124, 169–174. "Snick in Alabama," SNCC, Box 47, Folder 7; "2 rights groups," New York *Times*, (23 January 1966); "Politicians, leaders fight," *Southern Courier* (9–10 April 1966); "Negro leaders reveal how they worked strategy," *Southern Courier* (29–30 January 1966); Thornton, *Dividing Lines*, 141–379.

72. Evers in "2 rights groups," New York *Times* (23 January 1966).

73. Ibid.; Williams in "Civil rights leaders," *Southern Courier* (22–23 January 1966).

74. Williams in "SCLC proposes political group," *Southern Courier* (5–6 March 1965).

75. Williams in "Leaders in 15 counties meet to plan bloc vote," *Southern Courier* (12–13 March 1966); "Wallace stumps . . . SCLC plans," *Southern Courier* (23–24 October 1965); "Negro vote tempers racism by Alabama foes," New York *Times* (17 April 1966); "Rights group plans drive in Alabama," New York *Times* (4 November 1965).

76. "Dr. King bids Alabama Negroes conquer fears," New York *Times* (30 April 1966).

77. Turner in "Alabama sheriff opposed by Negro," New York *Times* (20 February 1966).

78. Williams in "Negro split endangers vote success," New York *Times* (April 1966).

79. "Wallace stumps . . . SCLC plans," *Southern Courier* (23–24 October 1965); "Rights group plans drive in Alabama," New York *Times* (4 November 1965); "Politicians, leaders fight over 'The Negro Vote,'" *Southern Courier* (9–10 April 1966); "SCLC proposes political group," *Southern Courier* (5–6 March 1965); "King criticizes Panthers," Birmingham *News* (27 April 1966); "The Black Panther Party," *Young Socialist* (May–June–July 1966); "Dr. King bids Alabama Negroes conquer fears and vote as bloc," New York *Times* (30 April 1966); "Alabama Negro candidates have an excellent chance," Michigan *Chronicle* (April 1966).

80. "Sabotage in Alabama," New York *Times* (21 April 1966).

81. Forman to Editors, (27 April 1966), SNCC, Box 47, Folder 13.

82. "SNCC's path? Carmichael answers," *National Guardian* (4 June 1966).

83. Courtland Cox, "What Would It Profit a Man . . . ? A Report on Alabama," SNCC, Box 46, Folder 14.

84. Carmichael in "Panther on the prowl," *Newsweek* (7 February 1966).

85. "Snick in Alabama," SNCC, Box 47, Folder 7.

86. Carmichael in "The Black Panther Party," *Young Socialist* (May–June–July 1966). See also "SNCC's path? Carmichael answers," *National Guardian* (4 June 1966).

87. "Snick in Alabama," SNCC, Box 47, Folder 8.

88. "A new freedom party," *The Militant* (2 May 1966); Harris to Staff (21 April 1966), SNCC, Box 35, Folder 9.

89. Hulett to Ryals, (n.d.), RMP, Box 1, Folder "Lowndes County Freedom Org., 1966–1968."

90. "Lowndes third party attracts 900," *Southern Courier* (7–8 May 1966); "Background Information on Freedom Elections in Alabama," (1966), SNCC, Box 45, Folder 12.

91. LCFO supporter in "Black Power in the Black Belt," *The Progressive* (October 1966).

92. Hulett in *The Black Panther Party*, 12; SNCC Press Release, (6 May 1966), SNCC, Box 35, Folder 9; "Lowndes third party attracts 900," *Southern Courier* (7–8 May 1966); "Background Information on Freedom Elections in Alabama," (1966), SNCC, Box 45, Folder 12.

93. Carmichael to Doar, (27 April 1966), in "Background Information on Freedom Elections in Alabama," (1966), SNCC, Box 45, Folder 12; "Lowndes third party attracts 900," *Southern Courier* (7–8 May 1966).

94. Hulett in *The Black Panther Party*, 13; SNCC Press Release, (6 May 1966), SNCC, Box 35, Folder 9.

95. Hulett in *The Black Panther Party*, 13.

96. Sidney Logan, Jr., defeated Jesse Favors for sheriff 492 to 381; Frank Miles, Jr., defeated Josephine Waginer for tax collector 489 to 362; Alice Moore and Emory Ross ran unopposed for tax assessor and coroner respectively and received 852 and 715 votes apiece; Robert Logan defeated Bernice Kelly for school board seat #3 559 to 330; John Hinson defeated Virginia White for school board seat #4 511 to 327; and Willie Mae Strickland defeated Annie Bell Scott for school board seat #5 604 to 241. LCFO Convention Results, (n.d.), SNCC, Box 47, Folder 13; SNCC Press Release, (6 May 1966), SNCC, Box 35, Folder 9; "Lowndes third party attracts 900," *Southern Courier* (7–8 May 1966); "Racists sweep Alabama primaries," *National Guardian* (14 May 1966).

97. "Interview with new SNCC chairman," *The Militant* (23 May 1966).

98. Logan in "Lowndes third party attracts 900," *Southern Courier* (7–8 May 1966).

99. Cosby in News of the Field #3, (6 May 1966), SNCC, Box 42, Folder 11.

100. Local farmer in SNCC Press Release, (6 May 1966), SNCC, Box 35, Folder 9.

101. Lurleen Wallace received 1,438 votes, presumably all from whites, while Richmond Flowers received 631 votes, mostly from African Americans. Carl Elliot received another 100 plus votes, presumably all from African Americans. "Election results," Lowndes *Signal* (5 May 1966); "Black Panther candidates optimistic," Birmingham *Post-Herald* (1 November 1966); "The changing times in Lowndes County," New York *Times* (31 October 1966).

102. Morgan, Crocker, and Bolden in "Alabama Negro candidates lead," New York *Times* (4 May 1966).

103. Taylor and Lawrence in "Negroes in Alabama" New York *Times* (4 May 1966).

104. Ibid.; "Negro voters double," New York *Times* (30 April 1966); "Alabama Negroes drive for office," New York *Times* (3 March 1966); "Alabama Negro candidates have an excellent chance," Michigan *Chronicle* (April 1966); "Negro nominated for sheriff's post in Alabama vote," New York *Times* (1 June 1966); "Several to face run-off races," *Southern Courier* (7–8 May 1966); "Racists sweep Alabama primaries," *National Guardian* (14 May 1966); "What's Happening in SNCC?" (3 June 1966), SNCC, Box 126, Folder 11.

105. "What's Happening in SNCC?" (3 June 1966), SNCC, Box 126, Folder 11; "The lair of the Black Panther," *New Republic* (13 August 1966); *The Black Panther Party*, 13–14.
106. "Lowndes County Freedom Organization leaders," *The Movement* (June 1966).

CHAPTER 6

1. Moore in "Candidates lose," *The Movement* (December 1966); "Candidate Profiles," RMP, Box 1, Folder "LCFO, Profile of Candidates."
2. Sellers, *River of No Return*, 155.
3. Ibid., 155.
4. Carmichael in SNCC Press Release, (1966), SNCC, Box 150, Folder 4.
5. Larry in Greenberg, *Circle of Trust*, 161.
6. Carmichael in "New leaders and new course," New York *Times* (22 May 1966).
7. "Integration is completely irrelevant," *The Movement* (June 1966).
8. "What's happening in SNCC?" (3 June 1966), SNCC, Box 126, Folder 11; "Freedom Voice," (May 1966), SNCC, Box 84, Folder 15.
9. Carmichael, *Ready for Revolution*, 466.
10. Ricks in "When they ask, 'What do you want?'" *Southern Courier* (25–26 June 1966).
11. Carmichael, *Ready for Revolution*, 479.
12. Moore to Carmichael, (29 August 1966), SNCC, Box 4, Folder 2.
13. Sellers in Greenberg, *Circle of Trust*, 159; Gaillard, *Cradle of Freedom*, 293.
14. "Lowndes County Freedom Organization leaders," *The Movement* (June 1966).
15. "The lair of the Black Panther," *New Republic* (13 August 1966).
16. Larry in Greenberg, *Circle of Trust*, 106; House Interview, (28 June 2000).
17. Cox in Greenberg, *Circle of Trust*, 109.
18. Minnis, "Lowndes County Freedom Organization," 10–11.
19. Minutes of LCFO meeting, (13 August 1966), RMP, Box 1, Folder "Election Work and Material"; WATS Report, (19 September 1966), SNCC, Box 41, Folder 10; "Black Panther candidates optimistic," Birmingham *Post-Herald* (1 November 1966).
20. Carmichael, *Ready for Revolution*, 490; "What's Happening in SNCC?" (3 June 1966), SNCC, Box 126, Folder 11; Sellers, *River of No Return*, 159–163.
21. "Mississippi reduces police protection for marchers," New York *Times* (17 June 1966); Hampton and Fayer, *Voices of Freedom*, 289–294.
22. "Troopers shove group resuming Meredith march," New York *Times* (8 June 1966); "Marchers stage Mississippi rally," New York *Times* (18 July 1966).
23. Don Smith, "Letter to the editor," New York *Times* (15 July 1966).

24. "Dr. King deplores 'Black Power' bid," New York *Times* (21 June 1966).

25. "Wilkins says Black Power leads only to black death," New York *Times* (6 July 1966). For more on anticommunism and NAACP see Martha Biondi, *To Stand and Fight: The Struggle for Civil Rights in Postwar New York City* (Cambridge, Mass.: Harvard University Press, 2003), 137–163.

26. Yuhuru Williams, "'A Red, Black and Green Liberation Jumpsuit': Roy Wilkins, the Black Panthers, and the Conundrum of Black Power," 167–192, in Joseph, *Black Power Movement*; "Militant rights groups feel pinch as gifts drop," New York *Times* (25 July 1966).

27. "President points to racial actions," New York *Times* (6 July 1966).

28. "Humphrey backs NAACP in fight on black racism," New York *Times* (7 July 1966).

29. "Black Power," New York *Times* (12 July 1966).

30. Carmichael, *Ready for Revolution*, 526, 541–547; "What's Happening in SNCC?" (3 June 1966), SNCC, Box 126, Folder 11; "Wilkins assails CORE and SNCC and hints full break," New York *Times* (8 July 1966); "A slogan, a chant, a threat," New York *Times* (10 December 1966); Carmichael and Hamilton, *Black Power*, 164–177.

31. "Black Power idea long in planning," New York *Times* (5 August 1966); "Black Power prophet," New York *Times* (5 August 1966).

32. "The politics of frustration," New York *Times* (7 August 1966).

33. "All but destroyed," New York *Times* (27 August 1966).

34. Ricks in Carson, *In Struggle*, 199.

35. SNCC Vine City Project, "Black Power," (Nashville: Southern Student Organizing Committee, 1966); Winston A. Grady-Willis, *Challenging U.S. Apartheid: Atlanta and Black Struggles for Human Rights* (Durham, N.C.: Duke University Press, 2006), 79–113; Carson, *In Struggle*, 192–200; Ogbar, *Black Power*, 72–81; Hill, *Deacons for Defense*, 220–223.

36. Moore to Carmichael, (10 August 1966), SNCC, Box 4, Folder 3.

37. Carmichael to Moore, (22 August 1966), SNCC, Box 4, Folder 3.

38. Moore to Carmichael, (29 August 1966), SNCC, Box 4, Folder 2.

39. "Black Power in the Black Belt," *The Progressive* (October 1966).

40. Residents in ibid., 22.

41. Carmichael and Hamilton, *Black Power*, 115.

42. Moore in "Black Power in the Black Belt," *The Progressive* (October 1966).

43. Calhoun Colored School Annual Report (1897), ADEP, LPR 139, Box 8; Loud to Land Trust Subscribers, (31 January 1931), PSC, MG 162, Box 25, Folder 16; Hulett Interview, (30 May 1968).

44. Minutes of LCFO Meeting, (13 August 1966), RMP, Box 1, Folder "Election Work and Material"; SNCC Volunteers, RMP, Box 1, Folder "Lowndes Co. Freedom Organization, 1966–1968"; "Agents of the Lowndes County Freedom Organization," SNCC, Box 46, Folder 14; Moore to Carmichael, (29 August 1966),

and Carmichael to Moore, (19 September 1966), SNCC, Box 4, Folder 2; Leaflets, SNCC, Box 44, Folder 15; Palm cards, SNCC, Box 46, Fold•r 14 and RMP, Box 1, Folder "Campaign literature"; "Freedom candidates campaign in Lowndes," *Southern Courier* (22–23 October 1966); "High hopes in Lowndes," *Southern Courier* (5–6 November 1966); Lawson Interview, (3 June 2000); WATS Report, (19 September 1966), and SNCC Field Report, (28 September 1966–8 October 1966), SNCC, Box 41, Folder 10.

45. Logan, Jr., and Miles in "Lowndes County Freedom Organization leaders," *The Movement* (June 1966); Aldridge Interview, (13 June 2000).

46. Sidney Logan, Jr., and Robert Logan in "High hopes in Lowndes," *Southern Courier* (5–6 November 1966); Tent City resident in "Freedom candidates campaign in Lowndes," *Southern Courier* (22–23 October 1966).

47. Hulett in "Black Panther candidates optimistic," Birmingham *Post-Herald* (1 November 1966).

48. May in "Black Power in the Black Belt," *The Progressive* (October 1966).

49. Landowner in "The changing times," New York *Times* (31 October 1966).

50. "Pull these levers first," Lowndes *Signal* (3 November 1966); Campbell, "The Lowndes County Freedom Organization," 74, 79.

51. Champion in "The changing times," New York *Times* (31 October 1966).

52. Purdue in "Freedom candidates," *Southern Courier* (22–23 October 1966).

53. "Candidates lose," *The Movement* (December 1966).

54. Leader in Carmichael and Hamilton, *Black Power*, 111; "List of assigned duties of poll watchers," (n.d), RMP, Box 1, Folder "Election Work and Materials."

55. Supporter in Carmichael and Hamilton, *Black Power*, 110; "List of property owners," RMP, Box 1, Folder "Election Work and Materials."

56. Meeting participant in Carmichael and Hamilton, *Black Power*, 111.

57. Ross in ibid., 111.

58. Ibid., 110–114.

59. Preacher and Hulett in "Candidates lose," *The Movement* (December 1966).

60. Carmichael and Hamilton, *Black Power*, 114.

61. "Candidates lose," *The Movement* (December 1966); "A good day to go voting," *Southern Courier* (12–13 November 1966).

62. "Carmichael's speech at Mt. Moriah Church," *The Movement* (December 1966).

63. Ibid.; Hulett and Carmichael in Carmichael and Hamilton, *Black Power*, 114; "Candidates lose," *The Movement* (December 1966).

64. "A good day to go voting," *Southern Courier* (12–13 November 1966); Carmichael and Hamilton, *Black Power*, 115; Aldridge Interview, (13 June 2000).

65. Voter in "Candidates lose," *The Movement* (December 1966).

66. "A good day to go voting," *Southern Courier* (12–13 November 1966); "Candidates lose," *The Movement* (December 1966).

67. Reports from poll watchers in Carmichael and Hamilton, *Black Power*, 116.

68. Ibid., 116; SNCC Newsletter, (November 1966), SNCC, Box 126, Folder 12.

69. SNCC Newsletter, (November 1966), SNCC, Box 126, Folder 12.

70. Ibid.; Andrew Jones Interview, (16 October 1998); "A good day to go voting," *Southern Courier* (12–13 November 1966).

71. Carmichael in "Candidates lose," *The Movement* (December 1966).

72. LCFO candidate for sheriff Sidney Logan, Jr., lost to Democrat Frank Ryals 1,643 to 2,320. LCFO candidate for coroner Emory Ross lost to Democrat Jack Golson 1,640 to 2,265. LCFO candidate for tax assessor Alice Moore lost to Democrat Charlie Sullivan 1,604 to 2,265. LCFO candidate for tax collector Frank Miles, Jr., lost to Democrat Iva Sullivan 1,603 to 2,268. LCFO candidate for school board seat #5 Willie Mae Strickland lost to Democrat C. B. Haigler 1,600 to 2,170. LCFO candidate for school board seat #3 Robert Logan lost to Republican candidate David Lyon 1,664 to 1,937. And LCFO candidate for school board seat #4 John Hinson lost to Republican candidate Tommy Coleman 1,666 to 1,966. "How Lowndes County voted," Lowndes *Signal* (10 November 1966); SNCC, "Election Reports," (10 November 1966), SNCC, Box 35, Folder 9; Carmichael and Hamilton, *Black Power*, 117–118.

73. Hulett in U.S. Commission on Civil Rights, *Hearing before the United States Commission on Civil Rights Held in Montgomery, Alabama* (Washington, D.C.: Government Printing Office), 596–603.

74. Moore in "Election aftermath," *Southern Courier* (19–20 November 1966).

75. Lillian McGill Interview, (29 May 1968); "Candidates lose," *The Movement* (December 1966); Campbell, "The Lowndes County Freedom Organization," 77.

76. "Candidates lose," *The Movement* (December 1966); Carmichael and Hamilton, *Black Power*, 116–117; Minnis, "Lowndes County Freedom Organization," 12.

77. Assuming that all 1,900 eligible white voters cast a ballot for sheriff Frank Ryals, who received 2,320 votes, then as many as 420 African Americans voted Democratic. This is also assuming that there was no ballot-box stuffing.

78. Connors in "Candidates lose," *The Movement* (December 1966).

79. Landowner in "The changing times," New York *Times* (31 October 1966).

80. Staff Report, "Voting and Political Participation by Blacks in the 16 Alabama Hearing Counties," in Commission on Civil Rights, *Hearing Held in Montgomery, Alabama*, 922—940.

81. Black voter in "Election aftermath," *Southern Courier* (19–20 November 1966); Commission on Civil Rights, *Hearing Held in Montgomery, Alabama*, 596–603; "Candidates lose," and "Interview with Sidney Logan, Jr.," *The Movement* (December 1966); Hulett Interview, (30 May 1968); Lillian McGill Interview, (29 May 1968).

82. "Candidates lose," and "Interview with John Hulett," *The Movement* (December 1966); Carmichael and Hamilton, *Black Power*, 116–117.

83. Jones in "Election aftermath," *Southern Courier* (19–20 November 1966).

84. "Interview with John Hulett," *The Movement* (December 1966).

85. Carmichael and Hamilton, *Black Power*, 120.

86. Carmichael, "What we want," *New York Review of Books* (22 September 1966); Donaldson to the Editors, (October 1966), SNCC, Box 126, Folder 12.

CHAPTER 7

1. Hulett in "Negro takes post as sheriff in Deep South," Los Angeles *Times* (17 January 1971); Denby, *Indignant Heart*, 219–220.

2. "Poverty war begins in old Hayneville church," *Southern Courier* (11–12 February 1967); "This is not the end of the program," *Southern Courier* (18–19 March 1967); McMeans in "Lowndes class gets a teacher," *Southern Courier* (16–17 March 1968).

3. "This is not the end of the program," *Southern Courier* (18–19 March 1967).

4. "Statement by Stokely Carmichael," SNCC, Box 5, Folder 14.

5. "Lowndes office re-opens at scene of church fire," *Southern Courier* (25–26 March 1967); "Lowndes County folks get plenty of advice," *Southern Courier* (1–2 April 1967); "Probe begins of possible arson in 3rd church fire," Alabama *Journal* (20 March 1967); "Good Hope rebuilt," Lowndes *Signal* (5 March 1970).

6. "Lowndes County folks get plenty of advice," *Southern Courier* (1–2 April 1967).

7. "This is not the end," *Southern Courier* (18–19 March 1967); "Lowndes office re-opens at scene of church fire," *Southern Courier* (25–26 March 1967); Taylor and participant in "Program heading for bitter dispute," *Southern Courier* (14–15 October 1967).

8. The leaders of the Lowndes County Co-op were unable to raise the capital necessary to start the businesses. Campbell, "The Lowndes County Freedom Organization," 83; "Co-op planned for Tent City," *Southern Courier* (8–9 April 1967).

9. "60 pupils fail," *Southern Courier* (3–4 June 1967).

10. Hulett in "Kids beaten in schools," *Southern Courier* (6–7 June 1968).

11. Miles in "People question Lowndes Program," *Southern Courier* (8–9 July 1967).

12. Smith in "Lowndes board fires head," *Southern Courier* (23–24 September 1967).

13. Moore in "Lowndes poverty program," *Southern Courier* (14–15 October 1967).

14. The LCCMHR received $225,514 from the OEO in 1968 to operate the farm workers adult education program. "Lowndes class gets a teacher," *Southern Courier* (16–17 March 1968); Ashmore, *Carry It On*, 272.

15. "John Hulett," *Southern Courier* (13–14 January 1968); Lillian McGill Interview, (29 May 1968); Elzie McGill Interview, (4 August 1968).

16. Carmichael, *Ready for Revolution*, 302; Minutes of the Central Committee Meeting, (22–23 October 1966), SNCC, Box 6, Folder "Cent. Comm. Minutes, Aug. and Oct. 1966."

17. "The Story of SNCC," New York *Times* (25 September 1966). For details of SNCC's final years see Carson, *In Struggle*; Grady-Willis, *Challenging U.S. Apartheid*; Countryman, *Up South*; Fleming, *Soon We Will Not Cry*; Sellers, *The River of No Return*; Forman, *The Making of Black Revolutionaries*; Carmichael, *Ready for Revolution*.

18. Hulett in "Black Power in the Black Belt," *The Progressive* (October 1966).

19. Miles in "War on Poverty hits Lowndes," *The Movement* (June 1967).

20. Lillian McGill Interview, (29 May 1968).

21. John Jackson Interview, (3 August 1968).

22. Mathew Jackson, Sr., Interview, (4 August 1968).

23. Hulett Interview, (30 May 1968).

24. "Not even an alternate," *Southern Courier* (30 September—1 October 1967).

25. Campbell, "The Lowndes County Freedom Organization," 90.

26. Hulett in "Judge withholds the names," New York *Times* (14 April 1968).

27. "Hammonds is named probate judge," Lowndes *Signal* (2 June 1950); "Judge Hammonds dies suddenly," Lowndes *Signal* (12 February 1987).

28. Elbert and Harriet Means Interview, (25 July 2000). Elbert Means was the Lowndes County tax assessor from 1978 to 1990.

29. Hammonds quoted in "Judge withholds the names," New York *Times* (14 April 1968).

30. "Uralee Haynes Interview, (23 September 1998); Means Interview, (25 July 2000); "Hammonds re-elected," Lowndes *Signal* (4 November 1964); U.S. Commission on Civil Rights, *Fifteen Years Ago . . . Rural Alabama Revisited* (Washington, D.C.: Government Printing Office, 1983).

31. Hammonds in "Judge withholds the names," New York *Times* (14 April 1968); John Jackson Interview, (3 August 1968).

32. In the 1968 election for county commission, Charles Smith lost to Ned T. Ellis, 1,557 votes to 2,231 votes, and R. L. Strickland lost to O. P. Woodruff, 1,550 votes to 2,122 votes. John Hinson lost his bid to win a seat on the board of education to Matt Holmes, 1,547 votes to 2,087 votes. African Americans did win two justice of the peace positions, but these no longer carried the power that they once did, partly because the local police and state troopers generally ignored black justices. Campbell, "The Lowndes County Freedom Organization," 89–93.

33. Hulett Interview, (1973).

34. Miller Interview, (1972).

35. Hardy T. Frye, *Black Parties and Black Power: A Case Study* (Boston: G. K. Hall, 1980), 62; Miller Interview, (1972).

36. Gaillard, *Cradle of Freedom*, 324; William "Bill" Edwards Interview, (28 February 1973); Frye, *Black Parties and Political Power*, 34, 87.

37. Edwards Interview, (28 February 1973).

38. John Jackson Interview, (14 July 2000).

39. "Frank Ryals candidate for probate judge," Lowndes *Signal* (5 March 1970); "The people's choice," *Southern Courier* (17–18 June 1967); Denby, *Indignant Heart*, 219.

40. Edwards Interview, (28 February 1973); Haynes Interview, (23 September 1998); John Jackson Interview, (14 July 2000).

41. Haynes Interview, (23 September 1998).

42. Lillian McGill Interview, (29 May 1968); Hulett Interview, (30 May 1968) and (2 August 2000).

43. The only other primary race that African Americans participated in was the gubernatorial contest. Black residents split their votes between incumbent governor Albert Brewer and white businessperson Charles Woods. Local whites, meanwhile, voted overwhelming for George Wallace. In the end, Brewer received 1,890 votes, Wallace received 1,075 votes, and Woods received 920 votes. Five other candidates received a combined 256 votes from white voters. "How Lowndes County voted," Lowndes *Signal* (5 May 1970); "Upset time," *Time* (18 May 1970).

44. Andrew Kopkind, "A Long Time Coming: Lowndes County, Alabama," *Working Papers for a New Society* Vol. 2 (1974–1975), 13–18.

45. Miller Interview, (1972); Edwards Interview, (28 February 1973); "McGhee announces candidacy," Lowndes *Signal* (7 March 1974); John Jackson Interview, (14 July 2000).

46. Haynes Interview, (23 September 1998). Hulett received 2,078 votes to John Julian's 1,868; McGhee received 1,942 votes to D. W. Nichols's 1,635; Miller received 1,909 votes to Bruce Davis' 1,769. "Election returns," Lowndes *Signal* (5 November 1970).

47. "Lowndes County [Public School] Survey, #317 (1976)," ADEP, SG 23324.

48. Miller Interview, (1972); Edwards Interview, (28 February 1973); King Interview, (17 July 2000); Haynes Interview, (23 September 1998); Denby, *Indignant Heart*, 220; "Final results," Lowndes *Signal* (9 November 1972).

49. Denby, *Indignant Heart*, 220; Haynes Interview, (23 September 1998).

50. "Haynes qualifies," Lowndes *Signal* (25 March 1976); "Haynes receives leadership award," Lowndes *Signal* (10 December 1981); Haynes Interview, (23 September 1998); Hulett Interview, (17 July 2000); King Interview, (17 July 2000).

51. Haynes Interview, (23 September 1998); Hulett Interview, (17 July 2000); King Interview, (17 July 2000); "Final results," Lowndes *Signal* (9 November 1972).

52. Edwards Interview, (28 February 1973).

53. Denby, *Indignant Heart*, 220.

54. Miller Interview, (1972); Kopkind, "A Long Time Coming," 17.

55. In the 1972 elections for county commissioners, William Cosby received 2,297 votes and lost to O. P. Woodruff, who received 2,367 votes; Sidney Logan, Jr., received 2,121 votes and lost to C. A. Day, who received 2,658 votes; and Charles Smith received 2,156 votes and defeated Democrat S. E. Ryals, who

received 2,138 votes, and Republican Willie Claude Bates III, who received 616 votes. In the elections for the school board, Threddie Stewart received 2,163 votes and lost to John Farrior, who received 2,448 votes, and Leroy Jenkins received 2,286 votes and lost to T. S. Coleman, who received 2,423 votes. John Jackson received 2,201 votes in his bid to become tax assessor and lost to Charlie Hutchison, who received 2,396 votes. May Bell Nelson, the NDPA nominee for tax collector, received 2,194 votes in her loss to J. Bruce Cook, who received 2,451 votes. Uralee Haynes received 2,440 votes in her loss to superintendent Hulda Coleman, who received 2,578 votes. "Final results in county races," Lowndes *Signal* (9 November 1972).

56. Denby, *Indignant Heart*, 221.

57. Edwards Interview, (28 February 1973).

58. Haynes Interview, (23 September 1998); Hulett Interview, (1973).

59. Local activist in Denby, *Indignant Heart*, 221.

60. Frye, *Black Parties and Political Power*, 151.

61. Local activist in Denby, *Indignant Heart*, 221.

62. "Hulett sets race for re-election," "Fountain announces candidacy," and "Wilson, Board of Education candidate," Lowndes *Signal* (7 March 1974); "Election results," Lowndes *Signal* (9 May 1974); Kopkind, "A Long Time Coming," 19. For a detailed examination of the struggle around health care see Couto, *Ain't Gonna Let Nobody Turn Me Round*.

63. Denby, *Indignant Heart*, 221–224.

64. Kopkind, "A Long Time Coming," 19.

65. "Coleman candidate for sheriff," Lowndes *Signal* (21 February 1974).

66. In the 1974 primary, Hulett received 2,753 votes to J. C. Coleman's 212. "Election results," Lowndes *Signal* (9 May 1974); Haynes Interview, (23 September 1998); Hulett Interview, (1978).

67. John Hulett (2,909 votes) defeated Lawrence Wells (1,400 votes) for sheriff. An analysis of county returns for state and local offices reveals that Hulett received at least 300 white votes. Willie Ed McGhee (2,538 votes) defeated Chester B. Seale, Sr. (1,599 votes), a Democratic primary candidate, for coroner. Elder Fletcher Fountain (2,535 votes) defeated Emily Holmes (1,702 votes) for board of education seat #1. Willie Wilson, Jr. (2,530 votes), defeated Tom Brown (1,649 votes), the second Democratic primary candidate, for board of education seat #2. "Election results," Lowndes *Signal* (9 May 1974) and (7 November 1974).

68. Commission on Civil Rights, *Fifteen Years Ago*, 56, 128; "Lowndes warned schools crowded," Montgomery *Advertiser* (7 November 1975); "Principal's salary won't prevent accreditation," Alabama *Journal* (5 January 1976); Catherine Coleman Flowers, "In Due Time," unpublished memoir in possession of author.

69. "An open letter to the people of Lowndes County," *Lowndes Signal* (28 August 1975); Haynes Interview, (23 September 1998); Commission on Civil Rights, *Fifteen Years Ago*, 56, 128.

298 *Notes to Chapter 7*

70. "Lowndes schools headed by black," Mobile *Register* (10 September 1975); "Lowndes board accepts faculty mixing order," Alabama *Journal* (3 May 1977); Commission on Civil Rights, *Fifteen Years Ago*, 58; "Lowndes County [Public School] Survey, #317 (1976)," ADEP, SG 23324.

71. "Lowndes board accepts faculty mixing order," Alabama *Journal* (3 May 1977); "Black named principal," Alabama *Journal* (9 August 1977); "Lowndes County [Public School] Survey, #460 (1995)," ADEP, SG 23324.

72. "Ground breaking re-set," Lowndes *Signal* (30 May 1974); "Fort Deposit Academy directors named," Lowndes *Signal* (20 June 1974); Champion quoted in "Lowndes Academy rises," Birmingham *News* (1 December 1969).

73. Couto, *Ain't Gonna Let Nobody Turn Me Round*, 93–116; "Bradley qualifies," Lowndes *Signal* (4 March 1976); "Blacks mount election push," Birmingham *News* (1976).

74. "Grand jury says no more public funds," Lowndes *Signal* (3 April 1975).

75. "Man, woman in race for Lowndes judgeship," Birmingham *News* (17 March 1976); "Sanders qualifies for district judge," Lowndes *Signal* (25 March 1976).

76. The population of Jefferson County, which included Birmingham, was 644,000 in 1976. The population of Lowndes County was less than 13,000. Hulett and Holmes in "Blacks may ask Justice voting probe," Birmingham *News* (27 April 1976).

77. Harrell Hammonds received 3,726 votes to William "Sam" Bradley's 712 votes. "Election returns," Lowndes *Signal* (6 May 1976).

78. Uralee Haynes received 2,839 votes to William R. Carnes' 1,341 votes. Alma Miller received 2,047 votes in her loss to Bruce Davis, who received 2,081 votes; and Rose Sanders received 1,974 votes in her loss to Ted Bozeman, who received 2,135 votes. In the county commissioner elections, Charles Smith received 2,223 votes to Joseph Barganier's 1,995 votes; Frank Miles, Jr., received 2,111 votes to C. A. Day's 2,110 votes; and America Daney received 1,923 votes to C. Raymond Dean's 1,809 votes and Lemon Bogan's 170 votes. Of the black candidates who lost, William Cosby received 1,872 votes to O. P. Woodruff's 2,103 votes; and Joe F. Brown received 1,996 votes to Snow Davis's 2,120 votes. "Election returns," Lowndes *Signal* (6 May 1976); "Circuit clerk election set for August 31," Lowndes *Signal* (12 August 1976); "Results," Lowndes *Signal* (2 September 1976).

79. In the November 1976 general election, probate judge Harrell Hammonds, superintendent Uralee Haynes, and commissioner Charles Smith ran unopposed. Black Democratic nominee Frank Miles, Jr., received 2,950 votes against C. A. Day, who received 1,891 votes in the race for county commission in District 2. In District 1, white Democratic nominee O. P. Woodruff (2,520 votes) defeated black independent Jake Williams (2,241 votes); in District 3, white Democratic nominee Snow Davis (2,611 votes) defeated black independent Joe Frank Brown (2,407 votes); and in District 5, white Democratic nominee C. Raymond Dean

(2,616 votes) defeated black independent Charlie Whiting, Jr. (2,239 votes). In the contest for circuit clerk, white Democratic nominee Bruce Davis (2,620 votes) defeated black independent Ida Searight (2,298 votes). "Lowndes County election returns," Lowndes *Signal* (4 November 1976).

80. Hulett Interview, (1978); Means Interview, (25 July 2000); John Jackson Interview, (14 July 2000); "Election returns," Lowndes *Signal* (7 September 1978).

81. Means Interview, (25 July 2000).

82. Ibid.

83. In the 1978 tax assessor's race, Elbert Means received 1,911 votes, Charlie Hutchinson 1,559, and Virginia Crook 922. In the sheriff's race, John Hulett received 3,709 votes and George Hammonds 1,551. All the Democratic nominees ran unopposed in the general election. "Election returns," Lowndes *Signal* (7 September 1978); Hulett Interview, (1978).

84. Means Interview, (25 July 2000); Means to Charles Graddick, (7 May 1984), AAGP, SG 18552, Folder "Lowndes County."

85. "Raids remove over \$1 million from streets," Lowndes *Signal* (29 August 1986); "Lowndes owners warned," Lowndes *Signal* (31 May 1990).

86. "County tax collector arrested," Lowndes *Signal* (17 June 1982); Harriet Means Interview, (25 July 2000).

87. In the 1980 Democratic primary for superintendent of education, Uralee Haynes received 2,456 votes to Ed Moore King's 1,406 votes. "Election results," Lowndes *Signal* (4 September 1980); Harriet Means Interview, (25 July 2000).

88. In the 1980 Democratic primary races for the county commission, William Cosby received 2,456 votes to O. P. Woodruff's 1,530 votes; Frank Miles, Jr., received 2,014 votes to Bill Jones's 1,251 votes (two other white candidates received 548 votes combined); Joe Frank Brown received 1,984 votes to Snow Davis's 1,676 votes; Charles Smith received 2,035 votes to Ned Ellis's 1,528 votes; and Thomas Pringle received 1,499 votes to Abdullah Shabazz's 519 votes and Dickson Farrior's 1,241 votes (two other white candidates received 665 votes combined). "Election results," Lowndes *Signal* (4 September 1980); Hulett Interview, (1978).

89. Commission on Civil Rights, *Fifteen Years Ago*, 56–58; "Food stamp recipients to see increase," Lowndes *Signal* (22 September 1983); "Poverty level declines," Lowndes *Signal* (11 December 1986); "Federal spending declines in Lowndes," Lowndes *Signal* (14 May 1987).

90. "County faces serious financial problems," Lowndes *Signal* (14 July 1983); Commission on Civil Rights, *Fifteen Years Ago*, 58.

91. GE gave one million dollars over five years to the Lowndes County board of education starting in 1987 to upgrade science and mathematics programs in the county's public schools. Although helpful, the grant was much less than GE would have paid in property taxes over the same period had it not received the tax exemption. "Construction to begin on GE plant in '83," Lowndes *Signal* (12 November 1981); "GE Plastics dedicates new facility," Lowndes *Signal* (30 April

1987); "GE Foundation Grant to benefit schools," Lowndes *Signal* (30 April 1987); "GE Foundation renews Lowndes grant," Lowndes *Signal* (4 June 1987); "GE grants $25,000 for Lowndes computerization," Lowndes *Signal* (7 April 1988); "Community leaders meet with GE officials," Lowndes *Signal* (10 October 1985); "Efforts increased to reduce unemployment," Lowndes *Signal* (25 June 1987); "GE lawsuit settled," Lowndes *Signal* (15 February 1996); Commission on Civil Rights, *Fifteen Years Ago*, 58–60.

92. "Citizens hold organizational meeting," Lowndes *Signal* (8 October 1981); "Hazardous waste committee meets," Lowndes *Signal* (22 October 1981); "Legislative act to limit hazardous waste dumps," Lowndes *Signal* (26 November 1981).

93. "Concerned Citizens Group," Lowndes *Signal* (17 March 1988).

94. "Foes to oppose landfill permit," Montgomery *Advertiser* (3 August 2000); "Activists turn attention to Lowndes County landfill," Montgomery *Advertiser* (25 August 2000).

95. "Hulett announces candidacy," Lowndes *Signal* (24 May 1984).

96. Means Interview, (25 July 2000); "Formal protest filed by Means," Lowndes *Signal* (6 September 1984). Ironically, Hulett engaged in ballot fraud at a time when the U.S. Justice Department systematically harassed black elected officials across the South under the aegis of investigating voting rights violations. Rumors swirled that Hulett was under investigation, but he was never charged with anything. Couto, *Ain't Gonna Let Nobody Turn Me Round*, 338, 399n21; Chestnut, *Black in Selma*, 321–323, 374–388.

97. Excluding absentee ballots cast in September 1984, Elbert Means received 1,962 votes to John E. Hulett's 1,871. Means estimated that the challenge cost him fourteen thousand dollars. "Lowndes County election returns," Lowndes *Signal* (6 September 1984); "Formal protest filed by Means," Lowndes *Signal* (6 September 1984); "Seaborn announces candidacy," Lowndes *Signal* (3 May 1984); Means Interview, (25 July 2000).

98. "Lowndes County election returns," Lowndes *Signal* (6 September 1984).

99. In 1990, Willie Ruth Myrick received 1,775 votes to Elbert Means's 1,699. In the general election, Means received 651 write-in votes. "Lowndes County unofficial election returns," Lowndes *Signal* (5 June 1986); "Judge favors Myrick's petition," Lowndes *Signal* (19 June 1990); Means Interview, (25 July 2000).

100. Jackson in Greenberg, *Circle of Trust*, 102

101. "Jackson reports on first term accomplishments," Lowndes *Signal* (22 September 1983); "White Hall mayor's progress report," Lowndes *Signal* (12 February 1987); W. Craig Remington and Thomas J. Kallsen, eds., *Historical Atlas of Alabama: Historical Locations by County Vol. 1* (Tuscaloosa: University of Alabama Press, 1997), 220.

102. "Lowndes County election results," Lowndes *Signal* (9 September 1982); "Probate Judge Harrell Hammonds," Lowndes *Signal* (6 December 1984); "Lowndes County unofficial election returns," Lowndes *Signal* (5 June 1986);

"Lowndes County unofficial vote returns," Lowndes *Signal* (9 June 1988); "Vaugh-ner to succeed Hulett as sheriff," Lowndes *Signal* (21 January 1993); "Lowndes County election results," Lowndes *Signal* (9 June 1994); "Lowndes County run-off election results," Lowndes *Signal* (30 June 1994). When Hammonds stepped down in 1984, he was the state's senior probate judge, having served for thirty-four years. "Probate Judge Harrell Hammonds," Lowndes *Signal* (6 December 1984); "Judge Hammonds dies suddenly," Lowndes *Signal* (12 February 1987).

103. Haynes Interview, (23 September 1998); Andrew Jones Interview, (25 July 2000); Means Interview, (25 July 2000).

104. John Jackson Interview, (14 July 2000).

105. Moorer quoted in Couto, *Ain't Gonna Let Nobody Turn Me Round*, 333.

106. Kelley, *Race Rebels*, 77–100. Minchin discusses the rise of police violence across the South in *From Rights to Economics*, 14–27. See also Tyson, *Blood Done Sign My Name*.

107. Governor George Wallace appointed O. P. Woodruff probate judge to com-plete the unexpired term of Harrell Hammonds. Woodruff placed a distant sec-ond to Hammonds in the 1982 Democratic primary. "Lowndes County election results," Lowndes *Signal* (9 September 1982); "Lowndes County unofficial vote returns," Lowndes *Signal* (9 June 1988).

108. "Lowndes has low voter turnout," Lowndes *Signal* (23 June 1994).

109. "Rights pioneer Hulett dies," Montgomery *Advertiser* (22 August 2006).

110. In 2006, there was one black student enrolled at Lowndes Academy. For education statistics for Lowndes County, see the Common Core of Data (CCD) public school district data and the Private School Universe Survey Data (PSS) from the National Center for Education Statistics, U.S. Department of Educa-tion, at http://www.nces.ed.gov/surveys/surveygroups.asp?group=1. For per capita income statistics by race or ethnicity, see U.S. Bureau of the Census, Twenty-second Census of the United States, 2000, at http://epodunk.com/cgi-bin/inco-meOverview.php?locIndex=12047; "No surprises most troubled school systems under funded," Birmingham *News* (26 June 2000); "High poverty rates plague most of state," Birmingham *News* (24 November 2000).

111. Carmichael and Hamilton, *Black Power*, 46–47.

EPILOGUE

1. Catherine Coleman Flowers, "In Due Time," unpublished memoir in pos-session of author.

2. Ibid.; Flowers Interview, (15 June 2008).

3. Flowers, "In Due Time."

4. Flowers Interview, (15 June 2008).

5. Ibid.

6. Ibid.

7. Ibid.; "Record turnout ousts Smitherman," Montgomery *Advertiser* (13 September 2000); "New seeds in a barren Black Belt," Montgomery *Advertiser* (20 January 2002); "Couple saved from jail time," Montgomery *Advertiser* (25 April 2002); "Tank legislation faces election year battle," Montgomery *Advertiser* (20 January 2002).

8. Flowers Interview, (15 June 2008); "Couple saved from jail time," Montgomery *Advertiser* (25 April 2002); "Flush septic tank worries," Montgomery *Advertiser* (13 March 2003); "Partners make sewer authority possible," Montgomery *Advertiser* (24 February 2004); "PAX show to shed light on Black Belt," Montgomery *Advertiser* (24 April 2004); "Destitute families may get new homes for Christmas," Montgomery *Advertiser* (15 December 2004); "Group gives 2nd woman new house," Montgomery *Advertiser* (19 January 2005); "Lowndes County snares supplier," Montgomery *Advertiser* (23 April 2003); "Extras bring jobs to town," Montgomery *Advertiser* (28 April 2003); "$2 million grant aimed at industry," Montgomery *Advertiser* (24 April 2004); "Hyundai supplier expands," Montgomery *Advertiser* (12 December 2007).

9. Flowers Interview, (15 June 2008).

10. Turner and Flowers in "Woman's home of 30 years damaged," Montgomery *Advertiser* (29 May 2008).

11. For more on the reverse migration see Carol Stack, *Call to Home: African Americans Reclaim the Rural South* (New York: Basic, 1996).

12. "Family gets new home," Montgomery *Advertiser* (30 August 2008).

Bibliography

MANUSCRIPT SOURCES

Alabama Department of Archives and History, Montgomery, Alabama
  Alabama Attorney General's Office Papers (AAGP)
  Alabama Church Records
  Alabama Department and Archives and History Papers (ADAH)
  Alabama Department of Education Papers (ADEP)
  Alabama Department of Public Health Papers
  Alabama Governors Papers (AGP)
  Lowndes County, Alabama, Probate Judges Records
  William Bonnell Hall Papers (WBHP)
  Works Progress Administration Papers (WPA)
Atlanta University Center Archives, Atlanta, Georgia
  Voter Education Project Papers
Auburn University Archives, Auburn, Alabama
  Agricultural Cooperative Extension Service Collection (ACES)
Martin Luther King, Jr., Center for Nonviolent Social Change, Atlanta, Georgia
  Robert Mants Papers (RMP)
  Southern Christian Leadership Conference Papers (SCLC)
  Student Nonviolent Coordinating Committee Papers (SNCC)
Schomburg Center for Research in Black Culture, New York, New York
  Phelps-Stokes Collection (PSC)
Tuskegee University Archives, Tuskegee, Alabama
  Tuskegee University Newspaper Clippings Collection

MANUSCRIPTS ON MICROFILM

Association of Southern Women for the Prevention of Lynching Papers (ASWPL)
Department of Justice Peonage Files (PF)
National Association for the Advancement of Colored People Papers (NAACP)
W. E. B. Du Bois Papers (DP)

INTERVIEWS CONDUCTED BY AUTHOR

Aldridge, Dorothy Dewberry, Detroit, Michigan, 13 June 2000 (with Taylor Branch).
Flowers, Catherine Coleman, Telephone, 15 June 2008.
Haynes, Uralee, Gordonsville, Alabama, 23 September 1998.
House, Gloria Larry, Detroit, Michigan, 28 June 2000 (with Taylor Branch).
Hulett, John, Hayneville, Alabama, 2 September 1998, 9 September 1998, 17 July 2000, and 2 August 2000.
Jackson, John, White Hall, Alabama, 14 July 2000.
Jones, Andrew, Calhoun, Alabama, 16 October 1998.
King, Ed Moore, White Hall, Alabama, 17 July 2000.
Lawson, Jennifer, Washington, D.C., 3 June 2000.
Logan, Sarah, Gordonsville, Alabama, 15 September 1998.
Mays, Timothy, Montgomery, Alabama, 27 July 2000.
McCall, Josephine, Montgomery, Alabama, 21 May 2008.
McDonald, Pattie, Hayneville, Alabama, 24 September 1998.
McGill, Lillian, Montgomery, Alabama, 2 August 2000.
McMeans, Bessie, Fort Deposit, Alabama, 13 October 1998.
Means, Elbert, Fort Deposit, Alabama, 25 July 2000.
Means, Harriet, Fort Deposit, Alabama, 25 July 2000.
Moses, Janet, Raleigh, North Carolina, 15 April 2000.
Norman, Martha Prescod, Detroit, Michigan, 28 June 2000 (with Taylor Branch).
Norman, Silas, Jr., Detroit, Michigan, 30 June 2000.
Patton, Gwen, Raleigh, North Carolina, 15 April 2000.
Ricks, Willie "Mukassa", Atlanta, Georgia, 13 September 1998.
Rogers, Jimmy, Raleigh, North Carolina, 15 April 2000.
Searight, Ida, Hayneville, Alabama, 8 October 1998.
Sellers, Cleveland, Raleigh, North Carolina, 15 April 2000.
Smith, Charles, Calhoun, Alabama, 14 September 1998.
White, Gardenia, Trickem, Alabama, 15 September 1998.
Williams, Jake, Montgomery, Alabama, 21 May 2008 (with Jeremiah Day).

INTERVIEWS CONDUCTED BY OTHERS

Alabama Center for Higher Education State Oral History Project, Alabama State University Archives, Montgomery, Alabama
Jones, Cornelius "C. J.," by Mildred Black, 25 July 1973.
Hardy T. Frye Oral History Collection, Auburn University Archives, Auburn, Alabama
Edwards, William "Bill," by Hardy T. Frye, 28 February 1973.
Hulett, John, by Hardy T. Frye, 1973, 1978.
Miller, Alma, by Hardy T. Frye, 1972.

Civil Rights Documentation Project, Moorland-Spingarn Research Center, Howard University, Washington, D.C.
Hulett, John, by Stanley Smith, 30 May 1968.
Jackson, Emma Lee, by Robert Wright, 4 August 1968.
Jackson, John, by Robert Wright, 3 August 1968.
Jackson, Sr., Mathew, by Robert Wright, 4 August 1968.
McGill, Mr. Elzie, by Robert Wright, 4 August 1968.
McGill, Mrs. Elzie, by Robert Wright, 4 August 1968.
McGill, Lillian, by Stanley Smith, 29 May 1968.

NEWSPAPERS AND OTHER SERIALS

Alabama *Journal* (Montgomery, Alabama)
Atlanta *Journal and Constitution* (Atlanta, Georgia)
Birmingham *Post-Herald* (Birmingham, Alabama)
Daily Worker
Emerge
Hayneville *Examiner* (Hayneville, Alabama)
Jet
Look
Los Angeles *Times* (Los Angeles, California)
Lowndes *Signal* (Fort Deposit, Alabama)
Militant
Montgomery *Advertiser* (Montgomery, Alabama)
Movement
Nation
National Guardian
New Republic
New York Review of Books
New York *Times* (New York, New York)
Newsweek
Outlook
Southern Courier (Montgomery, Alabama)
Wall Street *Journal* (New York, New York)
Washington *Post* (Washington, D.C)
Young Socialist

DISSERTATIONS, THESES, AND UNPUBLISHED MANUSCRIPTS

Campbell, David. "The Lowndes County (Alabama) Freedom Organization: The First Black Panther Party, 1965–1968." M.A. Thesis, Florida State University, 1970.

Flowers, Catherine Coleman. "In Due Time." Unpublished manuscript in possession of author.
Sisk, Glenn Nolan. "Alabama Black Belt: A Social History, 1875–1917." Ph.D. Dissertation, Duke University, 1951.

FILMS AND VIDEOS

Eyes on the Prize. Episode 7, "The Time Has Come (1964–1966)." Boston: Black-
side Inc., 1990.
Lowndes County Freedom Party: The Rise of the Black Panthers. Princeton, N.J.:
Films for the Humanities and Sciences, 1995.

GOVERNMENT PUBLICATIONS

U.S. Bureau of the Census. *Eighteenth Census of the United States, 1960, Vol. 1, Pt.
2.* Washington, D.C.: Government Printing Office, 1963.
U.S. Commission on Civil Rights. *Fifteen Years Ago . . . Rural Alabama Revisited.*
Washington, D.C.: Government Printing Office, 1983.
———. *Hearing before the United States Commission on Civil Rights Held in Mont-
gomery, Alabama.* Washington, D.C.: Government Printing Office, 1968.
———. *Political Participation.* Washington, D.C.: Government Printing Office,
1968.
———. *The Voting Rights Act . . . The First Months.* Washington, D.C.: Govern-
ment Printing Office, 1965.

ARTICLES AND BOOKS

Albaugh, June Middleton. *Collirene: The Queen Hill.* Montgomery: Herff Jones—
Paragon, 1977.
Anderson, Carol. *Eyes off the Prize: The United Nations and the African Ameri-
can Struggle for Human Rights, 1944–1955.* Cambridge: Cambridge University
Press, 2003.
Aptheker, Herbert, ed. *The Correspondence of W. E. B. Du Bois: Volume I Selec-
tion, 1877–1934.* Amherst: University of Massachusetts Press, 1973.
Arsenault, Raymond. *Freedom Riders: 1961 and the Struggle for Racial Justice.*
New York: Oxford University Press, 2006.
Ashmore, Susan Youngblood. *Carry It On: The War on Poverty and the Civil
Rights Movement in Alabama, 1964–1972.* Athens: University of Georgia Press,
2008.
Atkins, Leah R. "Populism in Alabama: Reuben F. Kolb and the Appeals to Mi-
nority Groups." *Alabama Historical Quarterly* Vol. 32, Nos. 3 and 4 (Fall and
Winter 1970), 167–180.

Austin, Curtis J. *Up against the Wall: Violence in the Making and Unmaking of the Black Panther Party.* Fayetteville: University of Arkansas Press, 2006.

Bailey, Richard. *Neither Carpetbaggers nor Scalawags: Black Officeholders during the Reconstruction of Alabama, 1867–1878.* Montgomery: R. Bailey, 1993.

Bedwell, Martha Ann Brinson. *Josiah's House.* Montgomery, Ala.: Colonial, 1993.

Belknap, Michael. *Civil Rights, the White House, and the Justice Department: 1945–1968.* New York: Barland, 1991.

Biondi, Martha. *To Stand and Fight: The Struggle for Civil Rights in Postwar New York City.* Cambridge, Mass.: Harvard University Press, 2003.

The Black Panther Party. New York: Merit, 1966.

Bolton, Charles. *The Hardest Deal of All: The Battle over School Integration in Mississippi, 1870–1980.* Jackson: University Press of Mississippi, 2005.

Bond, Horace M. *Negro Education in Alabama: A Study in Cotton and Steel.* Washington, D.C.: Associated, 1939.

Branch, Taylor. *At Canaan's Edge: America in the King Years, 1965–68.* New York: Simon & Schuster, 2006.

Brown, Elsa Barkley. "Negotiating and Transforming the Public Sphere: African American Political Life in the Transition from Slavery to Freedom," in *The Black Public Sphere: A Public Culture Book,* edited by Black Public Sphere Collective, 111–150. Chicago: University of Chicago Press, 1995.

Brown, Scot. *Fighting for US: Maulana Karenga, the US Organization, and Black Cultural Nationalism.* New York: New York University Press, 2005.

Bryant, Jonathan M. *How Curious a Land: Conflict and Change in Greene County, Georgia, 1850–1885.* Chapel Hill: University of North Carolina Press, 1996.

Burns, Stewart, ed. *Daybreak of Freedom: The Montgomery Bus Boycott.* Chapel Hill: University of North Carolina Press, 1997.

Bush, Rod. *We Are Not What We Seem: Black Nationalism and Class Struggle in the American Century.* New York: New York University Press, 1999.

Carmichael, Stokely, and Charles V. Hamilton. *Black Power: The Politics of Black Liberation in America.* New York: Vintage, 1967.

Carmichael, Stokely, with Ekwueme Michael Thelwell. *Ready for Revolution: The Life and Struggles of Stokely Carmichael (Kwame Ture).* New York: Scribner, 2003.

Carson, Clayborne. *In Struggle: SNCC and the Black Awakening of the 1960s.* Cambridge, Mass.: Harvard University Press, 1981.

———, ed. *The Movement, 1964–1970.* Westport, Conn.: Greenwood, 1993.

Carson, Clayborne, and Kris Shepard, eds. *A Call to Conscience: The Landmark Speeches of Dr. Martin Luther King, Jr.* New York: Warner, 2001.

Cha-Jua, Sundiata Keita, and Clarence Lang. "The 'Long Movement' as Vampire: Temporal and Spatial Fallacies in Recent Black Freedom Studies." *Journal of African American History* Vol. 92, Issue 4 (Fall 2007), 265–288.

Chafe, William. *Civilities and Civil Rights: Greensboro, North Carolina, and the Black Struggle for Freedom.* New York: Oxford University Press, 1980.

Chestnut, Jr. J. L., and Julia Cass. *Black in Selma: The Uncommon Life of J. L. Chestnut, Jr.* New York: Farrar, Straus and Giroux, 1990.

Corry, John. "A Visit to Lowndes County, Alabama." *New South* Vol. 27 (Winter 1972), 28–36.

Couto, Richard A. *Ain't Gonna Let Nobody Turn Me Round: The Pursuit of Racial Justice in the Rural South.* Philadelphia: Temple University Press, 1991.

Countryman, Matthew. *Up South: Civil Rights and Black Power in Philadelphia.* Philadelphia: University of Pennsylvania Press, 2006.

Crespino, Joseph. *In Search of Another Country: Mississippi and the Conservative Counterrevolution.* Princeton, N.J.: Princeton University Press, 2007.

Crosby, Emilye. *A Little Taste of Freedom: The Black Freedom Struggle in Claiborne County, Mississippi.* Chapel Hill: University of North Carolina Press, 2005.

Dalfiume, Richard. "The 'Forgotten Years' of the Negro Revolution." *Journal of American History* Vol. 55, No. 1 (June 1968), 90–160.

Daniel, Pete. *The Shadow of Slavery: Peonage in the South, 1901–1969.* Urbana: University of Illinois Press, 1972, 1990.

Davis, Belinda. "What's Left? Popular Political Participation in Postwar Europe." *American Historical Review* Vol. 113, No. 2 (April 2008), 363–390.

Dawson, Michael. *Black Visions: The Roots of Contemporary African-American Political Ideologies.* Chicago: University of Chicago Press, 2001.

de Jong, Greta. *A Different Day: African American Struggles for Justice in Rural Louisiana, 1900–1970.* Chapel Hill: University of North Carolina Press, 2002.

Demurth, Jerry. "Black Belt, Alabama." *Commonweal* Vol. 80 (August 7, 1964), 536–539.

Denby, Charles. *Indignant Heart: A Black Worker's Journal.* Boston: South End, 1978.

Dierenfield, Bruce J. *The Civil Rights Movement.* Harlow, England: Pearson, 2004.

Dittmer, John. *Local People: The Struggle for Civil Rights in Mississippi.* Urbana: University of Illinois Press, 1994.

Du Bois, W. E. B. *Dusk of Dawn: An Essay Toward an Autobiography of a Race Concept.* New Brunswick, N.J.: Transaction, 1940.

———. *The Souls of Black Folk.* New York: Vintage, 1903, 1990.

Dudziak, Mary L. *Cold War Civil Rights: Race and the Image of American Democracy.* Princeton, N.J.: Princeton University Press, 2000.

Eagles, Charles W. *Outside Agitator: Jon Daniels and the Civil Rights Movement in Alabama.* Chapel Hill: University of North Carolina Press, 1993.

Ellis, Rose Herlong. "The Calhoun School, Miss Charlotte Thorn's 'Lighthouse on the Hill' in Lowndes County, Alabama." *Alabama Review* Vol. 37, No. 3 (July 1984), 183–201.

Eskew, Glenn T. *But for Birmingham: The Local and National Movements in the Civil Rights Struggle.* Chapel Hill: University of North Carolina Press, 1997.

Fairclough, Adam. *To Redeem the Soul of America: The Southern Christian Leadership Conference and Martin Luther King, Jr.* Athens: University of Georgia Press, 1987.

———. "The Preachers and the People: The Origins and Early Years of the Southern Christian Leadership Conference, 1955–1959." *Journal of Southern History* Vol. 52, No. 3 (August 1986), 403–440.

Fleming, Cynthia Griggs. *In the Shadow of Selma: The Continuing Struggle for Civil Rights in the Rural South.* Lanham, Md.: Rowman and Littlefield, 2004.

———. *Soon We Will Not Cry: The Liberation of Ruby Doris Smith Robinson.* Lanham, Md.: Rowan and Littlefield, 1998.

Fleming, Walter L. *Civil War and Reconstruction in Alabama.* Spartanburg, S.C.: Reprint Co., 1978.

Foner, Philip S., ed. *W. E. B. Du Bois Speaks: Speeches and Addresses, 1890–1919.* New York: Pathfinder, 1970.

Forman, James. *The Making of Black Revolutionaries: A Personal Account.* New York: Macmillan, 1972.

Franklin, V. P. *Black Self-Determination: A Cultural History of African-American Resistance.* New York: Lawrence Hill, 1984, 1992.

Frye, Hardy T. *Black Parties and Political Power: A Case Study.* Boston: G. K. Hall, 1980.

Gaillard, Frye. *Cradle of Freedom: Alabama and the Movement That Changed America.* Tuscaloosa. University of Alabama Press, 2004.

Garrow, David J. *Bearing the Cross: Martin Luther King, Jr., and the Southern Christian Leadership Conference.* New York: Vintage, 1986.

———. *Protest at Selma: Martin Luther King, Jr., and the Voting Rights Act of 1965.* New Haven, Conn.: Yale University Press, 1978.

Geib, Paul. "From Mississippi to Milwaukee: A Case Study of Southern Black Migration to Milwaukee, 1940–1970." *Journal of Negro History* Vol. 83, No. 4 (Autumn 1998), 229–248.

Germany, Kent B. *New Orleans after the Promises: Poverty, Citizenship, and the Search for the Great Society.* Athens: University of Georgia Press, 2007.

Gilmore, Glenda Elizabeth. *Defying Dixie: The Radical Roots of Civil Rights, 1919–1950.* New York: Norton, 2008.

Gitlin, Todd. *The Sixties: Years of Hope, Days of Rage.* New York: Bantam, 1989.

Goldsmith, Glenn Davis. *Fort Deposit: History and Happenings.* Privately printed, 1982.

Goodwyn, Lawrence. *The Populist Moment: A Short History of the Agrarian Revolt in America.* Oxford: Oxford University Press, 1978.

Grady-Willis, Winston A. *Atlanta and Black Struggles for Human Rights, 1960–1977.* Durham, N.C.: Duke University Press, 2006.

Grant, Joanne. *Ella Baker: Freedom Bound.* New York: Wiley, 1998.

Green, Laurie. *Battling the Plantation Mentality: Memphis and the Black Freedom Struggle.* Chapel Hill: University of North Carolina Press, 2007.

Greenberg, Cheryl Lynn, ed. *A Circle of Trust: Remembering* SNCC. New Brunswick, N.J.: Rutgers University Press, 1998.

Greene, Christina. *Our Separate Ways: Women and the Black Freedom Movement in Durham, North Carolina.* Chapel Hill: University of North Carolina Press, 2005.

Greene, Melissa Fay. *Praying for Sheetrock.* New York: Fawcett Columbine, 1992.

Hahn, Steven. *A Nation under Our Feet: Black Political Struggles in the Rural South from Slavery to the Great Migration.* Cambridge, Mass.: Harvard University Press, 2003.

Halberstam, David. *The Children.* New York: Fawcett, 1998.

Hall, Jacquelyn Dowd. "The Long Civil Rights Movement and the Political Uses of the Past." *Journal of American History* Vol. 91, Issue 4 (March 2005), 1233–1263.

Hampton, Henry, and Steve Fayer, with Sarah Flynn. *Voices of Freedom: An Oral History of the Civil Rights Movement from the 1950s through the 1980s.* New York: Bantam, 1990.

Harlan, Louis R., ed. *The Booker T. Washington Papers.* 12 Vols. Urbana: University of Illinois Press, 1974–1982.

Hill, Lance. *Deacons for Defense: Armed Resistance and the Civil Rights Movement.* Chapel Hill: University of North Carolina Press, 2004.

Hogan, Wesley C. *Many Minds, One Heart:* SNCC's *Dream for A New America.* Chapel Hill: University of North Carolina Press, 2007.

Holly, Donald. "The Negro in the New Deal Resettlement Program." *New South* Vol. 27 (Winter 1972), 53–65.

Hurt, R. Douglas, ed. *African American Life in the Rural South, 1900–1950.* Columbia: University of Missouri Press, 2003.

Jackson, Thomas F. *From Civil Rights to Human Rights: Martin Luther King, Jr., and the Struggle for Economic Justice.* Philadelphia: University of Pennsylvania Press, 2007.

Johnson, Cedric. *Revolutionaries to Race Leaders: Black Power and the Making of African American Politics.* Minneapolis: University of Minnesota Press, 2007.

Jeffries, Hasan Kwame. "SNCC, Black Power, and Independent Political Party Organizing in Alabama, 1964–1966." *Journal of African American History* Vol. 91, No. 2 (Spring 2006), 171–193.

———. "Organizing for More than the Vote: The Political Radicalization of Local People in Lowndes County, Alabama, 1965–1966," in *Groundwork: Local Black Freedom Movements in America,* edited by Jeanne Theoharis and Komozi Woodard, 140–164. New York: New York University Press, 2005.

Jeffries, Judson, ed. *Comrades: A Local History of the Black Panther Party.* Bloomington: Indiana University Press, 2007.

Jeffries, Judson, ed. *Black Power in the Belly of the Beast*. Urbana: University of Illinois Press, 2006.

Johnson, Charles S., Edwin R. Embree, and Will Alexander. *The Collapse of Cotton Tenancy*. Chapel Hill: University of North Carolina Press, 1935.

Jones, Charles, ed., *The Black Panther Party [Reconsidered]*. Baltimore: Black Classic, 1998.

Joseph, Peniel E., ed. *The Black Power Movement: Rethinking the Civil Rights–Black Power Era*. New York: Routledge, 2006.

———. *Waiting 'Til the Midnight Hour: A Narrative History of Black Power in America*. New York: Henry Holt, 2006.

Kelley, Robin D. G. *Race Rebels: Culture, Politics, and the Black Working Class*. New York: Free Press, 1994.

———. *Hammer and Hoe: Alabama Communists during the Great Depression*. Chapel Hill: University of North Carolina, 1990.

Kolchin, Peter. *First Freedom: The Response of Alabama's Blacks to Emancipation and Reconstruction*. Westport, Conn.: Greenwood, 1972.

Kopkind, Andrew. "A Long Time Coming: Lowndes County, Alabama." *Working Papers for a New Society* Vol. 2 (Winter 1975), 13–20.

———. "Lowndes County, Alabama: The Great Fear Is Gone." *Ramparts* Vol. 13 (April 1975), 8–12, 53–55.

Korstad, Robert Rodgers. *Civil Rights Unionism: Tobacco Workers and the Struggle for Democracy in the Mid-Twentieth-Century South*. Chapel Hill: University of North Carolina Press, 2003.

Ladner, Joyce. "What Black Power Means to Negroes in Mississippi," in *The Transformation of Activism: Black Experience*, edited by August Meier, 131–154. Chicago: Aldine, 1970.

Lash-Quinn, Elisabeth. *Black Neighbors: Race and the Limits of Reform in the American Settlement House Movement, 1890–1945*. Chapel Hill: University of North Carolina Press, 1993.

Lau, Peter F. *Democracy Rising: South Carolina and the Fight for Black Equality since 1865* Lexington: University Press of Kentucky, 2006.

———. *From the Grassroots to the Supreme Court: Brown v. Board of Education and American Democracy*. Durham, N.C.: Duke University Press, 2004.

Lawson, Steven F. *In Pursuit of Power: Southern Blacks and Electoral Politics, 1965–1982*. New York: Columbia University Press, 1985.

———. *Black Ballots: Voting Rights in the South, 1944–1969*. New York: Columbia University Press, 1976.

Lazerow, Jama, and Yohuru Williams, eds. *In Search of the Black Panther Party: New Perspectives on a Revolutionary Movement*. Durham, N.C.: Duke University Press, 2006.

Lewis, John, with Michael D'Orso. *Walking with the Wind: A Memoir of the Movement*. New York: Simon & Schuster, 1998.

Litwack, Leon F. *Trouble in Mind: Black Southerners in the Age of Jim Crow.* New York: Knopf, 1998.

———. *Been in the Storm So Long: The Aftermath of Slavery.* New York: Knopf, 1979.

Long, Margaret. "Black Power in the Black Belt." *The Progressive* Vol. 30 (October, 1966), 22.

Lowndes County Historical Markers. Alabama: Lowndes County Historical Society, 1994.

Lowndesboro's Picturesque Legacies. Lowndesboro, Alabama: Lowndesboro Heritage Society, 1979.

Mannis, Andrew. *A Fire You Can't Put Out: The Civil Rights Life of Birmingham's Reverend Fred Shuttlesworth.* Tuscaloosa: University of Alabama Press, 1999.

May, Gary. *The Informant: The FBI, the Ku Klux Klan, and the Murder of Viola Liuzzo.* New Haven, Conn.: Yale University Press, 2005.

McAdam, Doug. *Freedom Summer.* New York: Oxford University Press, 1988.

———. *Political Process and the Development of Black Insurgency, 1930–1970.* Chicago: The University of Chicago Press, 1982.

McAdam, Doug, John D. McCarthy, and Mayer N. Zald, eds. *Comparative Perspectives on Social Movements: Political Opportunities, Mobilizing Structures, and Cultural Framings.* Cambridge: Cambridge University Press, 1996.

McMillen, Neil R. *Dark Journey: Black Mississippians in the Age of Jim Crow.* Urbana: University of Illinois Press, 1989.

———. *The Citizens' Council: Organized Resistance to the Second Reconstruction, 1954–64.* Urbana: University of Illinois Press, 1971.

McWhorter, Diane. *Carry Me Home: Birmingham, Alabama: The Climatic Battle of the Civil Rights Revolution.* New York: Simon & Schuster, 2001.

Minchin, Timothy J. *From Rights to Economics: The Ongoing Struggle for Black Equality in the U.S. South.* Gainesville: University Press of Florida, 2007.

Minnis, Jack. "The Story of the Development of an Independent Political Movement on the County Level." Louisville, Ky.: Southern Conference Educational Fund, 1967 [Duke University Library Pamphlet Collection].

Morris, Aldon D. *The Origins of the Civil Rights Movement: Black Communities Organizing for Change.* New York: Free Press, 1984.

Moses, Robert P., and Charles E. Cobb, Jr. *Radical Equations: Civil Rights from Mississippi to the Algebra Project.* Boston: Beacon, 2001.

Moses, Wilson Jeremiah. *The Golden Age of Black Nationalism, 1850–1925.* Oxford: Oxford University Press, 1978.

Moye, J. Todd. *Let the People Decide: Black Freedom and White Resistance Movements in Sunflower County, Mississippi, 1945–1986.* Chapel Hill: University of North Carolina Press, 2004.

Mueller, Carol. "Ella Baker and the Origins of 'Participatory Democracy,'" in *Women in the Civil Rights Movement: Trailblazers and Torchbearers, 1941–1965*, edited by Vicki L. Crawford, Jacqueline Anne Rouse, and Barbara Woods, 51–70. Bloomington: Indiana University Press, 1990, 1993.

Murray, Pauli. *Pauli Murray: The Autobiography of a Black Activist, Feminist, Lawyer, Priest, and Poet*. Knoxville: University of Tennessee Press, 1989.

Myers, John B. "The Alabama Freedmen and the Economic Adjustments during Presidential Reconstruction, 1865–1867." *Alabama Review* Vol. 26, No. 4 (October 1973), 252–266.

———. "The Freedmen and the Labor Supply: The Economic Adjustments in Post-bellum Alabama, 1865–1867." *Alabama Historical Quarterly* Vol. 32, Nos. 3 and 4 (Fall and Winter 1970), 157–167.

———. "The Freedmen and the Law in Post-bellum Alabama, 1865–1867." *Alabama Review* Vol. 23, No. 1 (January 1970), 55–69.

———. "Reaction and Adjustment: The Struggle of Alabama Freedmen in Post-bellum Alabama, 1865–1867." *Alabama Historical Quarterly* Vol. 32, Nos. 1 and 2 (Spring and Summer 1970), 5–22.

Nelson, Bruce. "Organized Labor and the Struggle for Black Equality in Mobile during World War II." *Journal of American History* Vol. 80, No. 3 (1993), 952–988.

Norrell, Robert J. "Labor at the Ballot Box: Alabama Politics from the New Deal to the Dixiecrat Movement," *Journal of Southern History* Vol. 57, No. 2 (May 1991), 201–234.

———. *Reaping the Whirlwind: The Civil Rights Movement in Tuskegee*. New York: Vintage, 1985.

———. "Reporters and Reformers: The Story of the *Southern Courier*." *South Atlantic Quarterly* Vol. 79 (Winter 1980), 93–104.

Ogbar, Jeffrey O. G. *Black Power: Radical Politics and African American Identity*. Baltimore: Johns Hopkins University Press, 2004.

Olson, Lynne. *Freedom's Daughters: The Unsung Heroines of the Civil Rights Movement from 1830 to 1970*. New York: Scribner, 2001.

Ortiz, Paul. *Emancipation Betrayed: The Hidden History of Black Organizing and White Violence in Florida from Reconstruction to the Bloody Election of 1920*. Berkeley and Los Angeles: University of California Press, 2005.

Parker, Frank R. *Black Votes Count: Political Empowerment in Mississippi after 1965*. Chapel Hill: University of North Carolina Press, 1990.

Payne, Charles M. *I've Got the Light of Freedom: The Organizing Tradition and the Mississippi Freedom Struggle*. Berkeley and Los Angeles: University of California Press, 1995.

Perry, Bruce. *Malcolm X: The Last Speeches*. New York: Pathfinder, 1989.

Rable, George C. *But There Was No Peace: The Role of Violence in the Politics of Reconstruction*. Athens: University of Georgia Press, 1984.

Ransby, Barbara. *Ella Baker and the Black Freedom Movement: A Radical Democratic Vision*. Chapel Hill: University of North Carolina Press, 2003.

Ransom, Roger L., and Richard Sutch. *One Kind of Freedom: The Economic Consequences of Emancipation*. Cambridge: Cambridge University Press, 1977.

Robnett, Belinda. *How Long? How Long? African-American Women in the Struggle for Civil Rights*. New York: Oxford University Press 1997.

Rouse, Jacqueline A. "'We Seek to Know . . . in Order to Speak the Truth': Nurturing the Seeds of Discontent—Septima P. Clark and Participatory Leadership," in *Sisters in the Struggle: African American Women in the Civil Rights–Black Power Movement*, edited by Bettye Collier-Thomas and V. P. Franklin, 95–120. New York: New York University Press, 2001.

Rozier, John. *Black Boss: Political Revolution in a Georgia County*. Athens: University of Georgia Press, 1982.

Russell, Mildred Brewer. *Lowndes County Court House: A Chronicle of Hayneville, an Alabama Black Belt Village, 1820–1900*. Montgomery, Ala.: Paragon, 1951.

Schweninger, Loren. "Alabama Blacks and the Congressional Reconstruction Acts of 1867." *Alabama Review* Vol. 31, No. 3 (July 1978), 182–189.

Scott, James. *Weapons of the Weak: Everyday Forms of Peasant Resistance*. New Haven, Conn.: Yale University Press, 1985.

Sellers, Cleveland, with Robert Terrell. *The River of No Return: The Autobiography of a Black Militant and the Life and Death of SNCC*. New York: Morrow, 1973.

Singh, Nikhil Pal. *Black Is a Country: Race and the Unfinished Struggle for Democracy*. Cambridge, Mass.: Harvard University Press, 2004.

Sitkoff, Harvard. "African American Militancy in the World War II South: Another Perspective," in *Remaking Dixie: The Impact of World War II on the American South*, edited by Neil R. McMillen, 70–92. Jackson: University Press of Mississippi, 1997.

Smethurst, James Edward. *The Black Arts Movement: Literary Nationalism in the 1960s and 1970s*. Chapel Hill: University of North Carolina Press, 2005.

Stack, Carol. *Call to Home: African Americans Reclaim the Rural South*. New York: Basic, 1996.

Stanton, Mary. *From Selma to Sorrow: The Life and Death of Viola Liuzzo*. Athens: University of Georgia Press, 1998.

Strain, Christopher. *Pure Fire: Armed Self-Defense as Activism in the Civil Rights Era*. Athens: University of Georgia Press, 2005.

Student Nonviolent Coordinating Committee. "The General Condition of the Alabama Negro." Atlanta: Student Nonviolent Coordinating Committee, 1965.

Sullivan, Patricia. *Days of Hope: Race and Democracy in the New Deal Era*. Chapel Hill: University of North Carolina Press, 1996.

Tate, Katherine. *From Protest to Politics: The New Black Voters in American Elections*. Cambridge, Mass.: Harvard University Press, 1994.

Theoharis, Jeanne F., and Komozi Woodard, eds. *Groundwork: Local Black Freedom Movements in America.* New York: New York University Press, 2005.
———. *Freedom North: Black Freedom Struggles outside the South, 1940–1980.* New York: Palgrave Macmillan, 2003.
Thornton, J. Mills. *Dividing Lines: Municipal Politics and the Struggle for Civil Rights in Montgomery, Birmingham, and Selma.* Tuscaloosa: University of Alabama Press, 2002.
Tugwell, Rexford G. "The Resettlement Idea." *Agricultural History* Vol. 33 (October 1959), 159–163.
Tyson, Timothy B. *Blood Done Sign My Name: A True Story.* New York: Crown, 2004.
———. *Radio Free Dixie: Robert F. Williams and the Roots of Black Power.* Chapel Hill: University of North Carolina Press, 1999.
Umoja, Akinyele O. "The Beginning of the End of Nonviolence in the Mississippi Freedom Movement." *Radical History Review* 85 (2003), 201–226.
Van Deburg, William L. *New Day in Babylon: The Black Power Movement and American Culture, 1965–1975.* Chicago: University of Chicago Press, 1993.
Von Eschen, Penny. *Race against Empire: Black Americans and Anticolonialism, 1937–1957.* Ithaca, N.Y.: Cornell University Press, 1997.
Walton, Hanes, Jr. *Black Political Parties: An Historical and Political Analysis.* New York: Free Press, 1972.
Wendt, Simon. *The Spirit and the Shotgun: Armed Resistance and the Struggle for Civil Rights.* Gainesville: University of Florida Press, 2007.
White, Kenneth B. "The Alabama Freedmen's Bureau and Black Education: The Myth of Opportunity." *Alabama Review* Vol. 34, No. 2 (April 1981), 107–124.
Williams, Heather Andrea. *Self-Taught: African American Education in Slavery and Freedom.* Chapel Hill: University of North Carolina Press, 2005.
Williams, Yohuru. *Black Politics/White Power: Civil Rights, Black Power, and the Black Panthers in New Haven.* New York: Brandywine, 2000.
Woodard, Komozi. *A Nation within a Nation: Amiri Baraka (LeRoi Jones) and Black Power Politics.* Chapel Hill: University of North Carolina Press, 1999.
Woodruff, Nan Elizabeth. *American Congo: The African American Freedom Struggle in the Delta.* Cambridge, Mass.: Harvard University Press, 2003.

Index

1966 general election in Lowndes County, Alabama, 192–206; African American turnout, 200–201, 202–203; African American votes for white incumbents, 204; African American voting against third-party candidates, 203; African American willingness to support white incumbents, 194, 195; Alabama Democratic Party, 134, 176; armed self-defense, 194, 202; ballot fraud, 196; beating of Andrew Jones, 201–202; black elite, 203; black moderates, 206; black nonparticipation, 202–203; Black Power, 180, 205–206; black professionals, 203; bloc voting by whites, 195, 203; blueprint for future political practice, 205; Braggs, Alabama, 204; Carmichael, Stokely, 198–199, 201, 205–206; Champion, Mac, Jr., 195; date, 200; Fort Deposit, Alabama, 201–202, 204; freedom politics, 177–178; freedom rights, 205; freedom struggle in Lowndes County, Alabama, 179; graveyard vote, 197; Hulett, John, 182–184, 194, 197, 199, 203, 204–205; illiterate or disabled voters, 196; intimidation of African Americans, 201, 202–203; irregularities, 201; LCFO candidates, 173; LCFO carpool system, 195–196,

204; LCFO defeat, 202–205, 293n72; LCFO hopes for victory, 194; LCFO leaflets, flyers, 192–193; LCFO organizational shortcomings, 204; LCFO poll watchers, 196–197, 201, 204; LCFO preparation, 182–185, 194; LCFO recognition as official political party, 205 (see also LCFP); LCFO strategizing, 176–177; LCFO vote share, 205, 293n72; Logan, Robert, 194; Logan, Sidney, Jr., 193, 194, 197; logistics, 194; May, R C., 194; McGill, Lillian, 203; Miles, Frank, Jr., 194; Moore, Alice, 197–198, 203; positions up for election, 151, 159; provisional ballots, 196; Ross, Emory, 196; Sandy Ridge, Alabama, 204; significance, 205–206; SNCC (Student Nonviolent Coordinating Committee), 179–180, 205–206; Strickland, Willie Mae, 193; third-party politics, 205; U.S. Civil Rights Commission report, 204; vote splitting, 194–195; voter registration roll, 197; votes cast, 289n101, 293n72; Wallace, Lurleen, 289n101; white attitudes towards black candidates, 194–195; white candidates' need for black votes, 195; white chicanery, 203; white "help" to black voters, 196, 201, 204; white turnout, 201

freedom struggle: black protest, 257n15; Dallas County, Alabama, 256n13; Macon County, Alabama, 256n13; Montgomery County, Alabama, 256n13
freedom struggle in Lowndes County, Alabama, 39–47, 66–74; 1930s, 26–27; 1930s and 1940s, 264n54; 1965 ASCS committee elections, 117–118, 128–131, 139, 141; 1966 general election, importance of, 179 (*see also* 1966 general election); 1970 general election, importance of, 222; 1970s, 2; 1980s and 1990s, 241; absence of newsworthy violence, 101–102; adult education classes, 208, 210–211; agricultural mechanization, 264n54; Alabama Democratic Party, 55–56; anti-landfill campaign, 238–239; armed self-defense (*see* armed self-defense); arson at poverty headquarters, 208–209; Baker, Ella, 150; black consciousness, 182; black elite, 72, 160, 166, 176, 203; black leaders, traditional, 4; black middle class, 122; Black Power, 191, 206; black professionals, 72, 166, 176–177, 203, 225; black protest, breadth of, 4; black protest, epicenters of, 3, 25; blacks' willingness to support white candidates, incumbents, 194, 195, 221–222, 226; Bloody Sunday (March 7, 1965), 43–44; Board of Education, 229–231; bombings and burning of churches, 209–210; canvassing, 66–68, 74, 87, 99, 102; churches, 45; civil rights meeting (March 19, 1965), 45–46; climatic event, 179 (*see also* 1966 general election); collective agitation/organized public protest, 26–27, 35;

control of county commission, 237–238; creation of parallel institutions to offset deficient existing ones, 99–100, 115; day laborers, 72; decline in black voter participation, 242–243; democratic tendencies, 45, 119–120; direct action protests, 94; domestic workers, 72; economic vulnerability of movement's base, 104; election of African Americans to public office, 243; electoral politics, 222, 245; eviction of participants, 71, 72, 104–106, 110, 116, 129, 215 (*see also* Tent City); federal government's involvement, effect of, 118–119, 134; firing of participants, 71, 72, 163; in Fort Deposit, 94; freedom rights, 2, 4; freedom songs and testimonials, 54; fundraising, material support, 71; generational divide, 225; grassroots insurgency, 2, 4; Great Depression, 26–27; harassment of participants, 100; institutional ostracism for participating, 45; jury discrimination, 131–133; leadership, 72–73; leadership struggle within poverty program, 211–212; local people in, 5; local whites in, 5; Lowndes Diaspora in, 4, 31, 71, 109, 116; murders of participants (*see* murders); mutual aid groups, 40–41, 69; neighboring and national events, 40; nonviolence, indifference to, 104, 116; outside forces, 4; outside organizers, 4; overestimation of sustainability of freedom politics, 243–245; persistence and possibility, 6; placing interest of individuals ahead of interests of the people, 162, 224–225, 244; poor people, 72;

Macon County Democratic Club
(MCDC), 166
Mahoney, Bill, 109
Malcolm X, 57, 192
Mants, Bob: 1966 general election, 192;
1984 general election, 240; in De-
troit, 71; on families of transfer stu-
dents, 91; on Fort Deposit, 94; free-
dom struggle in Lowndes County,
Alabama, 182; in Georgia, 60;
Hulett, John, 240; on withdrawal of
SNCC from Lowndes County, 213
March Against Fear (Mississippi,
1966), 185–188
Marengo County, Alabama, 79,
273n114
Marlette, M. E., Jr., 136, 138–139
Masonic orders, 69
May, Asa, 26
May, R. C., 194
Mays, Benjamin Elijah, 25
Mays, R. C., 215
Mays, Timothy, 85, 99
McCall, Andrew, 235
McCord, Robert, 84
MCDC (Macon County Democratic
Club), 166
McDonald, Leon, 100–101
McDonald, Pattie, 100–101
McDonald, Shirley Ann, 100–101
McDonald, Walter, 100–101
McDuffie, John, 14–15, 16, 261n18
McGhee, Willie Ed, 222, 226, 235,
297n67
McGill, Elzie Lee: civil rights meeting
(March 19, 1965), 46; literacy, 75–76;
Lowndes County Co-op, 211; Selma
to Montgomery March (1965), 49;
voter registration, 75–76, 212
McGill, Lillian: 1966 general election,
203; Alabama Area 22 grant pro-
posal, 122–123; boycott of LCTS, 87;

canvassing efforts, 67, 74; church
membership, 74; civil rights meeting (March 19, 1965), 46; community activism, 74; countywide CAP
action committee, 138; Department
of Agriculture job, 46, 67, 74; education, 46; on evictions of registered voters, 110; on Hammonds,
Harrell, 221; Hulett, John, 74; LCC-
MHR (Lowndes County Christian
Movement for Human Rights), 46,
74–75, 120–121; leadership skills,
74–75; *McGill v. Ryals*, 159; in Mont-
gomery, 46; Selma to Montgomery
March (1965), 49; SNCC (Student
Nonviolent Coordinating Commit-
tee), 214; son at Hayneville High,
97; transfer application for son, 92;
voter registration, 67, 74; on War on
Poverty, 120
McGill v. Ryals, 159–160
McKissick, Floyd, 188
McLelland, Warren, 230
McMeans, Bessie, 102, 208
McMeans, Clara, 201
McWilliams, Gerline, 70
Meadows, A. R., 112
Meadows, E. R., 36, 106
Meadows, Howard H., 36
Mealings, Edwin, 26
Means, Elbert: 1978 Democratic pri-
mary, 233–236, 299n83; 1984 general
election, 239–240, 300n97; 1990
general election, 300n99; activism,
234; Alabama's homestead exemp-
tion, 235–236; freedom rights, 234,
245; Hulett, John, 234–235; older
African Americans, 239–240; tax
assessments, 235–236
Means, Harriet, 234–235, 239
Meredith, James, 185
Meriwether, Annie May, 27

SNCC (Student Nonviolent Coordinating Committee) (*continued*): boycott of LCTS, 86, 99; canvassing, 66–68; CAP (Community Action Program), 120; Carmichael, Stokely, 213; chairmanship, 134, *183*; community-controlled institutions, 180; confrontation between Stokely Carmichael and police at LCTS, 62–63, 80; conscience, appeals to, 55–56; contact lists, 60; decline of, 5; Democratic Party, 55–56; direct action protests, 94; Domino Theory, 60; federal programs, taking advantage of, 116; freedom movements in Africa, 57; freedom politics, 243; Freedom Primer, *155–156*; freedom rights, 56; fundraising, 189, 213; government repression, 213; headquarters in Lowndes County, 63, 64, 66; Hulett, John, 61, 63, 214; information from paid informants, 133; on integration, 86; Jackson, John, 61–62, 64, 65; Jackson family, 64–65; Lafayette, Bernard, 54–55; Lafayette, Colia, 54–55; LCCMHR (Lowndes County Christian Movement for Human Rights), 61–63; LCFO (Lowndes County Freedom Organization), 1, 143–144, 145, 149–152, 153–157, 164, 180–181; leadership, 58; Lewis, John, 182; literacy requirements for voter registration, 76, 78; local students, 61–63; Lowndes County, interest in, 59–62; Lowndes County grassroots insurgency, 2; Lowndes County headquarters, 64–65; Lowndes Diaspora, 71; Malcolm X and, 57; March Against Fear (Mississippi, 1966), 185–188; McGill, Lillian, 214; *McGill v. Ryals,* 159; MFDP (Mississippi Freedom Democratic Party), 55, 57; in Mississippi, 149; Moses, Robert Parris "Bob," 57–58; murder of Jonathan Daniels, response to, 82; on nonviolence, 104; Norman, Silas, Jr., 55; organizing objectives/program, 57–58, 177, 179–180, 180, 205–206; political education program, workshops, 150–152, 153–157, 164, 177, 185; public criticism of LCFO, 169–171; publicity about violence in Lowndes County, 102; relationship with local people, 65; research department, 147, 151, 154; school desegregation, 86–87, 93; SCLC (Southern Christian Leadership Conference), 59–60, 167; Selma to Montgomery March (1965), 60, 80; staff retreat at Kingston Springs (1966), 180–181; staff size, 213; student demonstrations in Fort Deposit, 94; support for, 56; Tent City (Freedom City), 106; third-party politics, 148–152, 167, 177, 213; white hostility, southern, 56; white indifference, northern, 56; white organizers, 180, 181, 213; withdrawal from Lowndes County, 212–214

Snellings, Rolland, 190
Southern Christian Leadership Conference. *See* SCLC
Sparkman, John, 136
Staggers, William, 121
Steele, Rosie, 49
Steele, Sallie, 67
Stephenson, John, 109
Stewart, Threddie Lee, 106, 129–130, 296n55
Stines, Henri, 132
Strauder v. West Virginia, 282n34
Strickland, Edwin, 135

whites in Lowndes County, Alabama,
31–36; 1966 general election,
194–195, 201; African American
participation in Democratic primary elections, 174; anti-landfill
campaign, 238–239; attitude toward murder of white activists,
84; bloc voting, 176, 195, 203, 242;
Boswell Amendment to the Alabama Constitution, 31–32; defiance
of federal government, 114; Democratic Party, 15–16; discriminatory
tax policies, 236; federal participation in local affairs, 118, 140; Hammonds, Harrell, 216, 217, 219, 233;
Hulett, John, 83, 228; labor arrangements, 10, 32; lawlessness, 9;
lawlessness of, ending of, 241–242;
mass nomination of black ASCS
nominees, 128–129, 130; paramilitary units, 13; per capita income,
243; police violence, 34–35; political hegemony, 36; political
renaissance in late 1980s, early
1990s, 242; racial violence, 2, 9,
17–19, 24–25, 26–27, 32–34, 36,
66, 101–102, 116; registered voters
(1960), 253n1; resistance, evolution
of, 115–116; resistance, high-water
mark of, 114; school desegregation, opposition to, 89; Selma to
Montgomery March (1965), 49;
Selma voting rights campaign
(Voter Registration Campaign),
42; slaveholder mentality, 9, 36;
state government support for, 137;
unwillingness to share power equitably, 125; votes for black candidates (1970 general election), 222;
WCC (White Citizens' Council),
36; working-class, 219; World War
II, 264n54

Whiting, Charlie, Jr., 227, 298n79
Wilcox County, Alabama: African
American vote for white incum-
bents, 175–176; demonstrations in,
94; Lowndes County compared
to, 120; Ricks, Willie, 145; SCLC
(Southern Christian Leadership
Conference) in, 168
Wilcox County Freedom Organiza-
tion, 165
Wiley, Chris, 126
Wilkins, Collie, 51–52
Wilkins, Roy, 188–189, 189, 190
Williams, Hosea, 167–168, 169
Williams, Jake, 298n79
Williams, Robert F., 103
Wilson, Willie, Jr., 226, 229, 248,
297n67
women: armed self-defense, 103,
108; as candidates for public of-
fice, 163, 173, 193, 197–198, 222,
223, 224, 240, 293n72, 298n79,
300n99; canvassing, 67, 74; in
county government (*see* Coleman, Hulda; Haynes, Uralee);
in LCCMHR (Lowndes County
Christian Movement for Human
Rights) (*see* McGill, Lillian); in
LCFO (Lowndes County Freedom
Organization), 163 (*see also* Moore,
Alice; Strickland, Willie Mae;
Waginer, Josephine); leadership
roles, skills, 74–75, 80, 212
Woodruff, O. P.: 1968 general election, 295n32; 1972 general election,
296n55; 1976 Democratic primary,
298n78; 1976 general election,
298n79; 1980 Democratic primary,
299n88; 1988 general election, 242;
probate judgeship, 242; Wallace,
George, 301n107; White Citizens'
Council (WCC), 36

About the Author

HASAN KWAME JEFFRIES was born and raised in Brooklyn, New York. He moved to Atlanta, Georgia, in 1990 to attend Morehouse College. While at Morehouse, he was inducted into Phi Beta Kappa honor society and initiated into Kappa Alpha Psi Fraternity Inc. He graduated summa cum laude from Morehouse with a BA in history in 1994. That same year he enrolled at Duke University in Durham, North Carolina, where he earned a MA in American history in 1997, and a PhD in American history with a specialization in African American history in 2002. From 2002 to 2003, he was a Bankhead Fellow in the history department at the University of Alabama in Tuscaloosa, Alabama, where he taught American history and African American history. In 2003, he joined the faculty at Ohio State University where he currently holds a joint appointment in the history department and the Kirwan Institute for the Study of Race and Ethnicity.